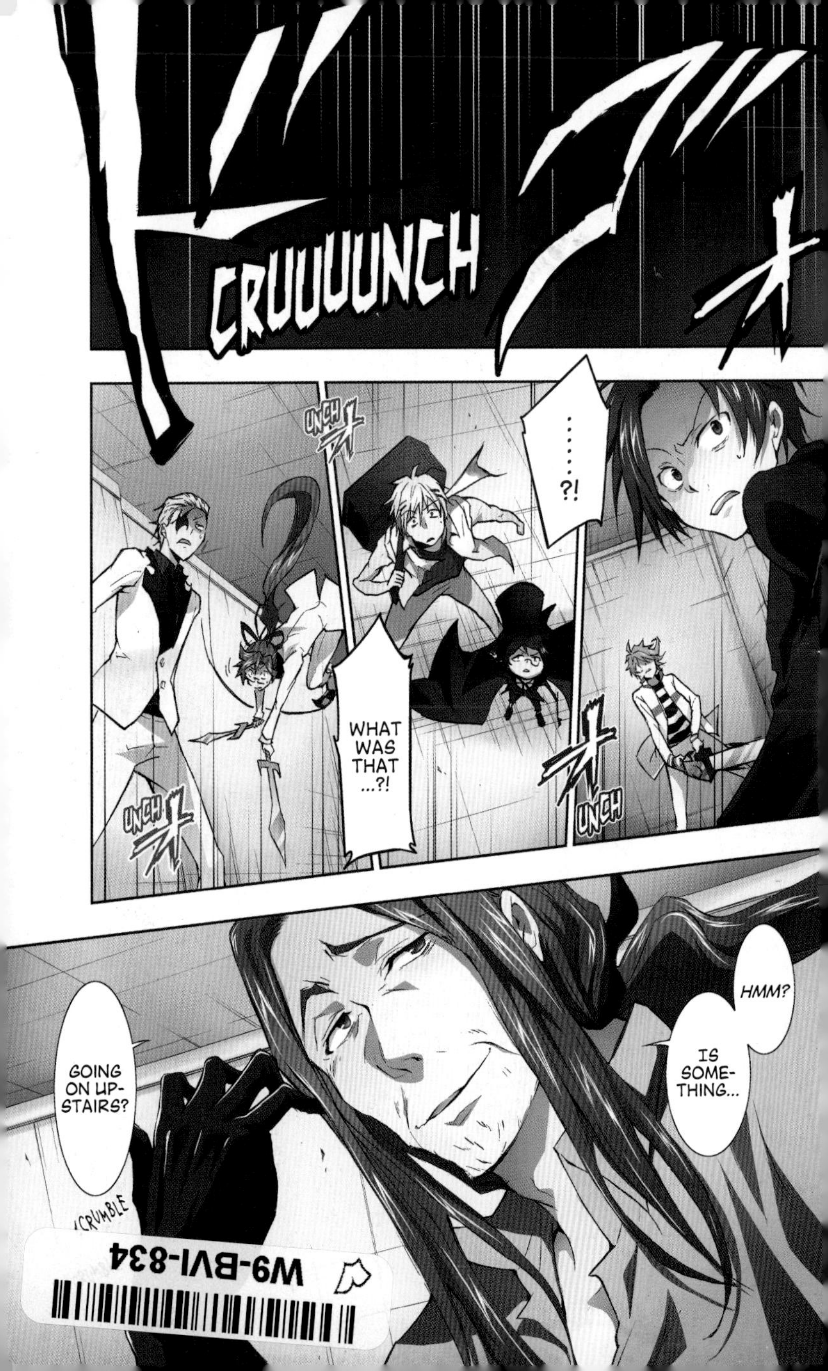
CRUUUUNCH
......?!
UNCH
UNCH
WHAT WAS THAT ...?!
UNCH
HMM?
IS SOME-THING...
GOING ON UP-STAIRS?
CRUMBLE

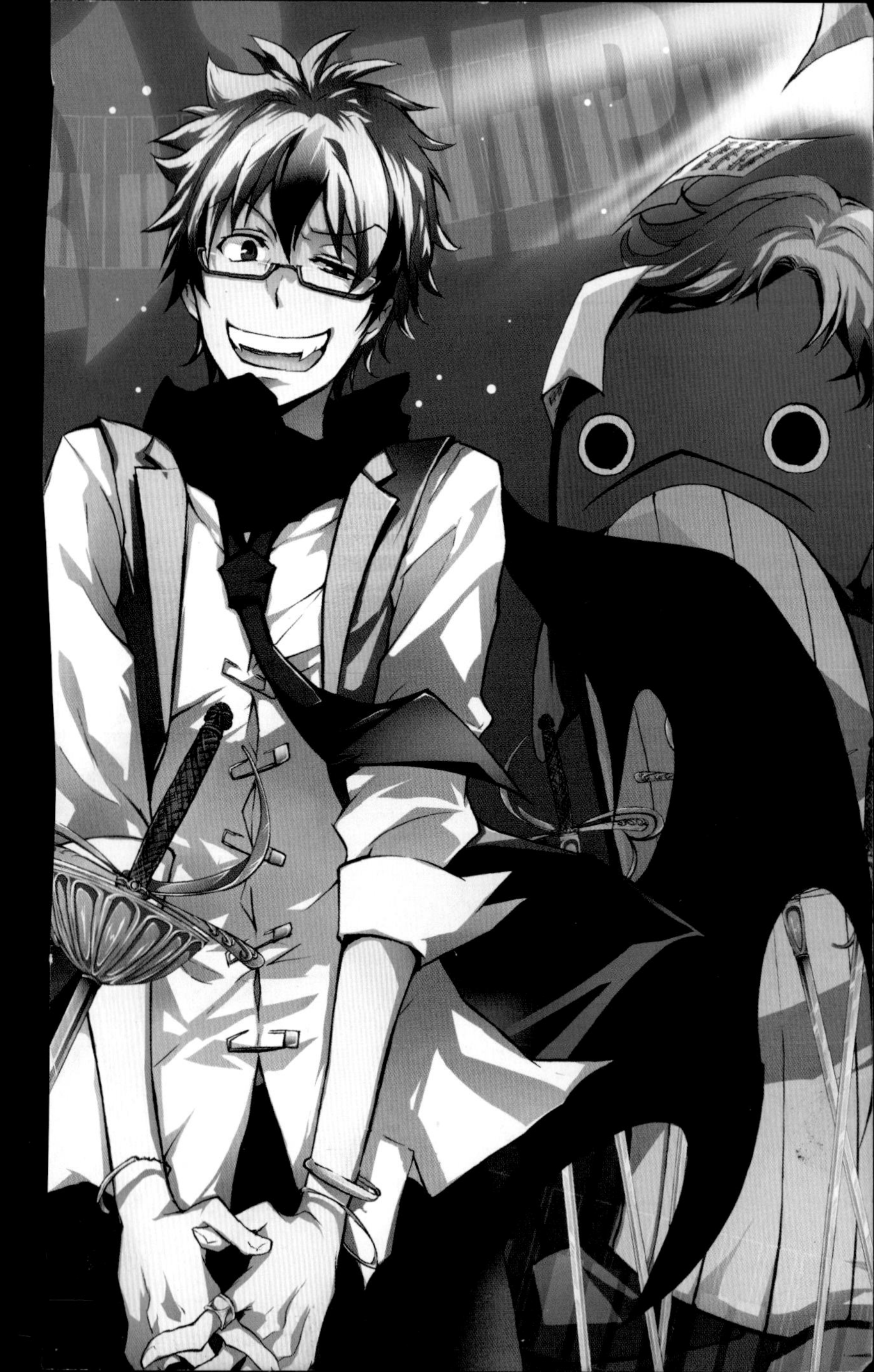

SEVEN SEAS ENTERTAINMENT PRESENTS

# SERVAMP

story by and art by STRIKE TANAKA VOLUME 7

TRANSLATION
**Wesley Bridges**

ADAPTATION
**Karis Page**

LETTERING
**Courtney Williams**

COVER DESIGN
**Nicky Lim**

PROOFREADER
**Janet Houck**
**Lee Otter**

PRODUCTION MANAGER
**Lissa Pattillo**

EDITOR-IN-CHIEF
**Adam Arnold**

PUBLISHER
**Jason DeAngelis**

SERVAMP VOL. 7


ISBN: 978-1-626923-17-1

Printed in Canada

First Printing: September 2016

10 9 8 7 6 5 4 3 2 1



## READING DIRECTIONS

This book reads from ***right to left***, Japanese style. If this is your first time reading manga, you start reading from the top right panel on each page and take it from there. If you get lost, just follow the numbered diagram here. It may seem backwards at first, but you'll get the hang of it! Have fun!!

1
2
3
4
5
6
7
8
9

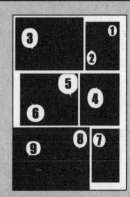

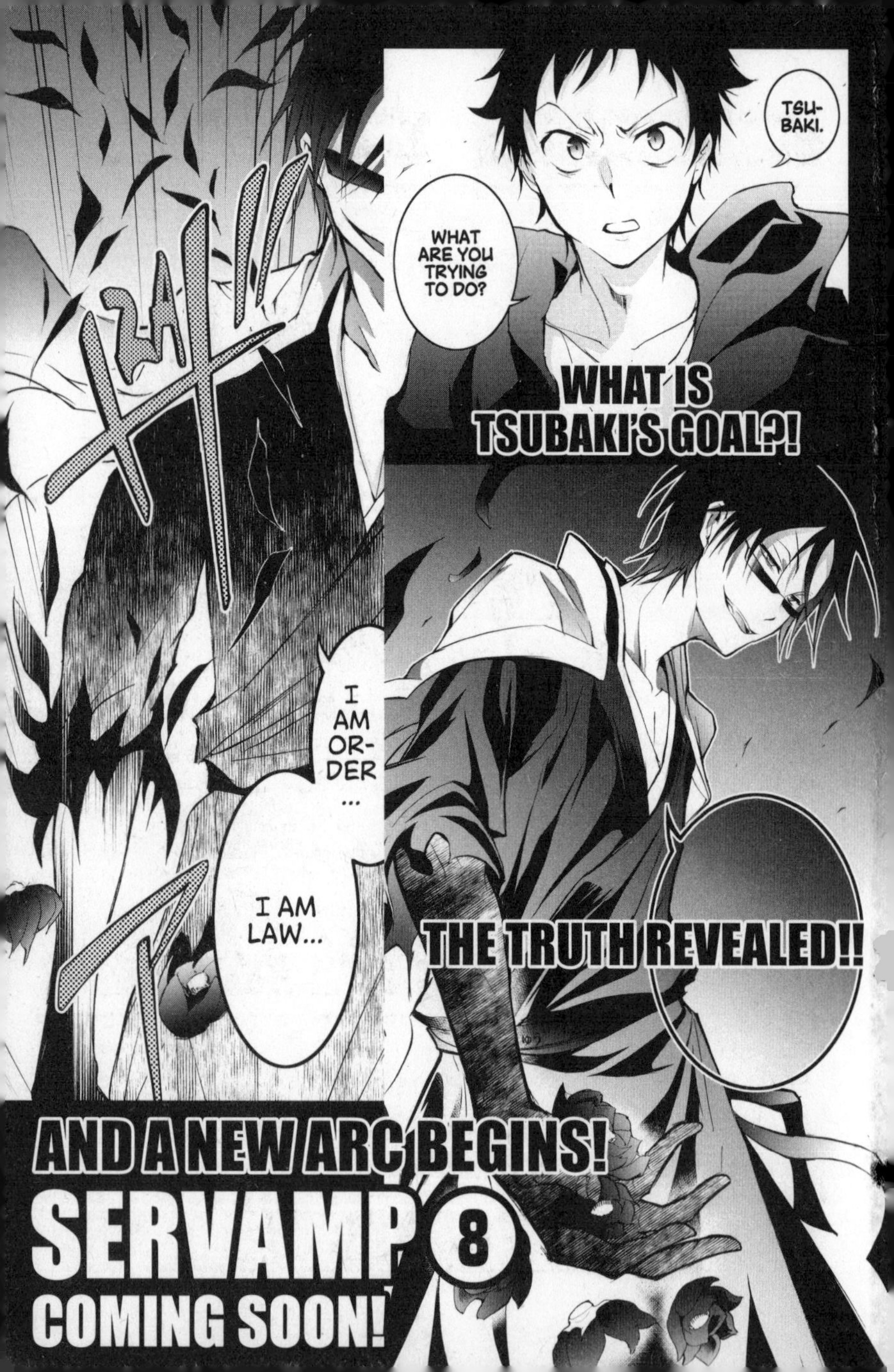
TSU-BAKI.
WHAT ARE YOU TRYING TO DO?
WHAT IS TSUBAKI'S GOAL?!
THE TRUTH REVEALED!!
ZAH!!
I AM ORDER...
I AM LAW...
AND A NEW ARC BEGINS!
SERVAMP 8
COMING SOON!

サーヴァンプ

# SERVAMP

## STORY

High school freshman Shirota Mahiru picked up a stray cat he named Kuro, but his new pet is actually a servant vampire, or Servamp. Mahiru is now his Eve--a vampire's master. That's when Tsubaki appeared, a Servamp who aims to kill his seven Servamp siblings. Lawless, the Servamp of Greed, and his eve, Licht, are currently being held captive. Misono comes up with a plan to rescue them, and has snuck into Tsubaki's hotel base along with Sendagaya and their Servamps, only to find Tsubaki's servants waiting for them. Meanwhile, Lawless and Licht have begun fighting each other, and Mahiru and Kuro haven't been seen since their recent journey of self-discovery...

## KEYWORDS

### THE SEVEN "PRIME" SERVAMPS

They rule all vampires and govern the seven sins of Sloth, Pride, Envy, Wrath, Gluttony, Greed and Lust. They forge contracts with human masters, called Eves. When Mahiru forges a contract with Kuro, he enters their surreal and dangerous world.

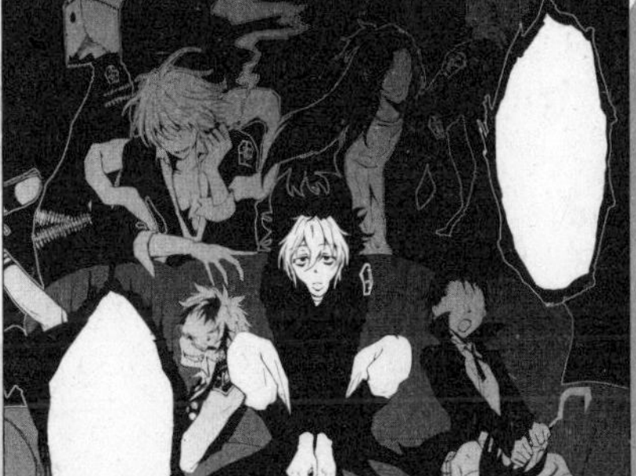

### THE FORGOTTEN 8TH

Tsubaki calls himself the 8th Servamp of Melancholy. But is he really a Prime Servamp?

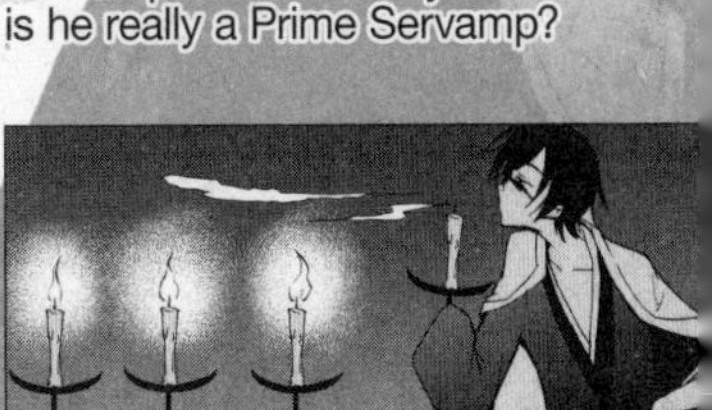

### SUB-VAMPS/SERVANTS

The Prime Vampires create these vampires. They must obey their Servamp masters.

# サーヴァンプ SERVAMP CHARACTERS

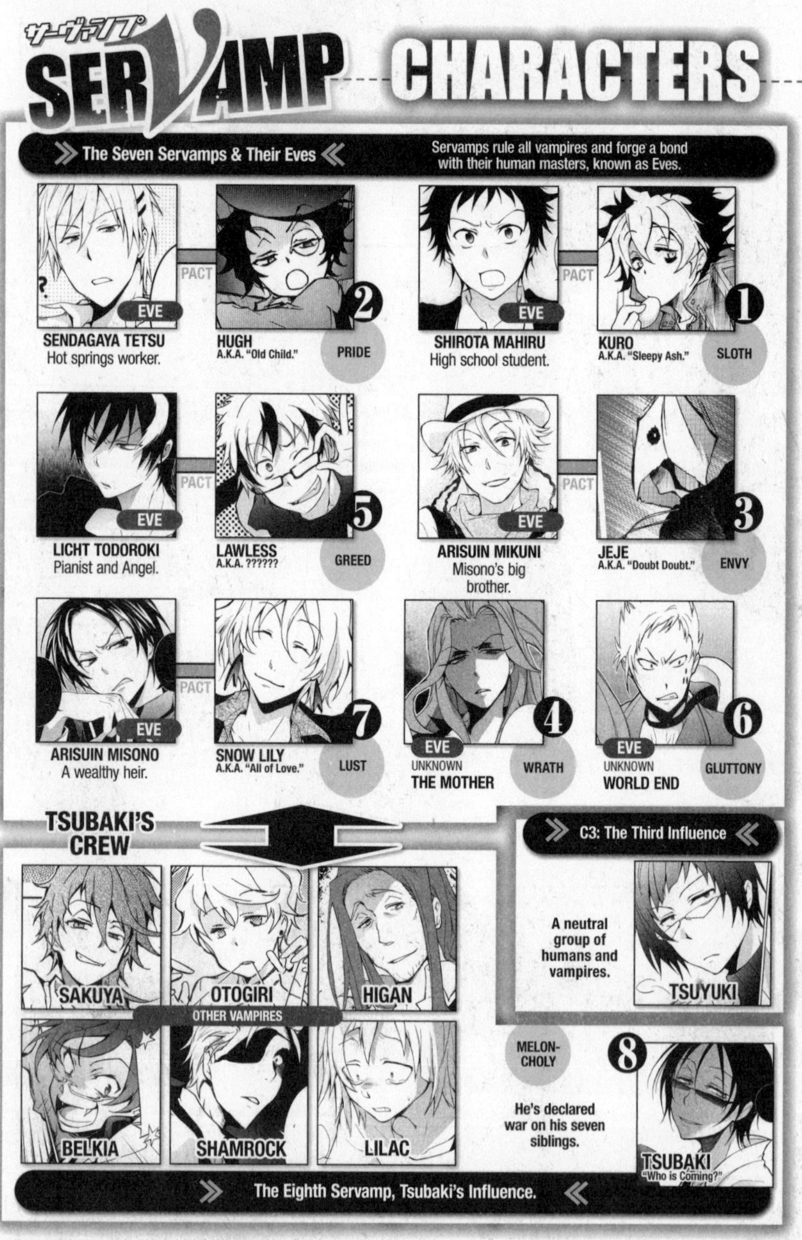

The Seven Servamps & Their Eves
Servamps rule all vampires and forge a bond with their human masters, known as Eves.
EVE
SENDAGAYA TETSU
Hot springs worker.
PACT
2
HUGH
A.K.A. "Old Child."
PRIDE
EVE
SHIROTA MAHIRU
High school student.
PACT
1
KURO
A.K.A. "Sleepy Ash."
SLOTH
EVE
LICHT TODOROKI
Pianist and Angel.
PACT
5
LAWLESS
A.K.A. ??????
GREED
EVE
ARISUIN MIKUNI
Misono's big brother.
PACT
3
JEJE
A.K.A. "Doubt Doubt."
ENVY
EVE
ARISUIN MISONO
A wealthy heir.
PACT
7
SNOW LILY
A.K.A. "All of Love."
LUST
4
EVE
UNKNOWN
THE MOTHER
WRATH
6
EVE
UNKNOWN
WORLD END
GLUTTONY
TSUBAKI'S CREW
C3: The Third Influence
A neutral group of humans and vampires.
TSUYUKI
SAKUYA
OTOGIRI
HIGAN
OTHER VAMPIRES
BELKIA
SHAMROCK
LILAC
MELON-CHOLY
8
He's declared war on his seven siblings.
TSUBAKI
"Who is Coming?"
The Eighth Servamp, Tsubaki's Influence.

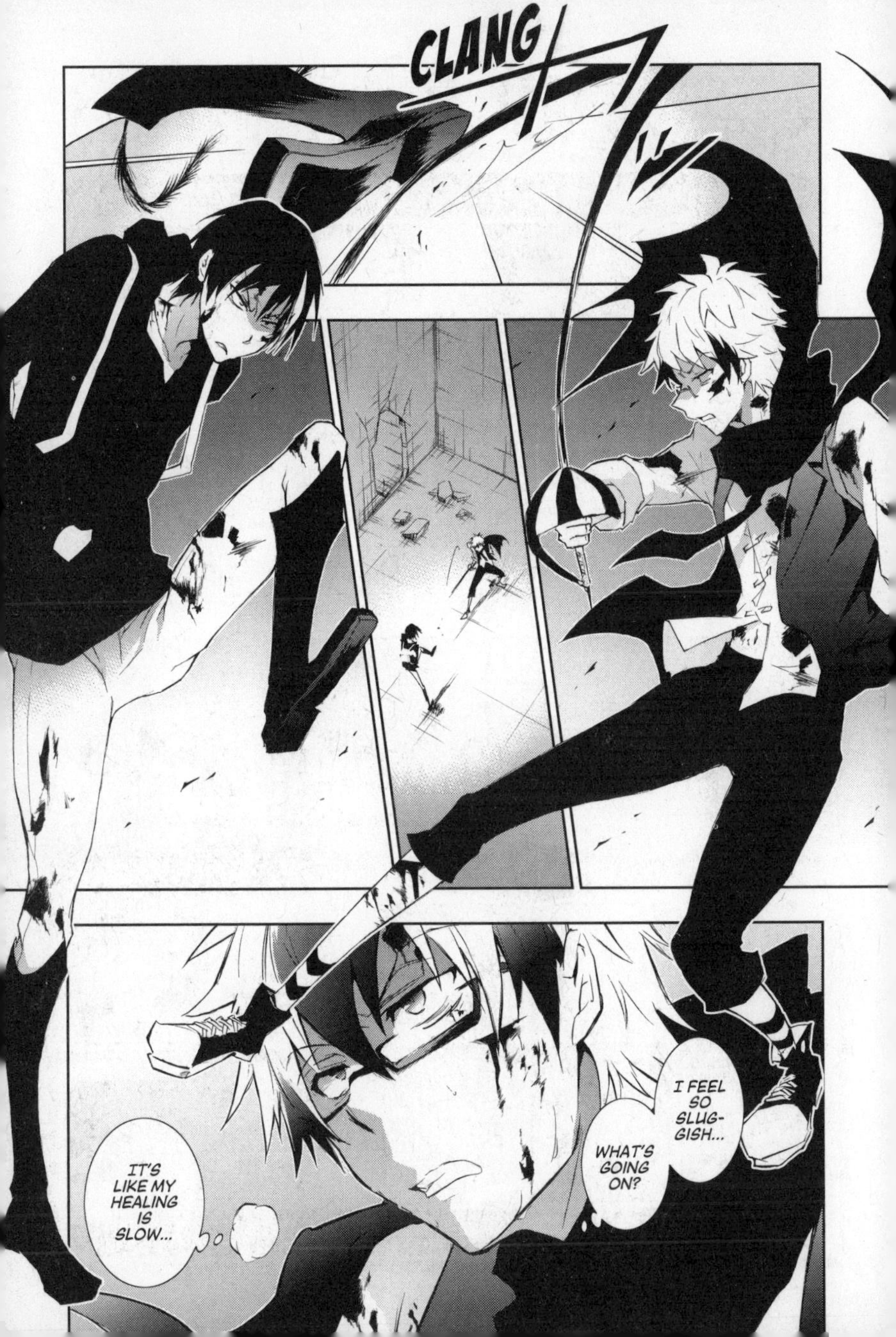
CLANG
I FEEL SO SLUG-GISH...
WHAT'S GOING ON?
IT'S LIKE MY HEALING IS SLOW...

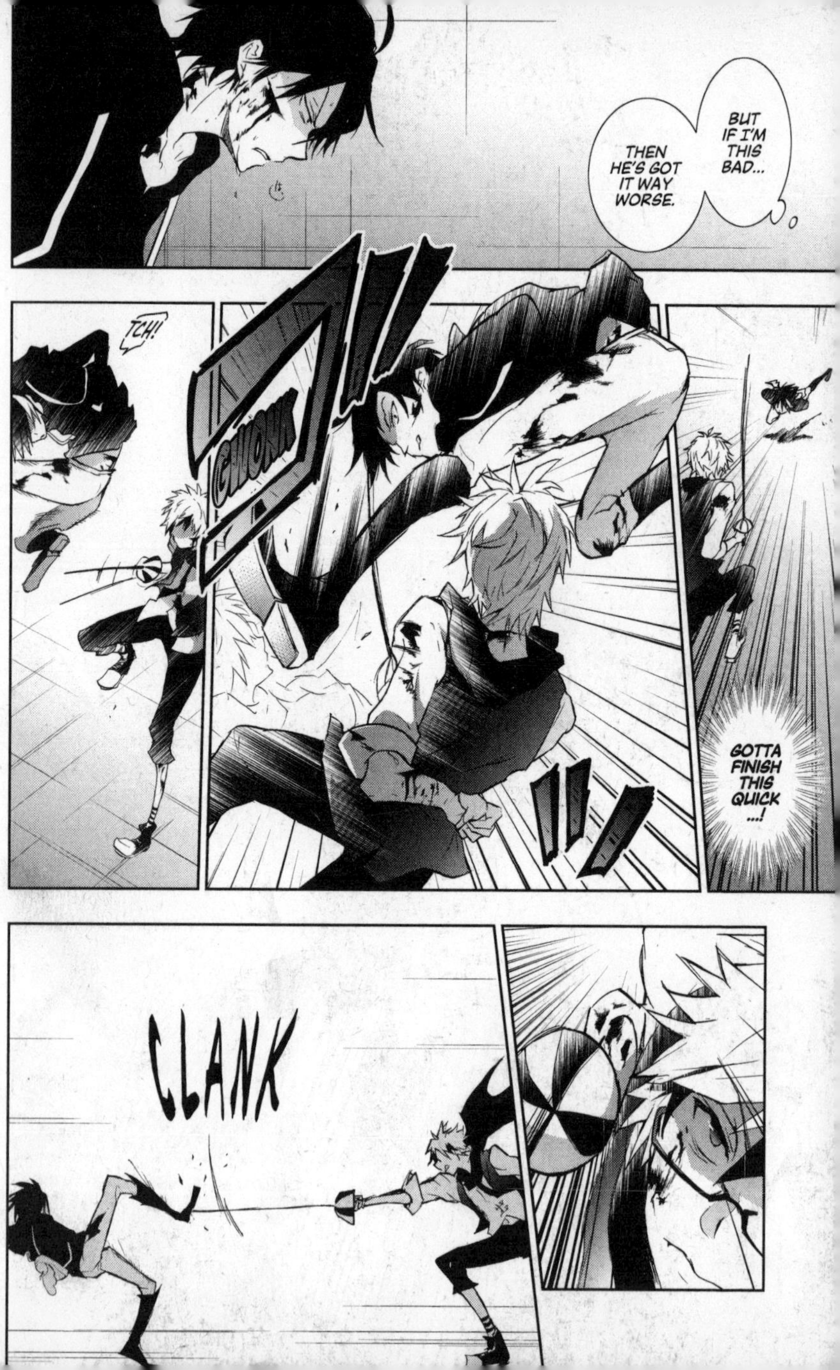
BUT IF I'M THIS BAD...
THEN HE'S GOT IT WAY WORSE.
GOTTA FINISH THIS QUICK...!
CHONK
TCH!
CLANK

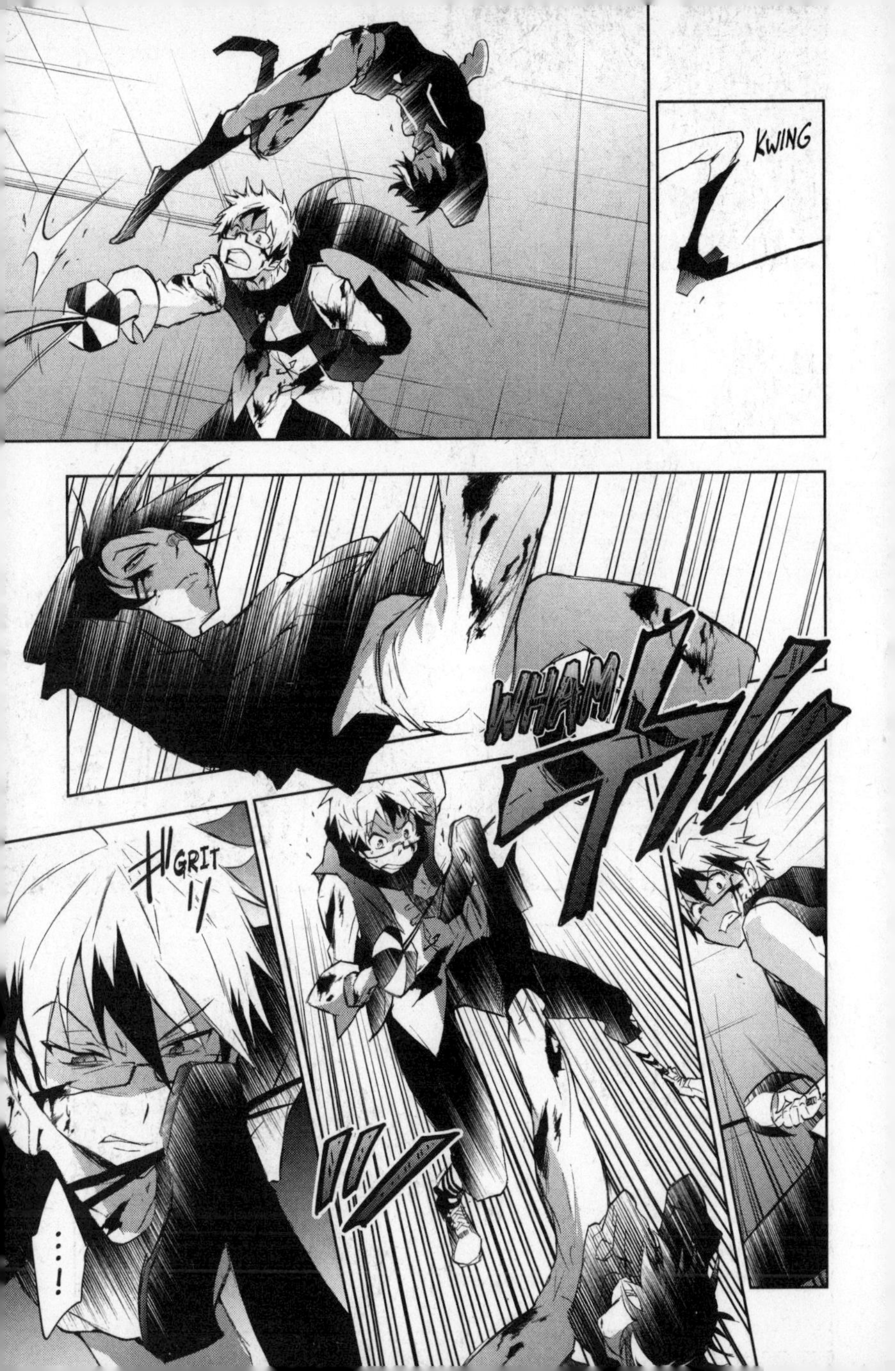
KWING
WHAM
GRIT
...!

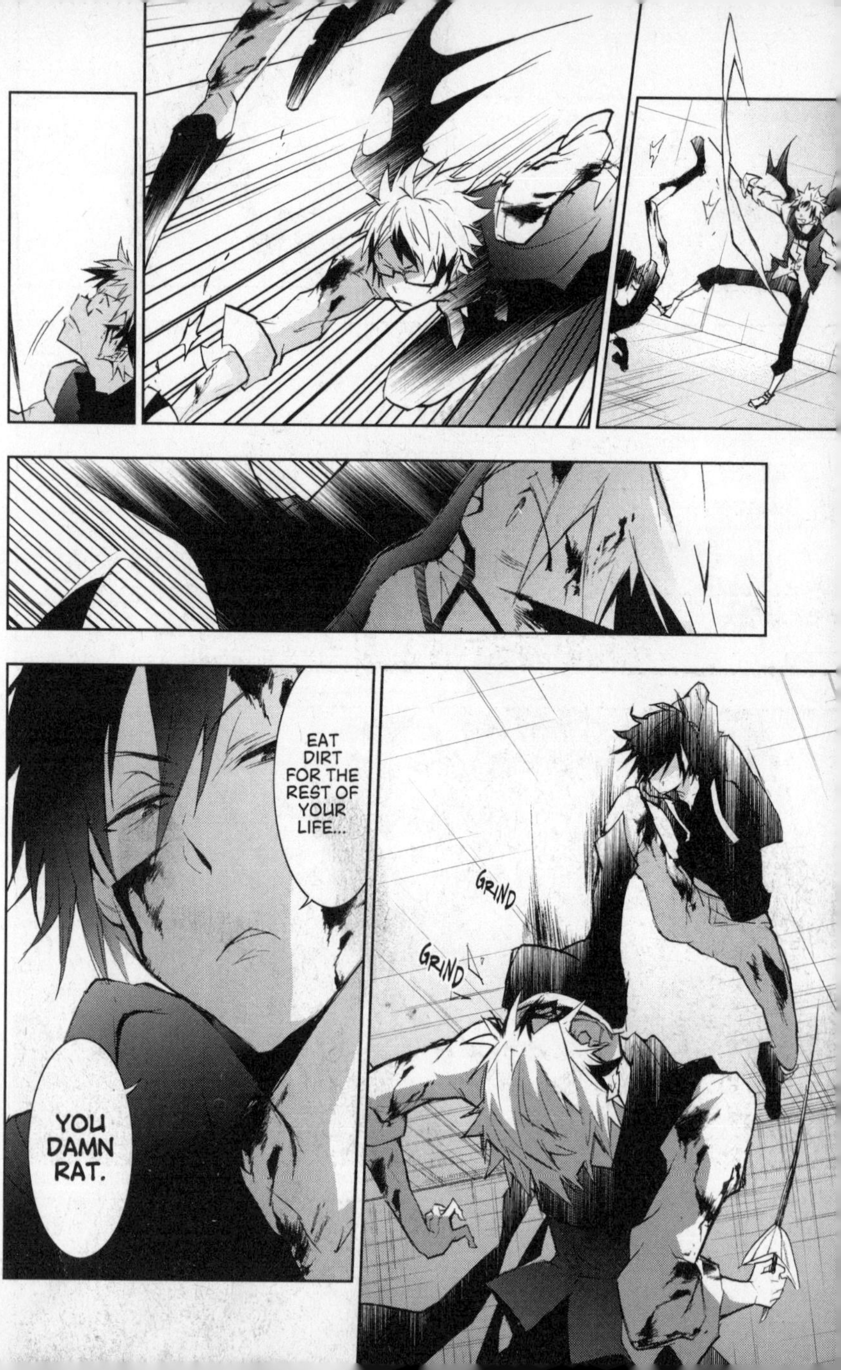
GRIND
GRIND
EAT DIRT FOR THE REST OF YOUR LIFE...
YOU DAMN RAT.

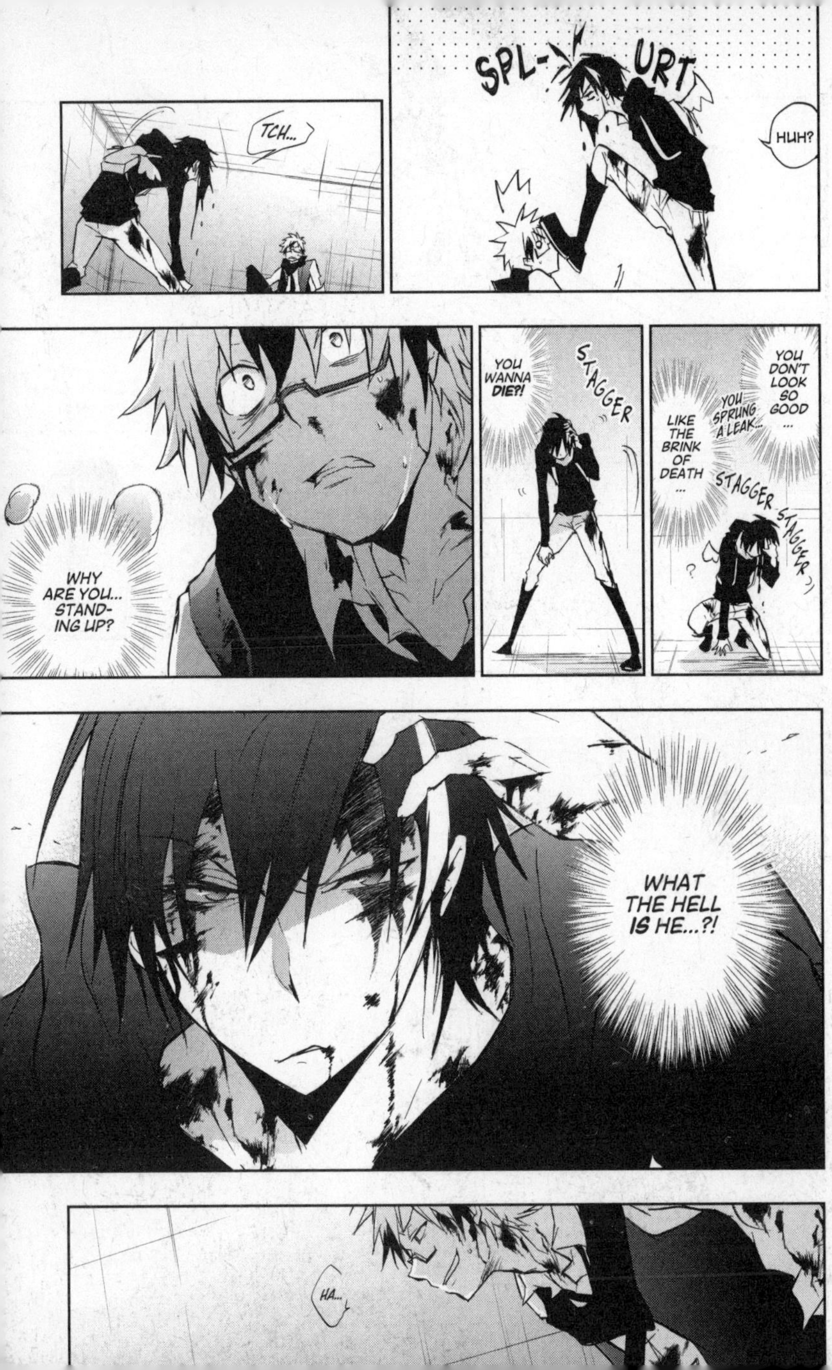
SPL- URT
HUH?
TCH...
YOU DON'T LOOK SO GOOD...
YOU SPRUNG A LEAK...
LIKE THE BRINK OF DEATH...
STAGGER STAGGER
YOU WANNA DIE?!
STAGGER
WHY ARE YOU... STAND-ING UP?
WHAT THE HELL IS HE...?!
HA...

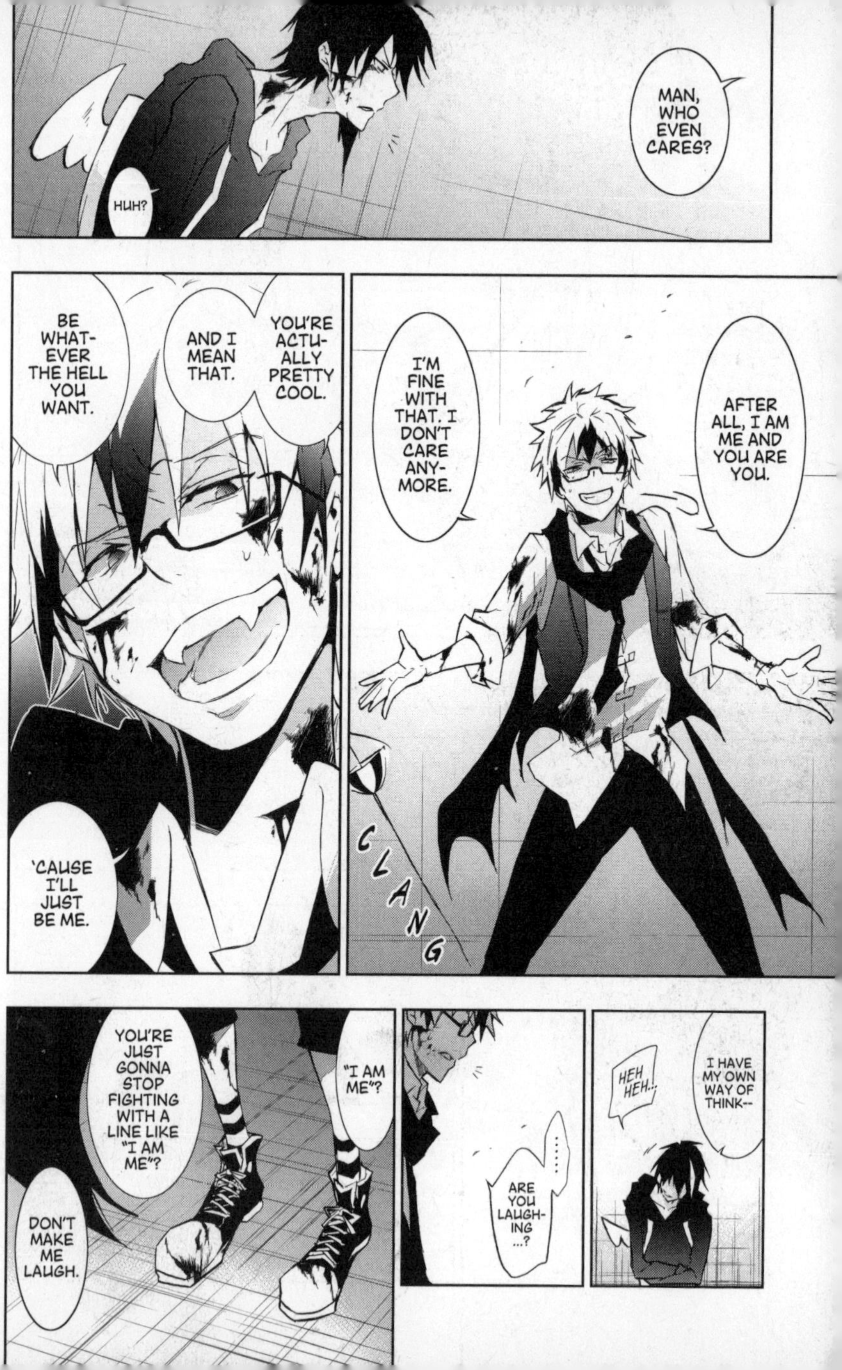

MAN, WHO EVEN CARES?
HUH?
AFTER ALL, I AM ME AND YOU ARE YOU.
I'M FINE WITH THAT. I DON'T CARE ANYMORE.
CLANG
YOU'RE ACTUALLY PRETTY COOL.
AND I MEAN THAT.
BE WHATEVER THE HELL YOU WANT.
'CAUSE I'LL JUST BE ME.
I HAVE MY OWN WAY OF THINK--
HEH HEH...
......
ARE YOU LAUGHING...?
"I AM ME"?
YOU'RE JUST GONNA STOP FIGHTING WITH A LINE LIKE "I AM ME"?
DON'T MAKE ME LAUGH.

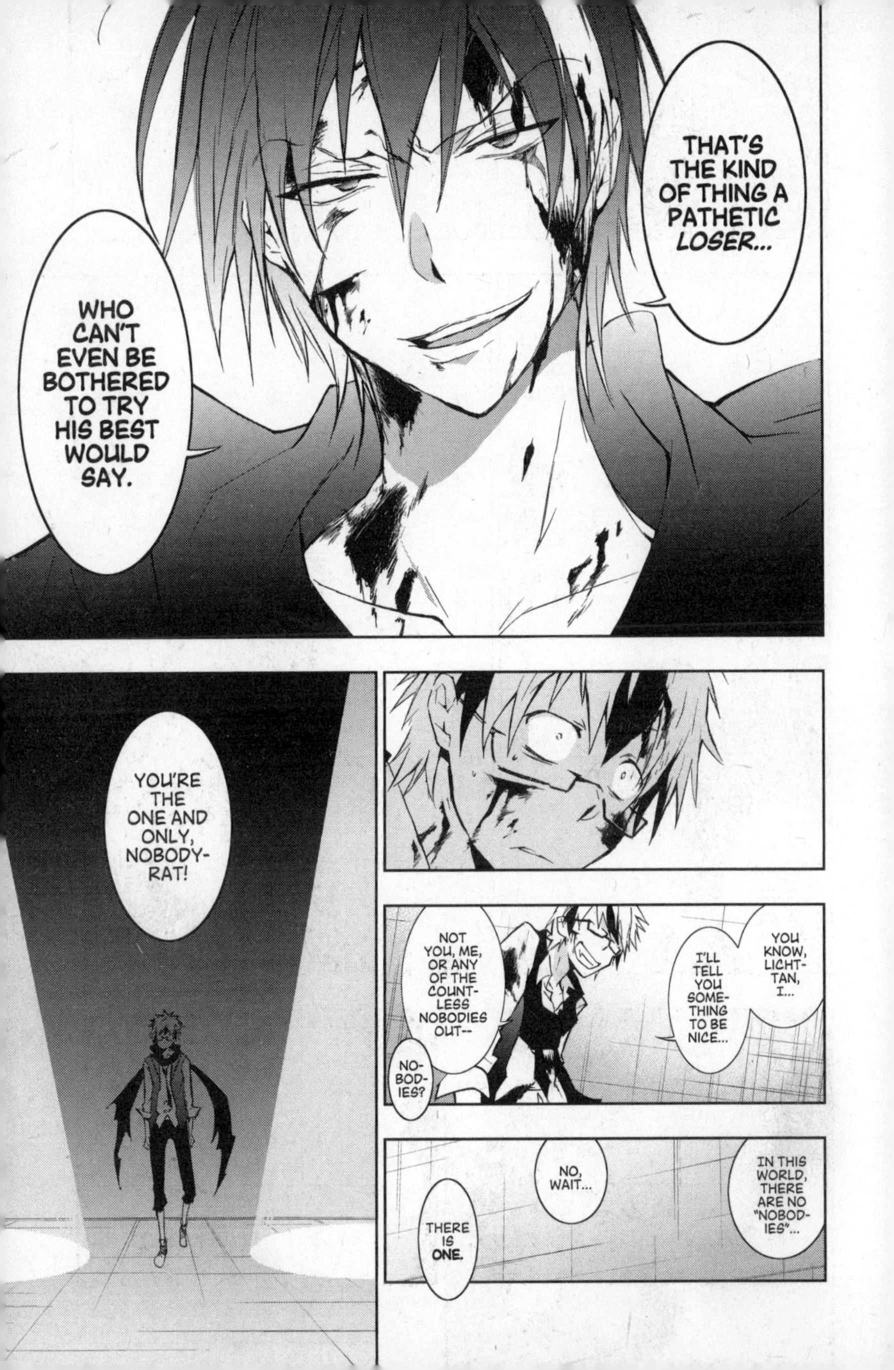
THAT'S THE KIND OF THING A PATHETIC *LOSER*...
WHO CAN'T EVEN BE BOTHERED TO TRY HIS BEST WOULD SAY.
YOU KNOW, LICHT-TAN, I...
I'LL TELL YOU SOMETHING TO BE NICE...
NOT YOU, ME, OR ANY OF THE COUNTLESS NOBODIES OUT--
NOBODIES?
IN THIS WORLD, THERE ARE NO "NOBODIES"...
NO, WAIT...
THERE IS **ONE.**
YOU'RE THE ONE AND ONLY, NOBODY-RAT!

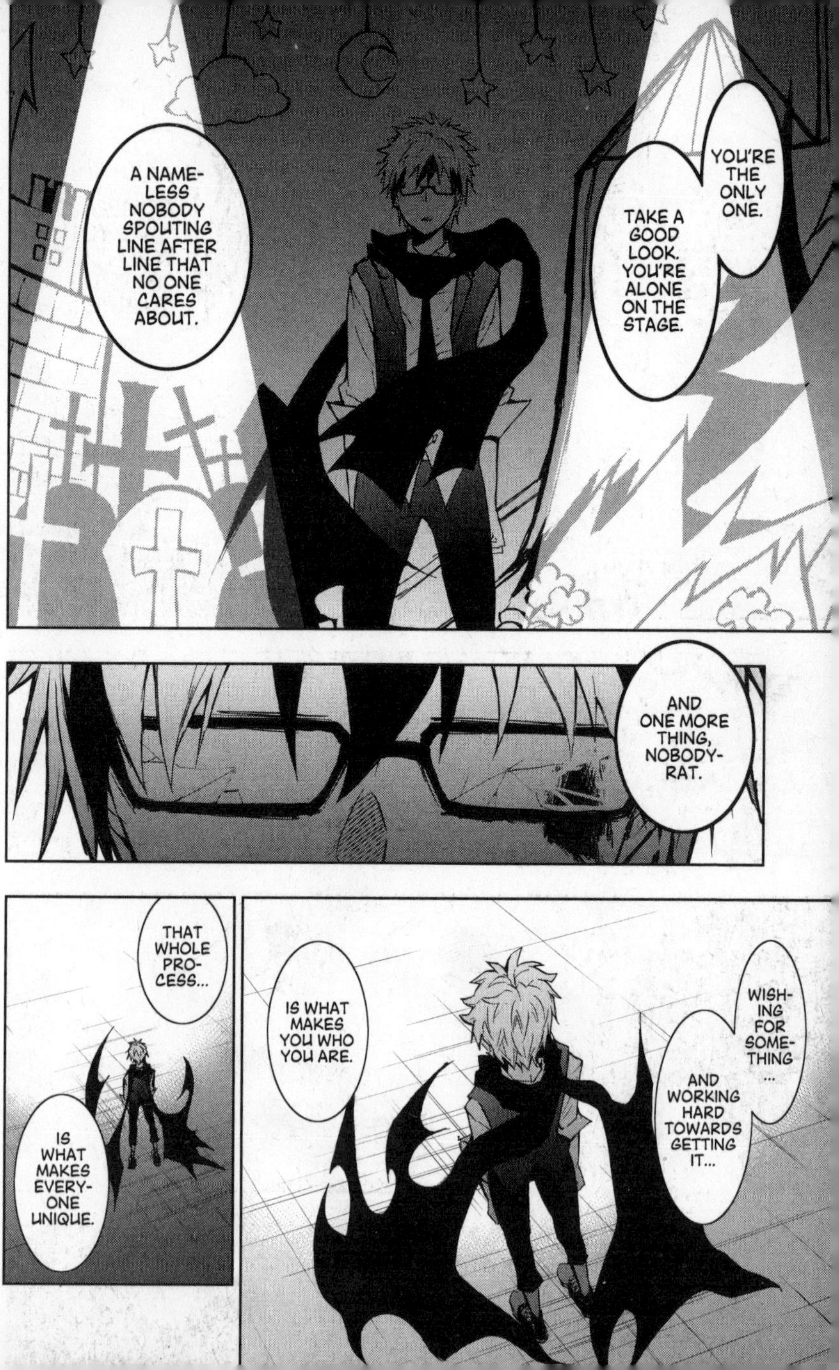
YOU'RE THE ONLY ONE.
TAKE A GOOD LOOK. YOU'RE ALONE ON THE STAGE.
A NAME-LESS NOBODY SPOUTING LINE AFTER LINE THAT NO ONE CARES ABOUT.
AND ONE MORE THING, NOBODY-RAT.
WISH-ING FOR SOME-THING...
AND WORKING HARD TOWARDS GETTING IT...
IS WHAT MAKES YOU WHO YOU ARE.
THAT WHOLE PRO-CESS...
IS WHAT MAKES EVERY-ONE UNIQUE.

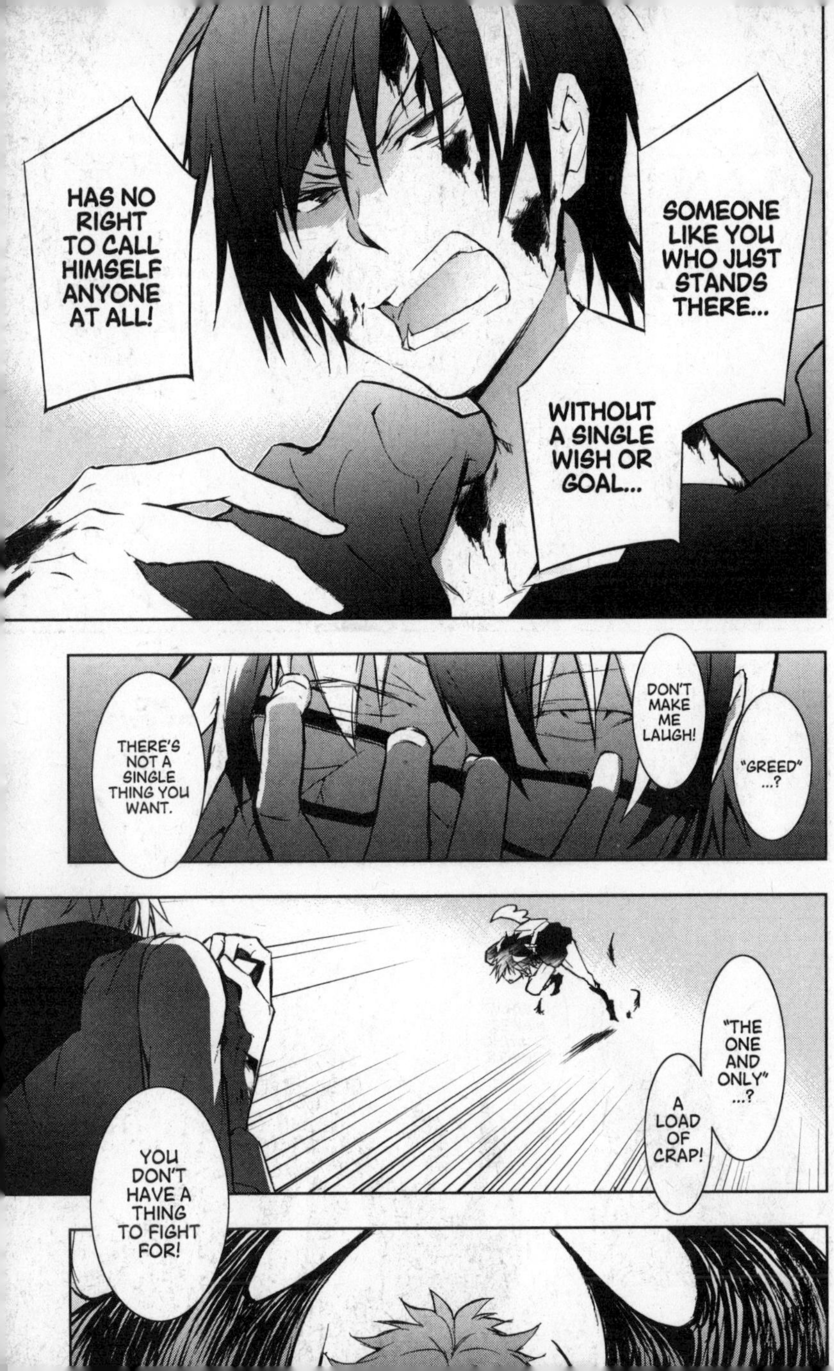
SOMEONE LIKE YOU WHO JUST STANDS THERE...
WITHOUT A SINGLE WISH OR GOAL...
HAS NO RIGHT TO CALL HIMSELF ANYONE AT ALL!
"GREED" ...?
DON'T MAKE ME LAUGH!
THERE'S NOT A SINGLE THING YOU WANT.
"THE ONE AND ONLY" ...?
A LOAD OF CRAP!
YOU DON'T HAVE A THING TO FIGHT FOR!

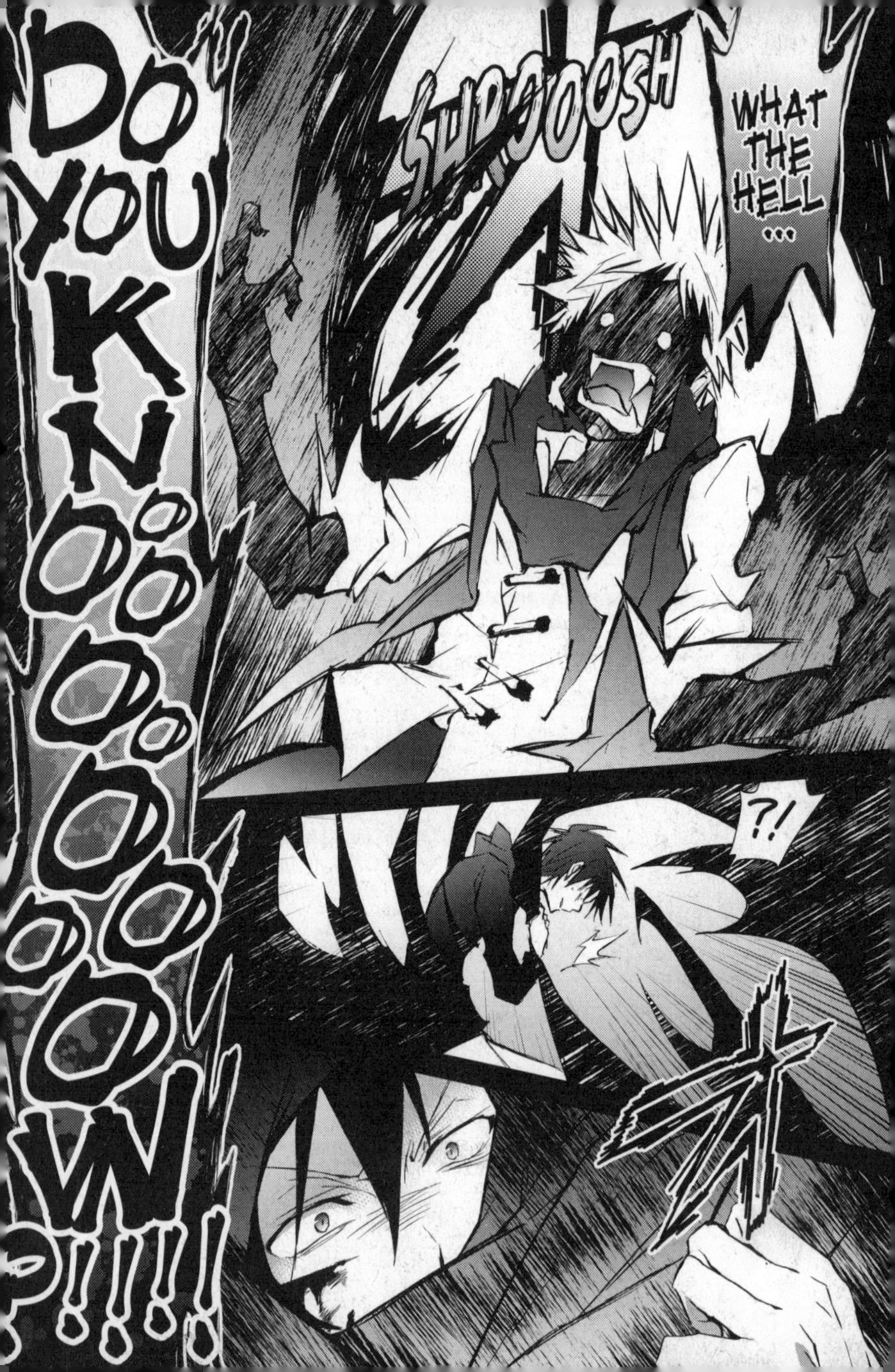
WHAT THE HELL ...
SHOOOOSH
?!
DO YOU KNOOOOOOOOOW?!!!

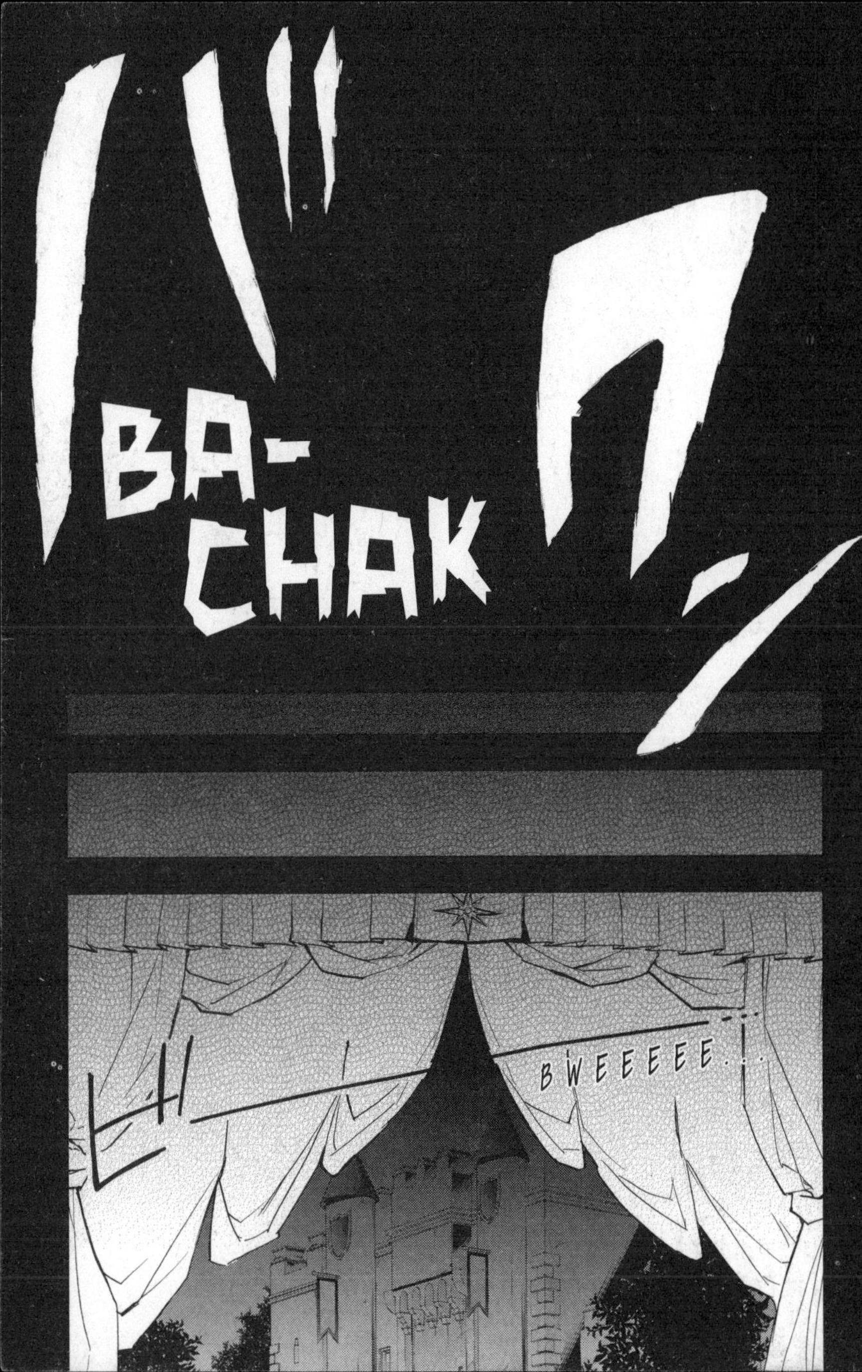
バシャッ
BA-CHAK
ピー
BWEEEEE...

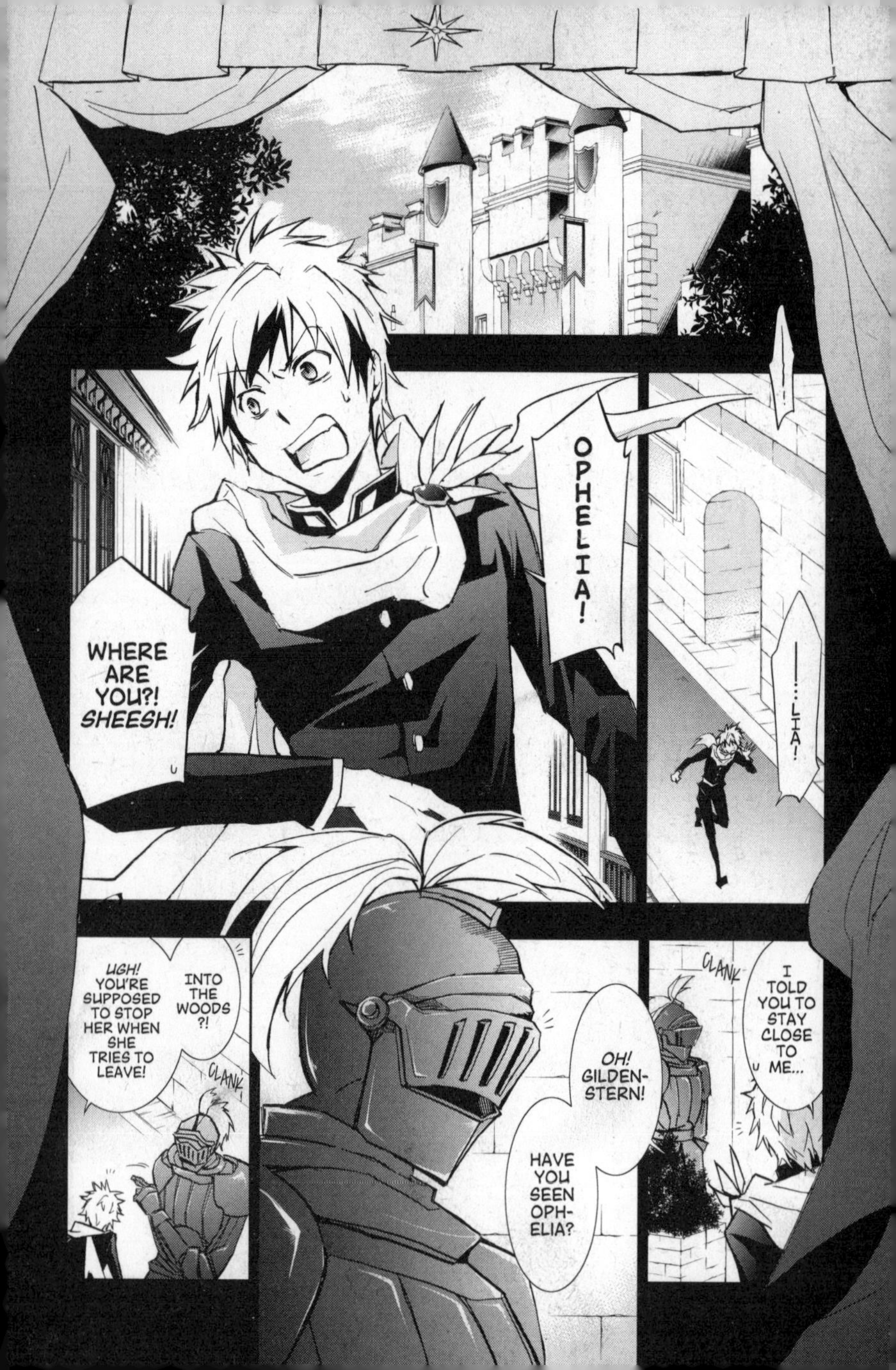

!
...LIA!
OPHELIA!
WHERE ARE YOU?! SHEESH!
CLANK
I TOLD YOU TO STAY CLOSE TO ME...
OH! GILDEN-STERN!
HAVE YOU SEEN OPH-ELIA?
INTO THE WOODS?!
UGH! YOU'RE SUPPOSED TO STOP HER WHEN SHE TRIES TO LEAVE!
CLANK

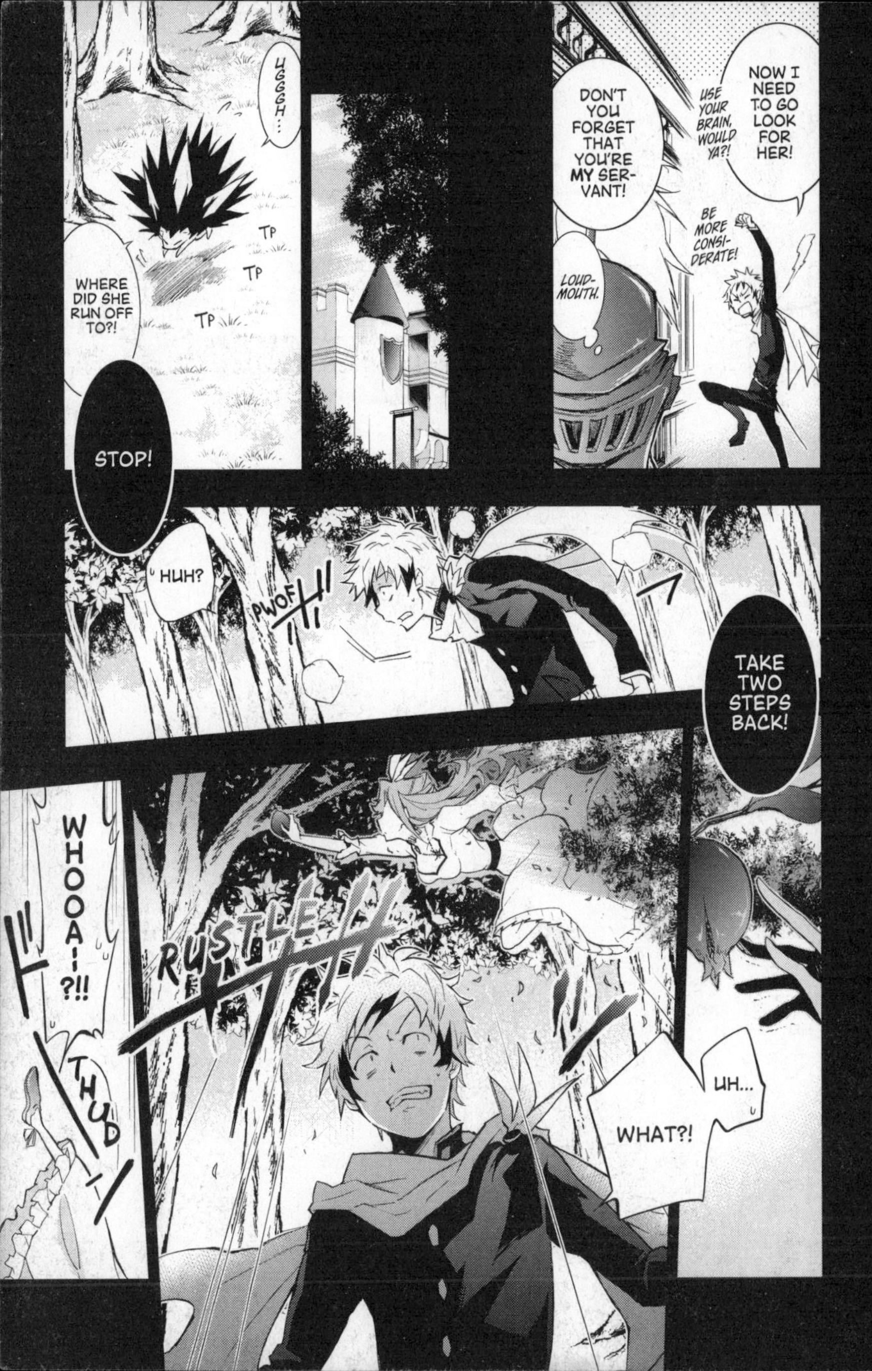
NOW I NEED TO GO LOOK FOR HER!
USE YOUR BRAIN, WOULD YA?!
BE MORE CONSIDERATE!
DON'T YOU FORGET THAT YOU'RE MY SERVANT!
LOUDMOUTH.
UGGGH...
TP
TP
TP
WHERE DID SHE RUN OFF TO?!
STOP!
TAKE TWO STEPS BACK!
HUH?
PWOF
UH...
WHAT?!
RUSTLE
WHOOAAI?!!
THUD

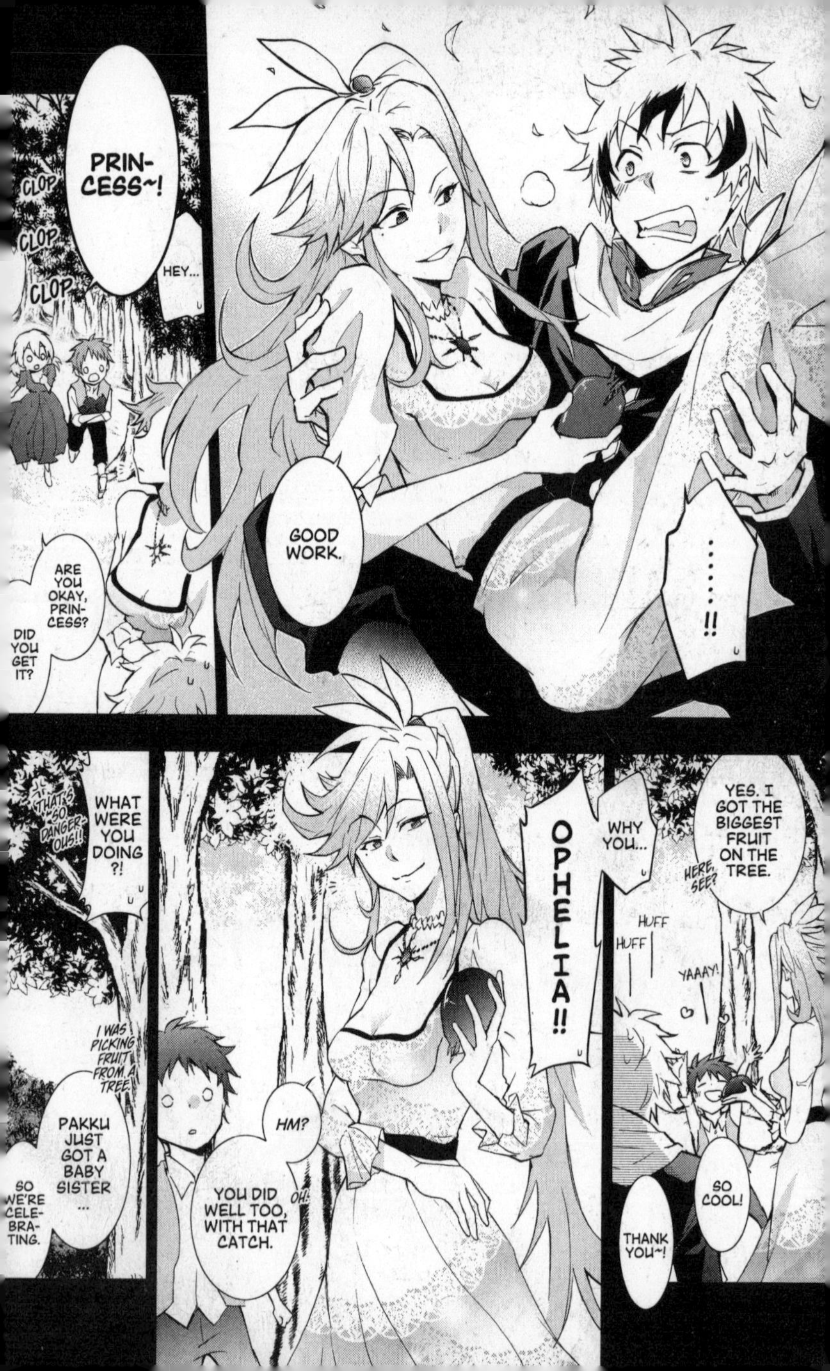

GOOD WORK.
......!!
PRIN-CESS~!
CLOP
CLOP
CLOP
HEY...
ARE YOU OKAY, PRIN-CESS?
DID YOU GET IT?
YES. I GOT THE BIGGEST FRUIT ON THE TREE.
HERE, SEE?
HUFF
HUFF
YAAAY!
SO COOL!
THANK YOU~!
WHY YOU...
OPHELIA!!
HM?
OH!
YOU DID WELL TOO, WITH THAT CATCH.
THAT'S SO DANGER-OUS!!
WHAT WERE YOU DOING ?!
I WAS PICKING FRUIT FROM A TREE.
PAKKU JUST GOT A BABY SISTER ...
SO WE'RE CELE-BRA-TING.

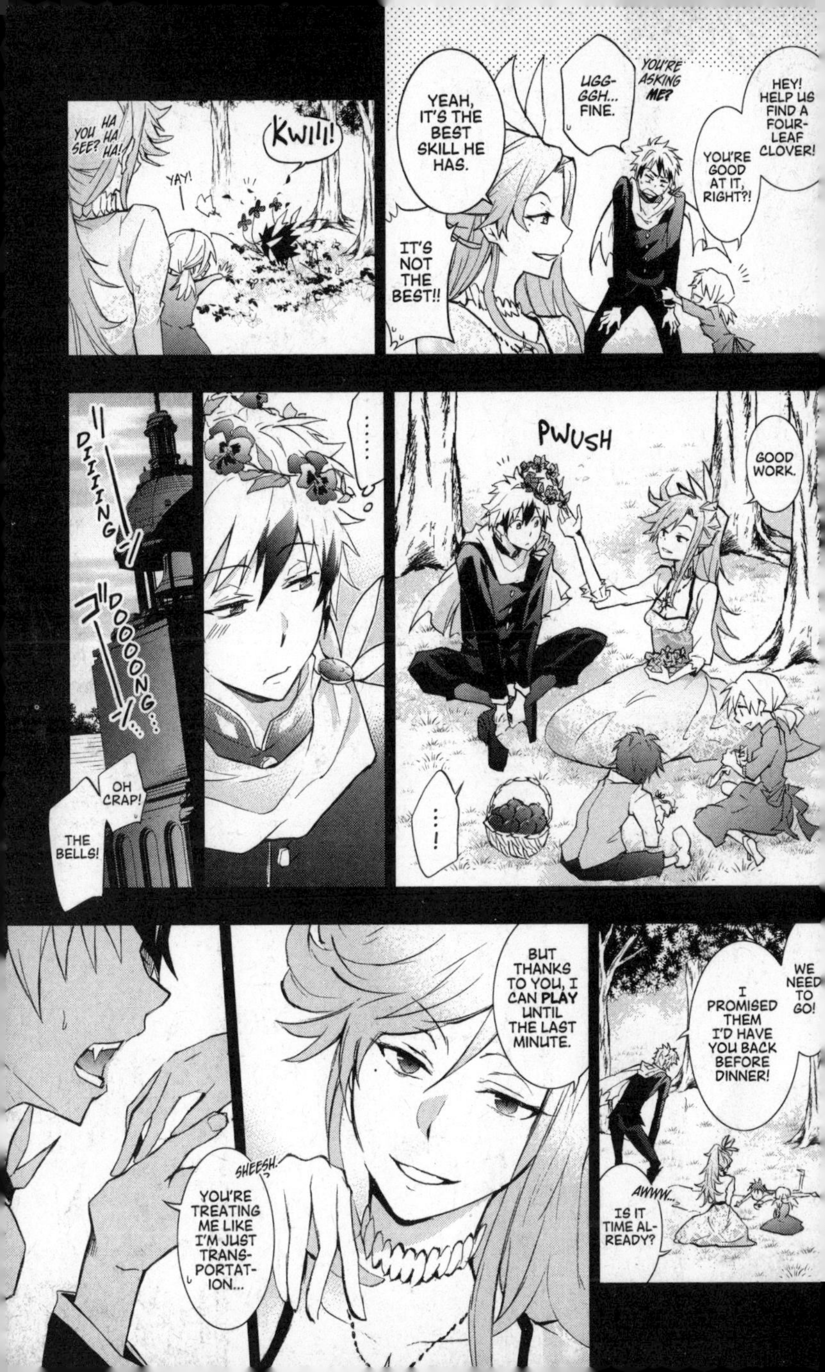
HEY! HELP US FIND A FOUR-LEAF CLOVER!
YOU'RE GOOD AT IT, RIGHT?!
YOU'RE ASKING **ME?**
UGG-GGH... FINE.
YEAH, IT'S THE BEST SKILL HE HAS.
IT'S NOT THE BEST!!
KWIII!
YOU SEE? HA HA HA!
YAY!
GOOD WORK.
PWUSH
...!
......
DIIIIING
DOOOOONG...
OH CRAP!
THE BELLS!
WE NEED TO GO!
I PROMISED THEM I'D HAVE YOU BACK BEFORE DINNER!
AWWW...
IS IT TIME AL-READY?
BUT THANKS TO YOU, I CAN **PLAY** UNTIL THE LAST MINUTE.
SHEESH.
YOU'RE TREATING ME LIKE I'M JUST TRANS-PORTAT-ION...

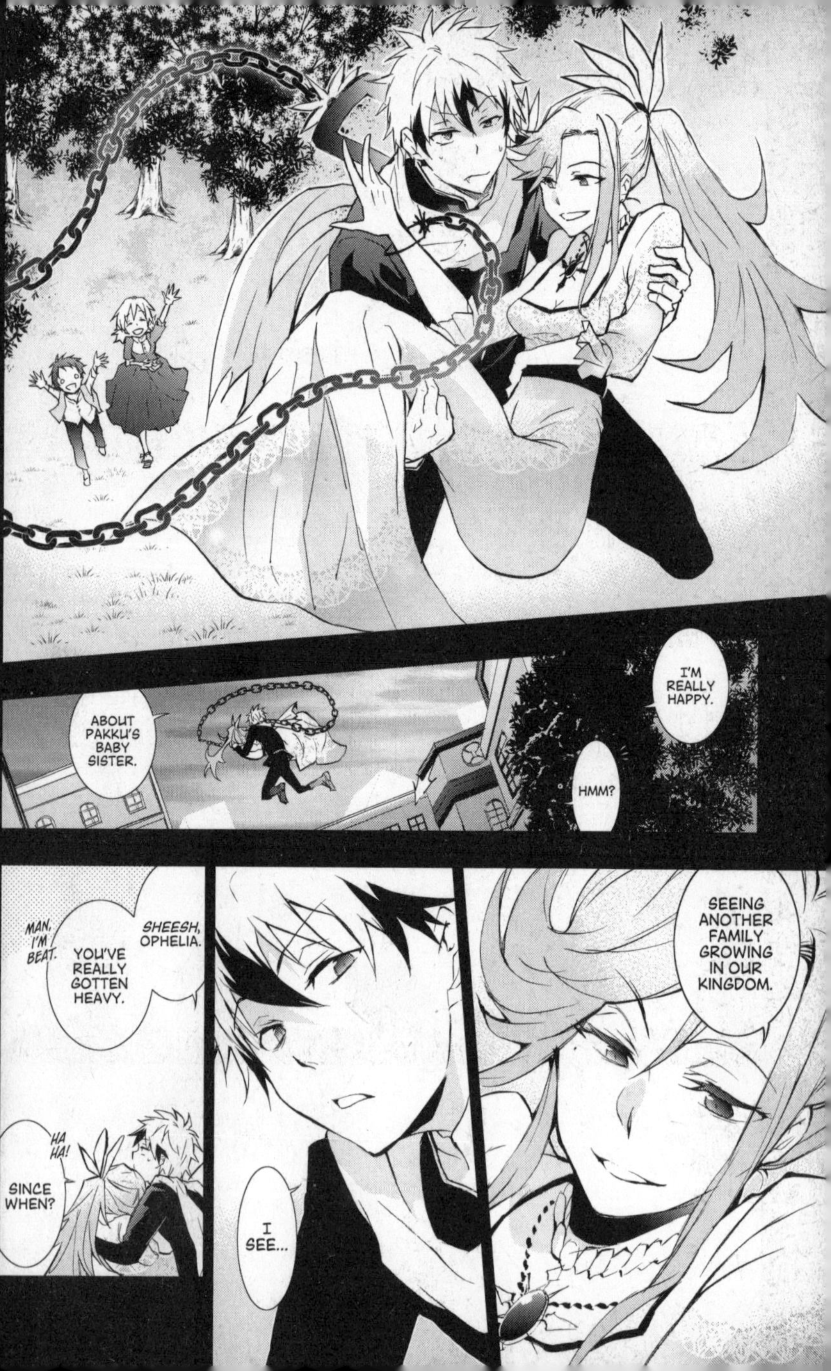
I'M REALLY HAPPY.
HMM?
ABOUT PAKKU'S BABY SISTER.
SEEING ANOTHER FAMILY GROWING IN OUR KINGDOM.
I SEE...
SHEESH, OPHELIA.
YOU'VE REALLY GOTTEN HEAVY.
MAN, I'M BEAT.
HA HA!
SINCE WHEN?

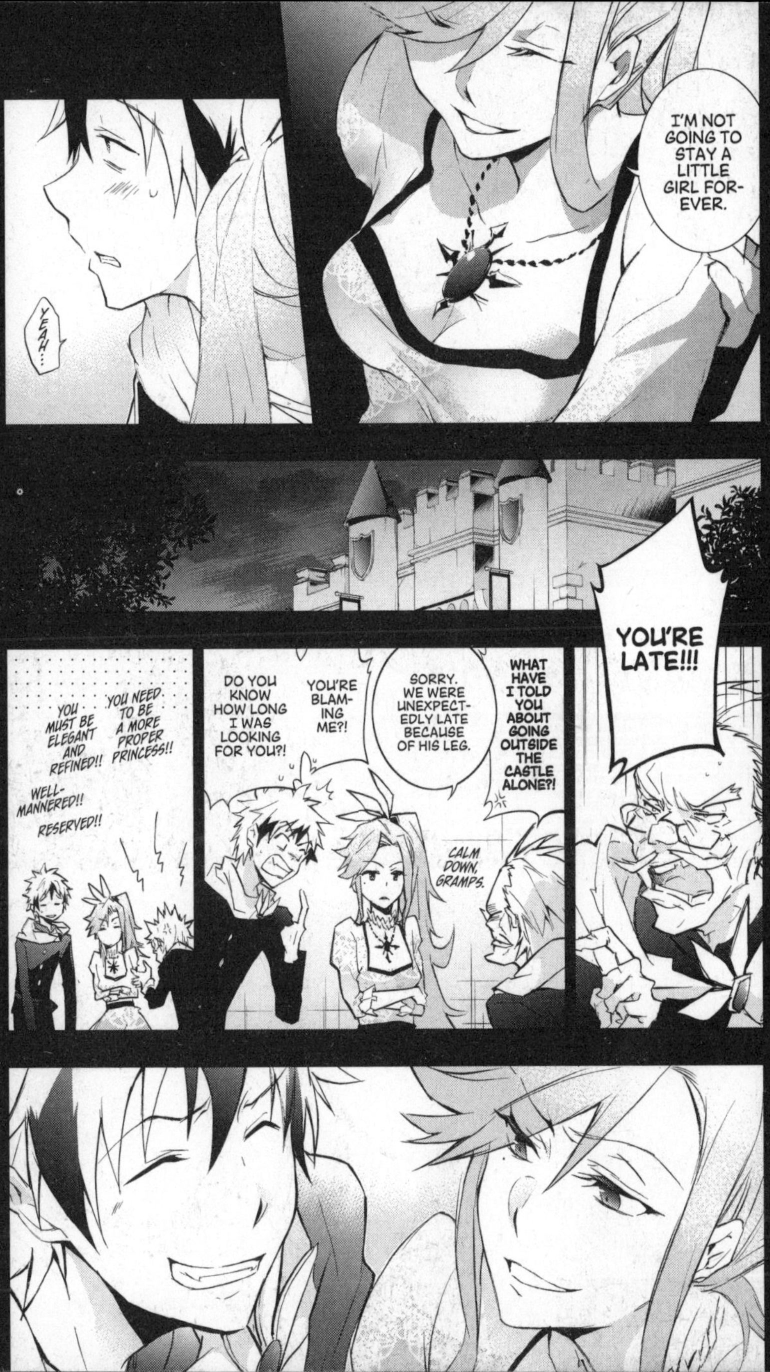
I'M NOT GOING TO STAY A LITTLE GIRL FOREVER.
YEAH...
YOU'RE LATE!!!
WHAT HAVE I TOLD YOU ABOUT GOING OUTSIDE THE CASTLE ALONE?!
SORRY. WE WERE UNEXPECTEDLY LATE BECAUSE OF HIS LEG.
YOU'RE BLAMING ME?!
DO YOU KNOW HOW LONG I WAS LOOKING FOR YOU?!
CALM DOWN, GRAMPS.
YOU NEED TO BE A MORE PROPER PRINCESS!!
YOU MUST BE ELEGANT AND REFINED!!
WELL-MANNERED!!
RESERVED!!

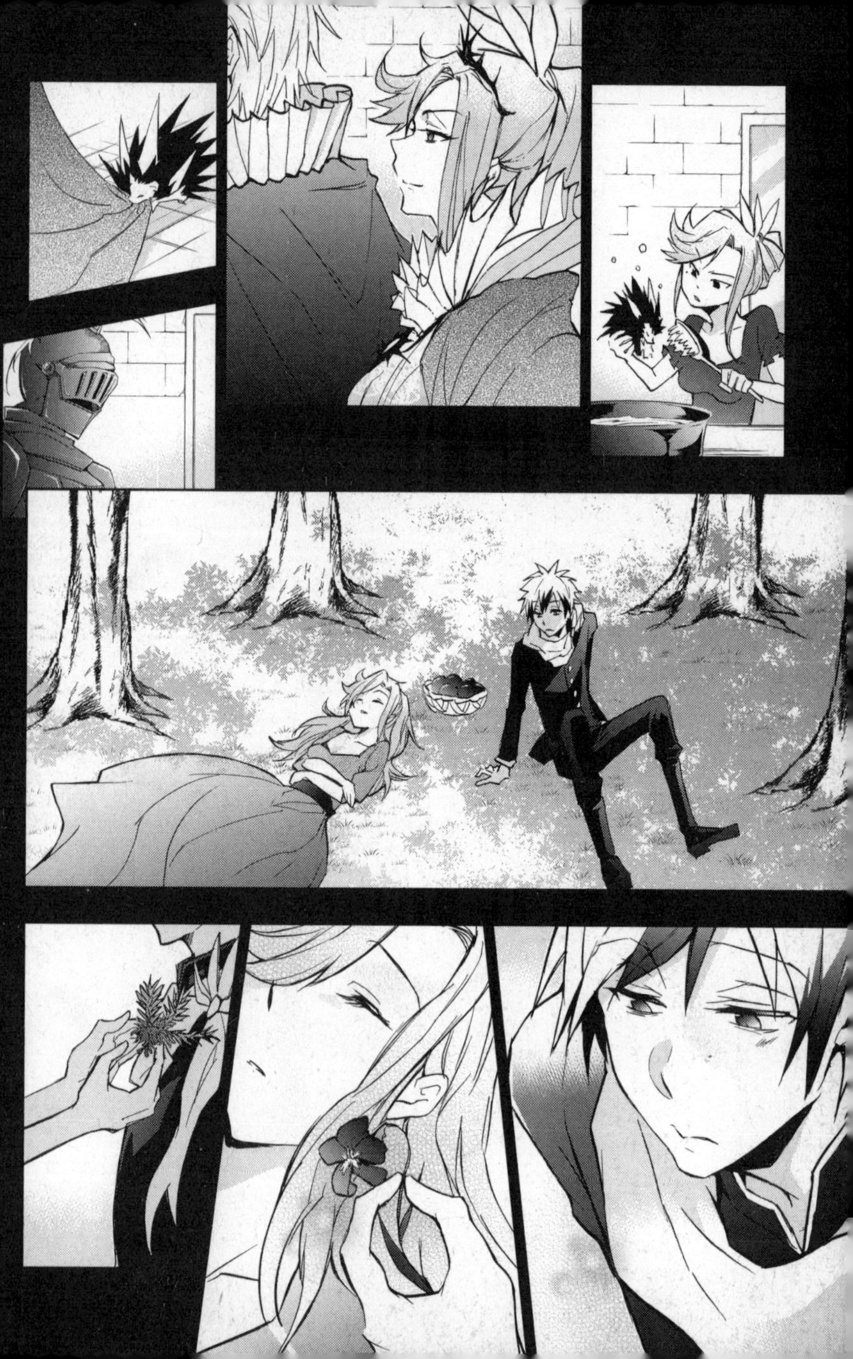

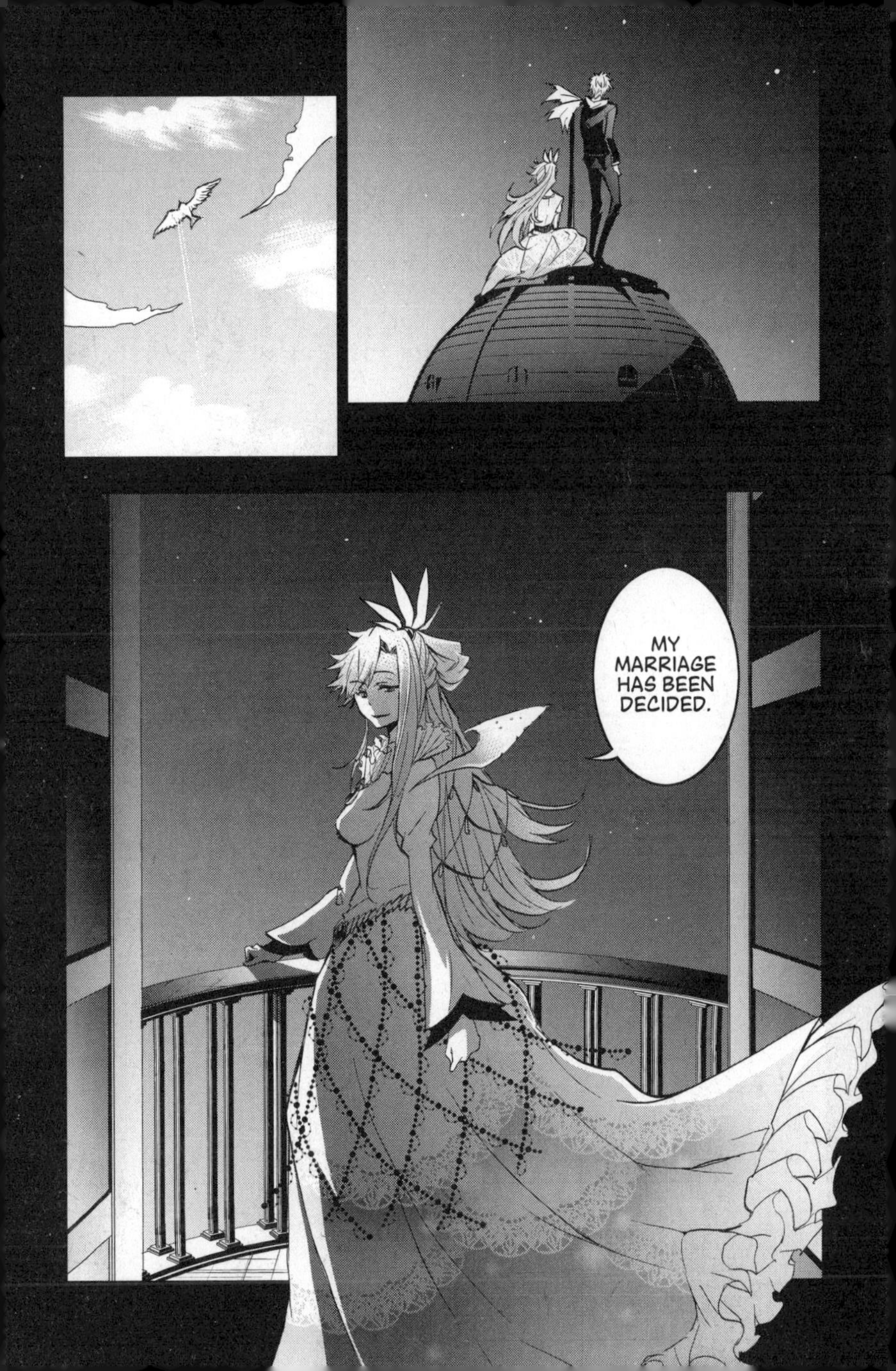
MY MARRIAGE HAS BEEN DECIDED.

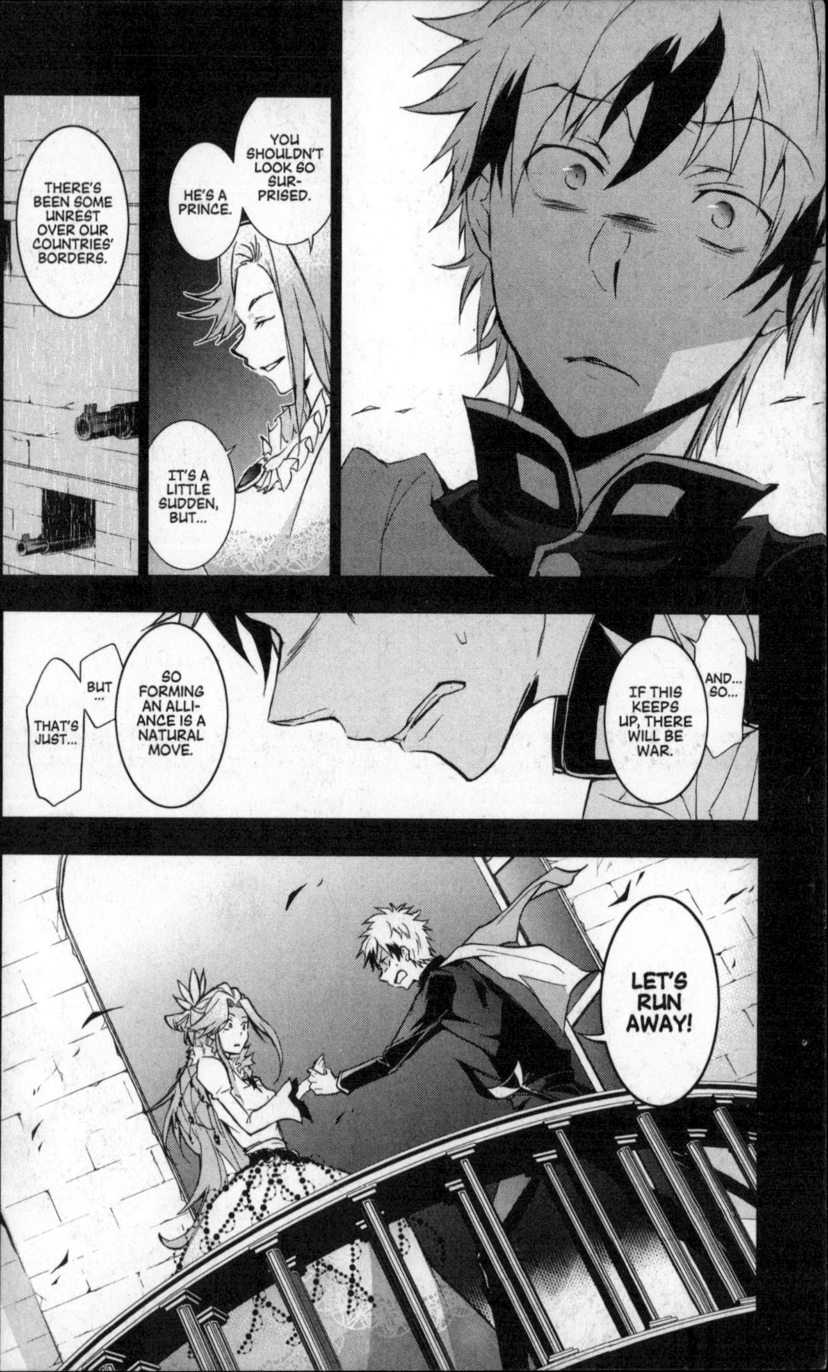
YOU SHOULDN'T LOOK SO SUR-PRISED.
HE'S A PRINCE.
IT'S A LITTLE SUDDEN, BUT...
THERE'S BEEN SOME UNREST OVER OUR COUNTRIES' BORDERS.
AND... SO...
IF THIS KEEPS UP, THERE WILL BE WAR.
SO FORMING AN ALLI-ANCE IS A NATURAL MOVE.
BUT...
THAT'S JUST...
LET'S RUN AWAY!

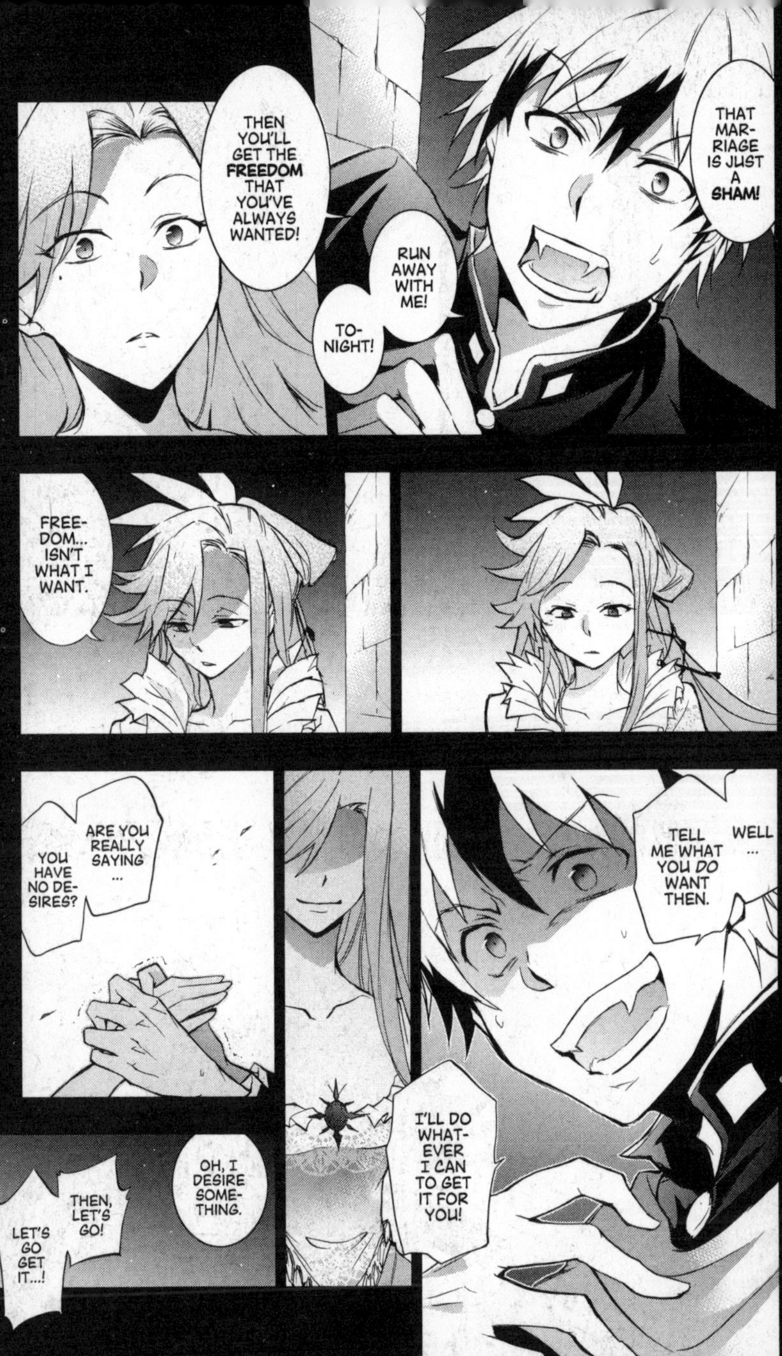
THAT MARRIAGE IS JUST A **SHAM!**
RUN AWAY WITH ME!
TO-NIGHT!
THEN YOU'LL GET THE **FREEDOM** THAT YOU'VE ALWAYS WANTED!
FREEDOM... ISN'T WHAT I WANT.
WELL ...
TELL ME WHAT YOU *DO* WANT THEN.
I'LL DO WHATEVER I CAN TO GET IT FOR YOU!
ARE YOU REALLY SAYING ...
YOU HAVE NO DESIRES?
OH, I DESIRE SOMETHING.
THEN, LET'S GO!
LET'S GO GET IT...!

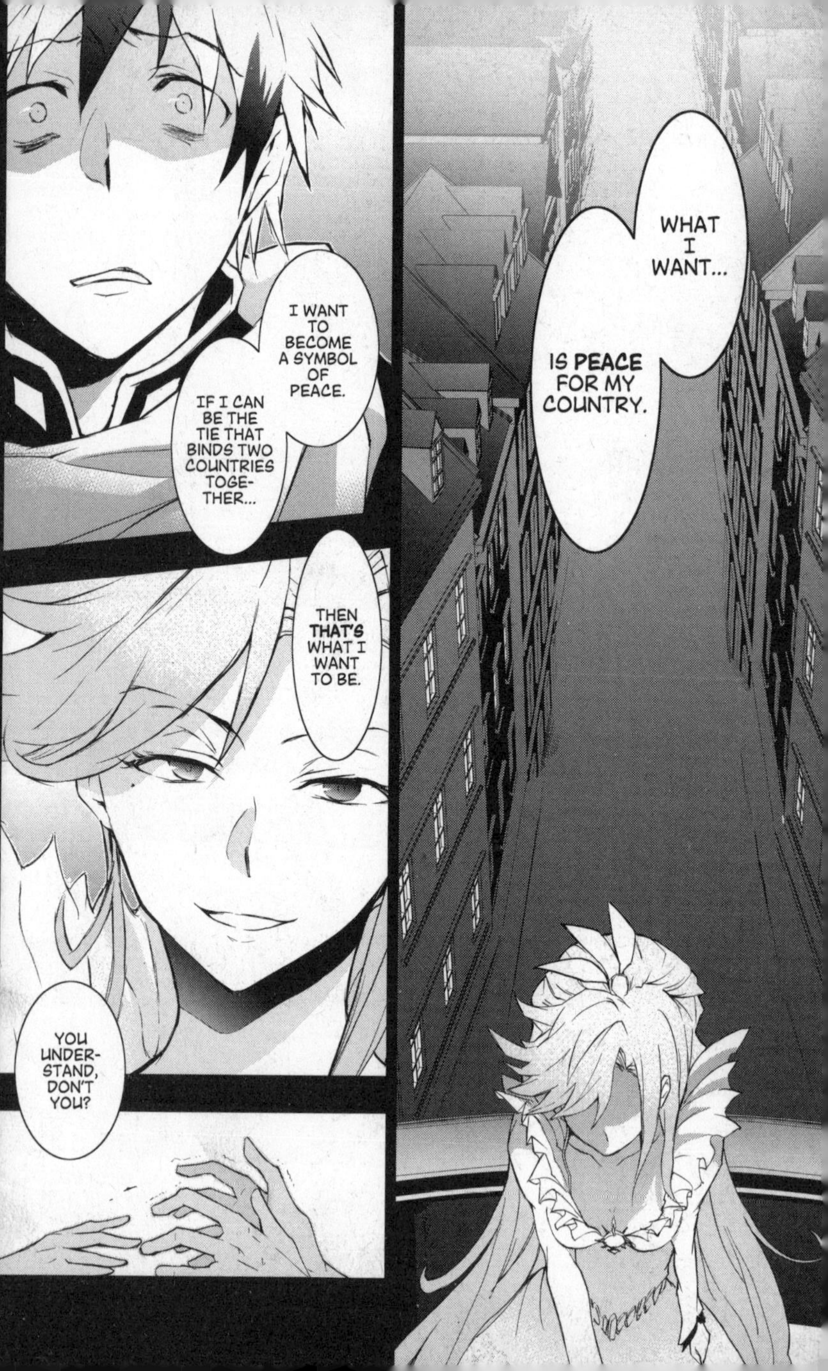
WHAT I WANT...
IS PEACE FOR MY COUNTRY.
I WANT TO BECOME A SYMBOL OF PEACE.
IF I CAN BE THE TIE THAT BINDS TWO COUNTRIES TOGE-THER...
THEN THAT'S WHAT I WANT TO BE.
YOU UNDER-STAND, DON'T YOU?

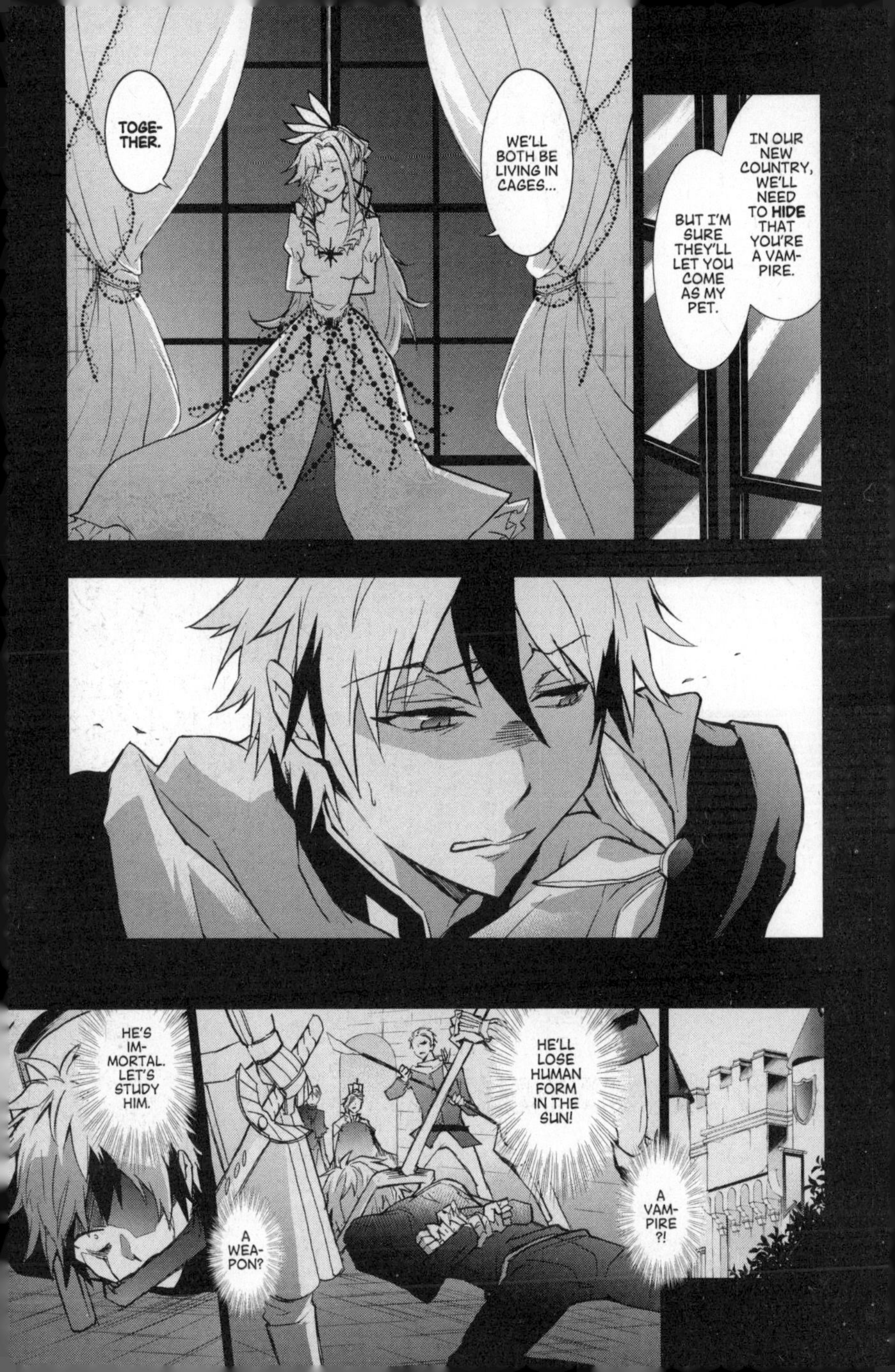
IN OUR NEW COUNTRY, WE'LL NEED TO **HIDE** THAT YOU'RE A VAM-PIRE.
BUT I'M SURE THEY'LL LET YOU COME AS MY PET.
WE'LL BOTH BE LIVING IN CAGES...
TOGE-THER.
HE'LL LOSE HUMAN FORM IN THE SUN!
A VAM-PIRE ?!
HE'S IM-MORTAL. LET'S STUDY HIM.
A WEA-PON?

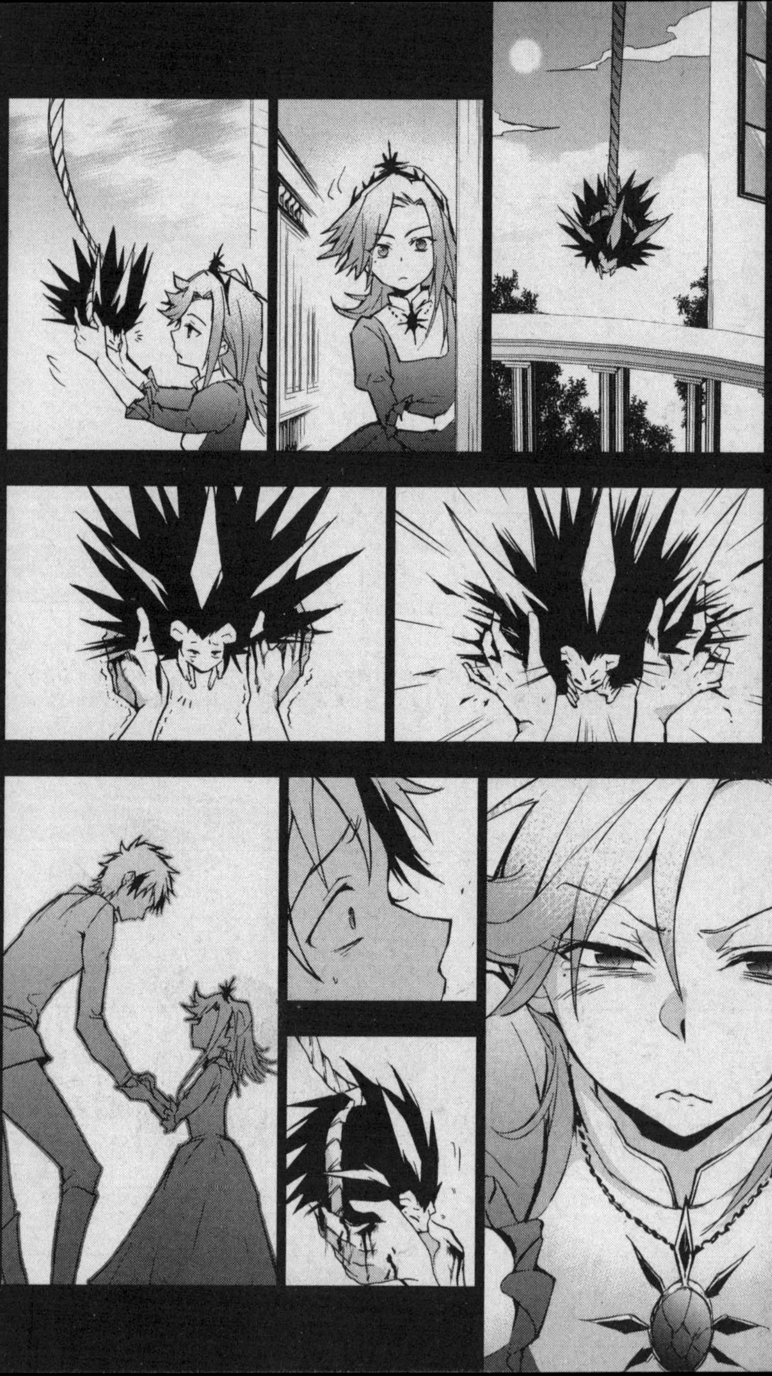

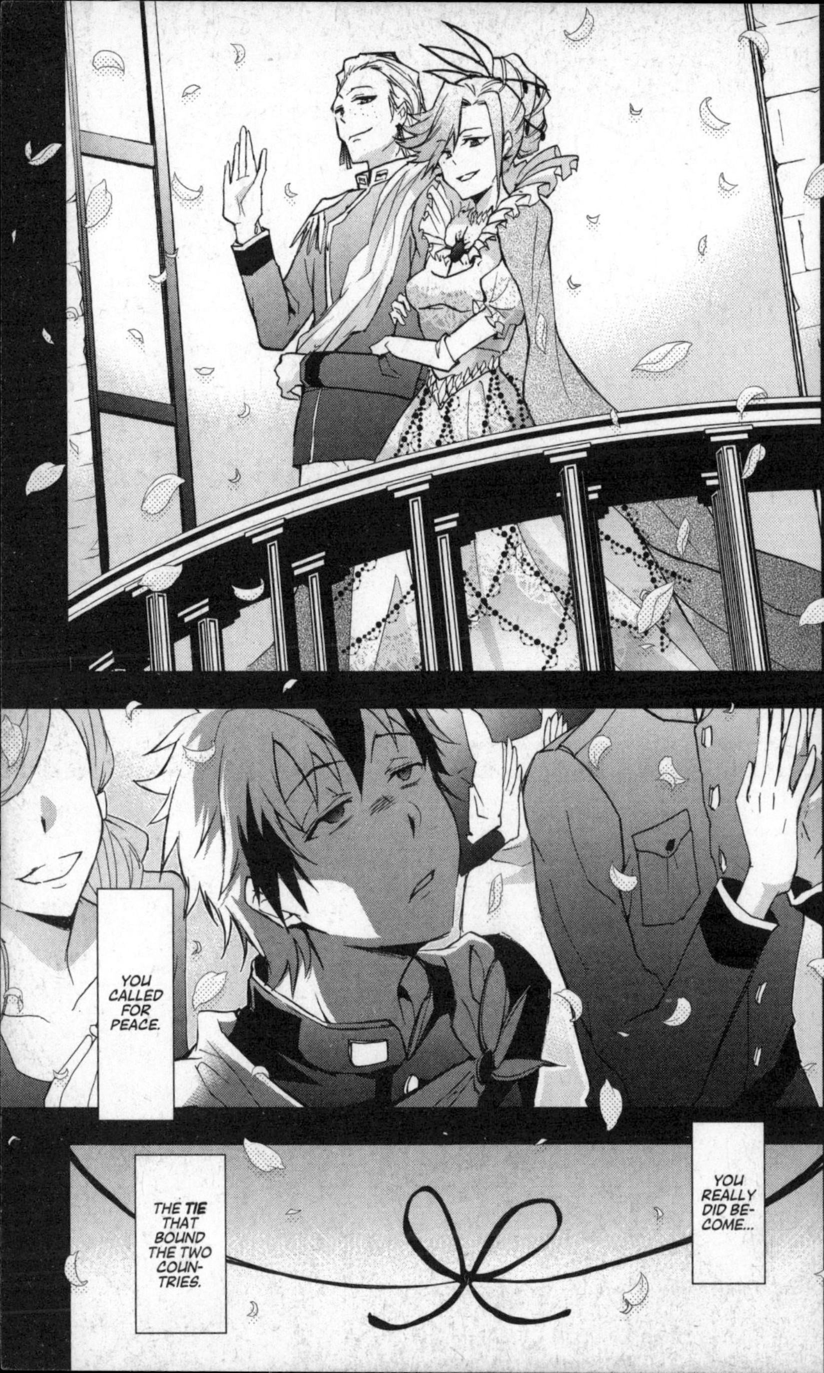
YOU CALLED FOR PEACE.
YOU REALLY DID BE-COME...
THE TIE THAT BOUND THE TWO COUN-TRIES.

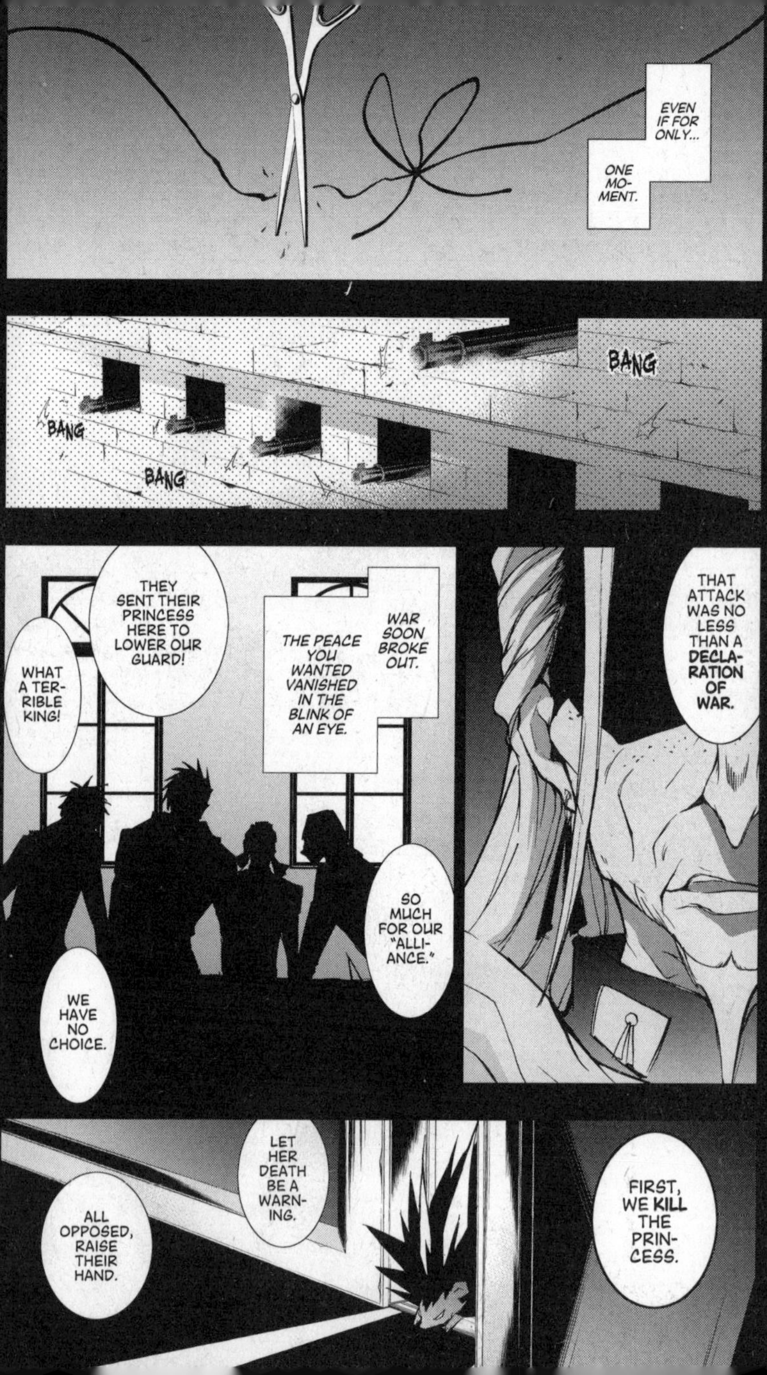
EVEN IF FOR ONLY...
ONE MOMENT.
BANG
BANG
BANG
THAT ATTACK WAS NO LESS THAN A **DECLARATION OF WAR.**
WAR SOON BROKE OUT.
THE PEACE YOU WANTED VANISHED IN THE BLINK OF AN EYE.
THEY SENT THEIR PRINCESS HERE TO LOWER OUR GUARD!
WHAT A TERRIBLE KING!
SO MUCH FOR OUR "ALLIANCE."
WE HAVE NO CHOICE.
FIRST, WE **KILL** THE PRINCESS.
LET HER DEATH BE A WARNING.
ALL OPPOSED, RAISE THEIR HAND.

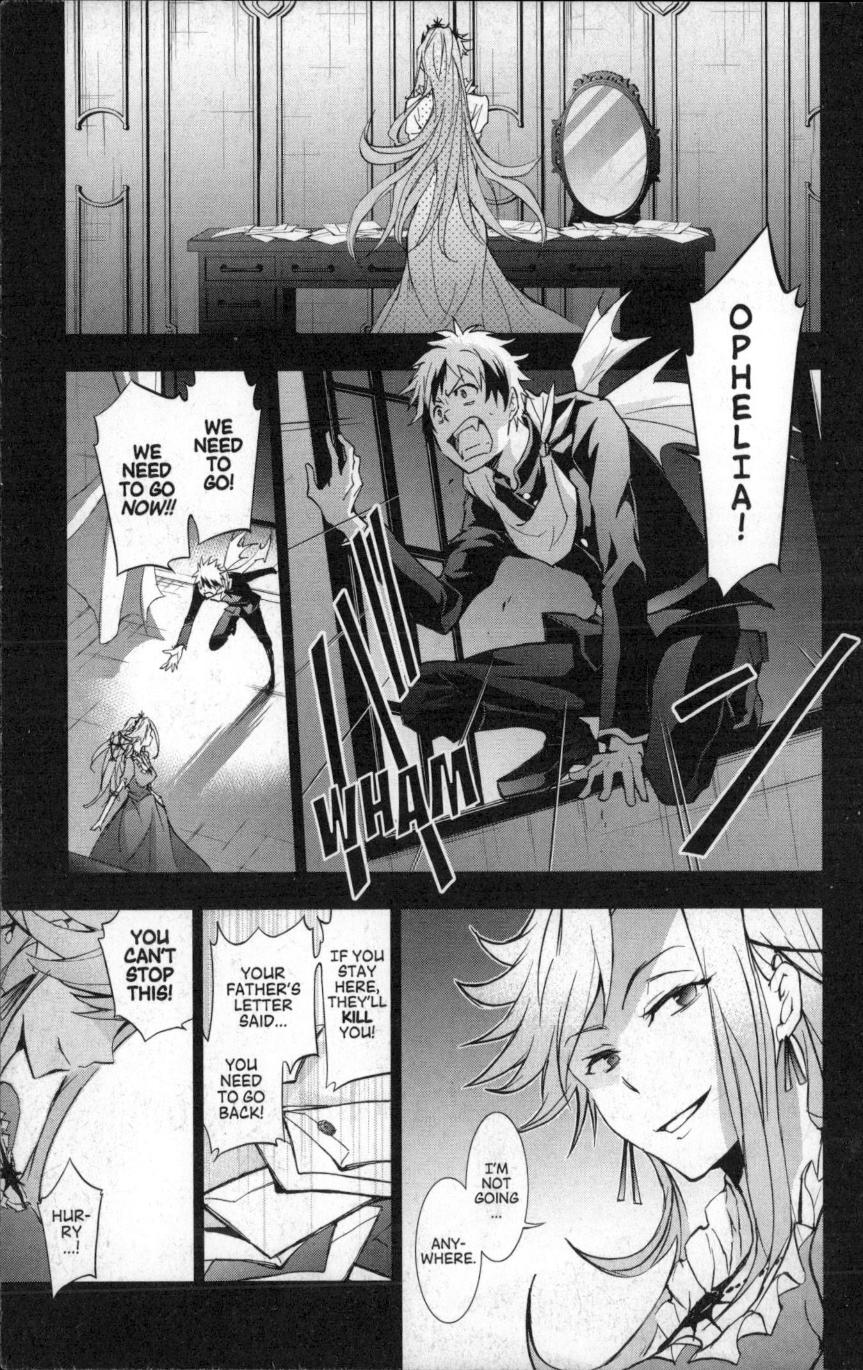
OPHELIA!
WHAM
WE NEED TO GO!
WE NEED TO GO NOW!!
I'M NOT GOING...
ANYWHERE.
YOUR FATHER'S LETTER SAID...
IF YOU STAY HERE, THEY'LL KILL YOU!
YOU NEED TO GO BACK!
YOU CAN'T STOP THIS!
HURRY...!

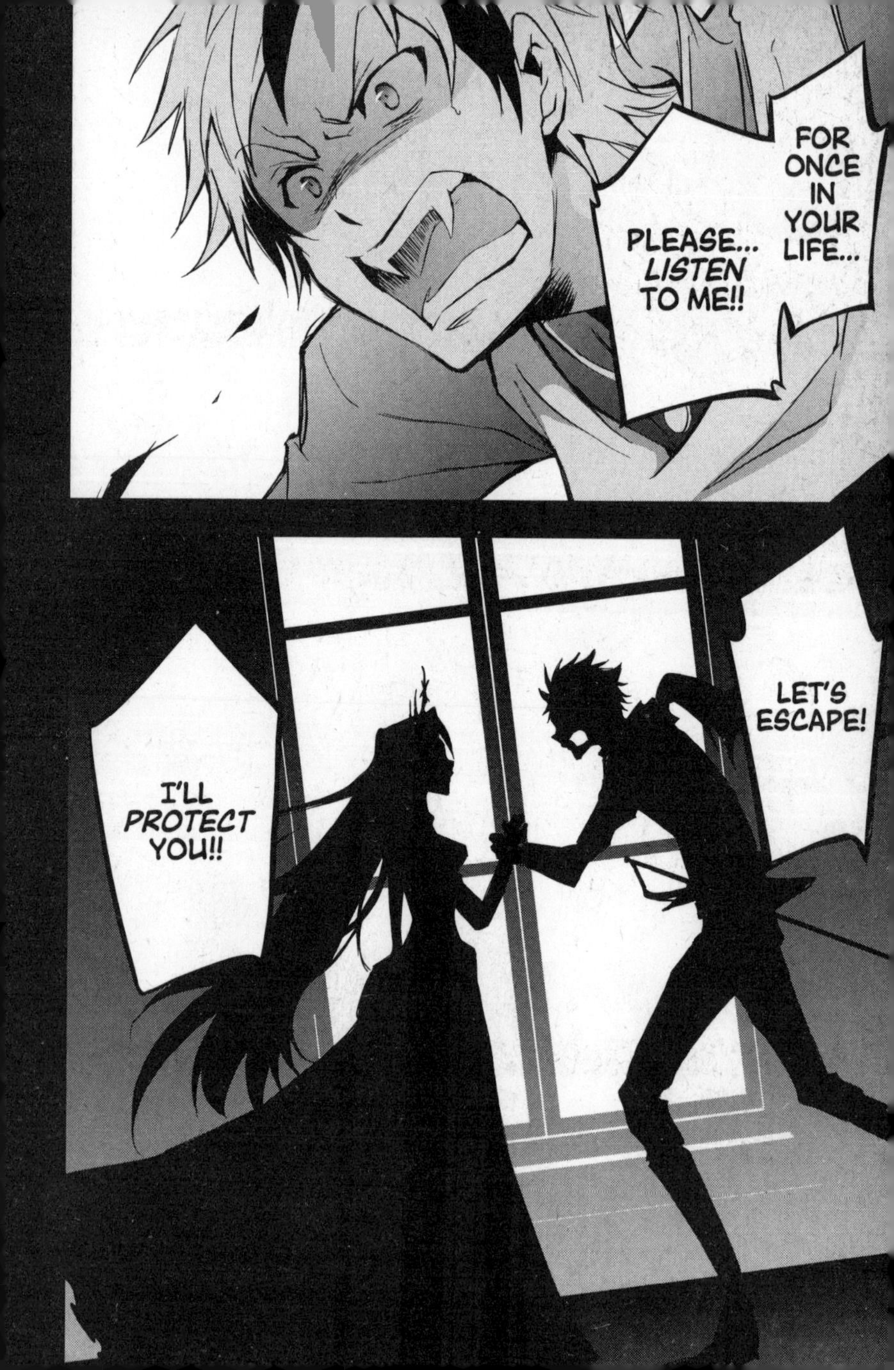
FOR ONCE IN YOUR LIFE...
PLEASE... *LISTEN* TO ME!!
LET'S ESCAPE!
I'LL *PROTECT* YOU!!

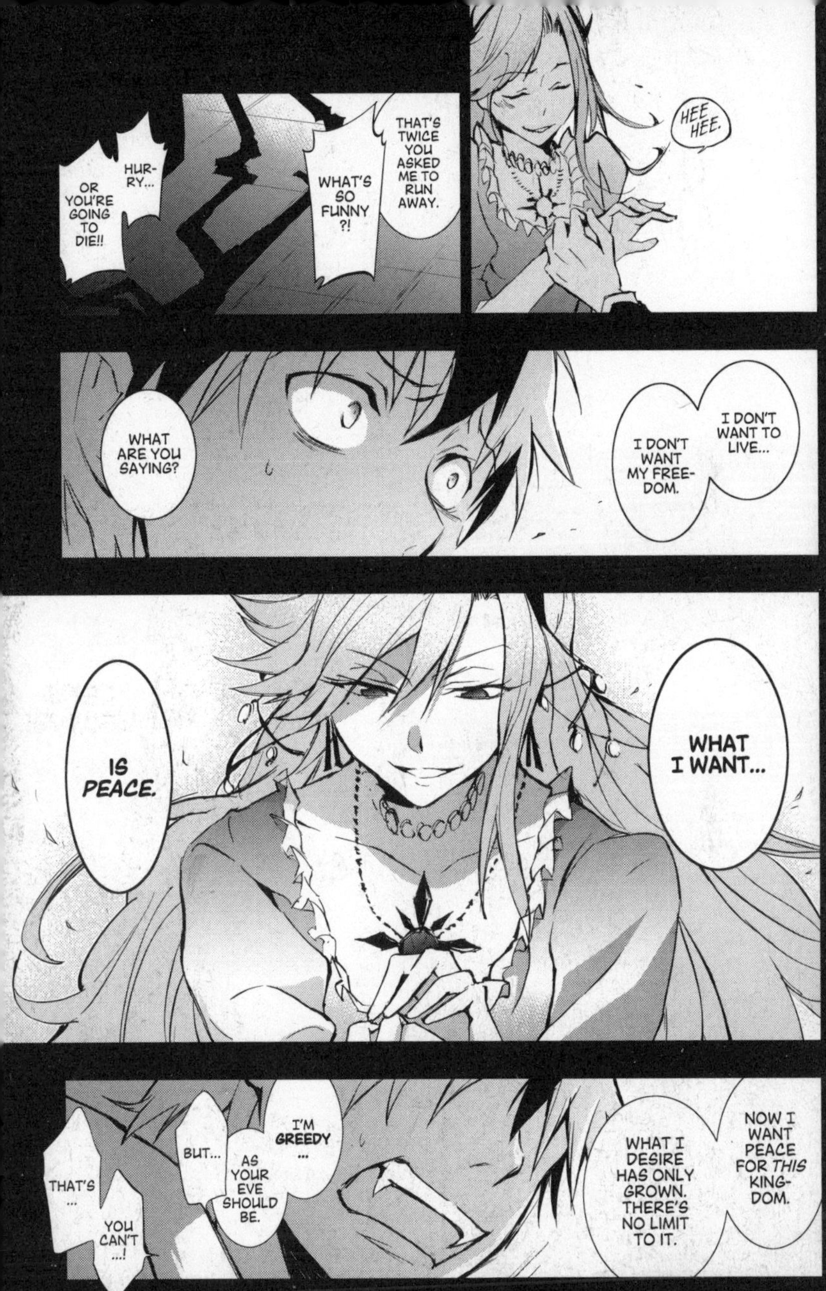
HEE HEE.
THAT'S TWICE YOU ASKED ME TO RUN AWAY.
WHAT'S SO FUNNY?!
HUR-RY...
OR YOU'RE GOING TO DIE!!
I DON'T WANT TO LIVE...
I DON'T WANT MY FREE-DOM.
WHAT ARE YOU SAYING?
WHAT I WANT...
IS PEACE.
NOW I WANT PEACE FOR *THIS* KING-DOM.
WHAT I DESIRE HAS ONLY GROWN. THERE'S NO LIMIT TO IT.
I'M **GREEDY**...
AS YOUR EVE SHOULD BE.
BUT...
THAT'S...
YOU CAN'T...!

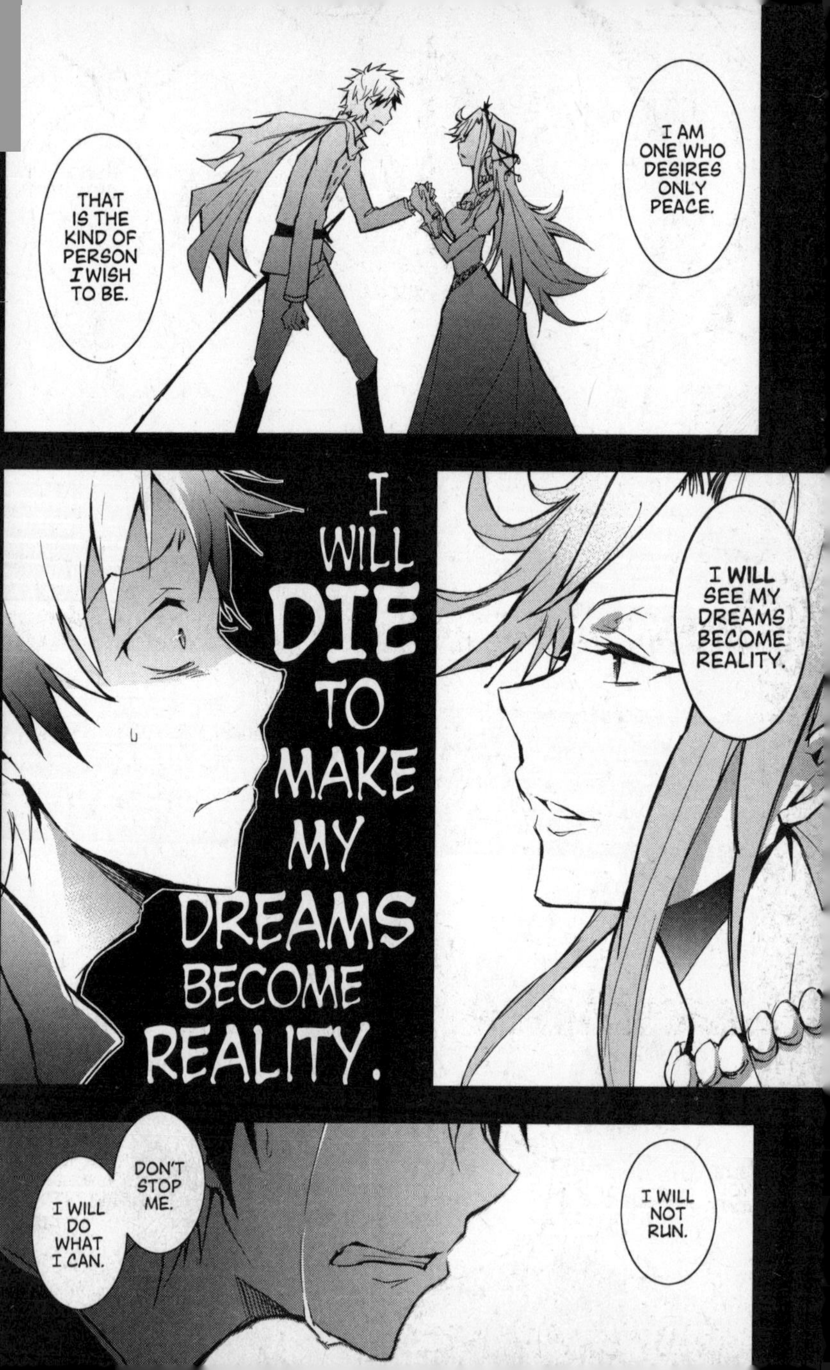
I AM ONE WHO DESIRES ONLY PEACE.
THAT IS THE KIND OF PERSON *I* WISH TO BE.
I **WILL** SEE MY DREAMS BECOME REALITY.
I WILL **DIE** TO MAKE MY DREAMS BECOME REALITY.
I WILL NOT RUN.
DON'T STOP ME.
I WILL DO WHAT I CAN.

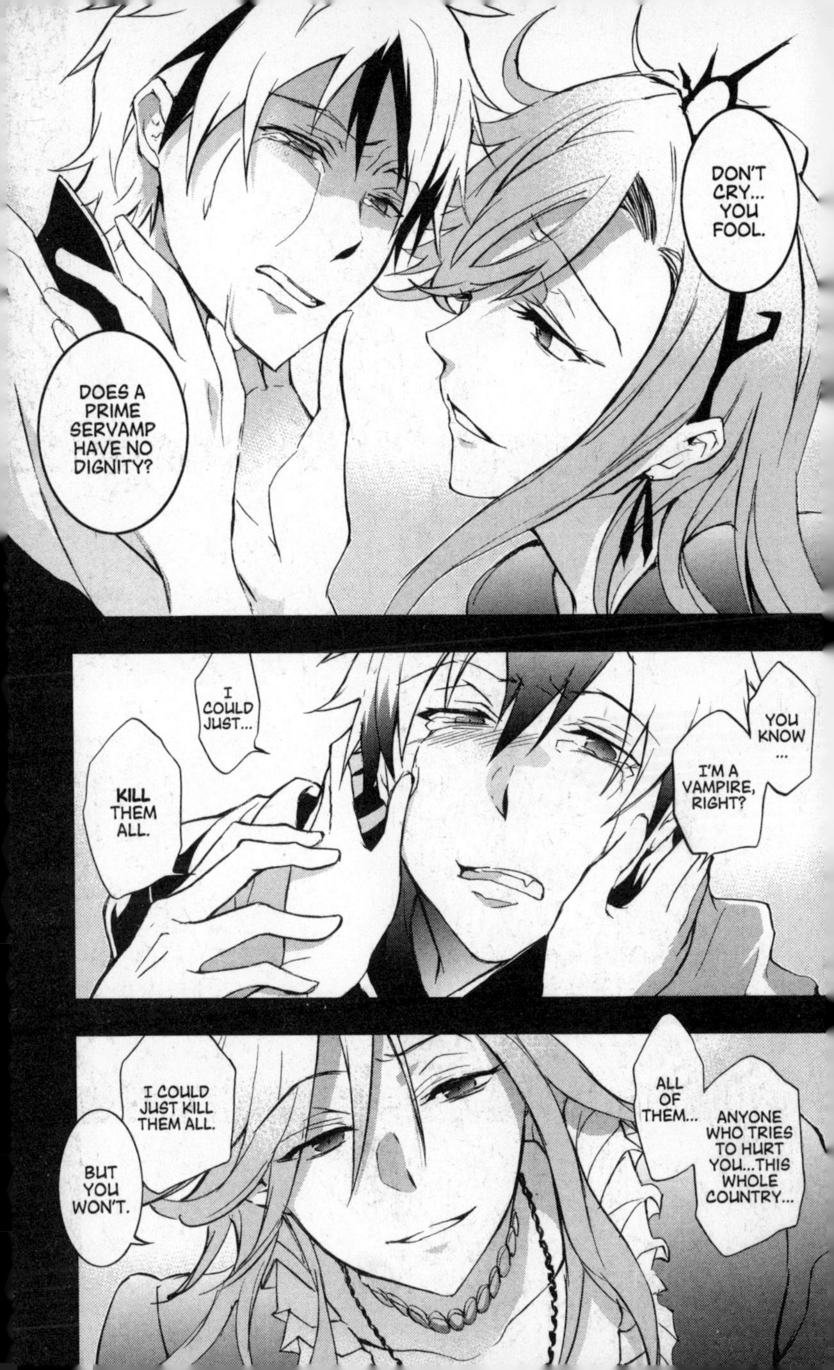
DON'T CRY... YOU FOOL.
DOES A PRIME SERVAMP HAVE NO DIGNITY?
YOU KNOW ... I'M A VAMPIRE, RIGHT?
I COULD JUST...
**KILL** THEM ALL.
ANYONE WHO TRIES TO HURT YOU...THIS WHOLE COUNTRY...
ALL OF THEM...
I COULD JUST KILL THEM ALL.
BUT YOU WON'T.

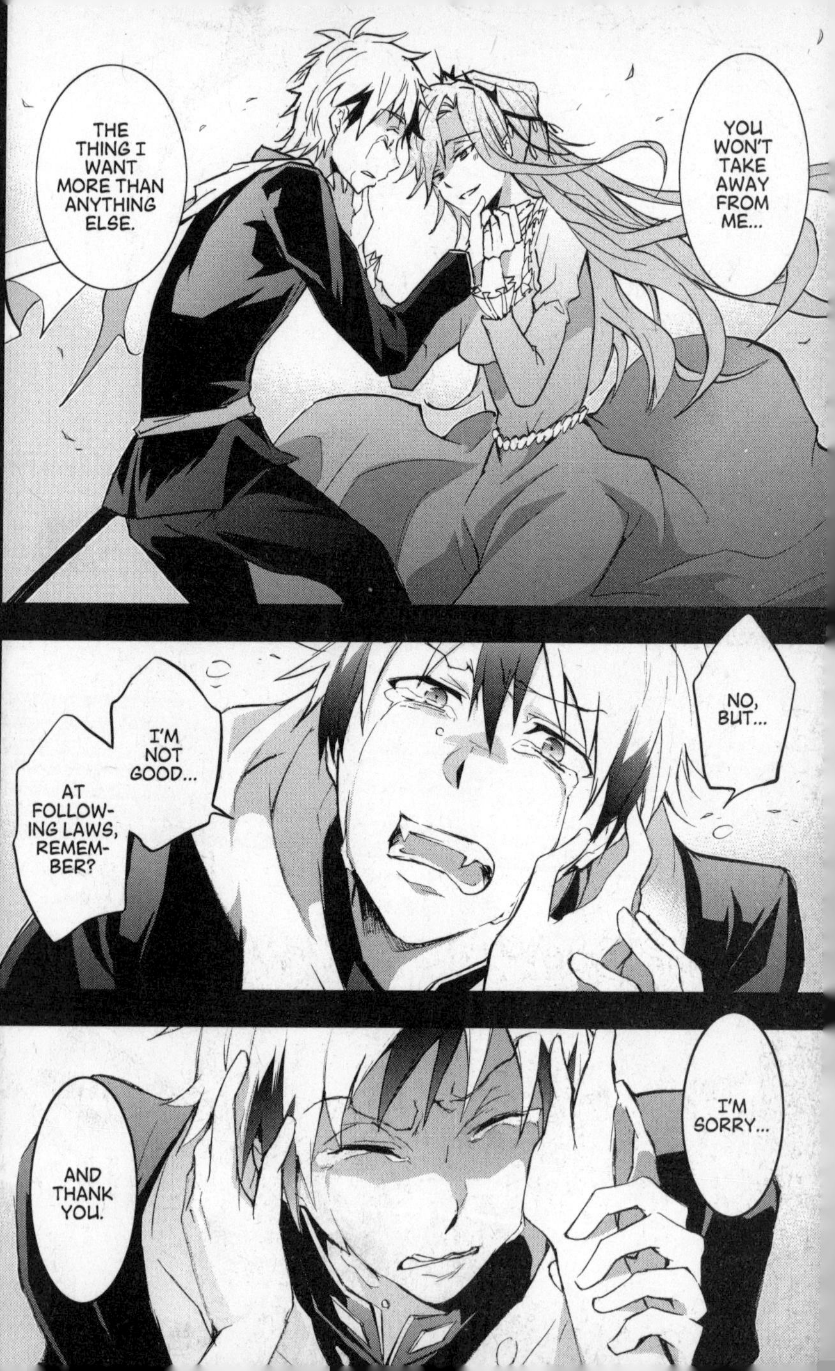
YOU WON'T TAKE AWAY FROM ME...
THE THING I WANT MORE THAN ANYTHING ELSE.
NO, BUT...
I'M NOT GOOD...
AT FOLLOW-ING LAWS, REMEMBER?
I'M SORRY...
AND THANK YOU.

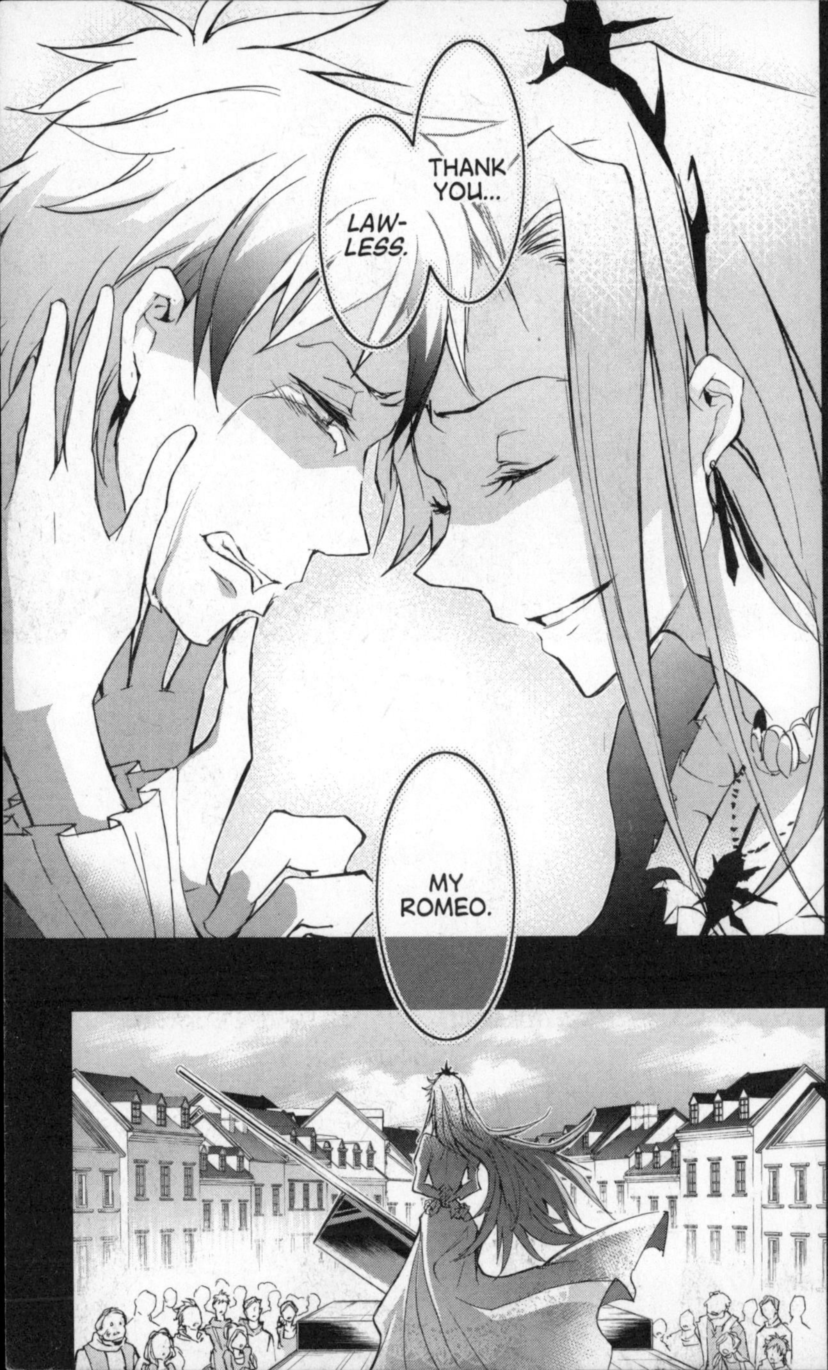
THANK YOU...
LAW-LESS.
MY ROMEO.

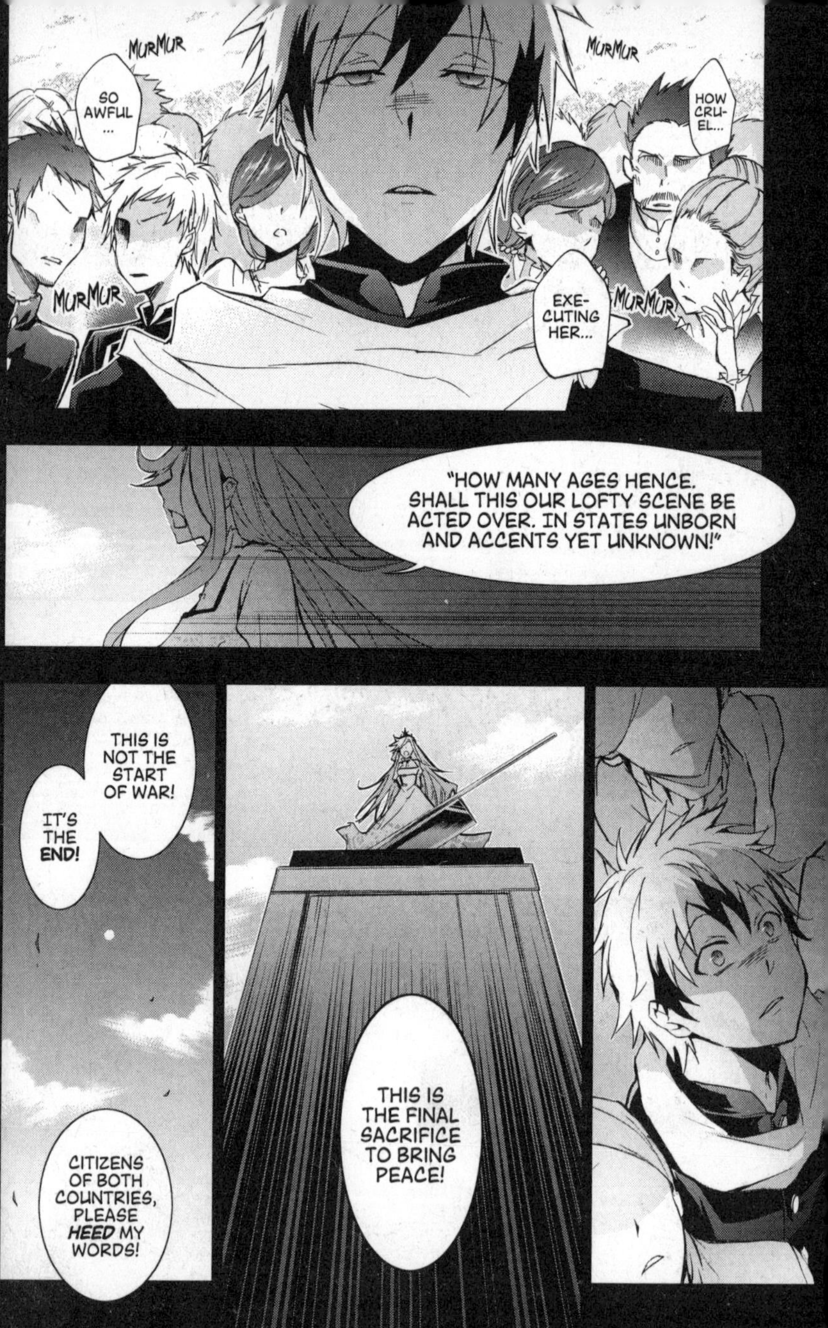
MURMUR
HOW CRUEL...
MURMUR
SO AWFUL ...
EXECUTING HER...
MURMUR
MURMUR
"HOW MANY AGES HENCE. SHALL THIS OUR LOFTY SCENE BE ACTED OVER. IN STATES UNBORN AND ACCENTS YET UNKNOWN!"
THIS IS THE FINAL SACRIFICE TO BRING PEACE!
THIS IS NOT THE START OF WAR!
IT'S THE **END!**
CITIZENS OF BOTH COUNTRIES, PLEASE ***HEED*** MY WORDS!

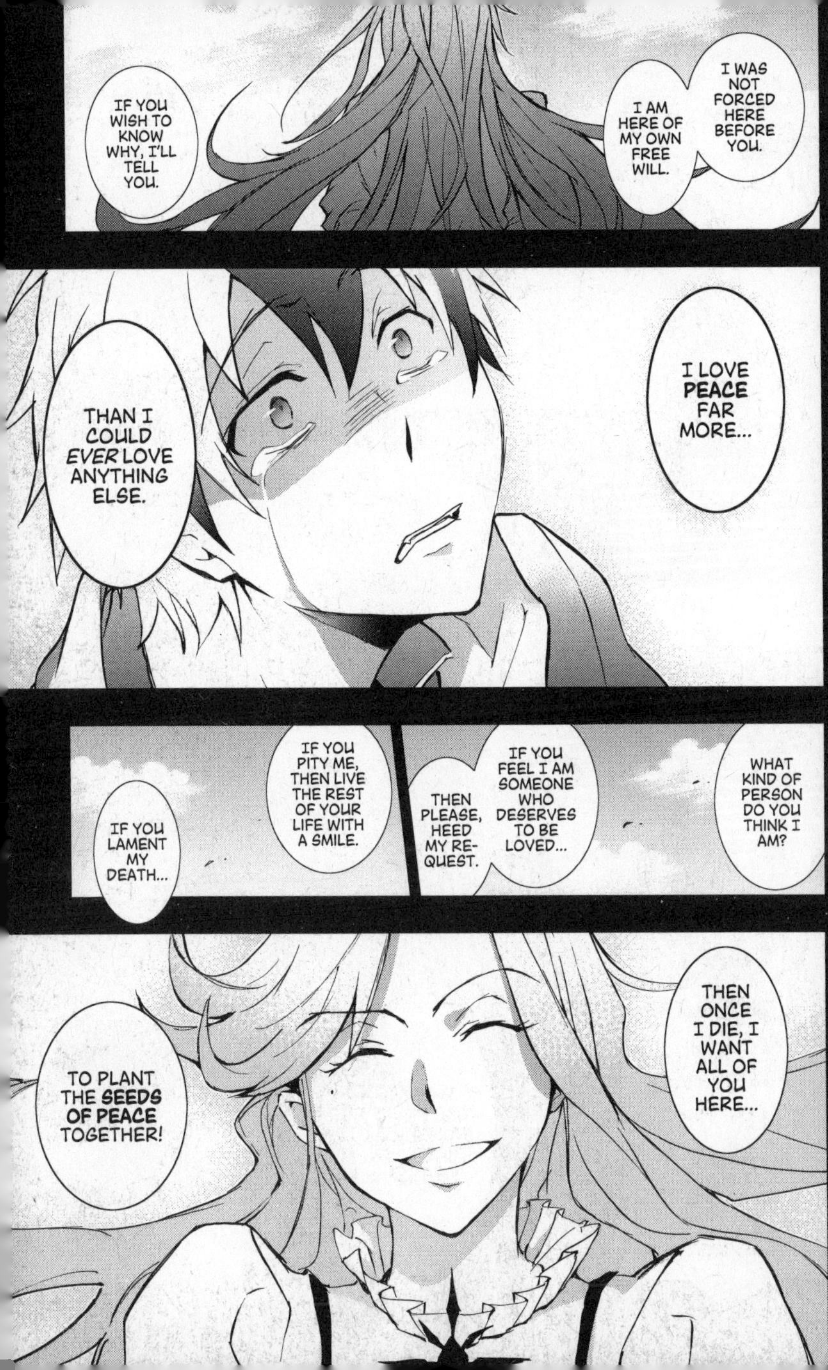
I WAS NOT FORCED HERE BEFORE YOU.
I AM HERE OF MY OWN FREE WILL.
IF YOU WISH TO KNOW WHY, I'LL TELL YOU.
I LOVE **PEACE** FAR MORE...
THAN I COULD *EVER* LOVE ANYTHING ELSE.
WHAT KIND OF PERSON DO YOU THINK I AM?
IF YOU FEEL I AM SOMEONE WHO DESERVES TO BE LOVED...
THEN PLEASE, HEED MY RE-QUEST.
IF YOU PITY ME, THEN LIVE THE REST OF YOUR LIFE WITH A SMILE.
IF YOU LAMENT MY DEATH...
THEN ONCE I DIE, I WANT ALL OF YOU HERE...
TO PLANT THE **SEEDS OF PEACE** TOGETHER!

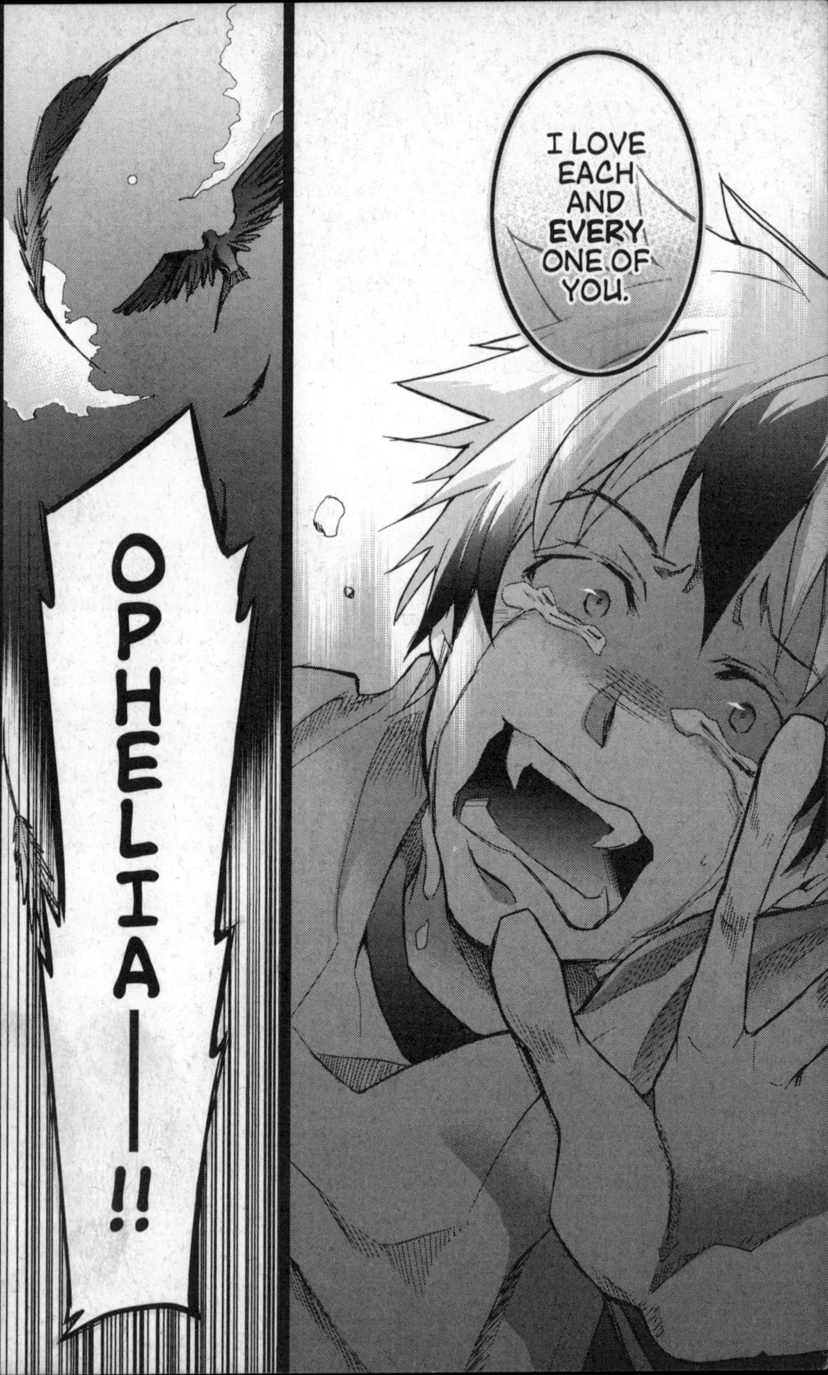
I LOVE EACH AND EVERY ONE OF YOU.
OPHELIA—!!

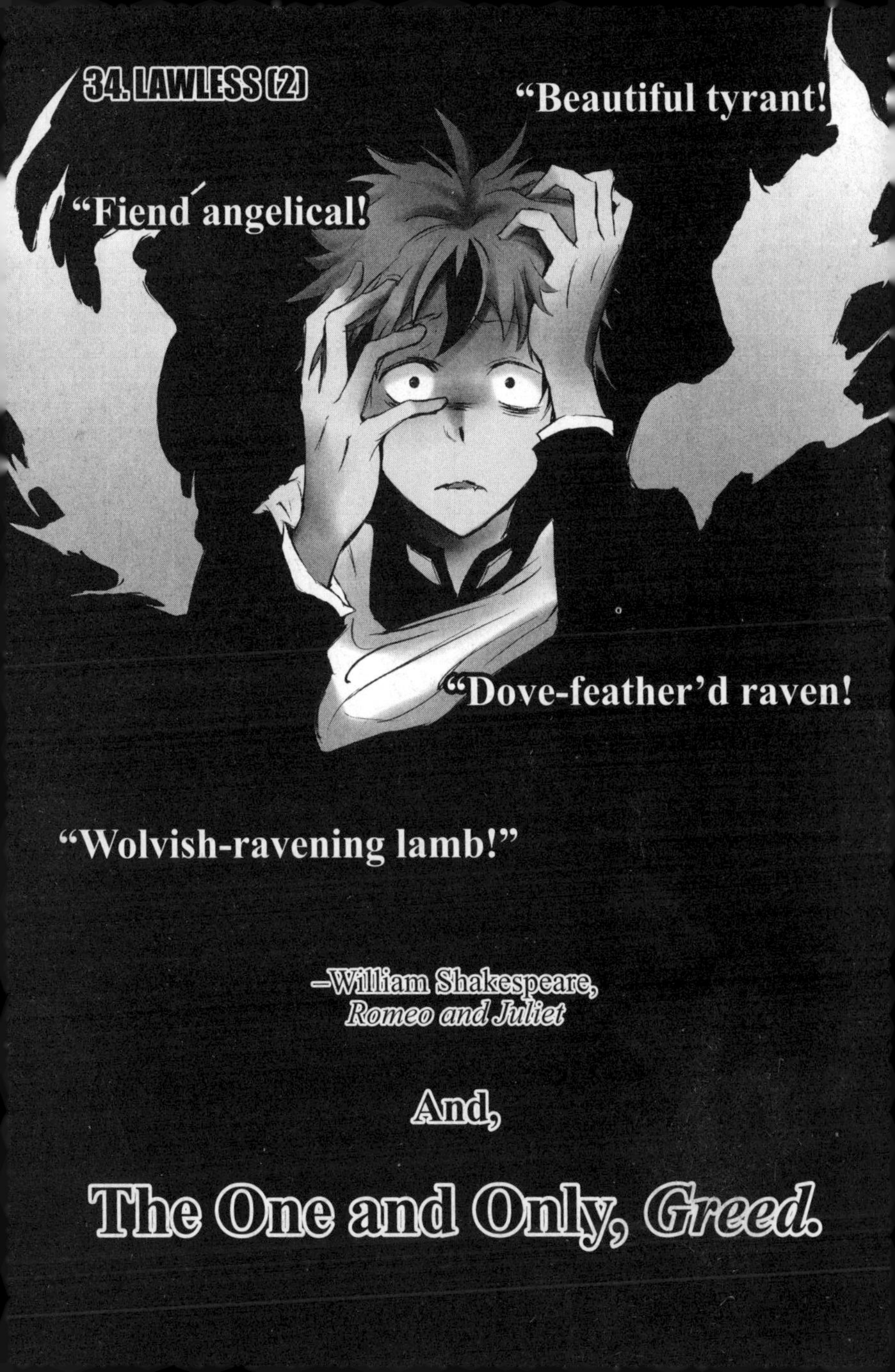
34. LAWLESS (2)
"Beautiful tyrant!
"Fiend angelical!
"Dove-feather'd raven!
"Wolvish-ravening lamb!"
–William Shakespeare,
*Romeo and Juliet*
And,
The One and Only, *Greed.*

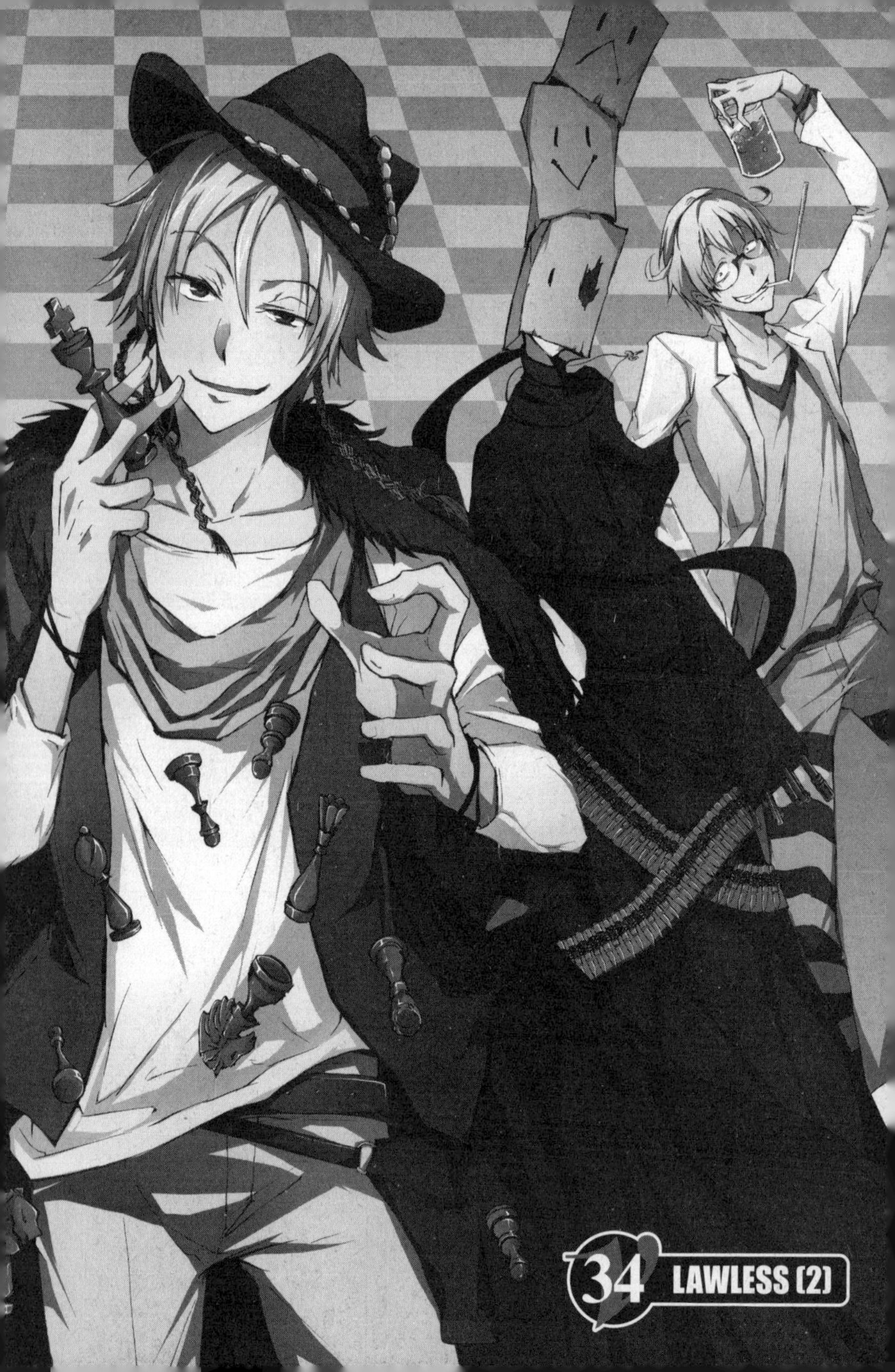
34 LAWLESS (2)

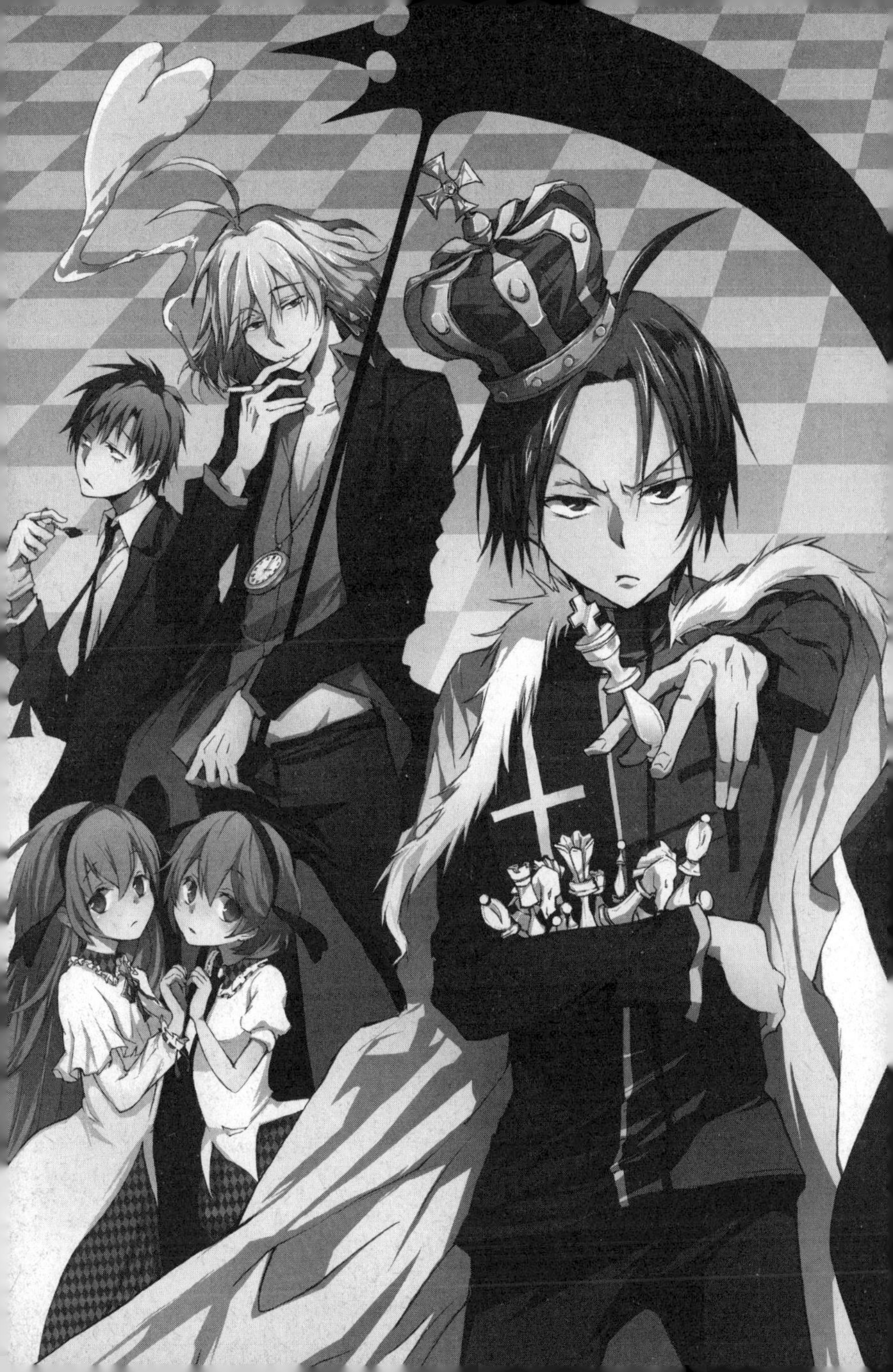

SERVAMP

STRIKE TANAKA

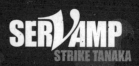

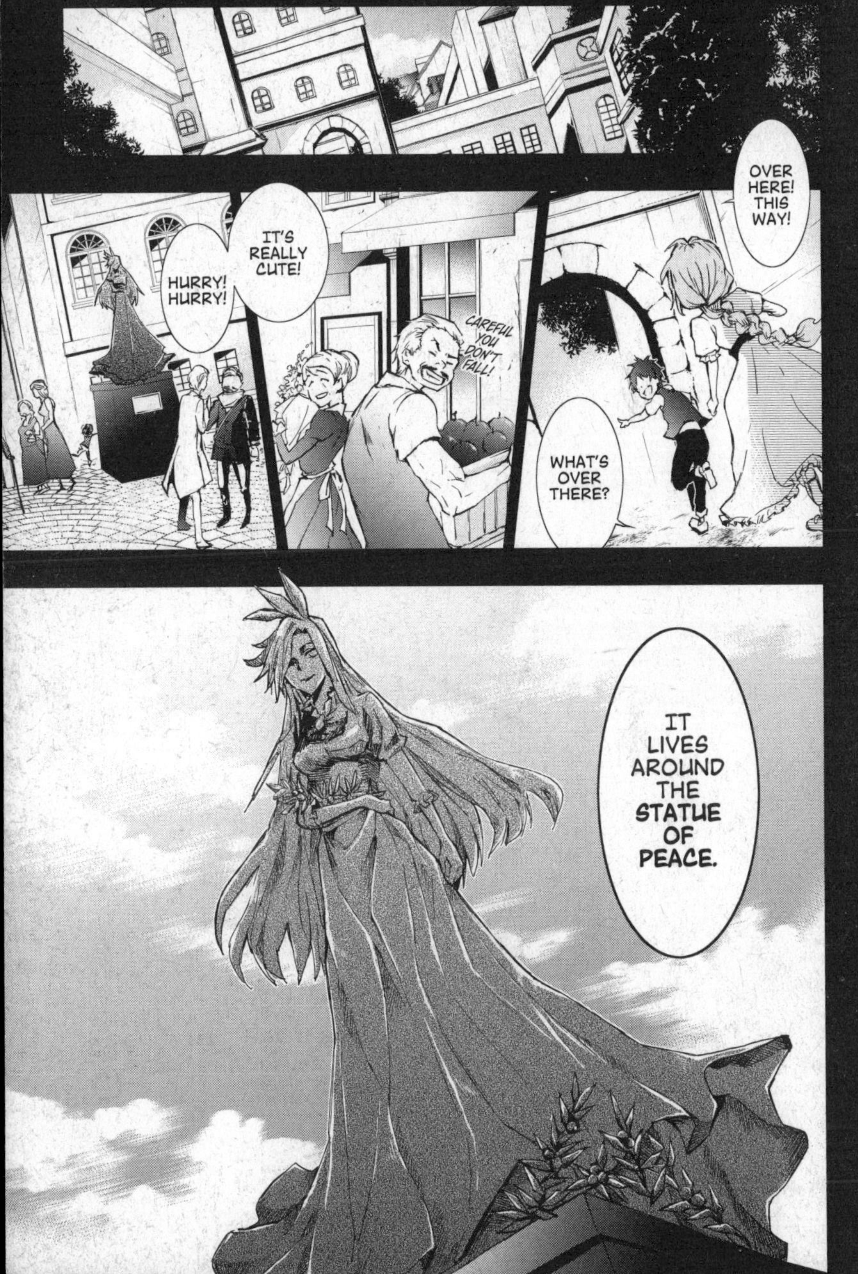
OVER HERE! THIS WAY!
WHAT'S OVER THERE?
CAREFUL YOU DON'T FALL!
IT'S REALLY CUTE!
HURRY! HURRY!
IT LIVES AROUND THE STATUE OF PEACE.

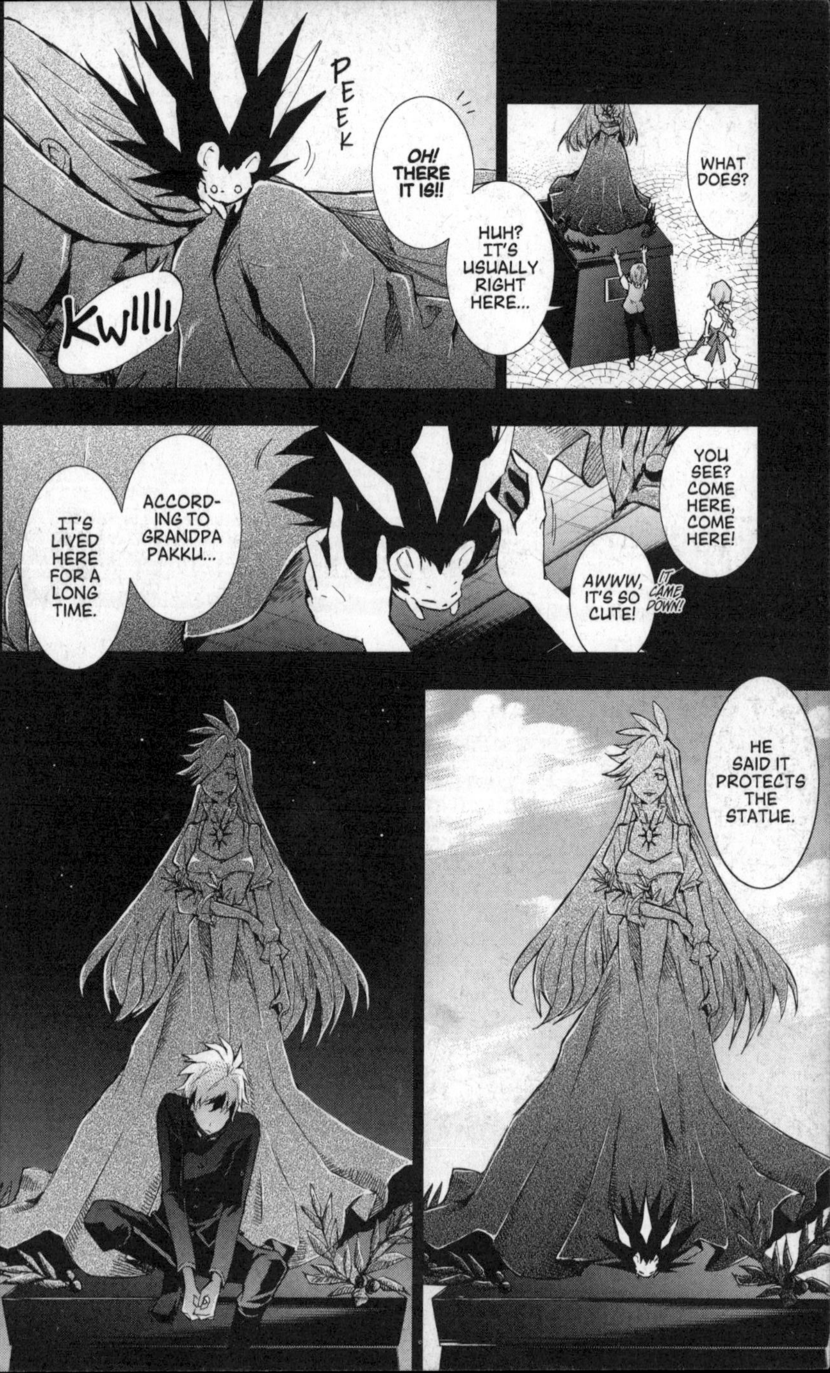
WHAT DOES?
OH! THERE IT IS!!
HUH? IT'S USUALLY RIGHT HERE...
PEEK
KWIIII
YOU SEE? COME HERE, COME HERE!
IT CAME DOWN!
AWWW, IT'S SO CUTE!
ACCORDING TO GRANDPA PAKKU...
IT'S LIVED HERE FOR A LONG TIME.
HE SAID IT PROTECTS THE STATUE.

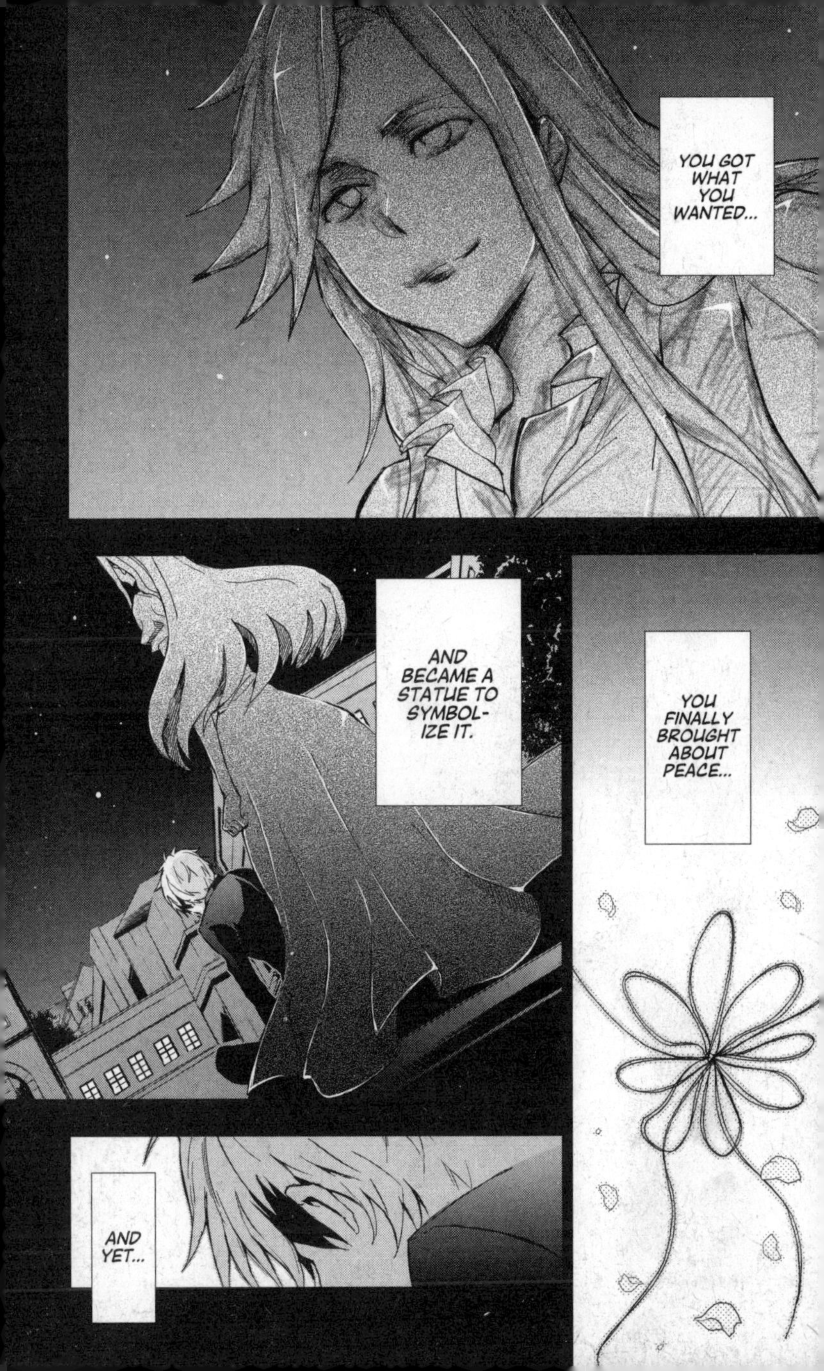
YOU GOT WHAT YOU WANTED...
YOU FINALLY BROUGHT ABOUT PEACE...
AND BECAME A STATUE TO SYMBOL-IZE IT.
AND YET...

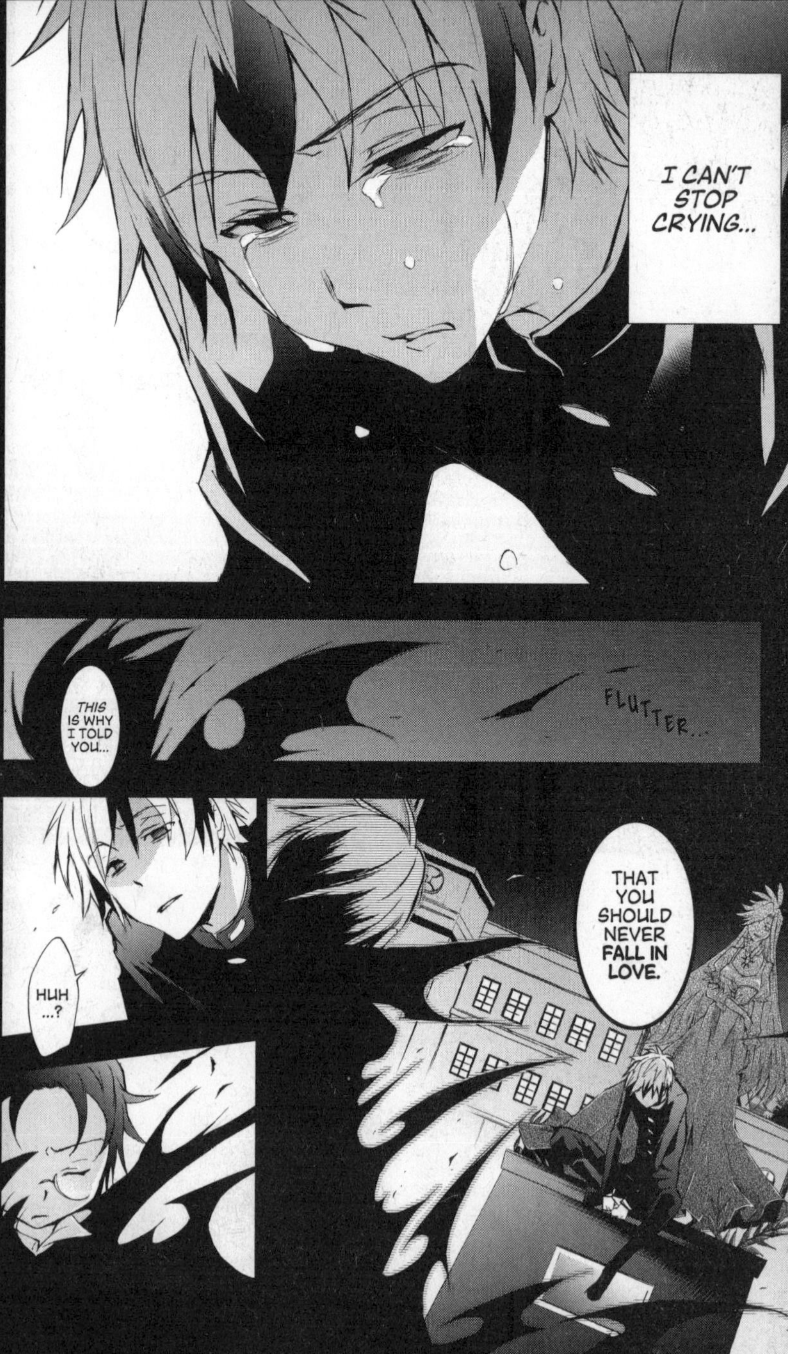
I CAN'T STOP CRYING...
FLUTTER...
THIS IS WHY I TOLD YOU...
THAT YOU SHOULD NEVER FALL IN LOVE.
HUH ...?

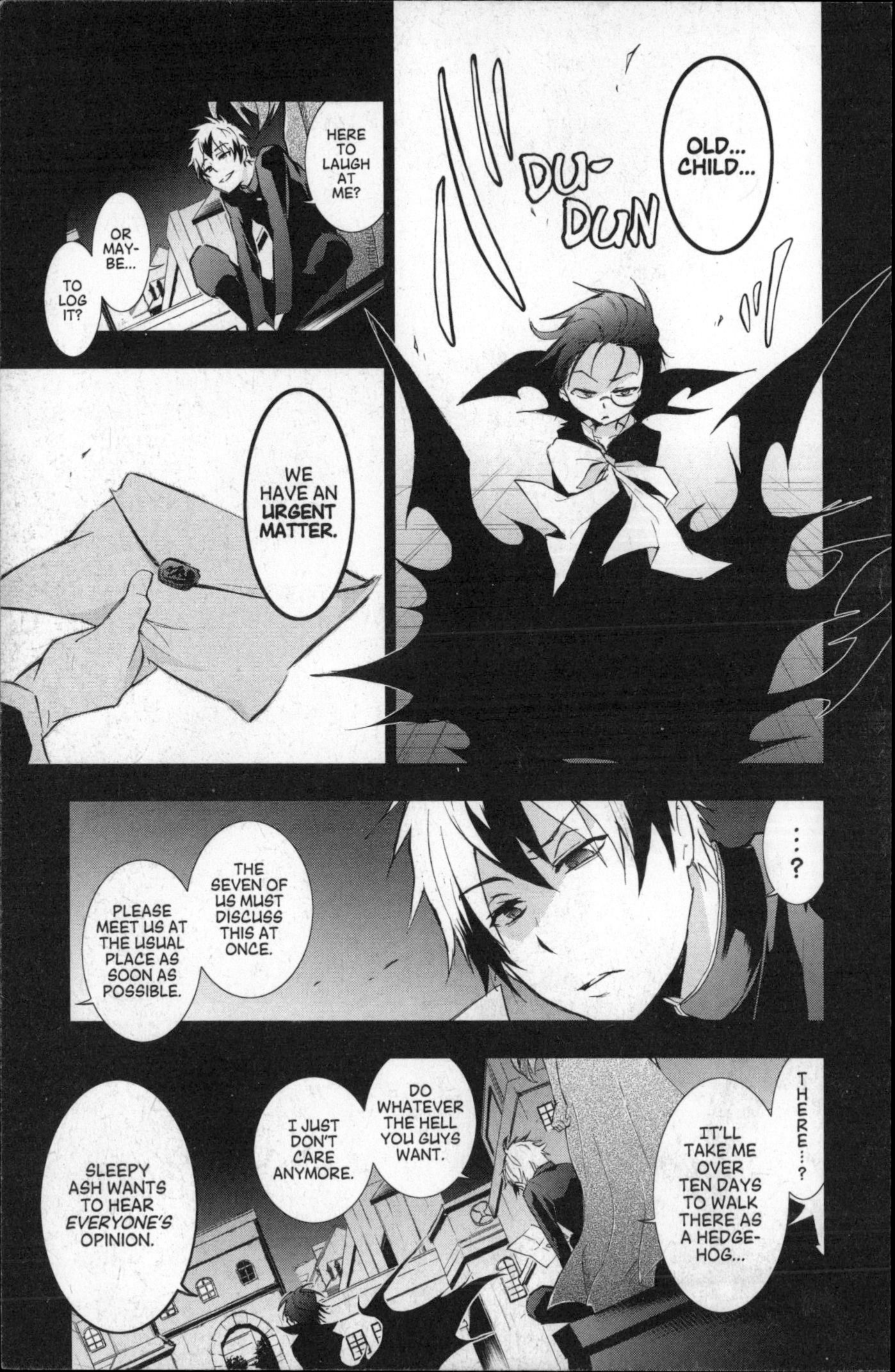
OLD... CHILD...
DU-DUN
HERE TO LAUGH AT ME?
OR MAY-BE...
TO LOG IT?
WE HAVE AN **URGENT MATTER.**
...?
THE SEVEN OF US MUST DISCUSS THIS AT ONCE.
PLEASE MEET US AT THE USUAL PLACE AS SOON AS POSSIBLE.
THERE...?
IT'LL TAKE ME OVER TEN DAYS TO WALK THERE AS A HEDGE-HOG...
DO WHATEVER THE HELL YOU GUYS WANT.
I JUST DON'T CARE ANYMORE.
SLEEPY ASH WANTS TO HEAR *EVERYONE'S* OPINION.

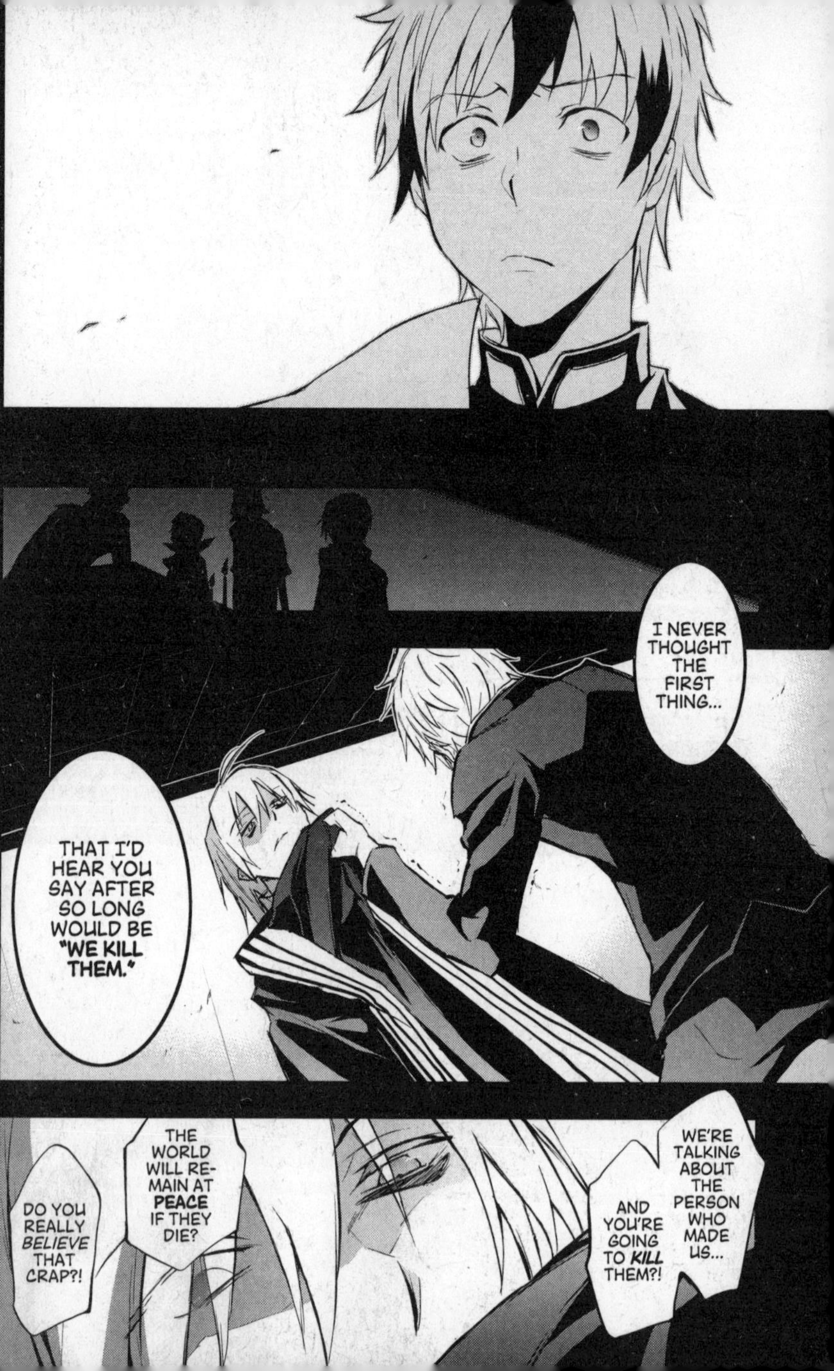
I NEVER THOUGHT THE FIRST THING...
THAT I'D HEAR YOU SAY AFTER SO LONG WOULD BE **"WE KILL THEM."**
WE'RE TALKING ABOUT THE PERSON WHO MADE US...
AND YOU'RE GOING TO *KILL* THEM?!
THE WORLD WILL RE-MAIN AT **PEACE** IF THEY DIE?
DO YOU REALLY *BELIEVE* THAT CRAP?!

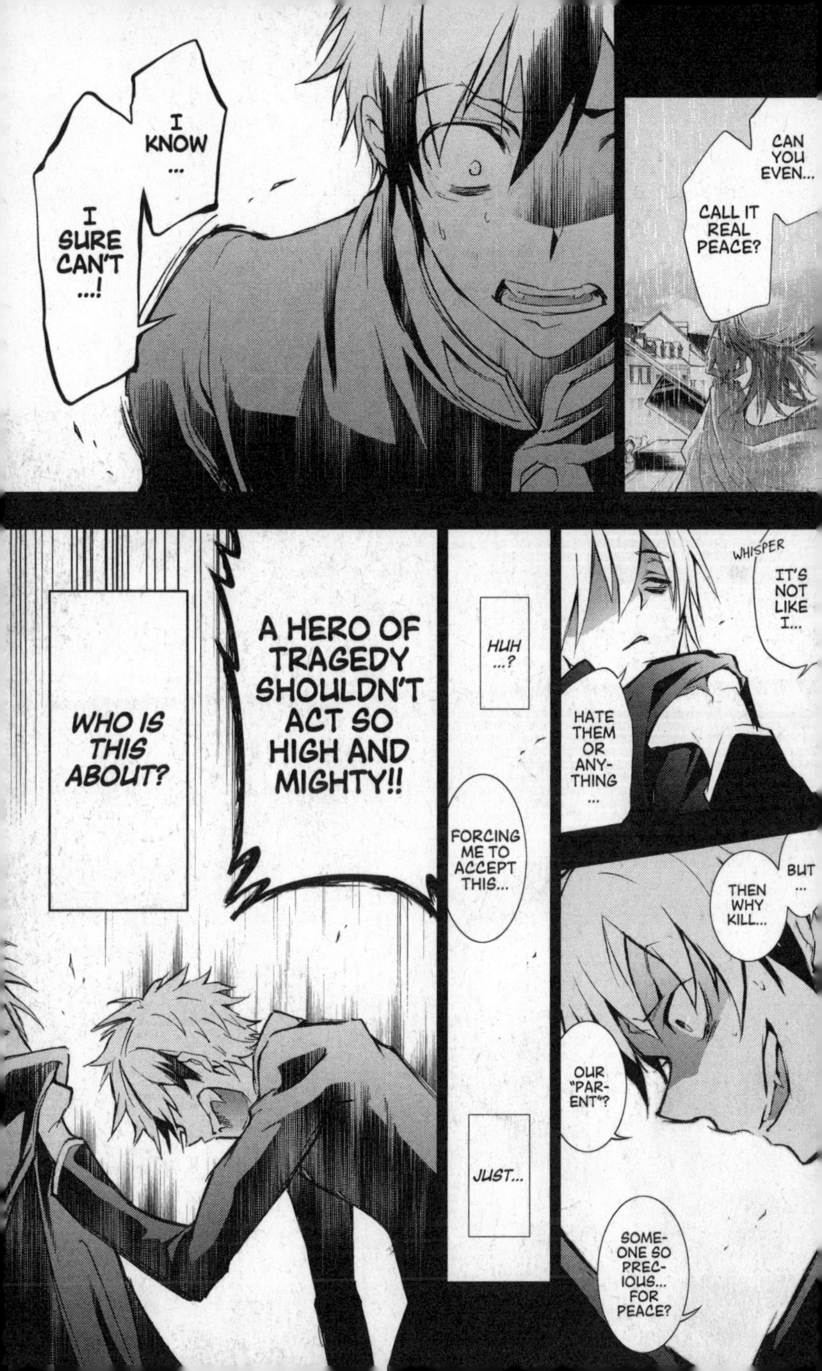
CAN YOU EVEN...
CALL IT REAL PEACE?
I KNOW...
I SURE CAN'T...!
WHISPER
IT'S NOT LIKE I...
HATE THEM OR ANY-THING...
BUT...
THEN WHY KILL...
OUR "PAR-ENT"?
SOME-ONE SO PREC-IOUS... FOR PEACE?
HUH...?
FORCING ME TO ACCEPT THIS...
JUST...
A HERO OF TRAGEDY SHOULDN'T ACT SO HIGH AND MIGHTY!!
WHO IS THIS ABOUT?

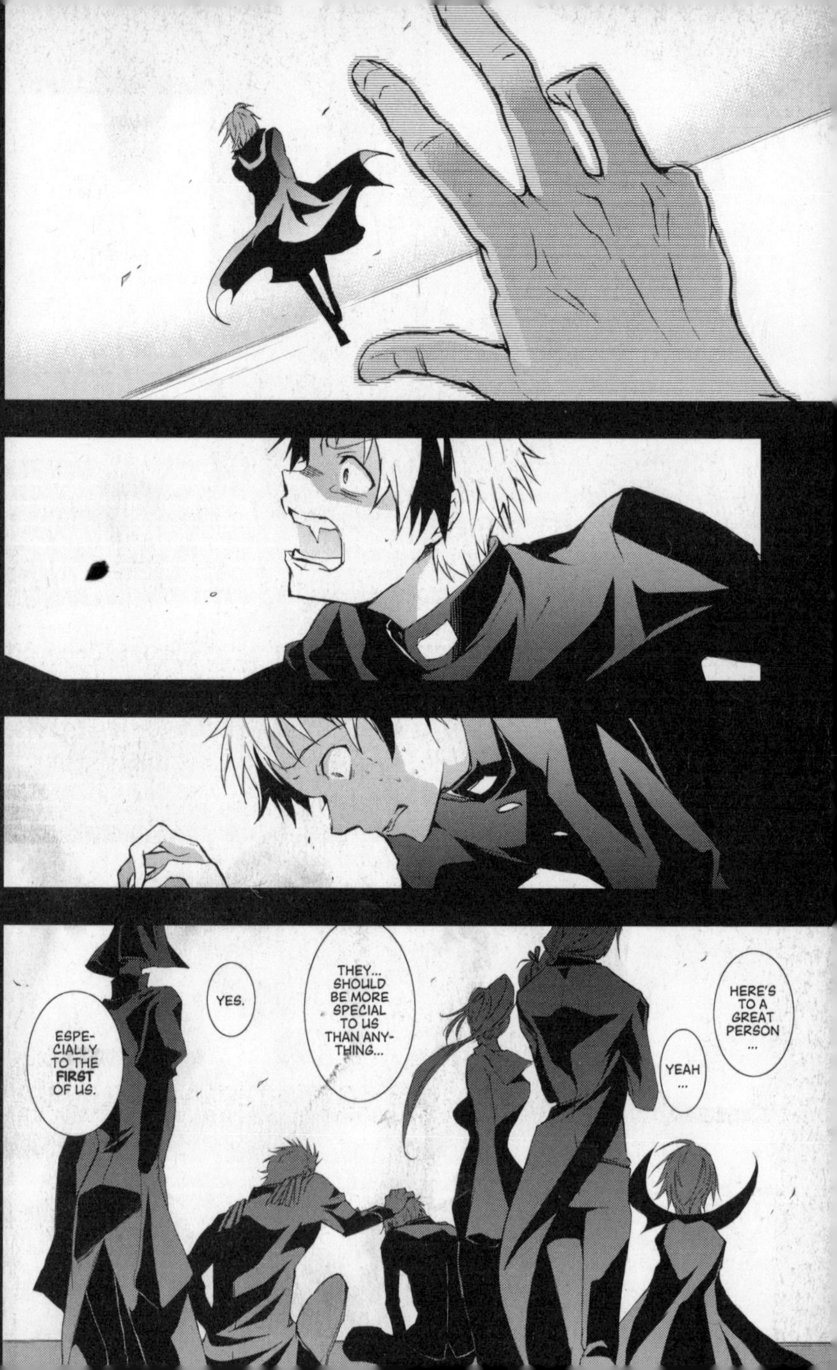
HERE'S TO A GREAT PERSON ...
YEAH ...
THEY... SHOULD BE MORE SPECIAL TO US THAN ANY-THING...
YES.
ESPE-CIALLY TO THE **FIRST** OF US.

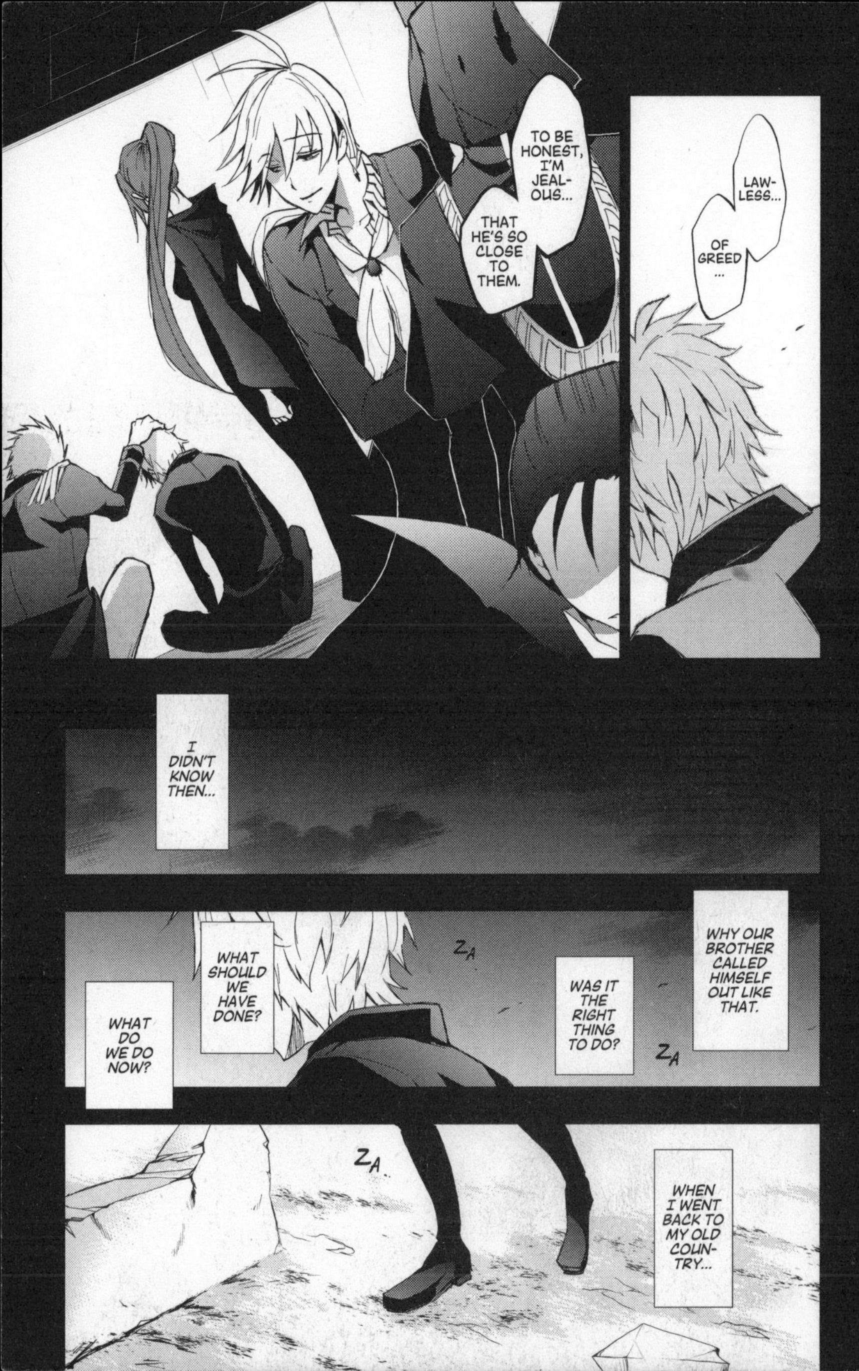
LAW-LESS...
OF GREED ...
TO BE HONEST, I'M JEAL-OUS...
THAT HE'S SO CLOSE TO THEM.
I DIDN'T KNOW THEN...
WHY OUR BROTHER CALLED HIMSELF OUT LIKE THAT.
ZA
WAS IT THE RIGHT THING TO DO?
ZA
WHAT SHOULD WE HAVE DONE?
WHAT DO WE DO NOW?
WHEN I WENT BACK TO MY OLD COUN-TRY...
ZA..

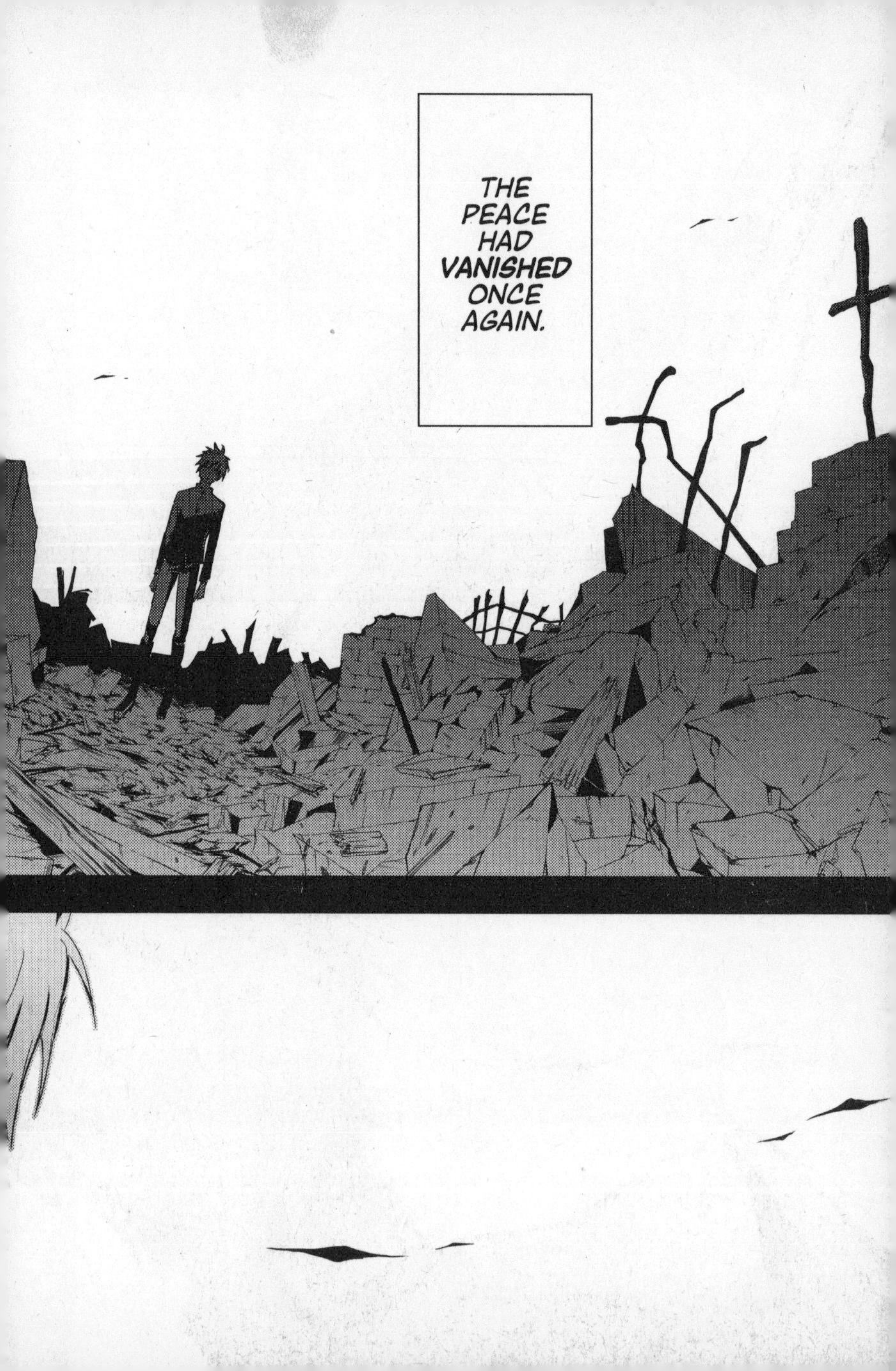
THE PEACE HAD VANISHED ONCE AGAIN.

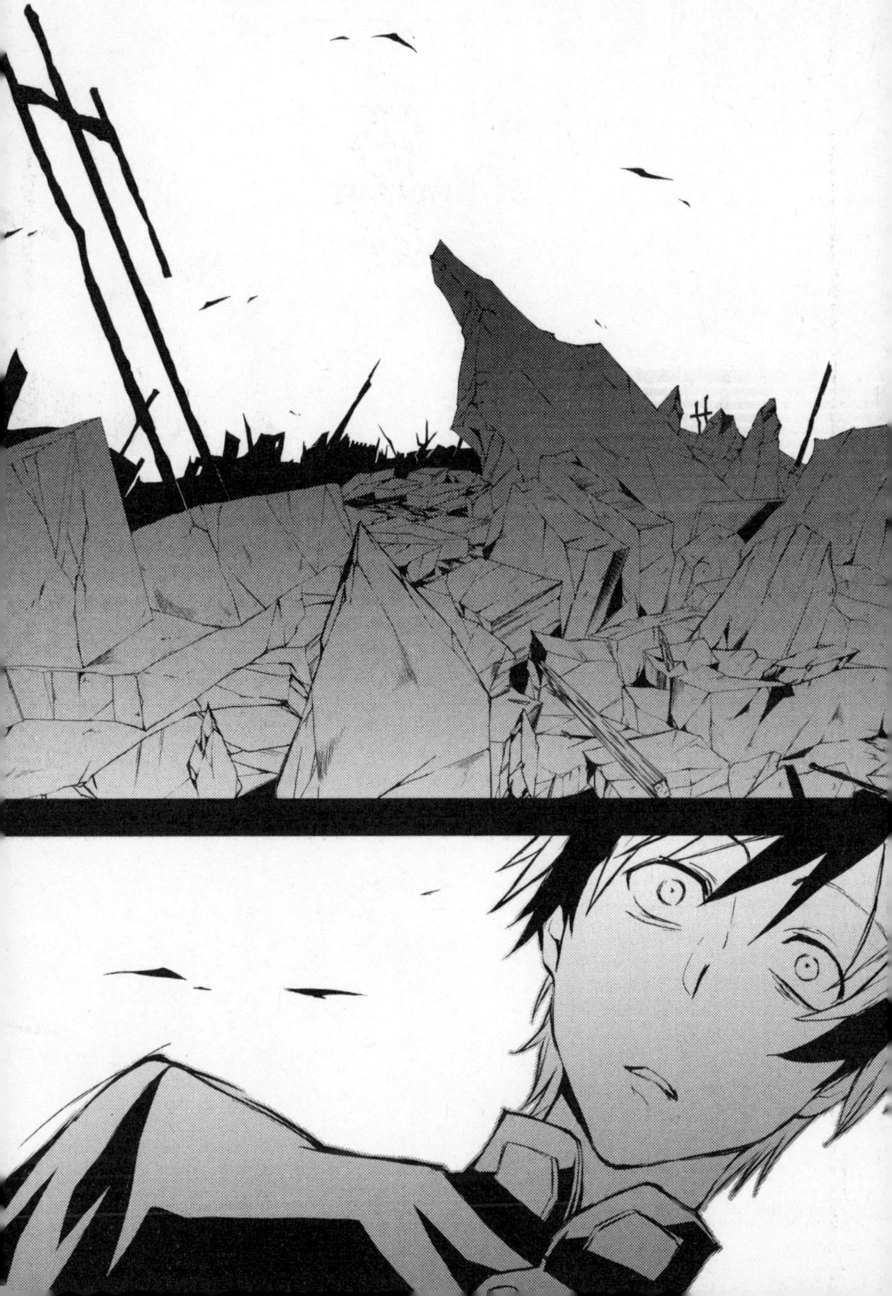

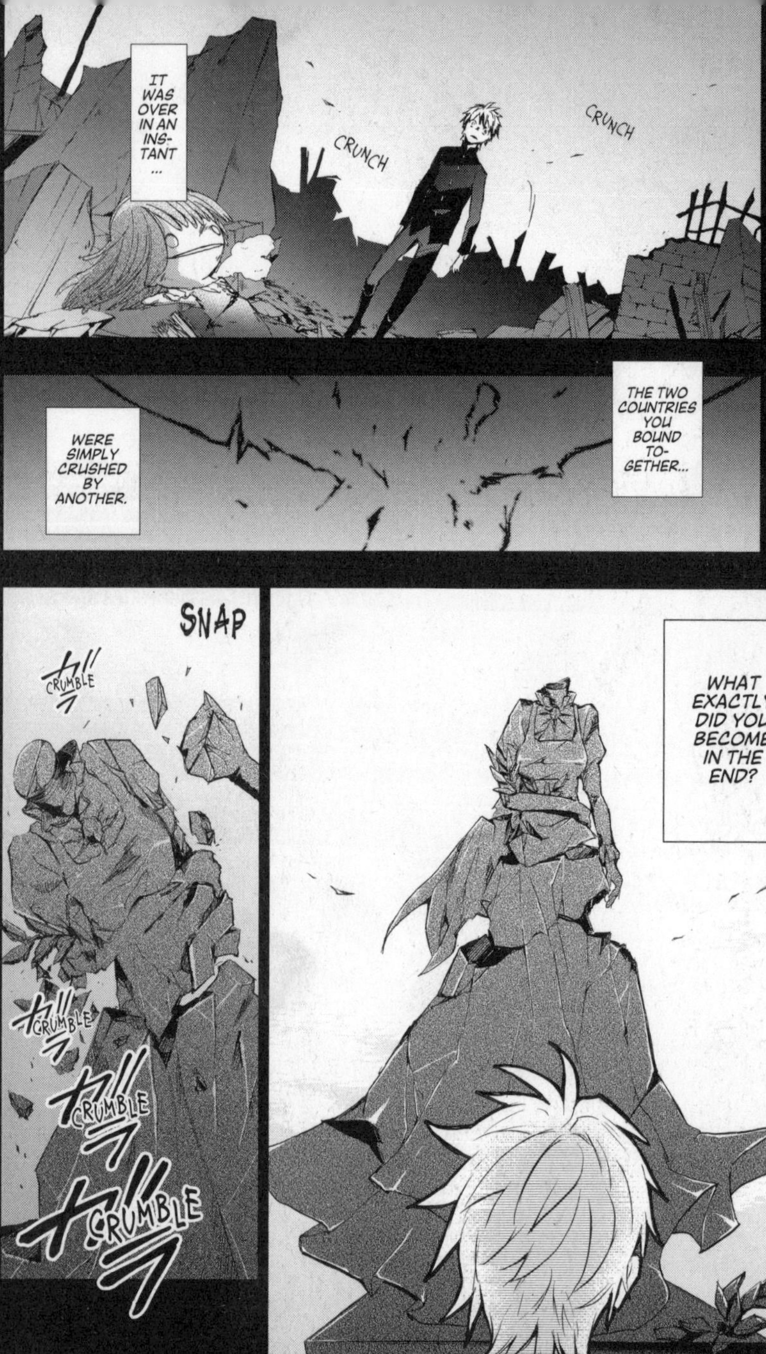
IT WAS OVER IN AN INS-TANT ...
CRUNCH
CRUNCH
THE TWO COUNTRIES YOU BOUND TO-GETHER...
WERE SIMPLY CRUSHED BY ANOTHER.
WHAT EXACTLY DID YOU BECOME IN THE END?
SNAP
CRUMBLE
CRUMBLE
CRUMBLE
CRUMBLE

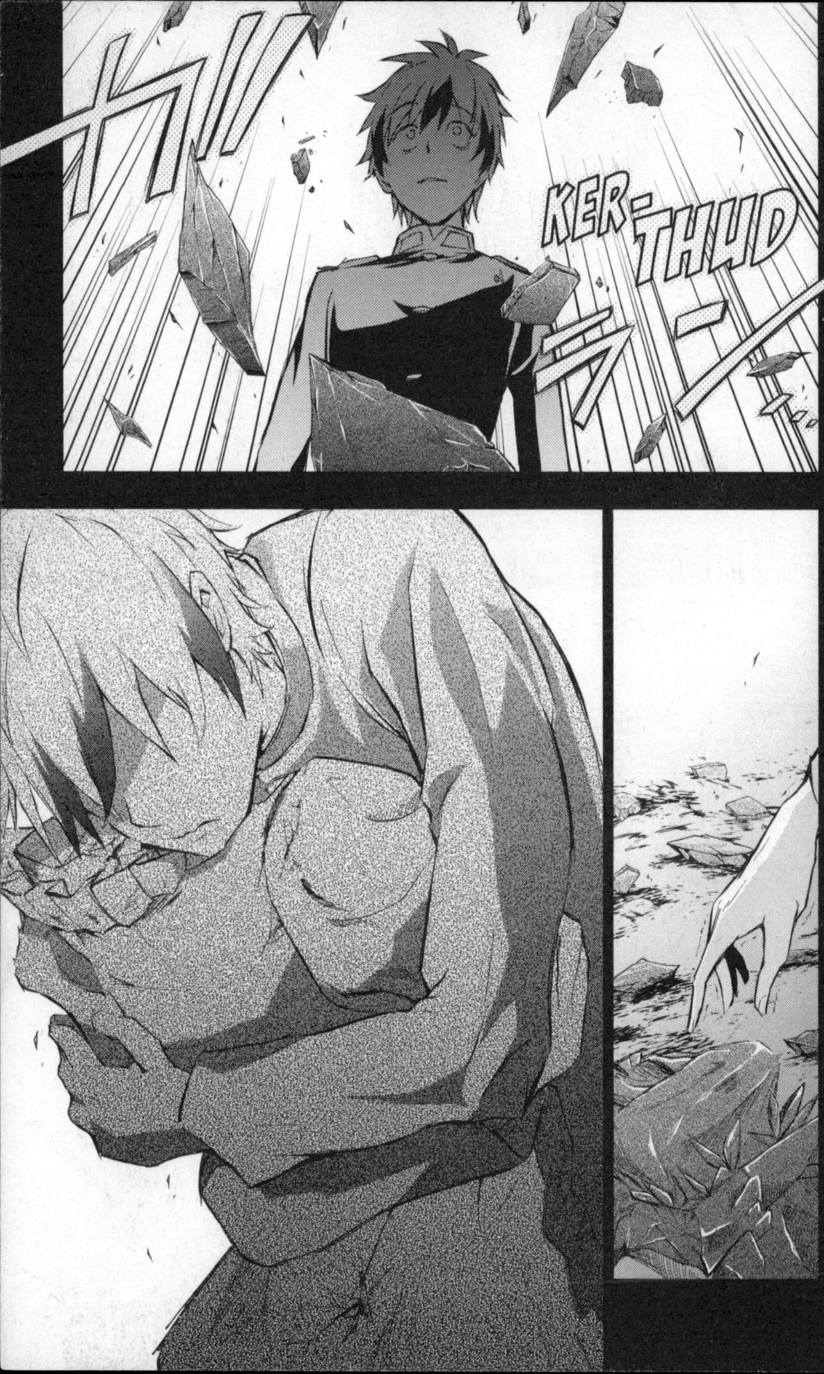
KER-THUD

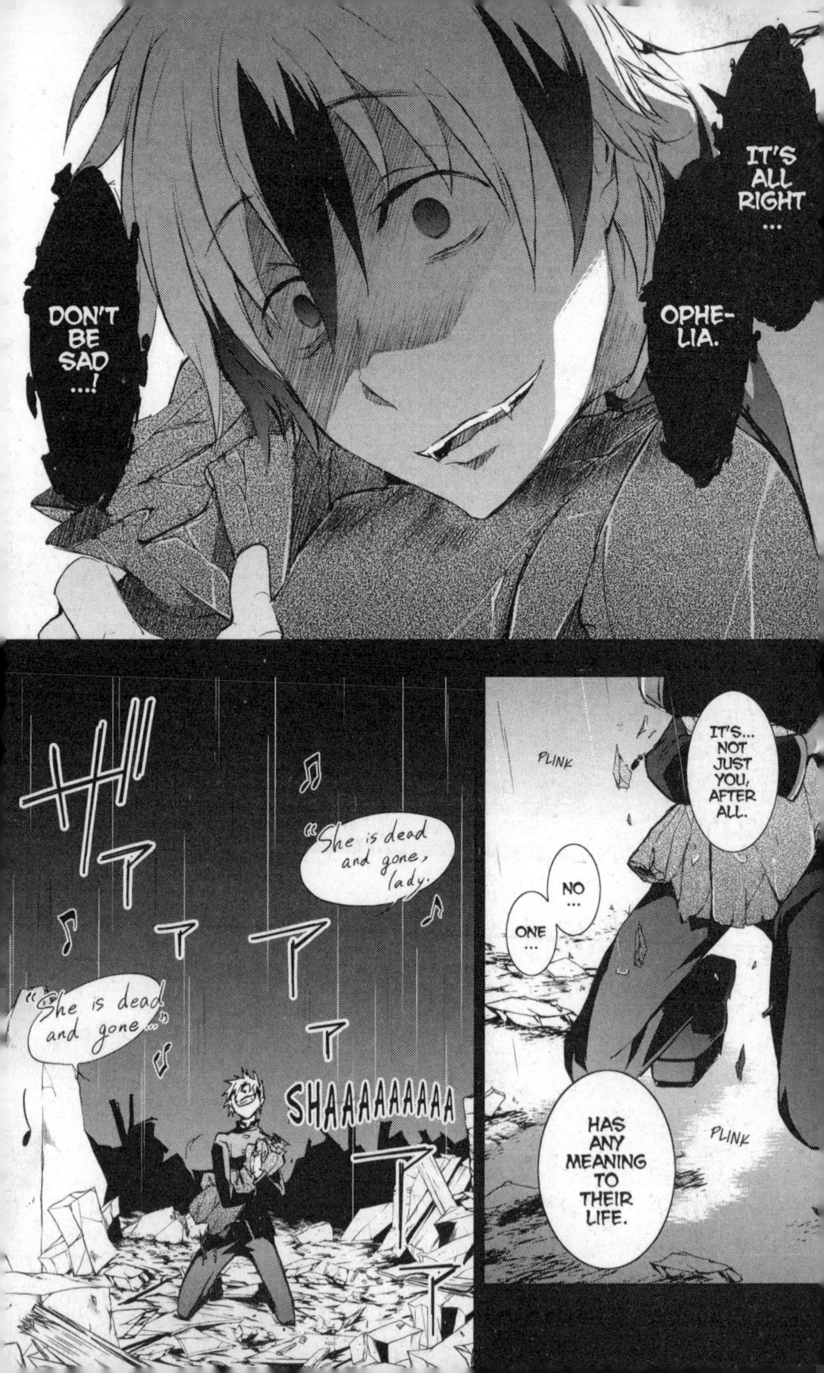
IT'S ALL RIGHT...
OPHELIA.
DON'T BE SAD...!
IT'S... NOT JUST YOU, AFTER ALL.
PLINK
NO...
ONE...
HAS ANY MEANING TO THEIR LIFE.
PLINK
"She is dead and gone, lady."
"She is dead and gone..."
SHAAAAAAAA

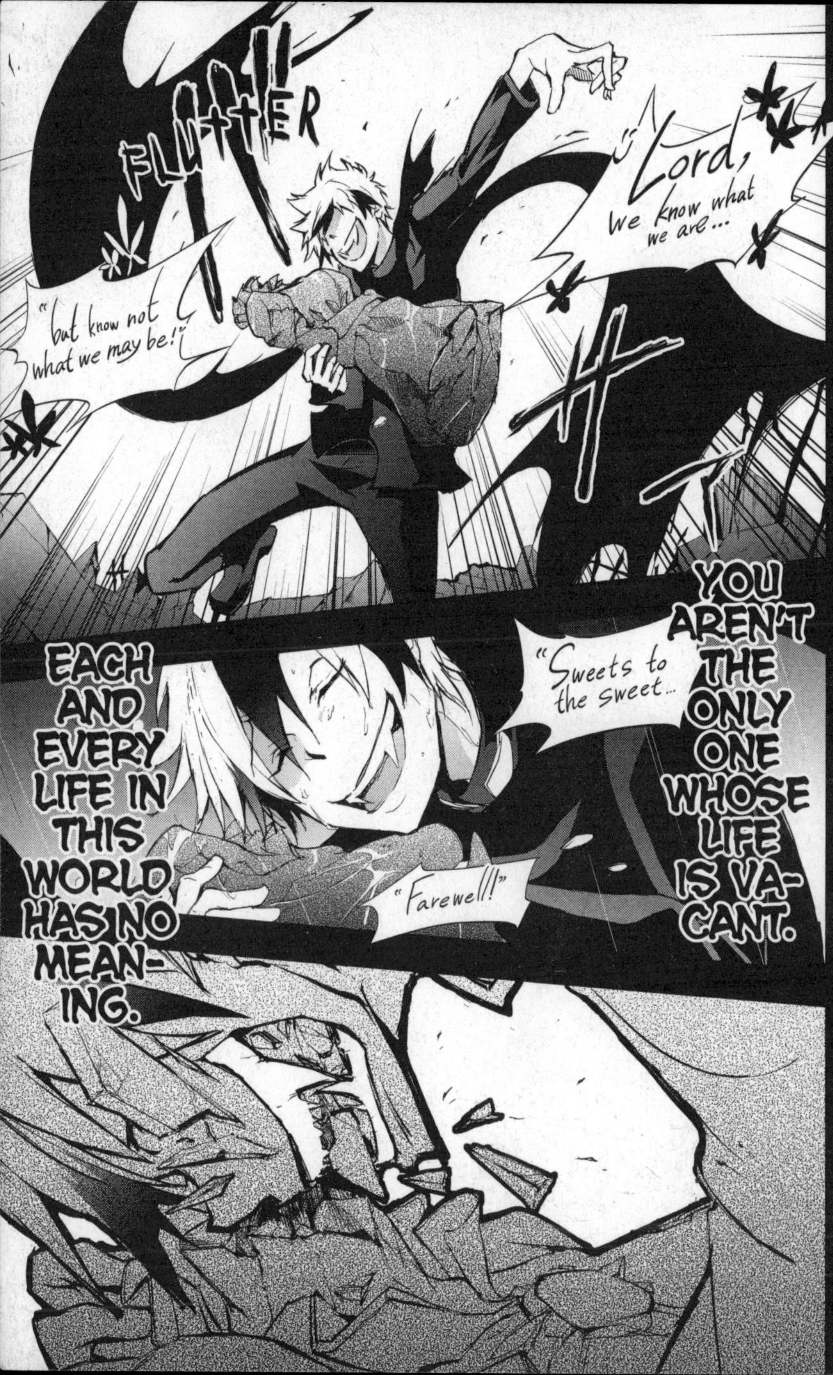

FLUTTER
"Lord, we know what we are...
"but know not what we may be!"
YOU AREN'T THE ONLY ONE WHOSE LIFE IS VA-CANT.
"Sweets to the sweet...
"Farewell!"
EACH AND EVERY LIFE IN THIS WORLD HAS NO MEAN-ING.

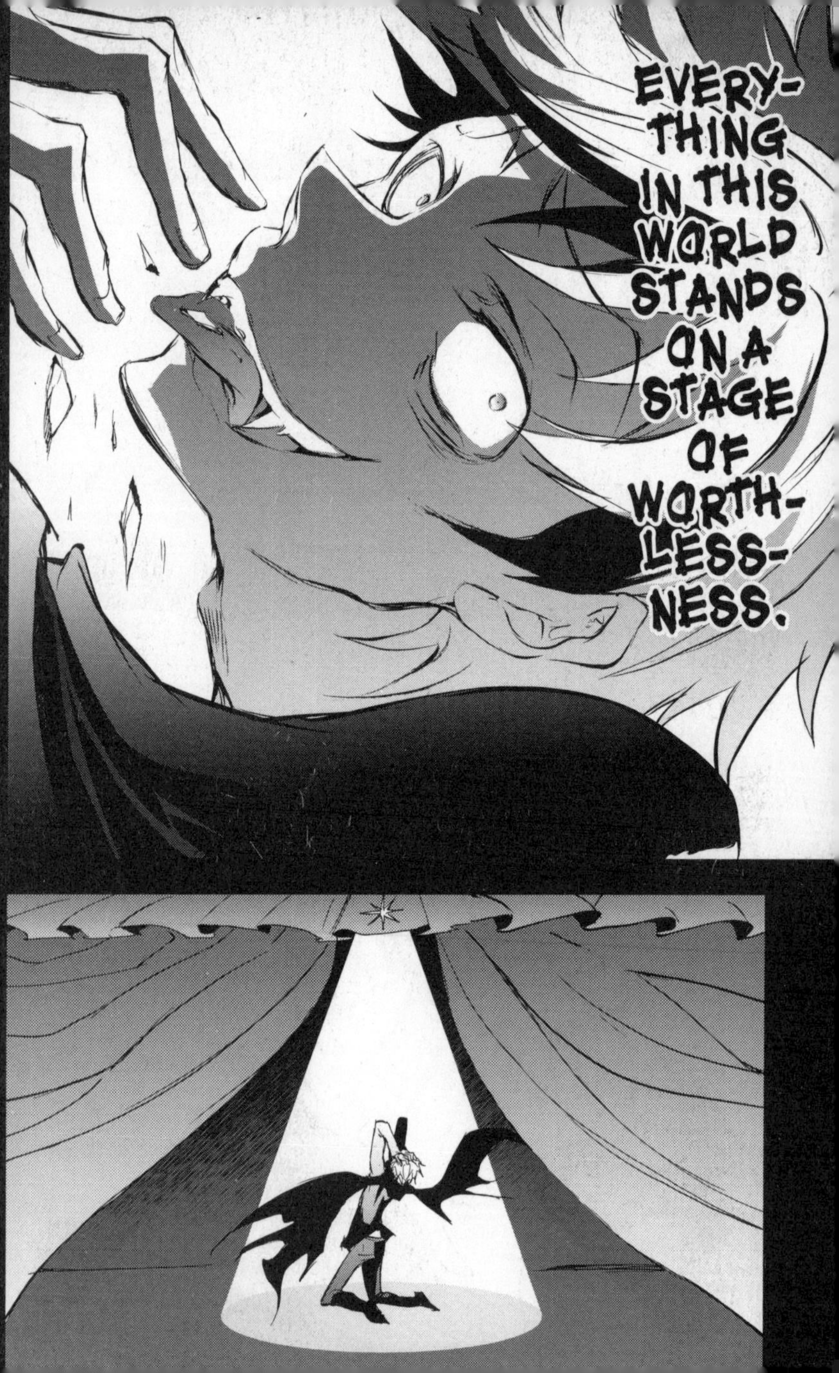
EVERY-THING IN THIS WORLD STANDS ON A STAGE OF WORTH-LESS-NESS.

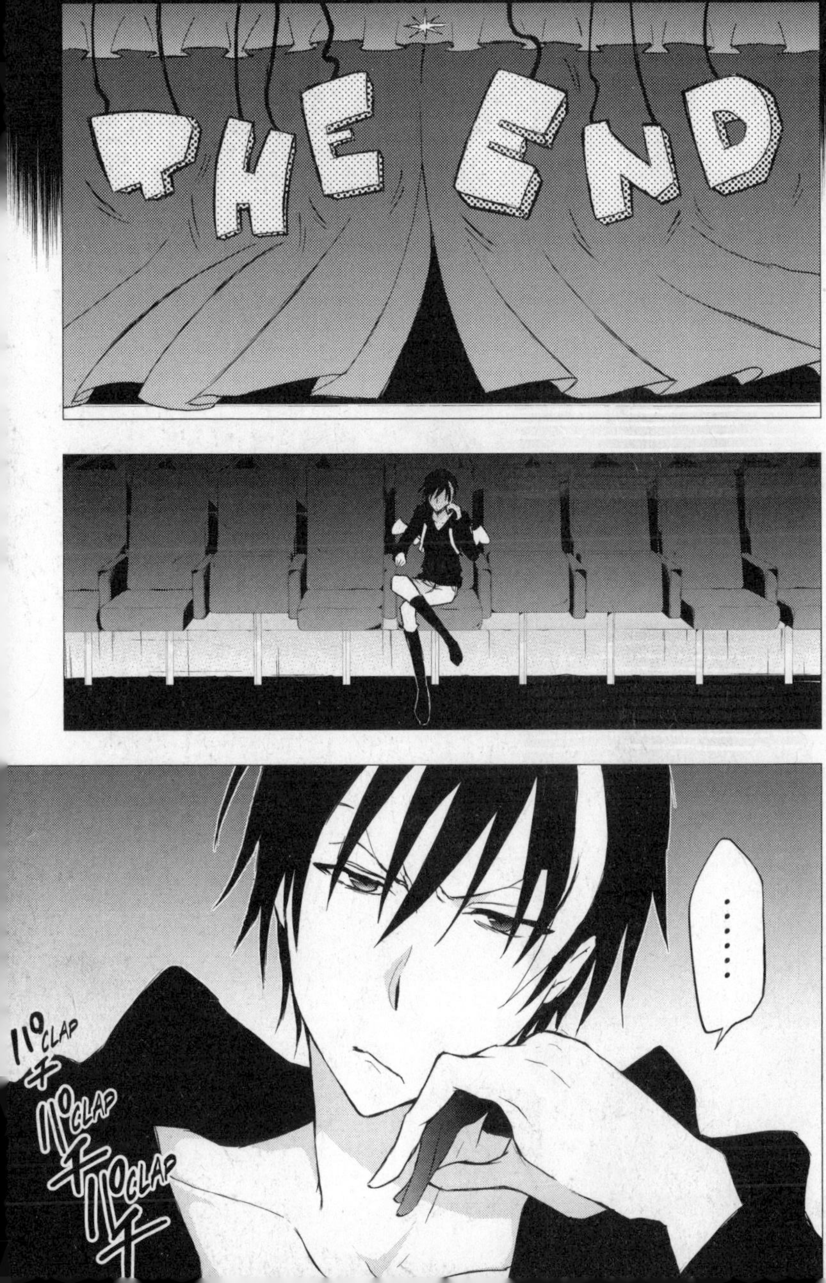
THE END
......
パチ CLAP
パチ CLAP
パチ CLAP

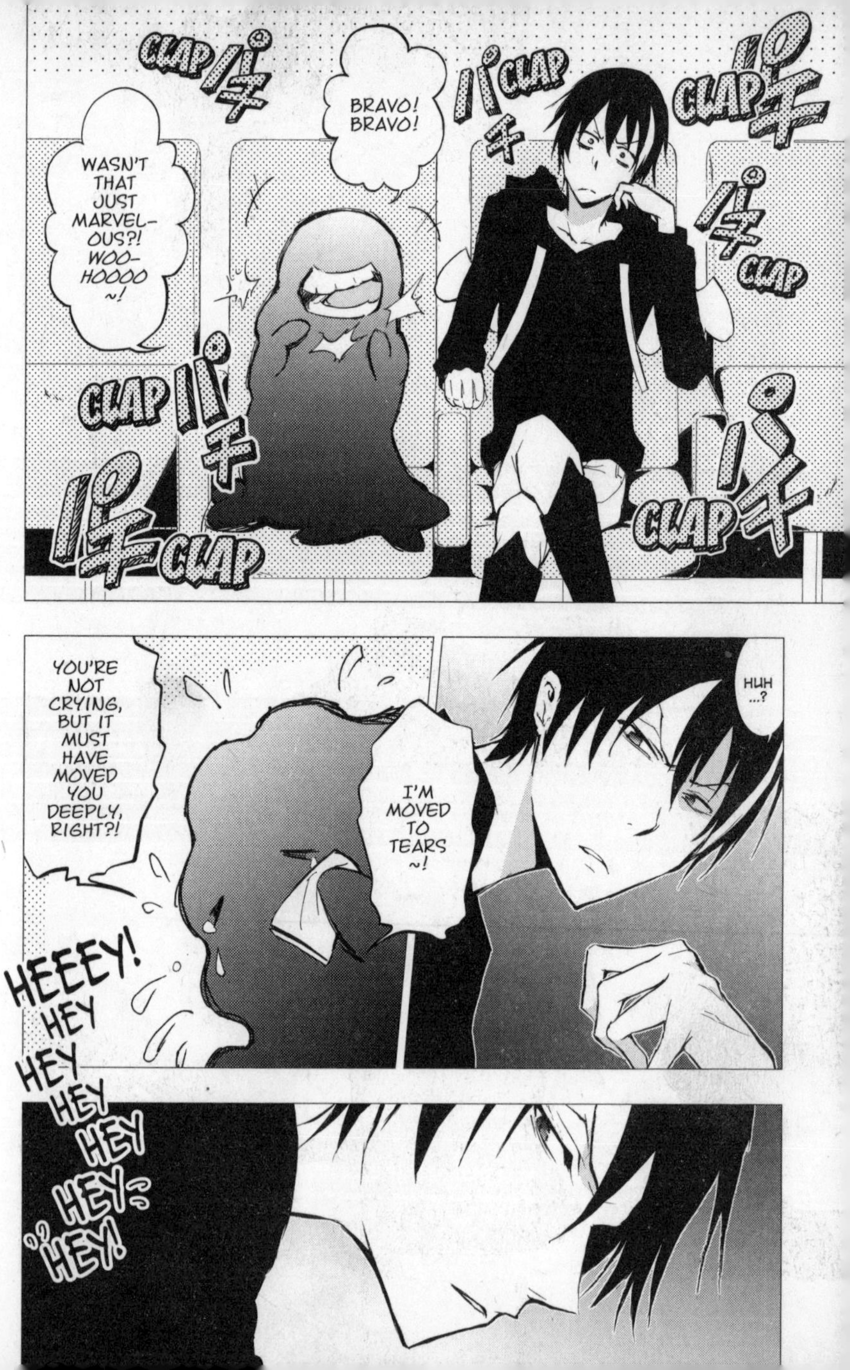
CLAP パチ
CLAP パチ
BRAVO! BRAVO!
パチ CLAP
パチ CLAP
WASN'T THAT JUST MARVELOUS?! WOO-HOOOOO ~!
CLAP パチ
パチ CLAP
パチ CLAP
パチ CLAP
HUH ...?
I'M MOVED TO TEARS ~!
YOU'RE NOT CRYING, BUT IT MUST HAVE MOVED YOU DEEPLY, RIGHT?!
HEEEY! HEY HEY HEY HEY HEY, HEY!

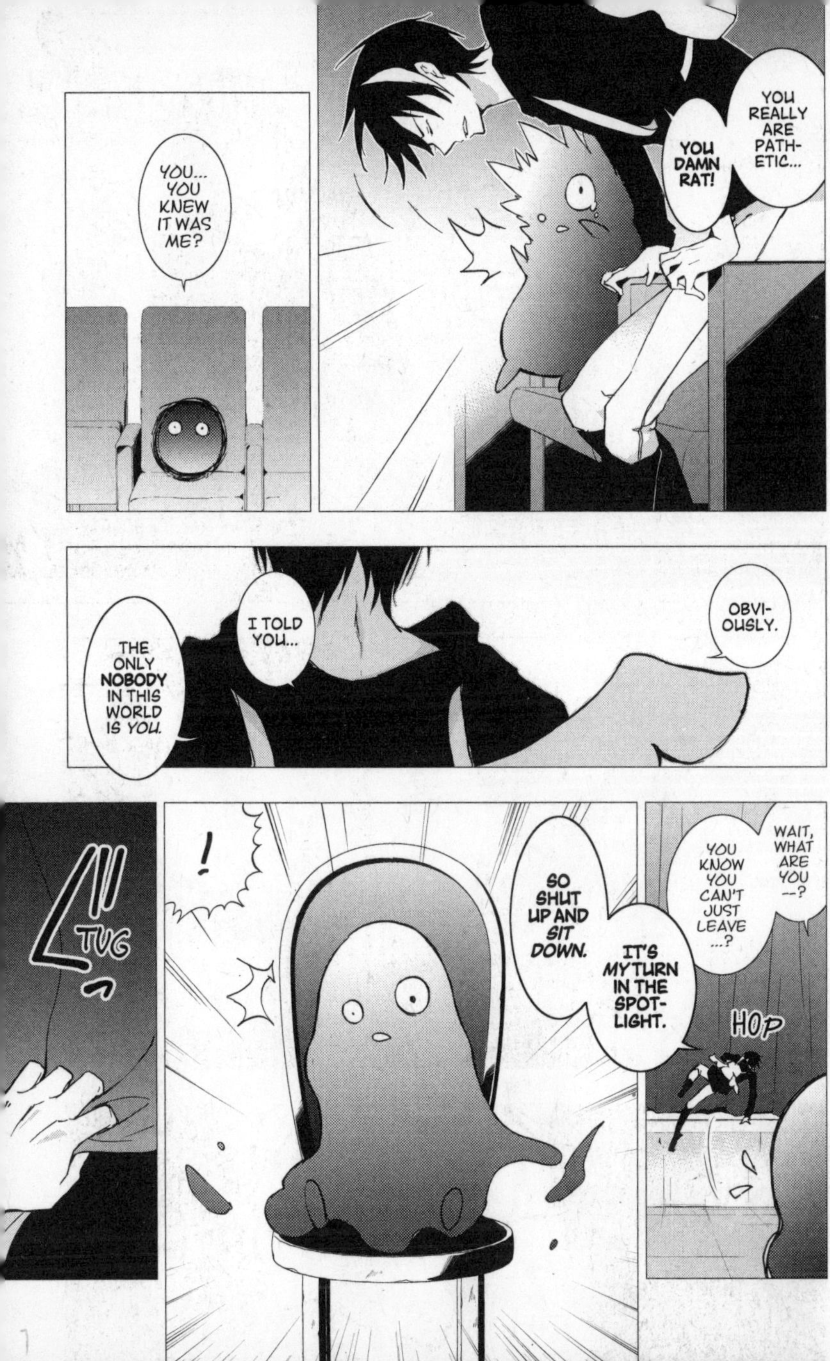
YOU REALLY ARE PATH-ETIC...
YOU DAMN RAT!
YOU... YOU KNEW IT WAS ME?
OBVI-OUSLY.
I TOLD YOU...
THE ONLY NOBODY IN THIS WORLD IS YOU.
WAIT, WHAT ARE YOU --?
YOU KNOW YOU CAN'T JUST LEAVE ...?
HOP
SO SHUT UP AND SIT DOWN.
IT'S MY TURN IN THE SPOT-LIGHT.
!
TUG

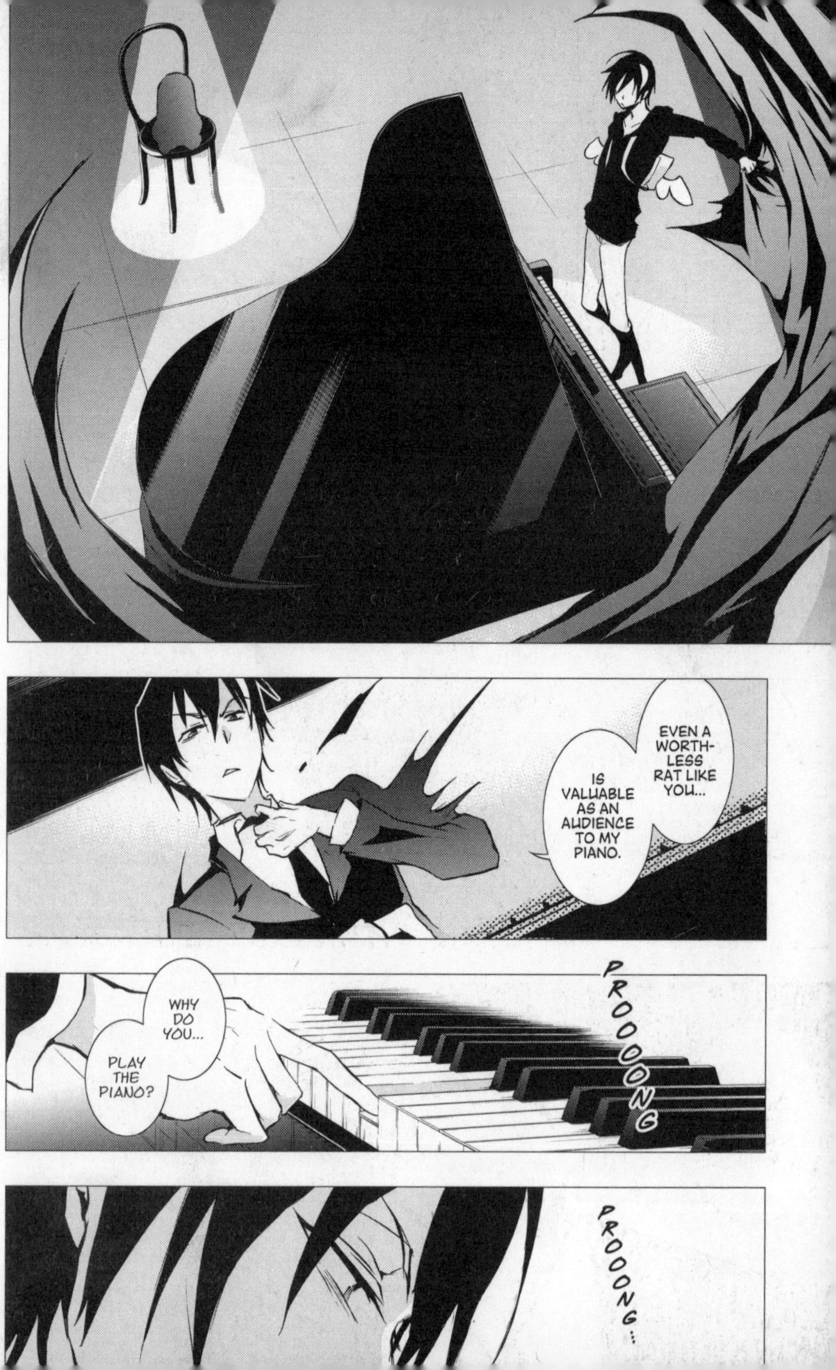
EVEN A WORTHLESS RAT LIKE YOU...
IS VALUABLE AS AN AUDIENCE TO MY PIANO.
PROOOONG
WHY DO YOU...
PLAY THE PIANO?
PROOONG...

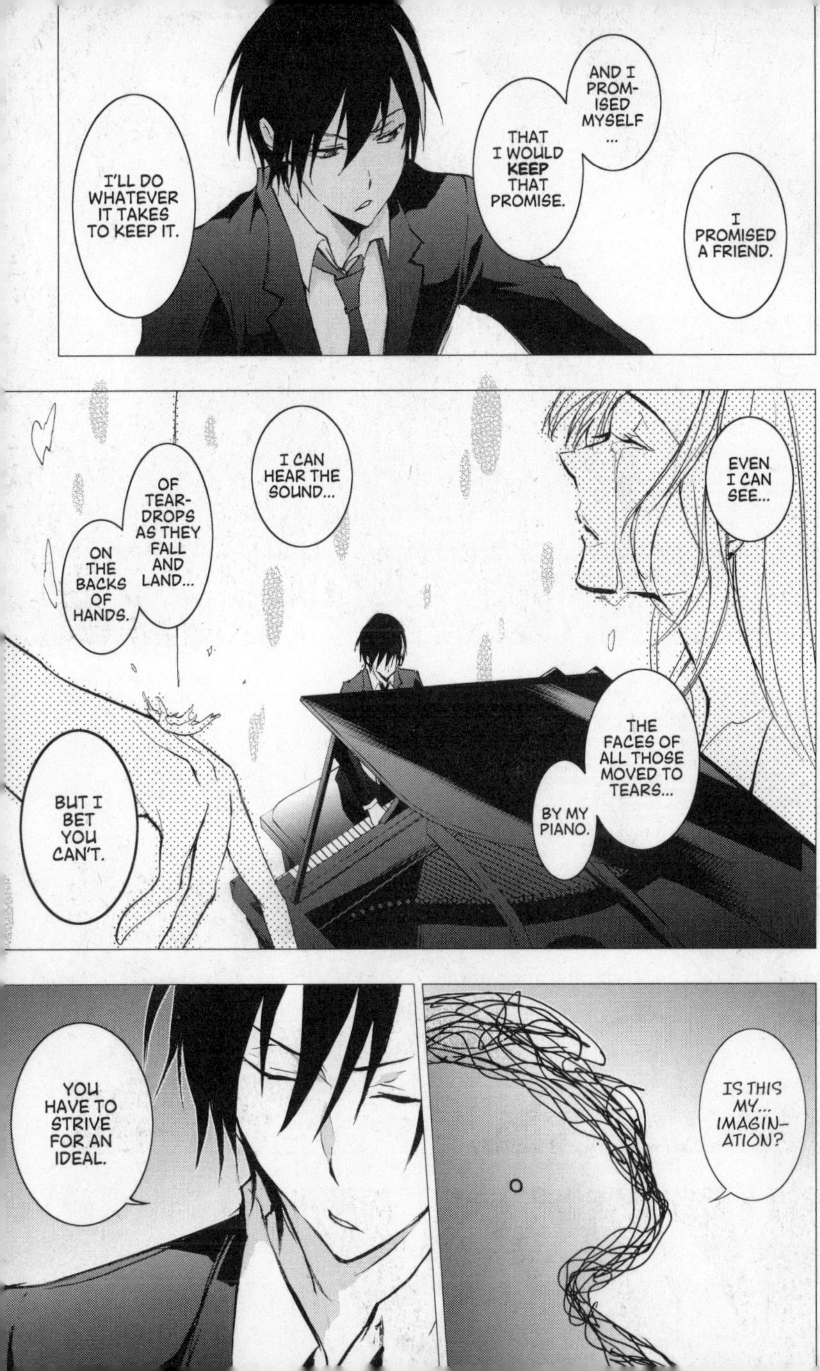
I PROMISED A FRIEND.
AND I PROMISED MYSELF ...
THAT I WOULD **KEEP** THAT PROMISE.
I'LL DO WHATEVER IT TAKES TO KEEP IT.
EVEN I CAN SEE...
THE FACES OF ALL THOSE MOVED TO TEARS...
BY MY PIANO.
I CAN HEAR THE SOUND...
OF TEAR-DROPS AS THEY FALL AND LAND...
ON THE BACKS OF HANDS.
BUT I BET YOU CAN'T.
IS THIS MY... IMAGINATION?
YOU HAVE TO STRIVE FOR AN IDEAL.

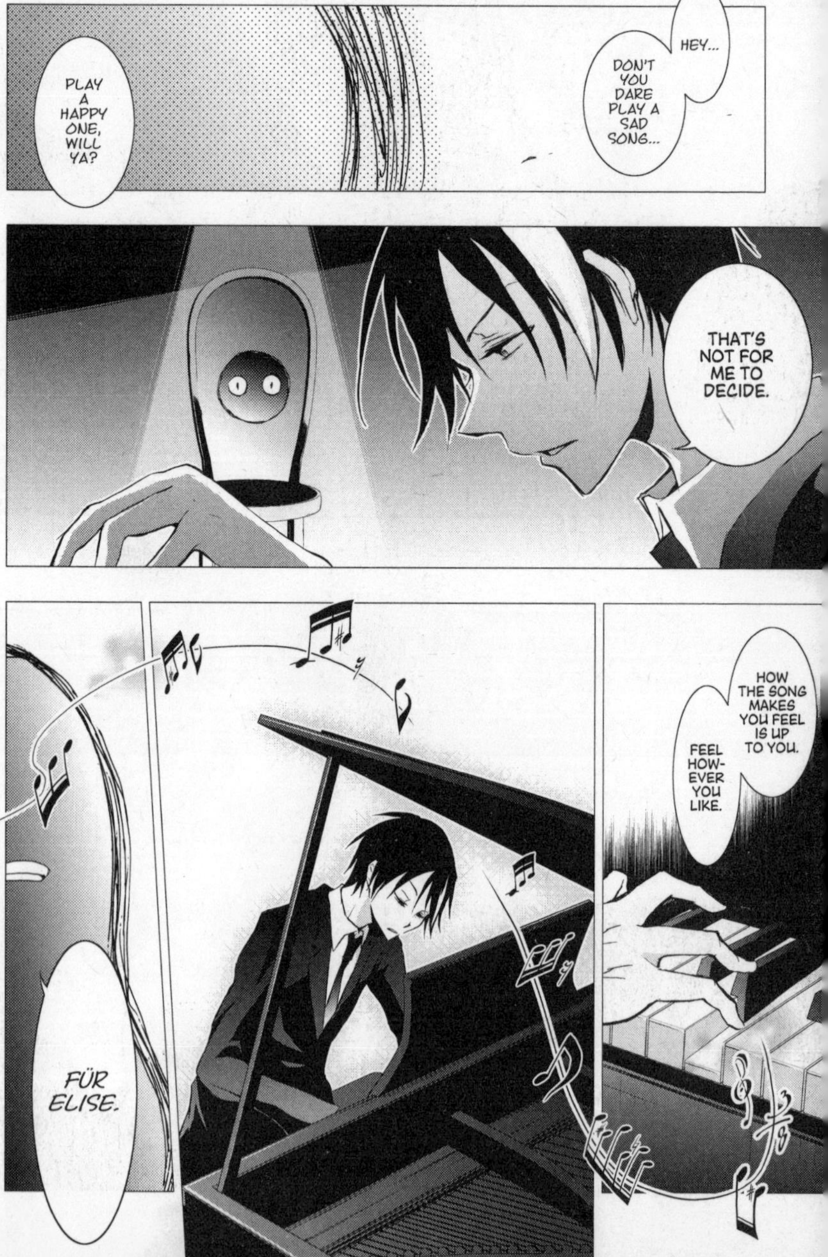
HEY...
DON'T YOU DARE PLAY A SAD SONG...
PLAY A HAPPY ONE, WILL YA?
THAT'S NOT FOR ME TO DECIDE.
HOW THE SONG MAKES YOU FEEL IS UP TO YOU.
FEEL HOW-EVER YOU LIKE.
FÜR ELISE.

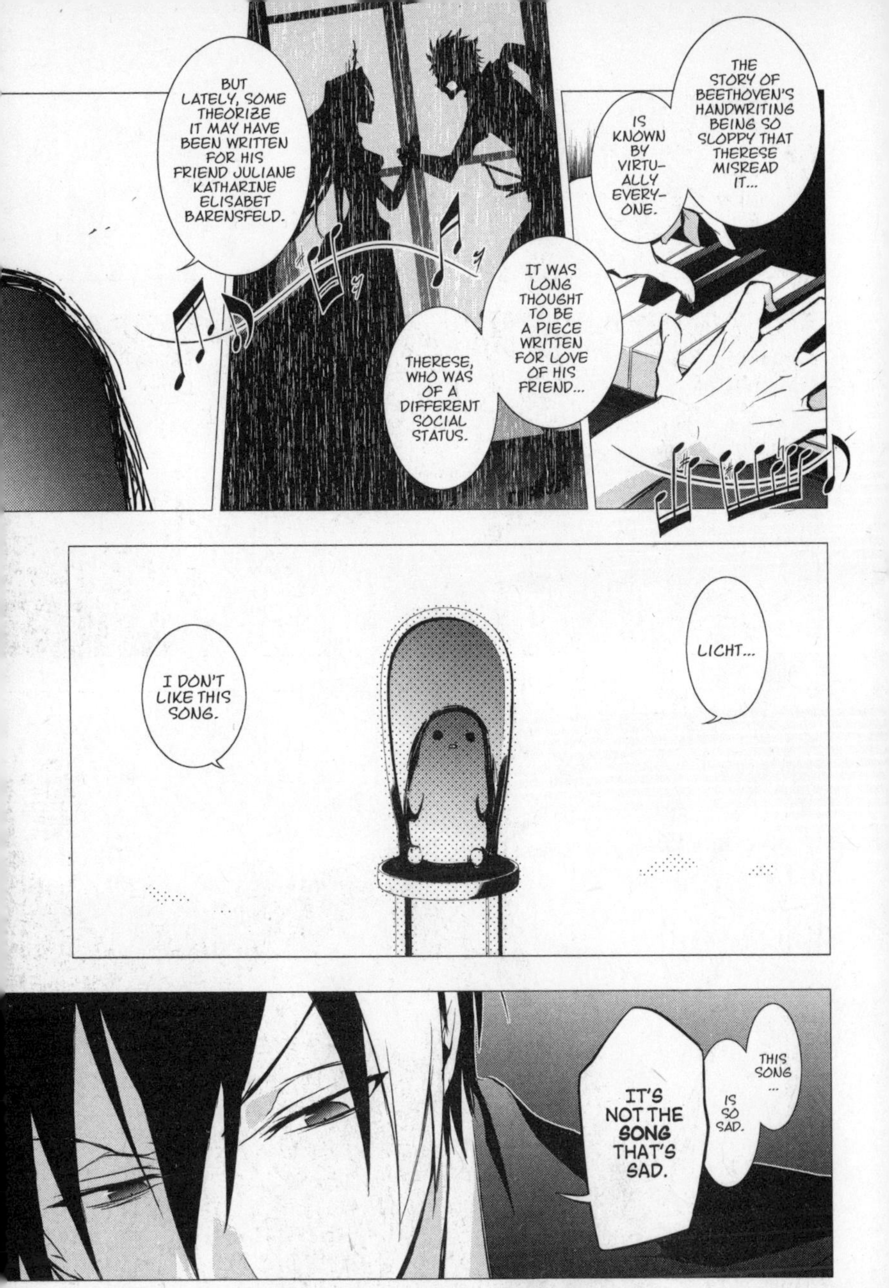
THE STORY OF BEETHOVEN'S HANDWRITING BEING SO SLOPPY THAT THERESE MISREAD IT...
IS KNOWN BY VIRTU-ALLY EVERY-ONE.
IT WAS LONG THOUGHT TO BE A PIECE WRITTEN FOR LOVE OF HIS FRIEND...
THERESE, WHO WAS OF A DIFFERENT SOCIAL STATUS.
BUT LATELY, SOME THEORIZE IT MAY HAVE BEEN WRITTEN FOR HIS FRIEND JULIANE KATHARINE ELISABET BARENSFELD.
LICHT...
I DON'T LIKE THIS SONG.
THIS SONG...
IS SO SAD.
IT'S NOT THE SONG THAT'S SAD.

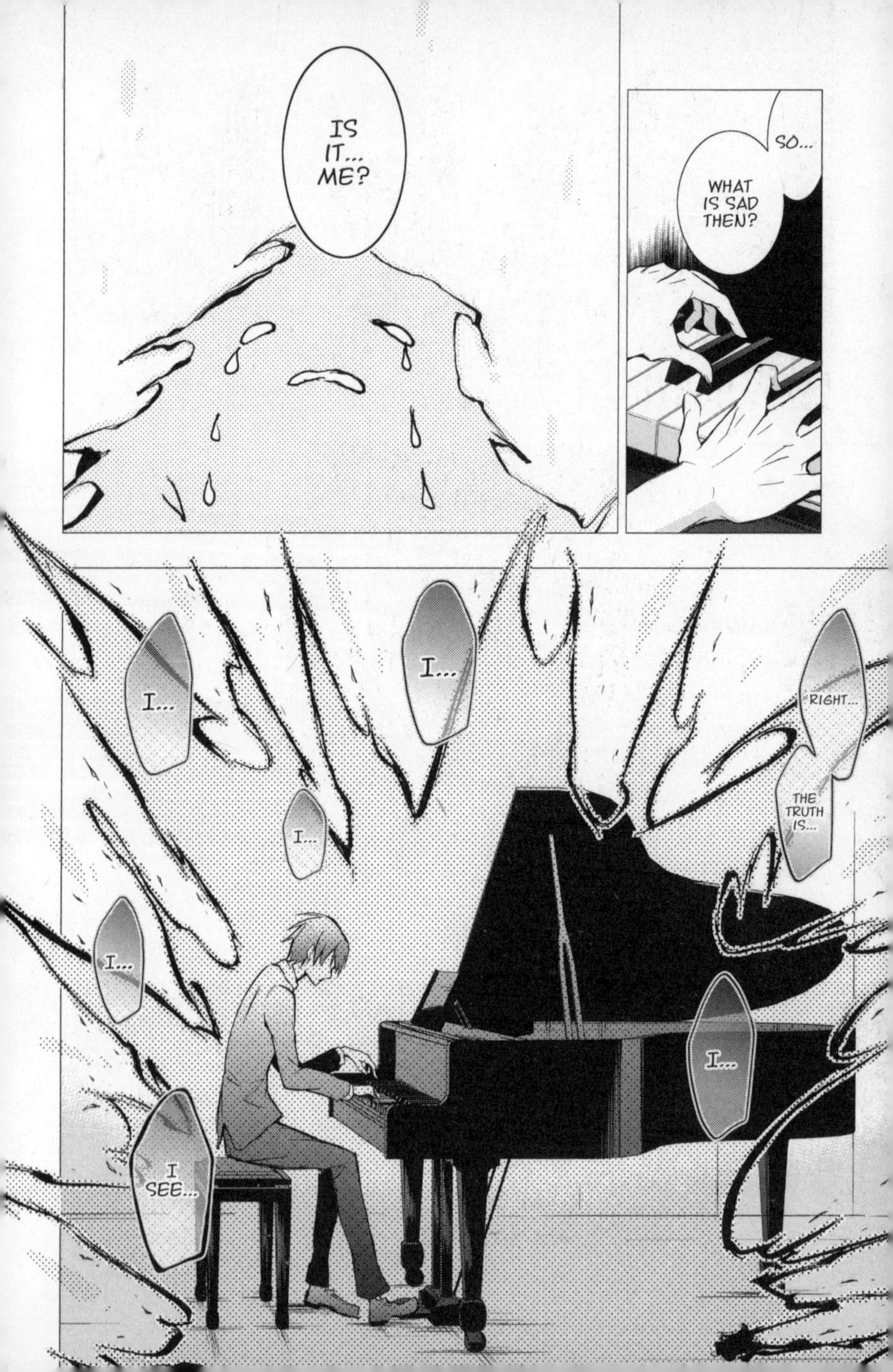
SO...
WHAT IS SAD THEN?
IS IT... ME?
RIGHT...
THE TRUTH IS...
I...
I...
I...
I...
I...
I SEE...

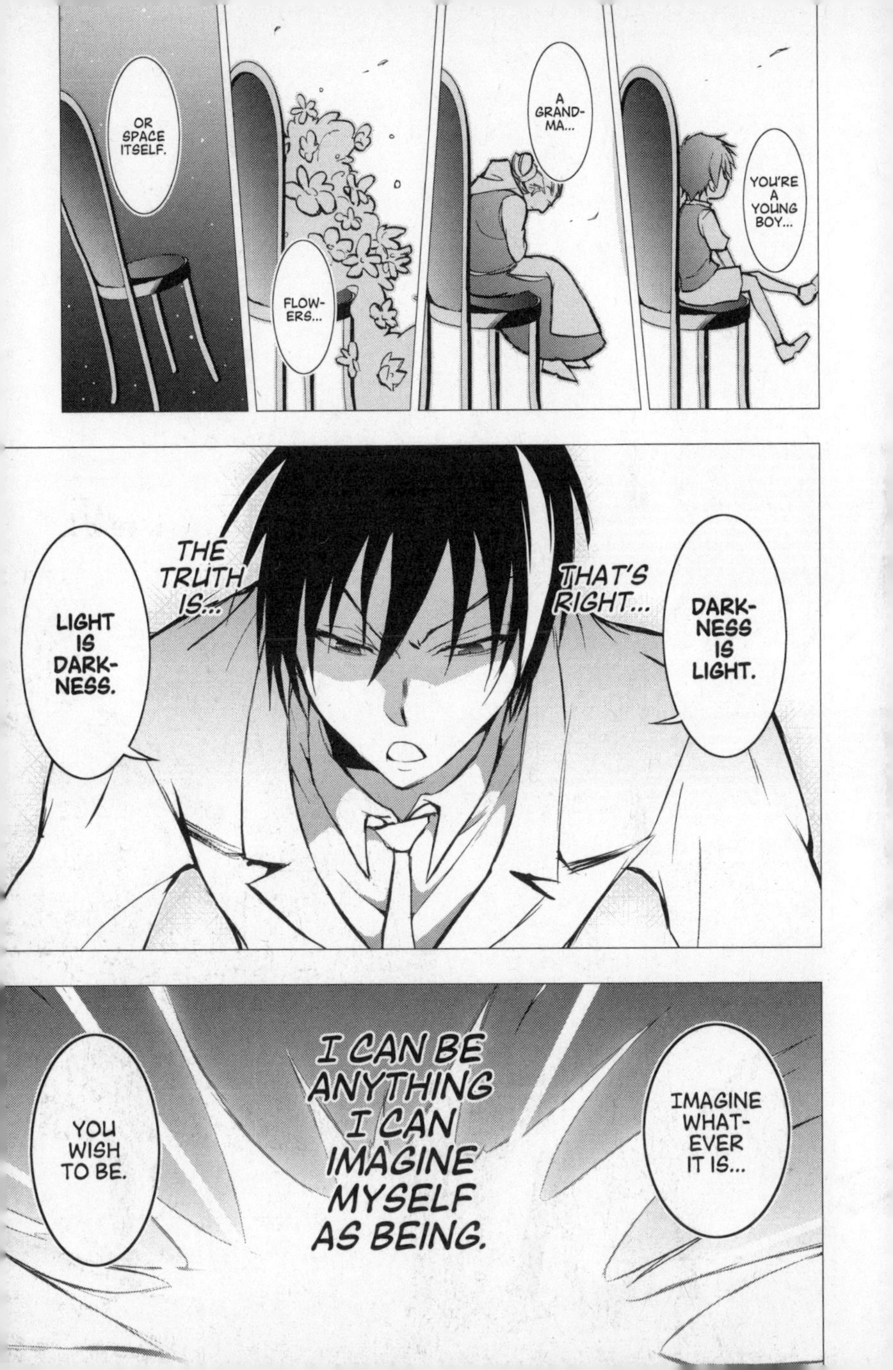
YOU'RE A YOUNG BOY...
A GRANDMA...
FLOWERS...
OR SPACE ITSELF.
THAT'S RIGHT...
DARKNESS IS LIGHT.
THE TRUTH IS...
LIGHT IS DARKNESS.
IMAGINE WHATEVER IT IS...
I CAN BE ANYTHING I CAN IMAGINE MYSELF AS BEING.
YOU WISH TO BE.

WHAT AM I?
I WAS THE ONE WHO DIDN'T WANT TO LEAVE YOUR SIDE.
I WAS THE ONE WHO WANTED TO PROTECT YOU.
I WAS THE ONE WHO WANTED TO PROTECT EVERYTHING YOU WANTED TO PROTECT.
WHY IS IT...
I WAS THE ONE...
WHO WANTED TO TELL YOU... THAT I LOVED YOU.
THAT I WASN'T ABLE TO BECOME ANYTHING IN THE END?

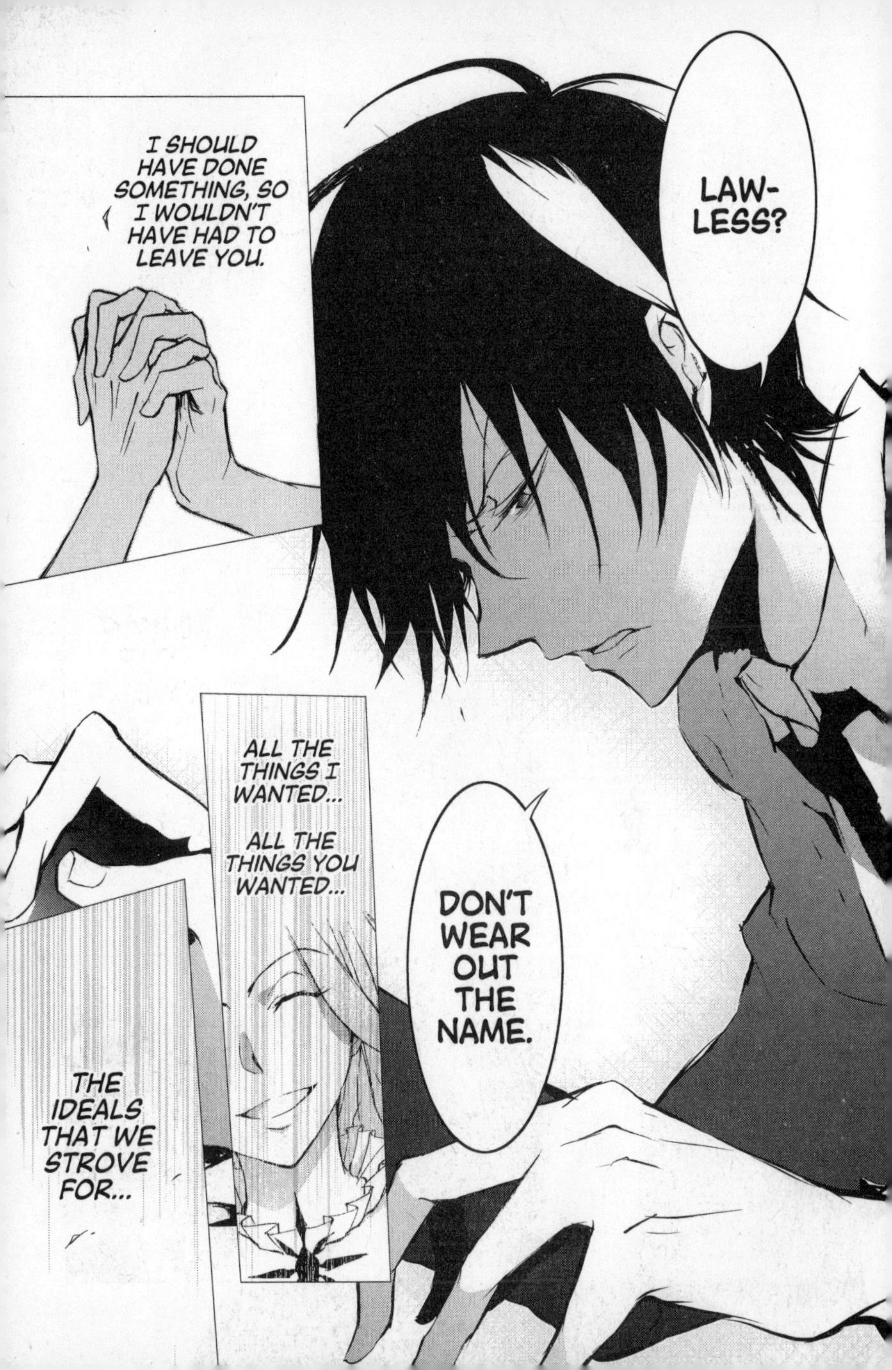
LAW-LESS?
I SHOULD HAVE DONE SOMETHING, SO I WOULDN'T HAVE HAD TO LEAVE YOU.
DON'T WEAR OUT THE NAME.
ALL THE THINGS I WANTED...
ALL THE THINGS YOU WANTED...
THE IDEALS THAT WE STROVE FOR...

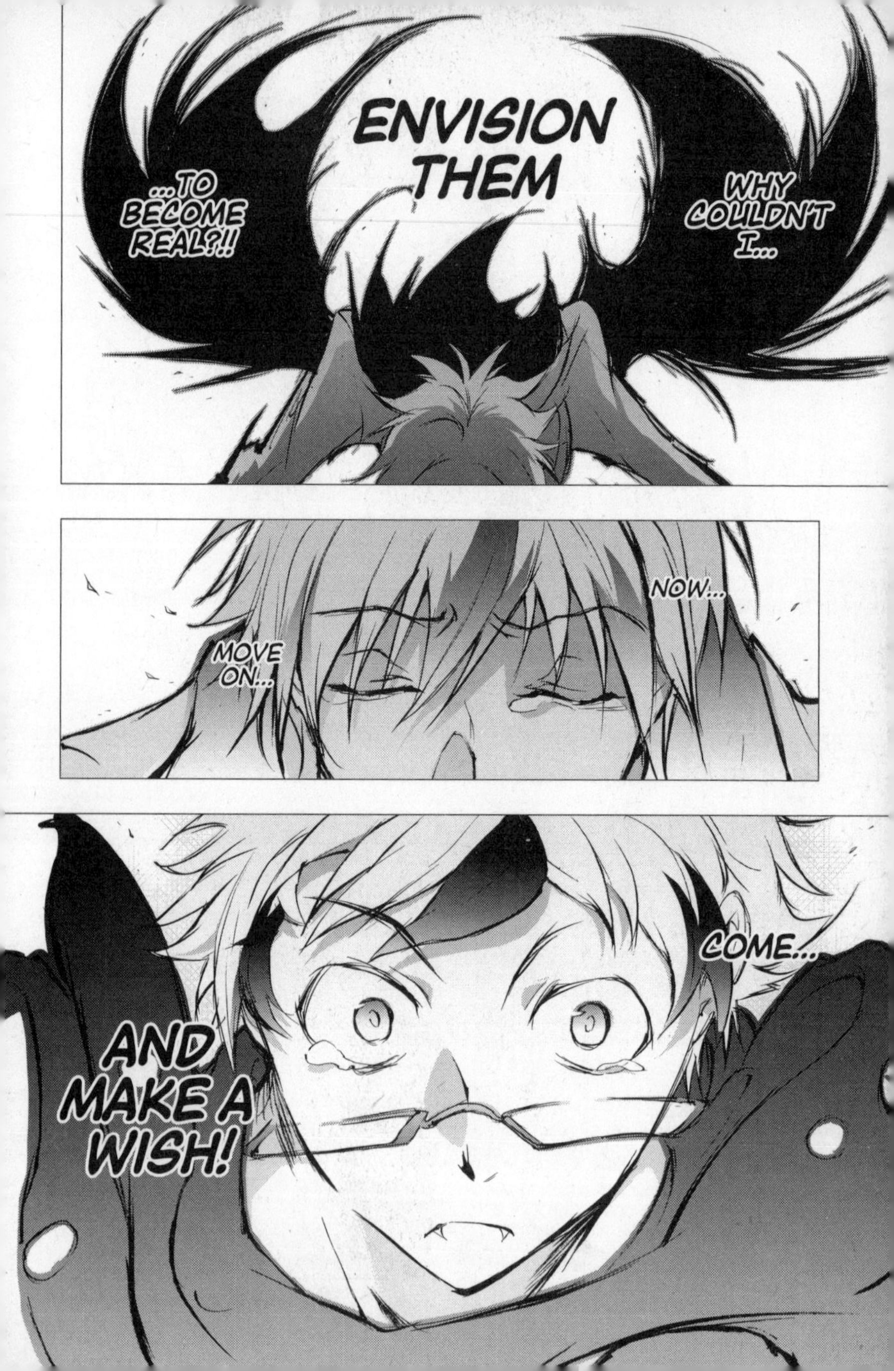
WHY COULDN'T I...
ENVISION THEM
...TO BECOME REAL?!!
NOW...
MOVE ON...
COME...
AND MAKE A WISH!

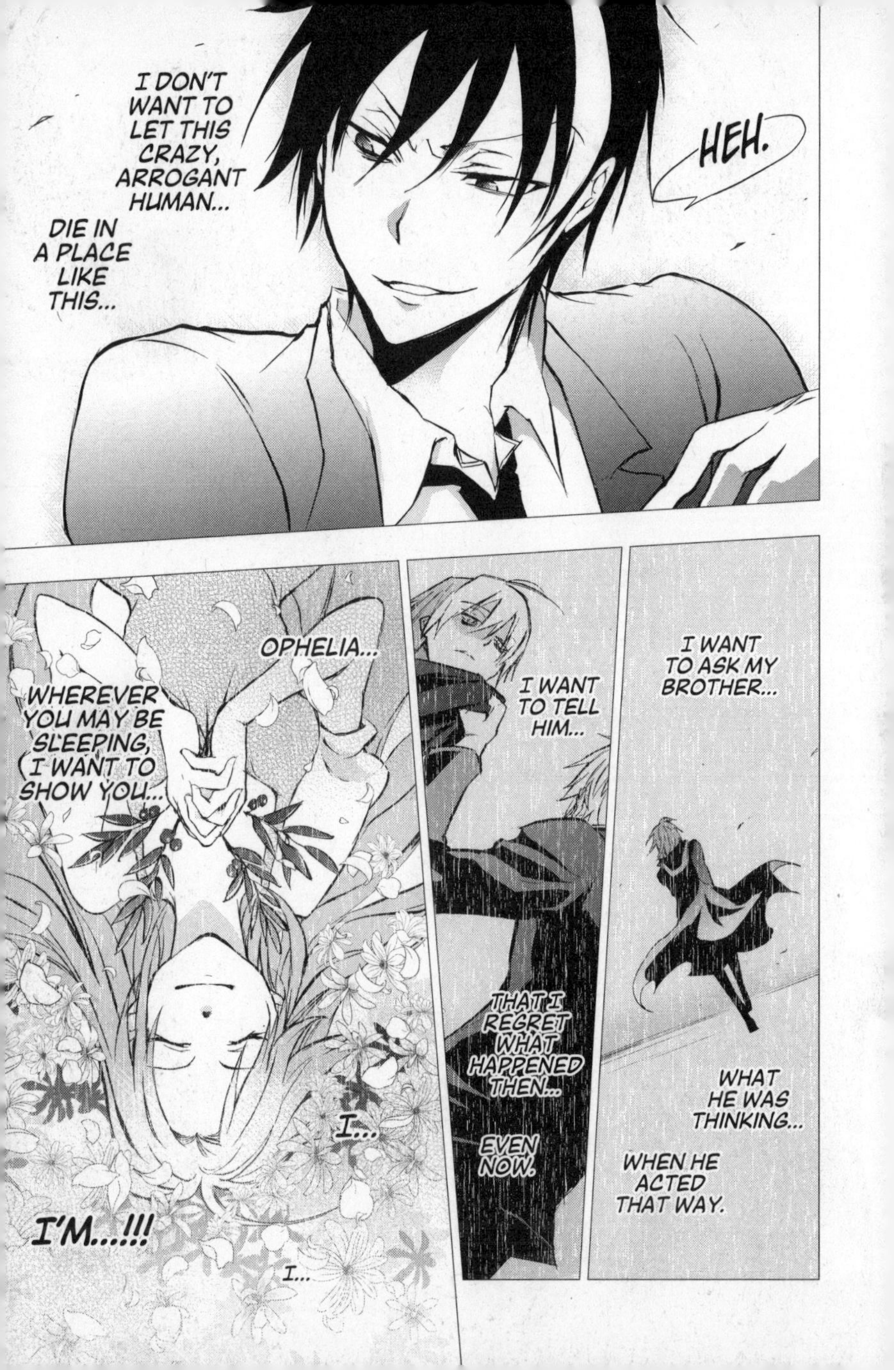
HEH.
I DON'T WANT TO LET THIS CRAZY, ARROGANT HUMAN...
DIE IN A PLACE LIKE THIS...
I WANT TO ASK MY BROTHER...
WHAT HE WAS THINKING...
WHEN HE ACTED THAT WAY.
I WANT TO TELL HIM...
THAT I REGRET WHAT HAPPENED THEN...
EVEN NOW.
OPHELIA...
WHEREVER YOU MAY BE SLEEPING, I WANT TO SHOW YOU...
I...
I'M...!!!
I...

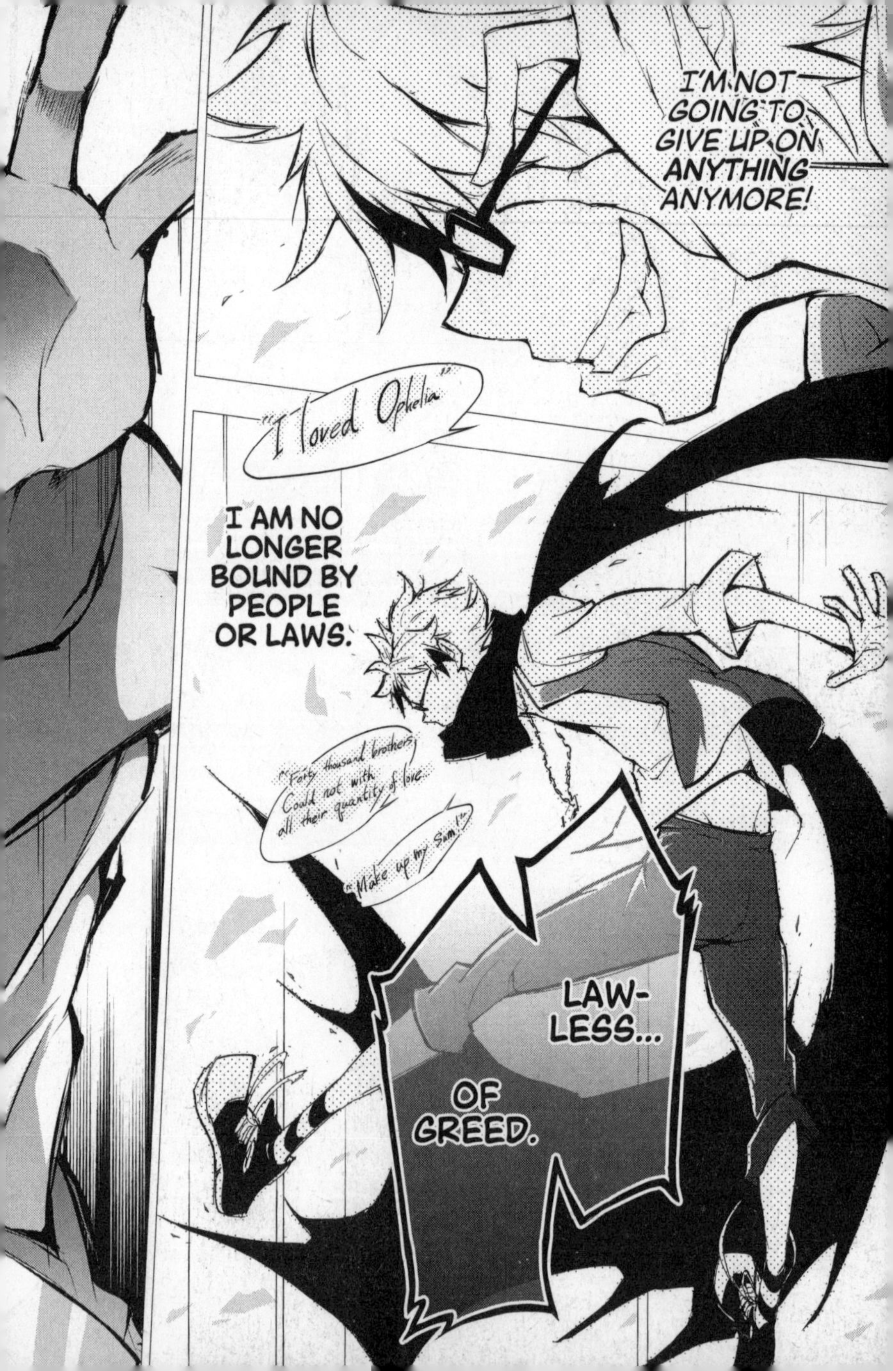
I'M NOT GOING TO GIVE UP ON ANYTHING ANYMORE!
"I loved Ophelia"
I AM NO LONGER BOUND BY PEOPLE OR LAWS.
"Forty thousand brothers Could not with all their quantity of love...
"Make up my Sum!"
LAW-LESS...
OF GREED.

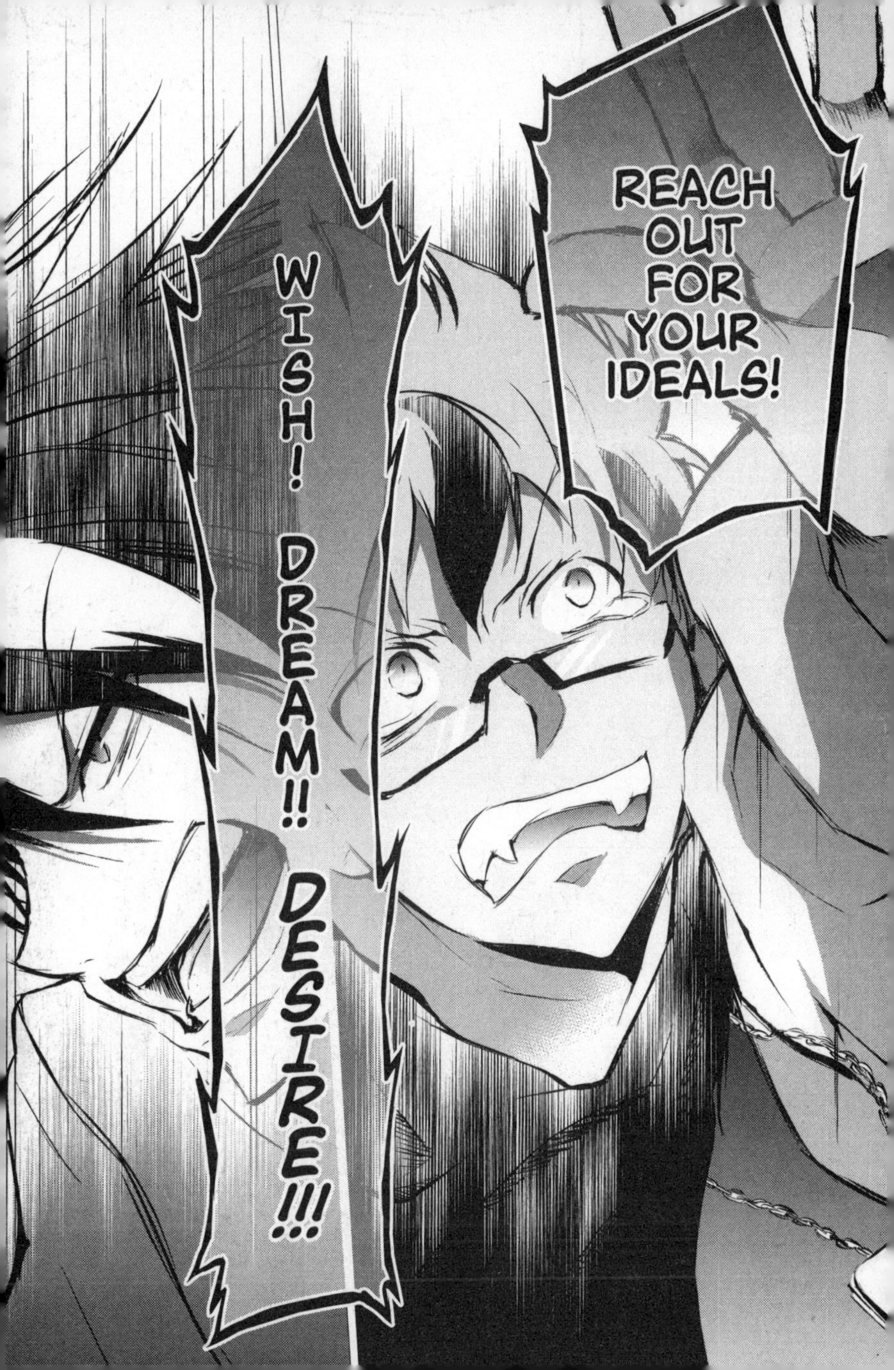
REACH OUT FOR YOUR IDEALS!
WISH! DREAM!! DESIRE!!!

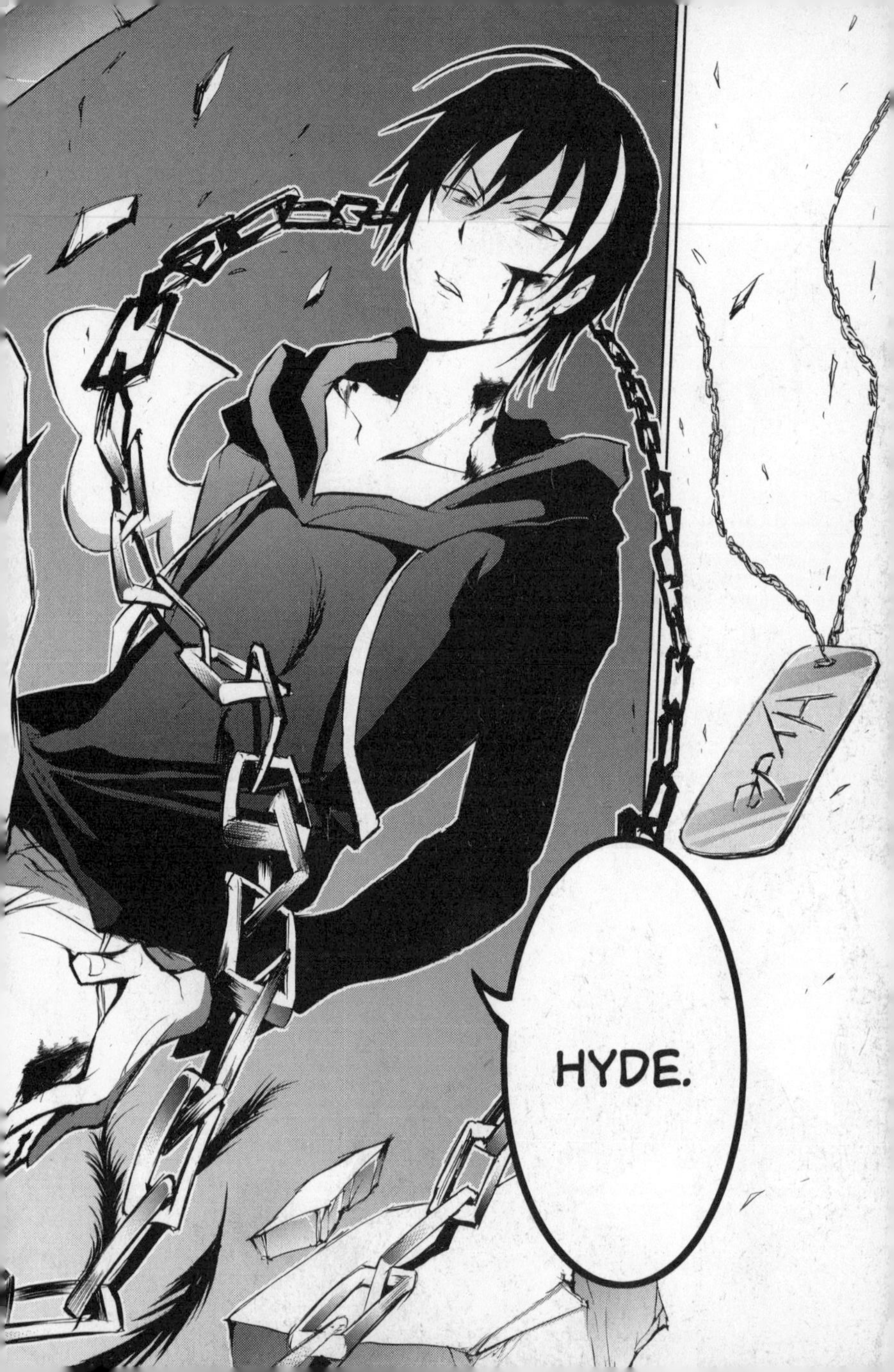
HYDE.

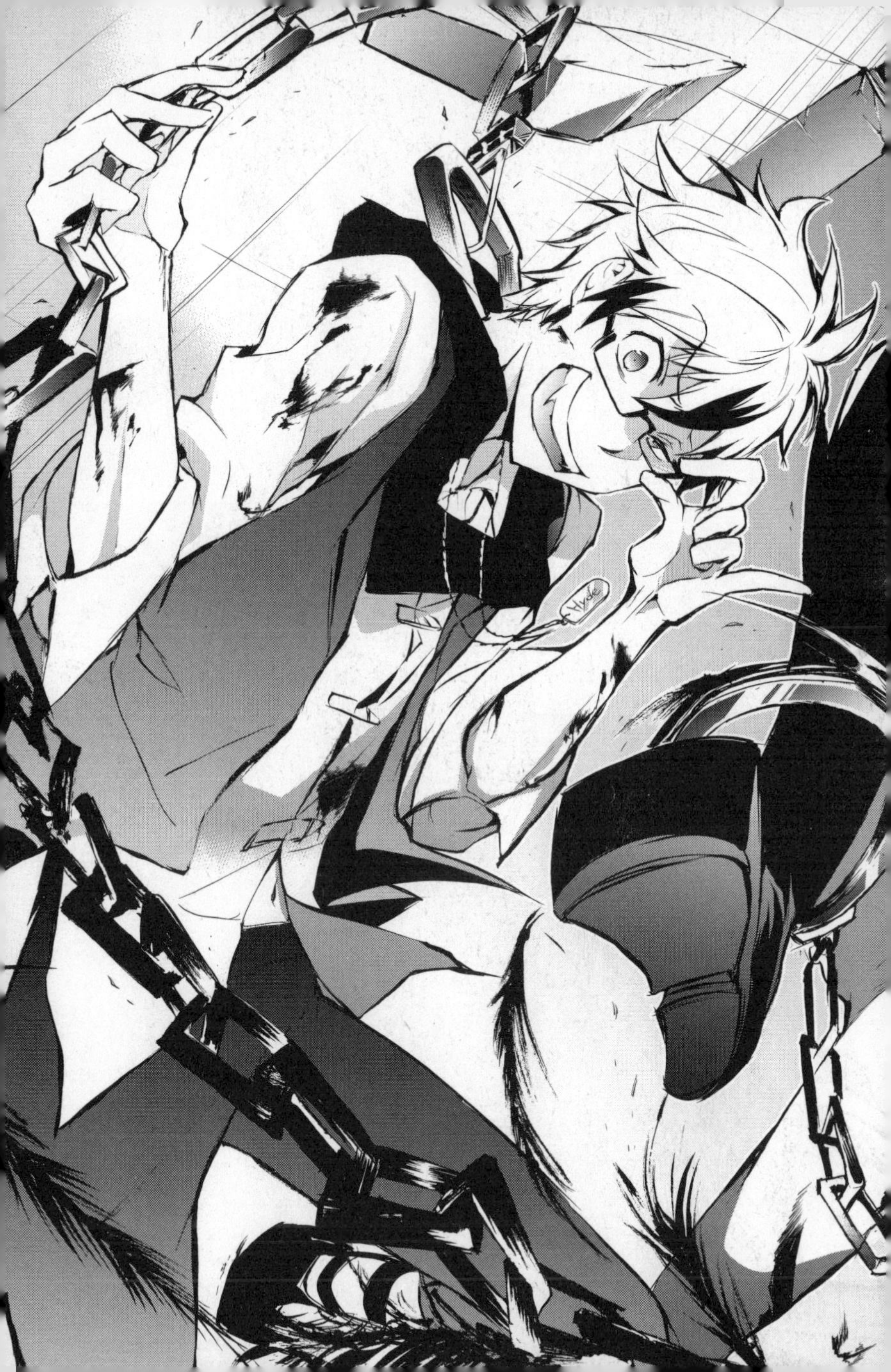
Hyde

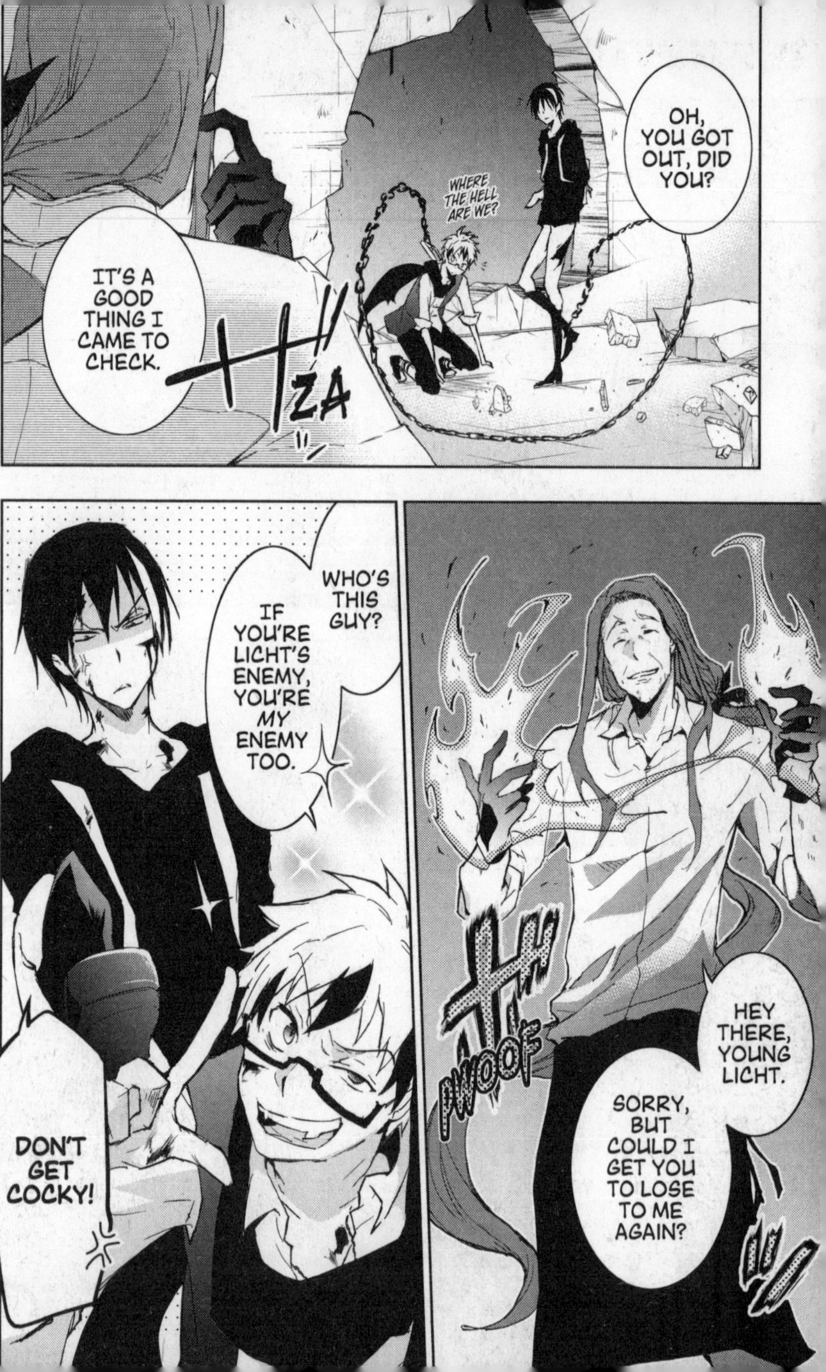
OH, YOU GOT OUT, DID YOU?
WHERE THE HELL ARE WE?
ZA
IT'S A GOOD THING I CAME TO CHECK.
HEY THERE, YOUNG LICHT.
FWOOF
SORRY, BUT COULD I GET YOU TO LOSE TO ME AGAIN?
WHO'S THIS GUY?
IF YOU'RE LICHT'S ENEMY, YOU'RE *MY* ENEMY TOO.
DON'T GET COCKY!

# 35. SCORPIO'S FLAME

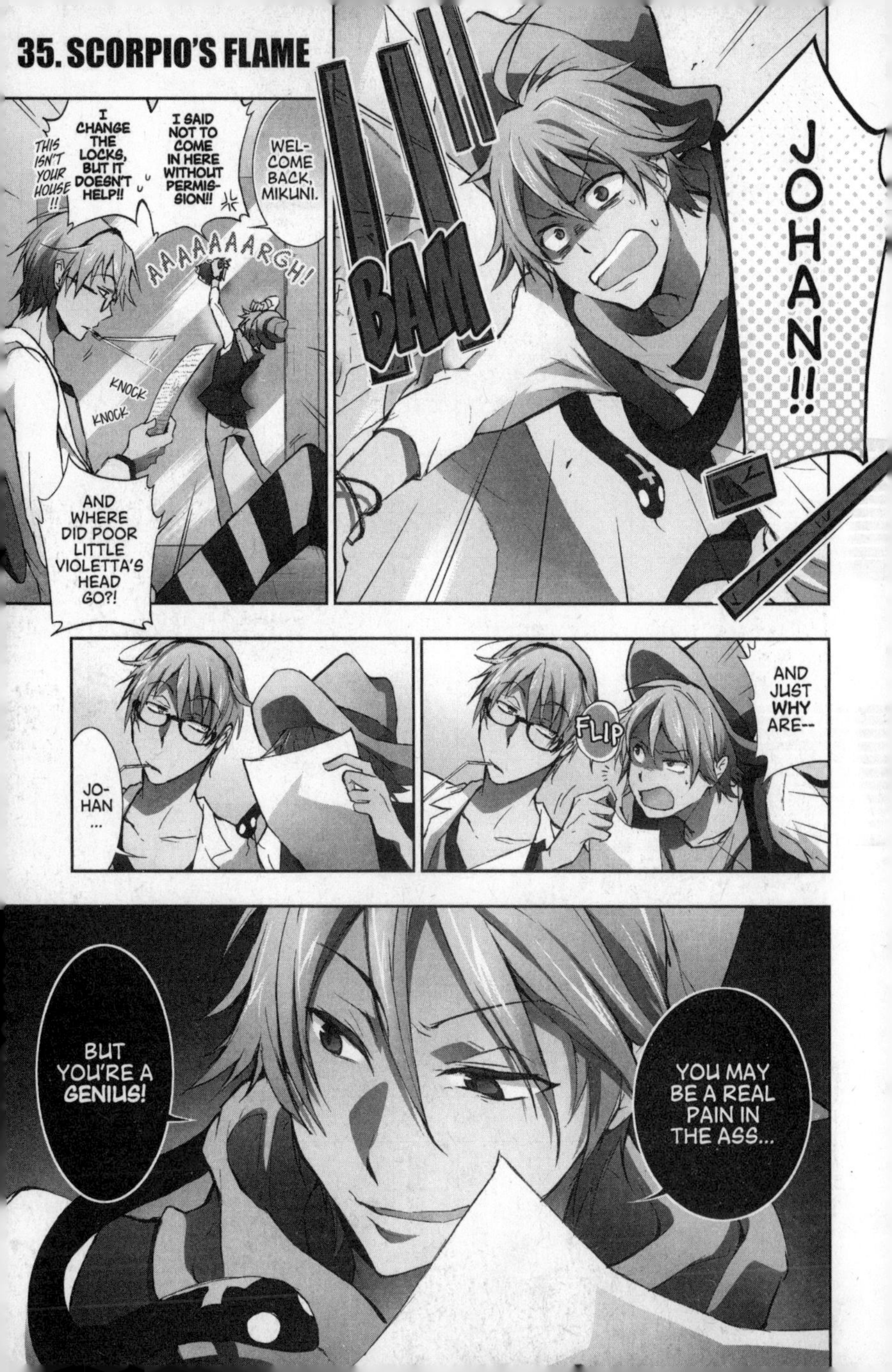
JOHAN!!
BAM
WEL-COME BACK, MIKUNI.
I SAID NOT TO COME IN HERE WITHOUT PERMIS-SION!!
I CHANGE THE LOCKS, BUT IT DOESN'T HELP!!
THIS ISN'T YOUR HOUSE!!
AAAAAAARGH!
KNOCK
KNOCK
AND WHERE DID POOR LITTLE VIOLETTA'S HEAD GO?!
AND JUST WHY ARE--
FLIP
JO-HAN...
YOU MAY BE A REAL PAIN IN THE ASS...
BUT YOU'RE A GENIUS!

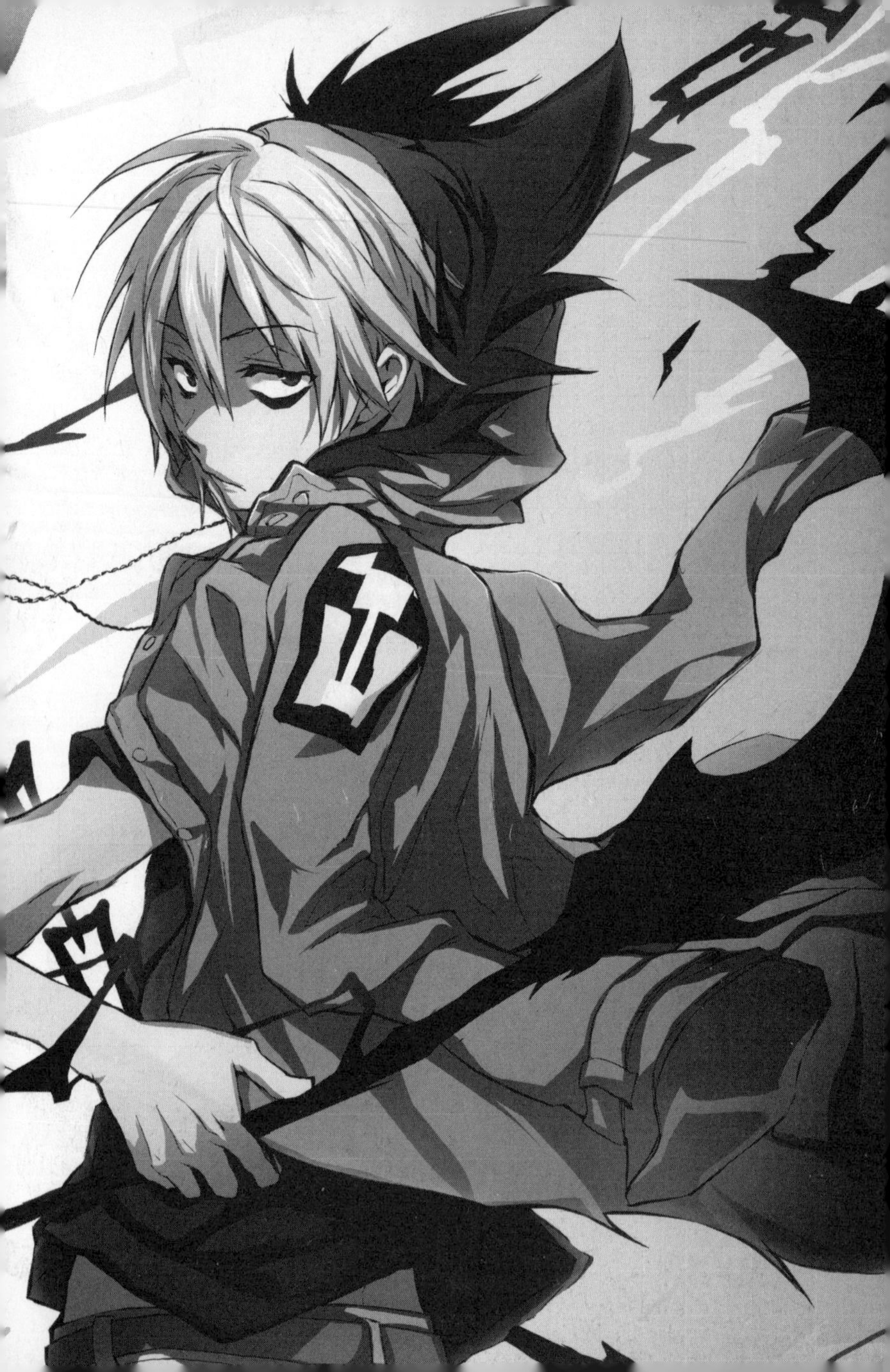

# 35 SCORPIO'S FLAME

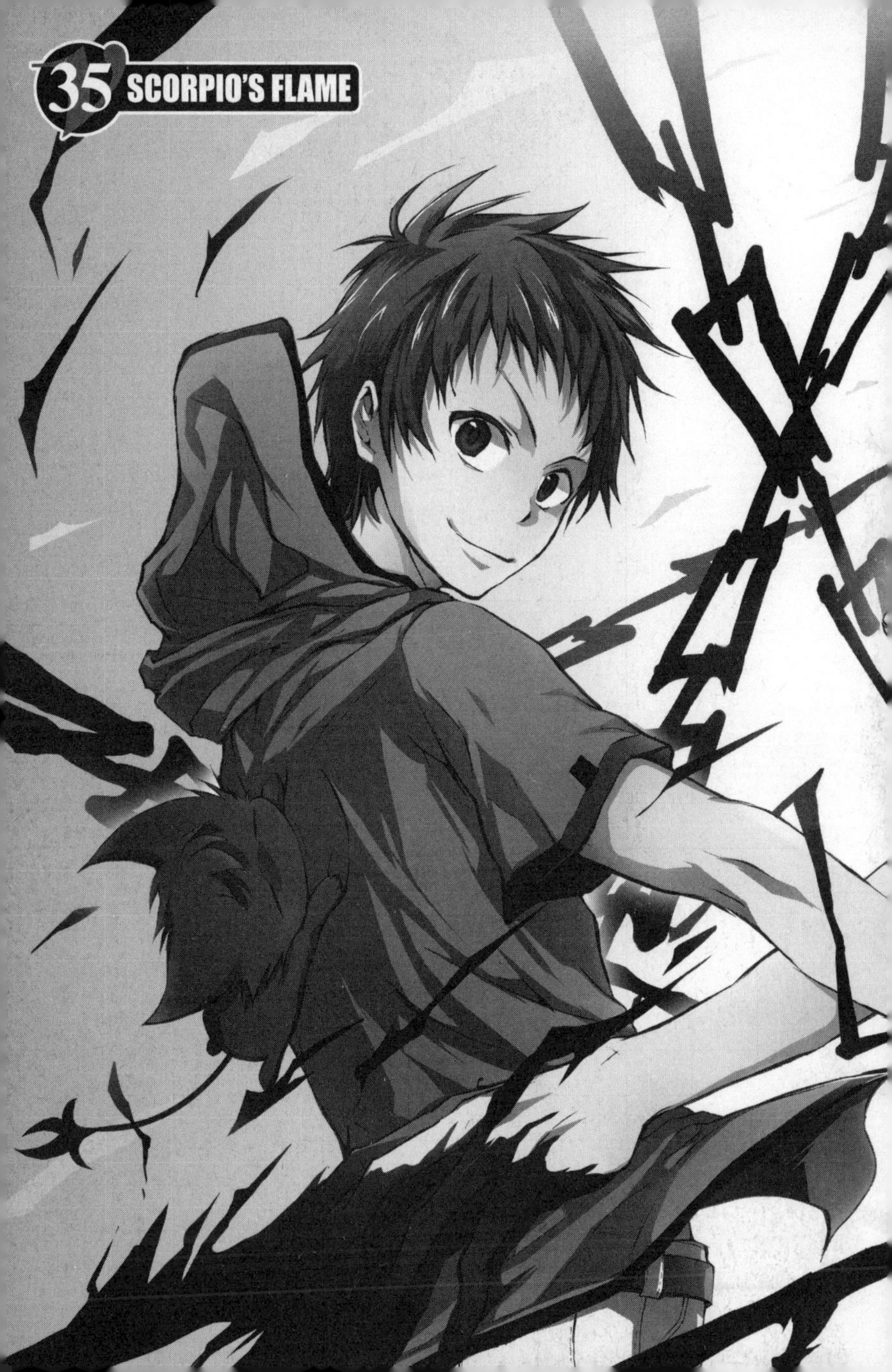

SERVAMP

STRIKE TANAKA

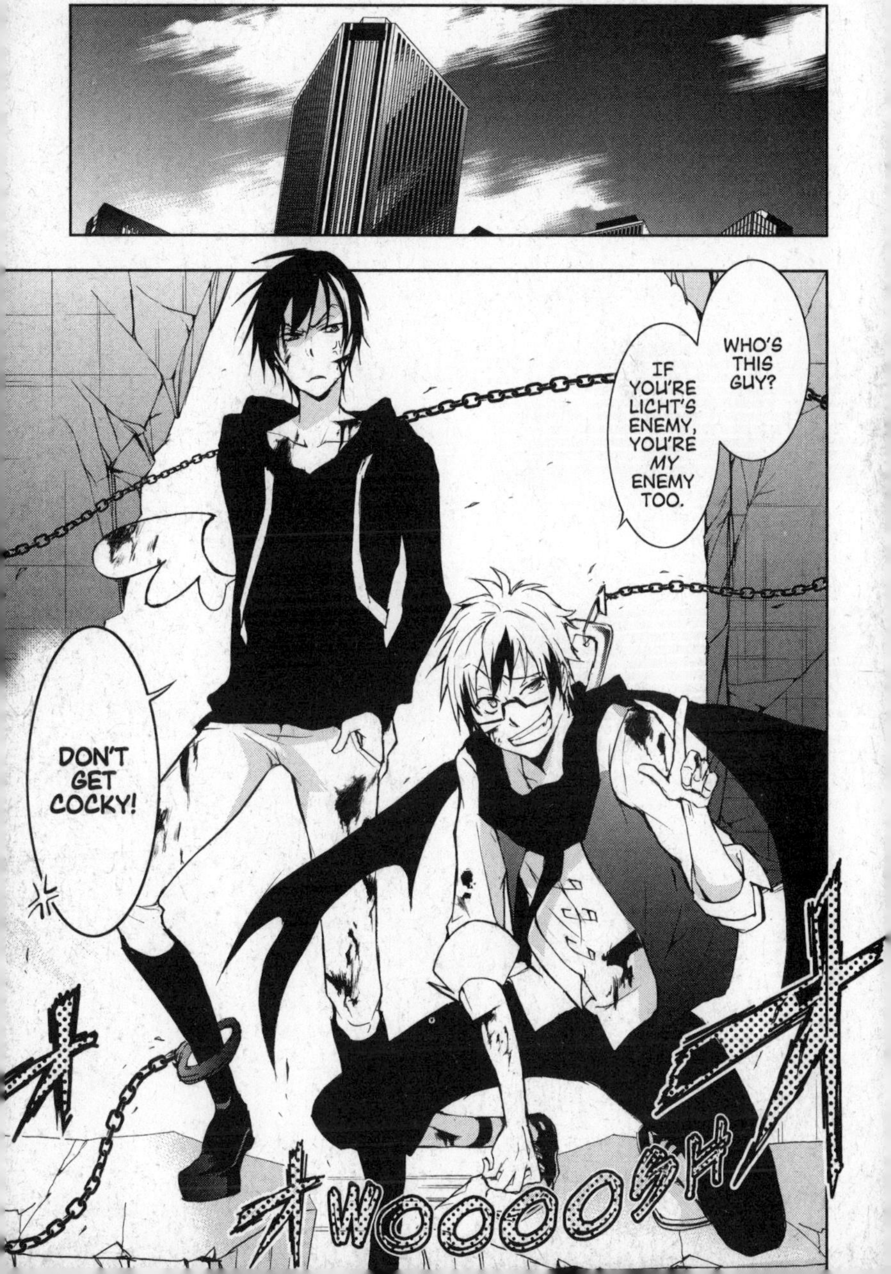
WHO'S THIS GUY?
IF YOU'RE LICHT'S ENEMY, YOU'RE MY ENEMY TOO.
DON'T GET COCKY!
WOOOOOSH

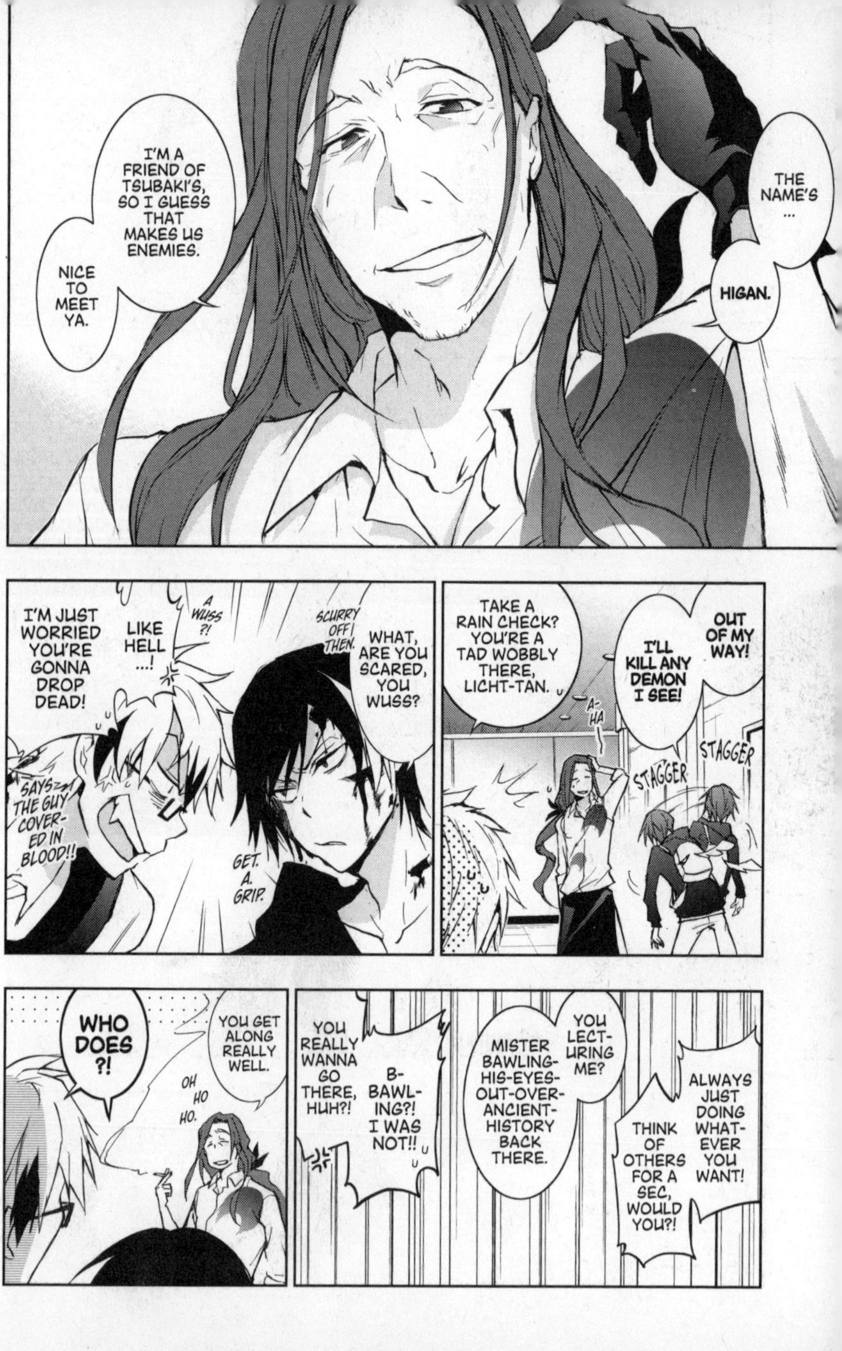
THE NAME'S ...
HIGAN.
I'M A FRIEND OF TSUBAKI'S, SO I GUESS THAT MAKES US ENEMIES.
NICE TO MEET YA.
OUT OF MY WAY!
I'LL KILL ANY DEMON I SEE!
STAGGER
STAGGER
TAKE A RAIN CHECK? YOU'RE A TAD WOBBLY THERE, LICHT-TAN.
A-HA
SCURRY OFF THEN.
WHAT, ARE YOU SCARED, YOU WUSS?
A WUSS?!
LIKE HELL ...!
I'M JUST WORRIED YOU'RE GONNA DROP DEAD!
GET. A. GRIP.
SAYS THE GUY COVERED IN BLOOD!!
YOU LECTURING ME?
ALWAYS JUST DOING WHATEVER YOU WANT!
THINK OF OTHERS FOR A SEC, WOULD YOU?!
MISTER BAWLING-HIS-EYES-OUT-OVER-ANCIENT-HISTORY BACK THERE.
B-BAWLING?! I WAS NOT!!
YOU REALLY WANNA GO THERE, HUH?!
YOU GET ALONG REALLY WELL.
OH HO HO.
WHO DOES?!

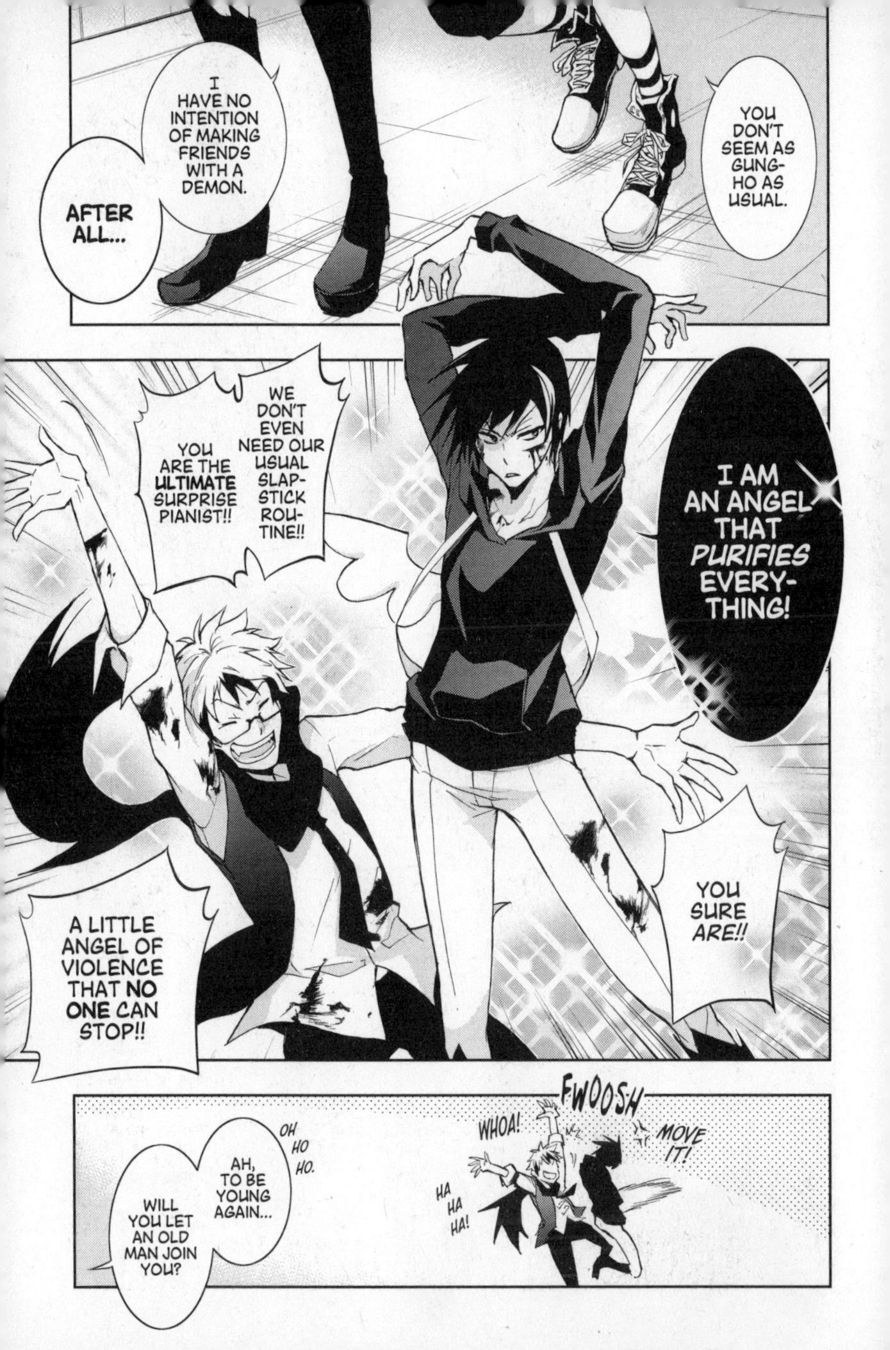
YOU DON'T SEEM AS GUNG-HO AS USUAL.
I HAVE NO INTENTION OF MAKING FRIENDS WITH A DEMON.
AFTER ALL...
I AM AN ANGEL THAT PURIFIES EVERYTHING!
WE DON'T EVEN NEED OUR USUAL SLAPSTICK ROUTINE!!
YOU ARE THE ULTIMATE SURPRISE PIANIST!!
YOU SURE ARE!!
A LITTLE ANGEL OF VIOLENCE THAT NO ONE CAN STOP!!
FWOOSH
MOVE IT!
WHOA!
HA HA HA!
OH HO HO.
AH, TO BE YOUNG AGAIN...
WILL YOU LET AN OLD MAN JOIN YOU?

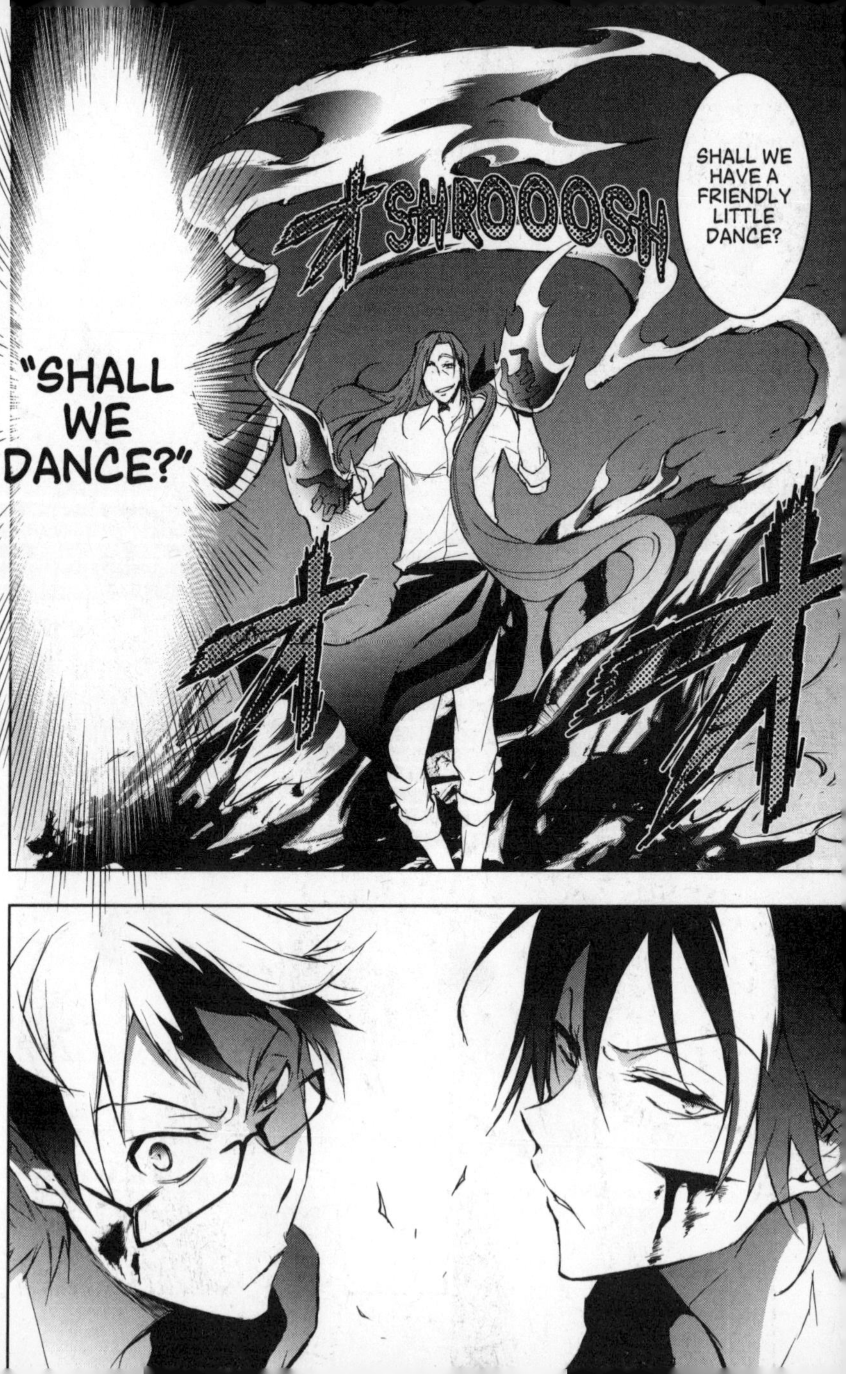
SHALL WE HAVE A FRIENDLY LITTLE DANCE?
SHROOOSH
"SHALL WE DANCE?"

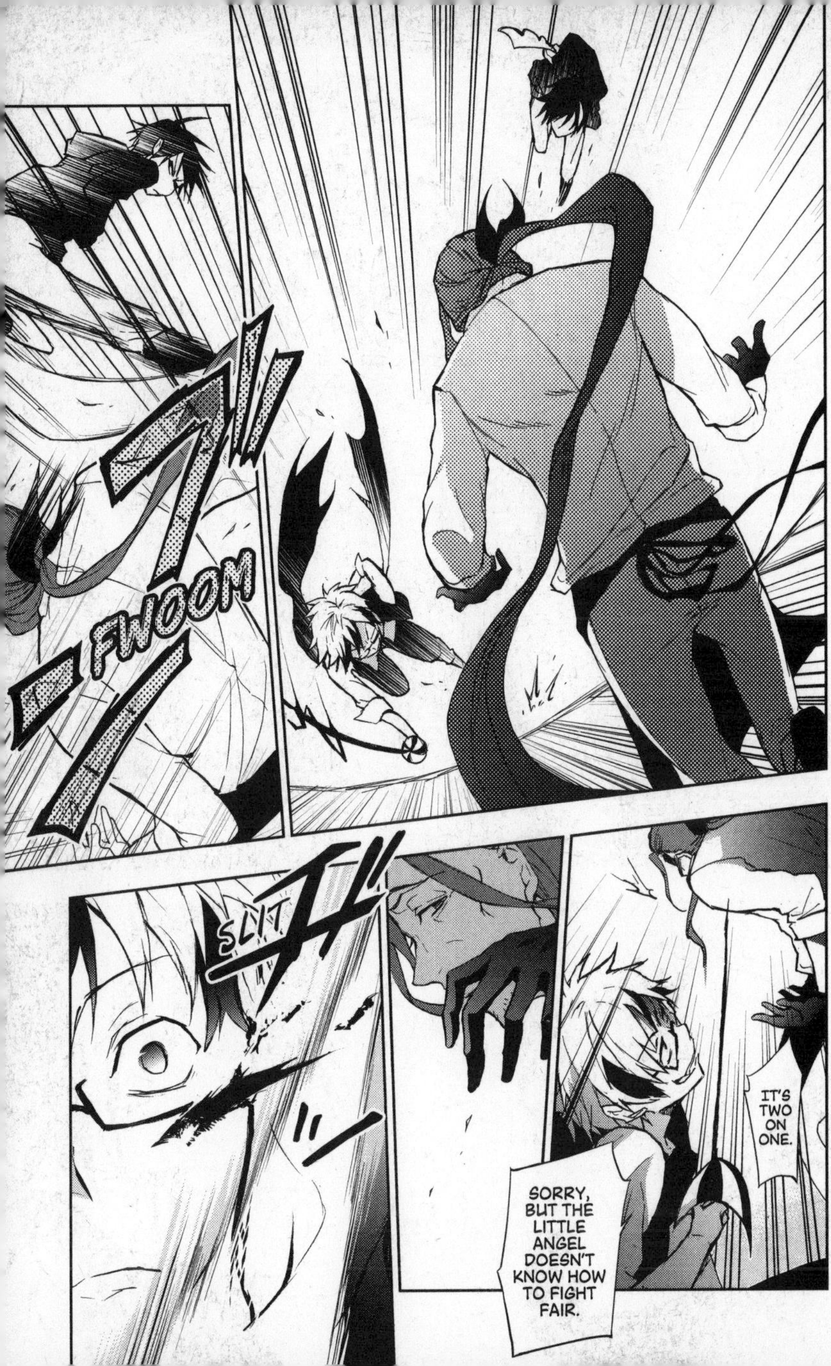
FWOOM
IT'S TWO ON ONE.
SORRY, BUT THE LITTLE ANGEL DOESN'T KNOW HOW TO FIGHT FAIR.
SLIT

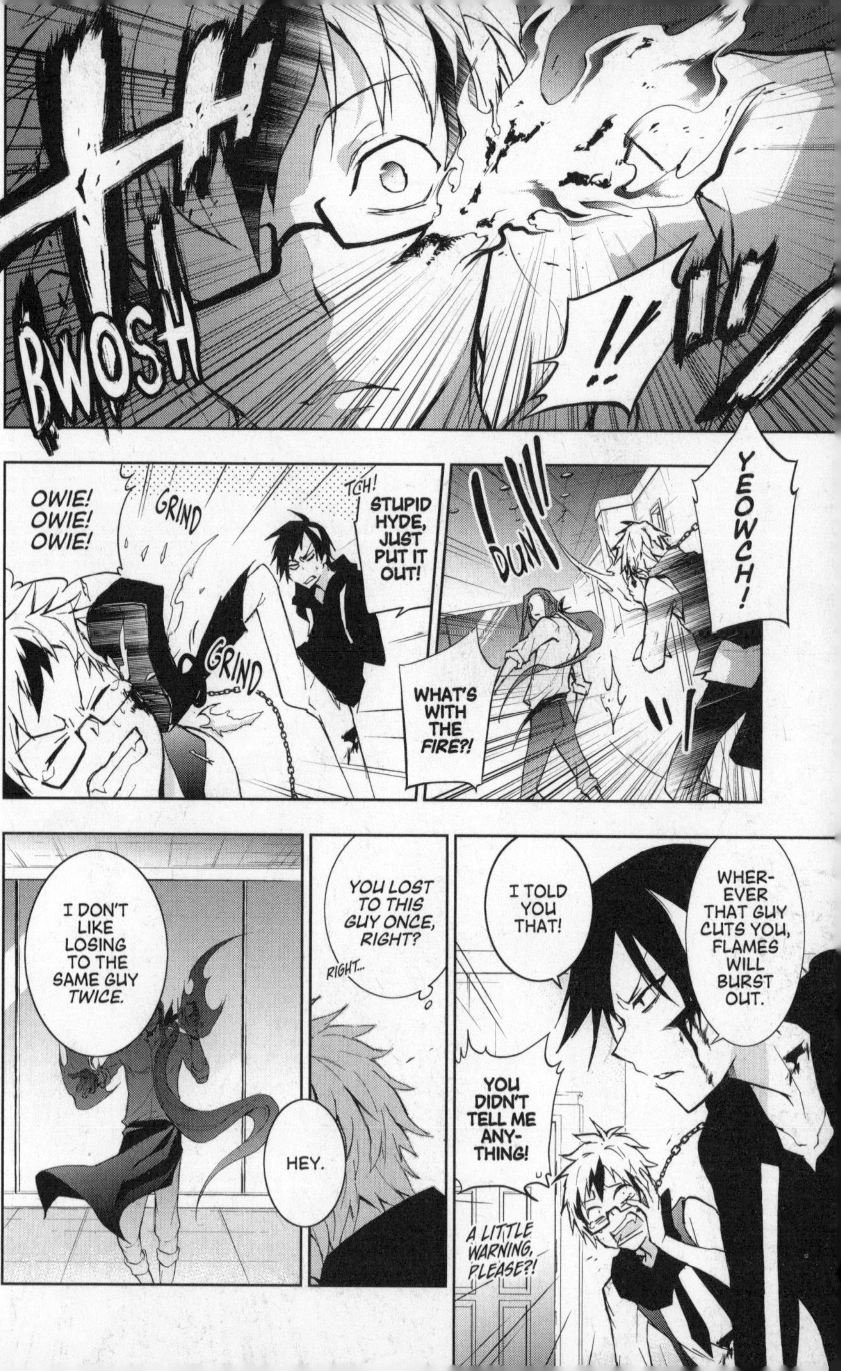
BWOSH
!!
YEOWCH!
DUN
WHAT'S WITH THE FIRE?!
TCH!
STUPID HYDE, JUST PUT IT OUT!
GRIND
GRIND
OWIE! OWIE! OWIE!
WHER-EVER THAT GUY CUTS YOU, FLAMES WILL BURST OUT.
I TOLD YOU THAT!
YOU DIDN'T TELL ME ANY-THING!
A LITTLE WARNING, PLEASE?!
YOU LOST TO THIS GUY ONCE, RIGHT?
RIGHT...
HEY.
I DON'T LIKE LOSING TO THE SAME GUY TWICE.

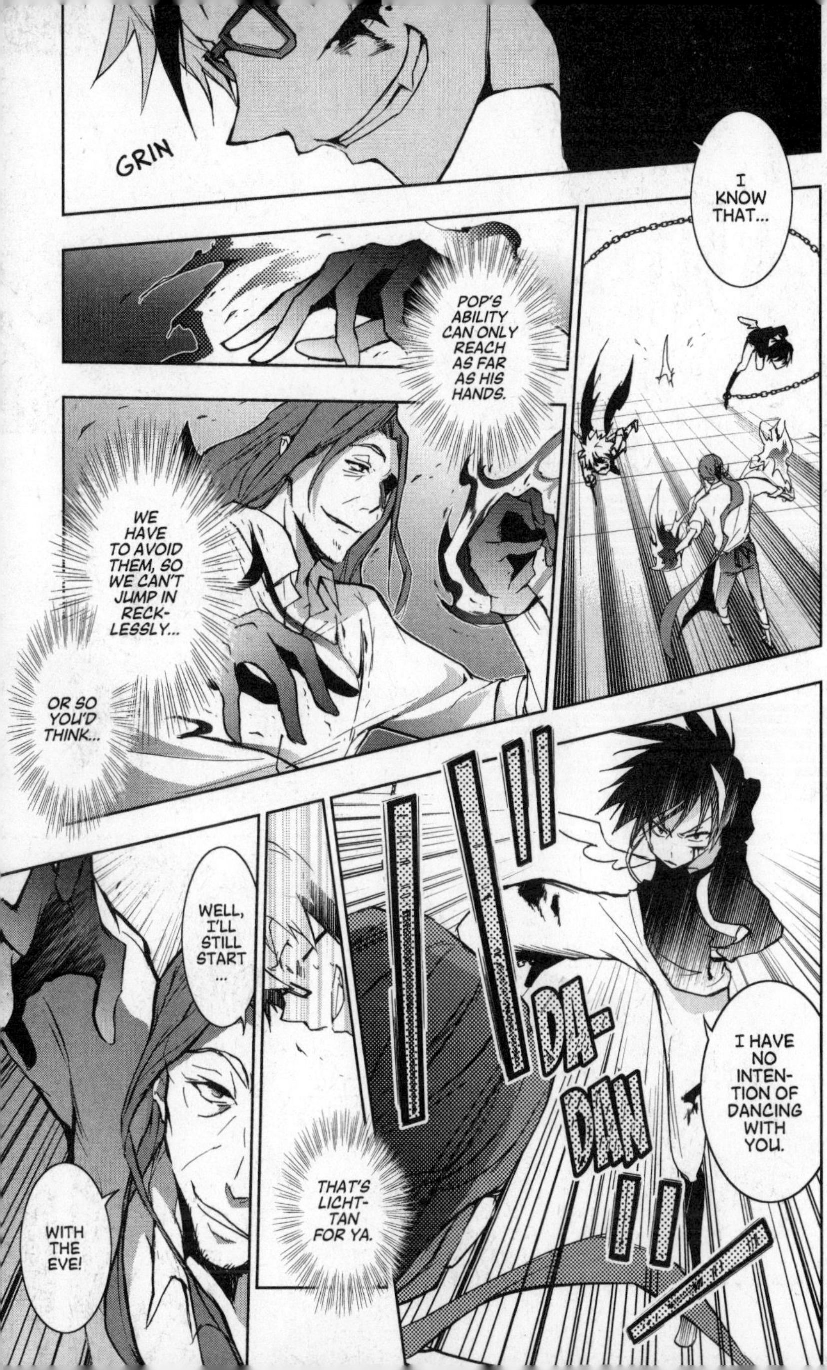
GRIN
I KNOW THAT...
POP'S ABILITY CAN ONLY REACH AS FAR AS HIS HANDS.
WE HAVE TO AVOID THEM, SO WE CAN'T JUMP IN RECK-LESSLY...
OR SO YOU'D THINK...
I HAVE NO INTEN-TION OF DANCING WITH YOU.
DA-DAN
WELL, I'LL STILL START ...
THAT'S LICHT-TAN FOR YA.
WITH THE EVE!

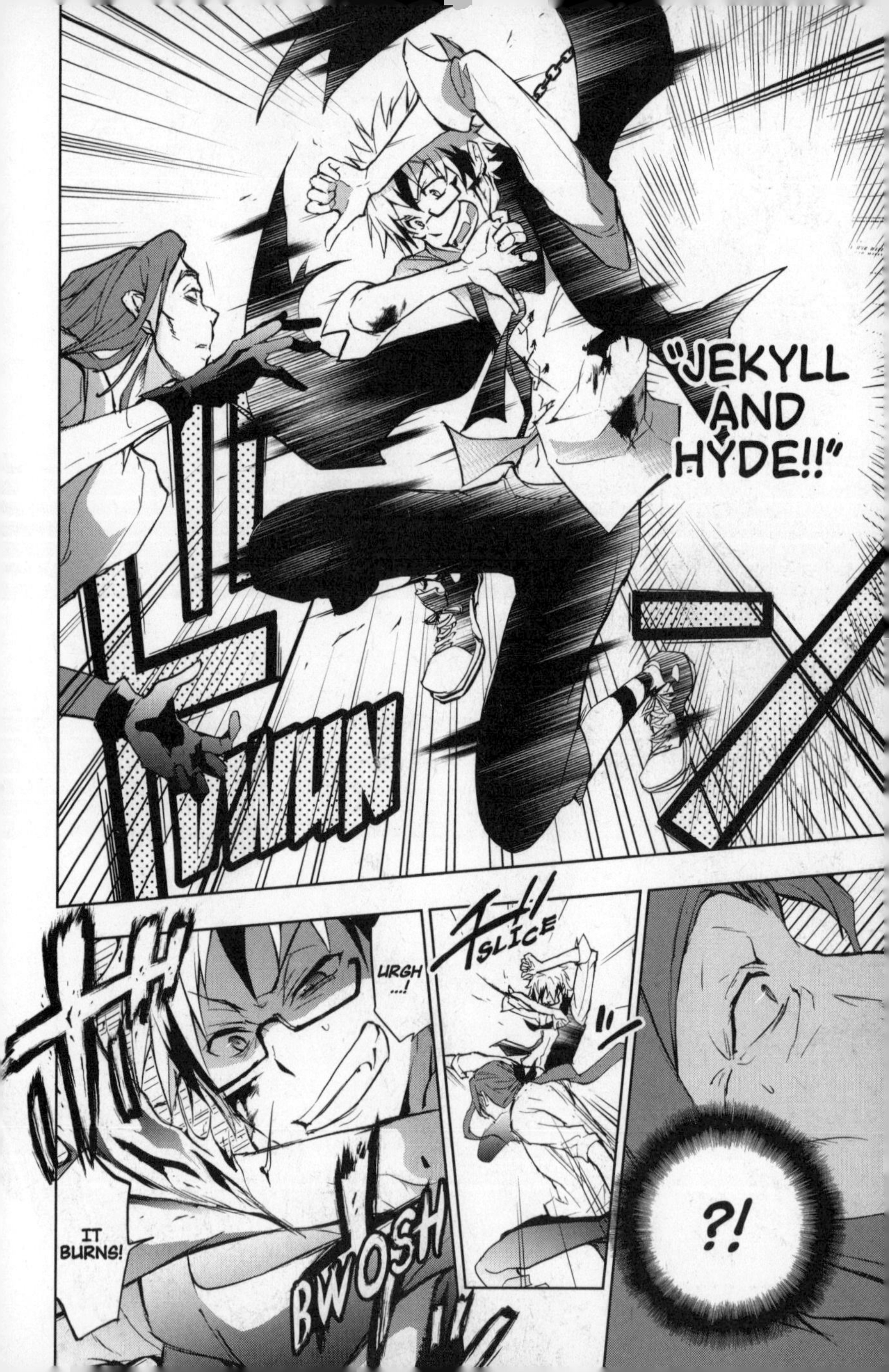
"JEKYLL AND HYDE!!"
?!
SLICE
URGH ...!
IT BURNS!
BWOSH

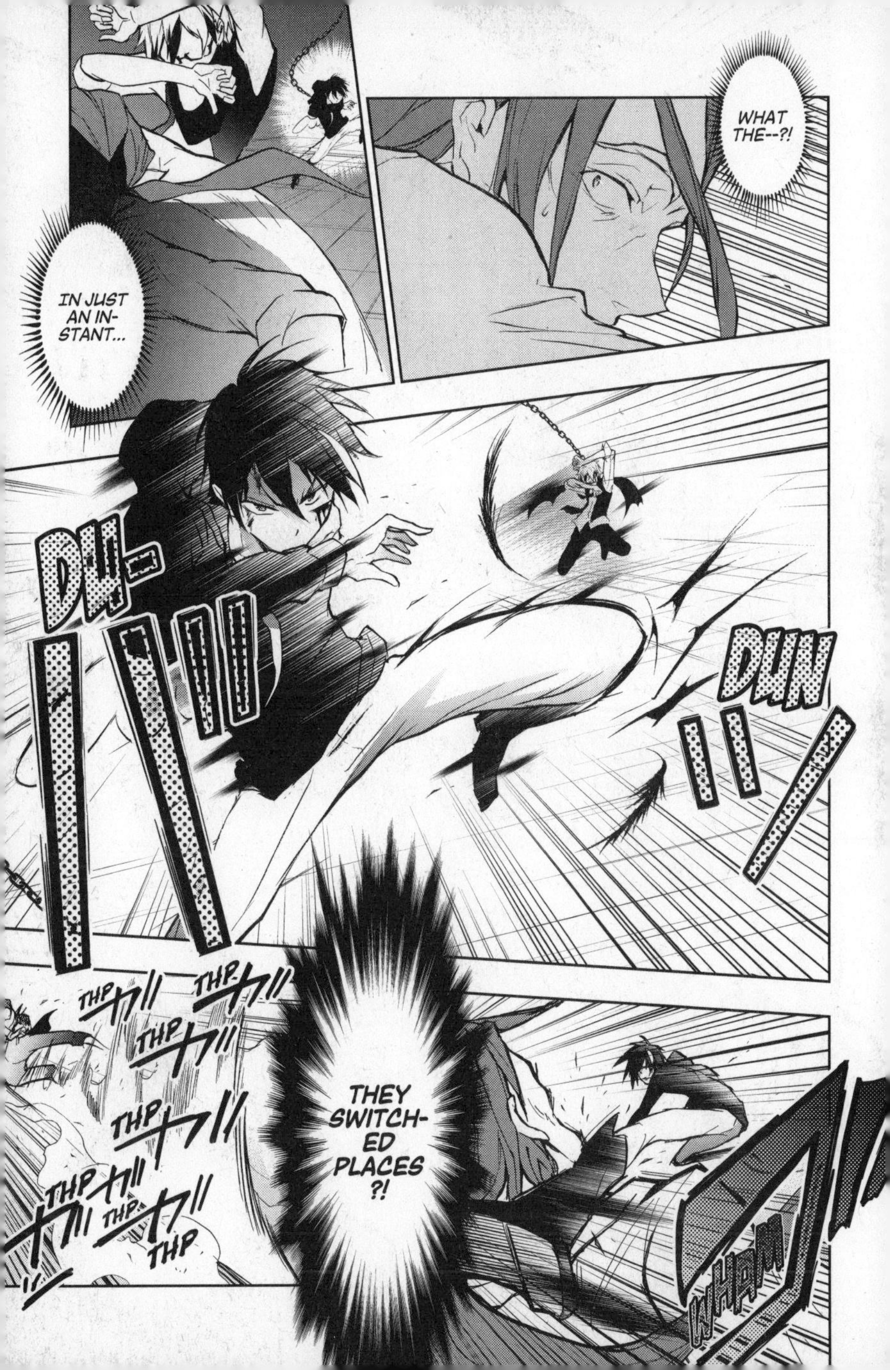

WHAT THE--?!
IN JUST AN IN-STANT...
DUN
DU-N!!
WHAM
THEY SWITCH-ED PLACES?!
THP
THP
THP
THP
THP
THP
THP

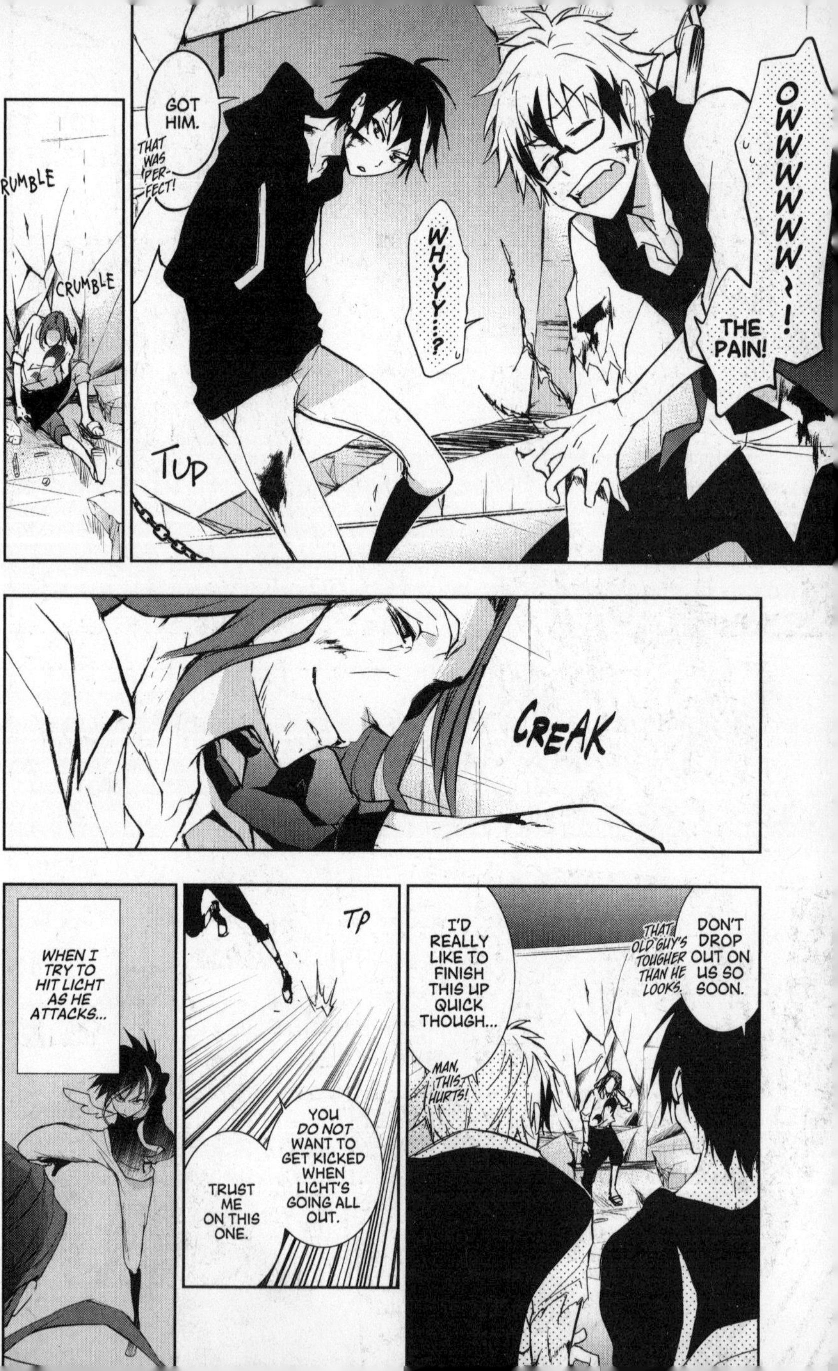
OWWWWWWW~!
THE PAIN!
GOT HIM.
THAT WAS PER-FECT!
WHYYY...?
TUP
CRUMBLE
CRUMBLE
CREAK
DON'T DROP OUT ON US SO SOON.
THAT OLD GUY'S TOUGHER THAN HE LOOKS.
I'D REALLY LIKE TO FINISH THIS UP QUICK THOUGH...
MAN, THIS HURTS!
TP
YOU DO NOT WANT TO GET KICKED WHEN LICHT'S GOING ALL OUT.
TRUST ME ON THIS ONE.
WHEN I TRY TO HIT LICHT AS HE ATTACKS...

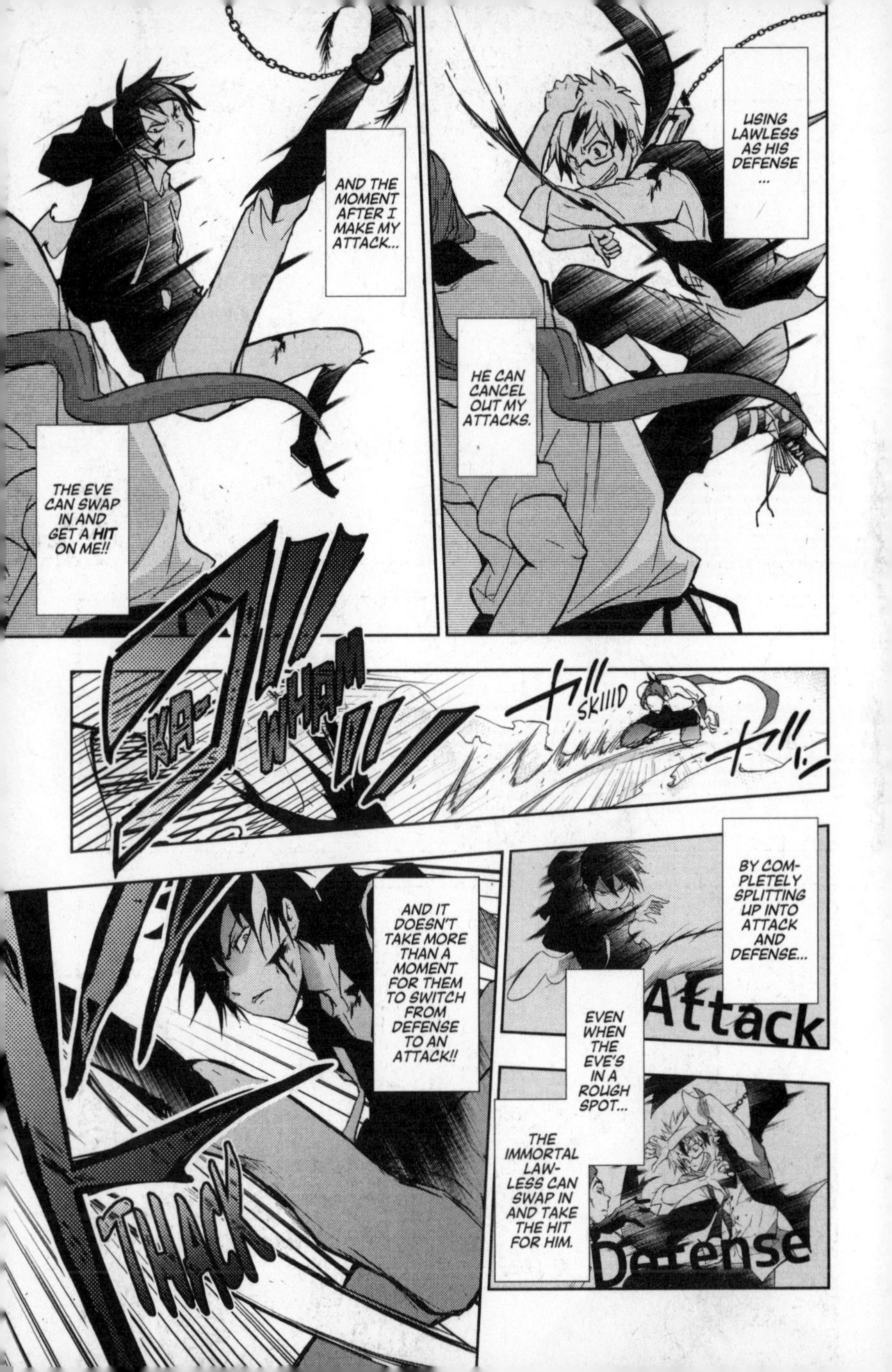
USING LAWLESS AS HIS DEFENSE ...
HE CAN CANCEL OUT MY ATTACKS.
AND THE MOMENT AFTER I MAKE MY ATTACK...
THE EVE CAN SWAP IN AND GET A HIT ON ME!!
SKIIID
KA-WHAM!!
BY COM-PLETELY SPLITTING UP INTO ATTACK AND DEFENSE...
Attack
EVEN WHEN THE EVE'S IN A ROUGH SPOT...
THE IMMORTAL LAW-LESS CAN SWAP IN AND TAKE THE HIT FOR HIM.
Defense
AND IT DOESN'T TAKE MORE THAN A MOMENT FOR THEM TO SWITCH FROM DEFENSE TO AN ATTACK!!
THACK

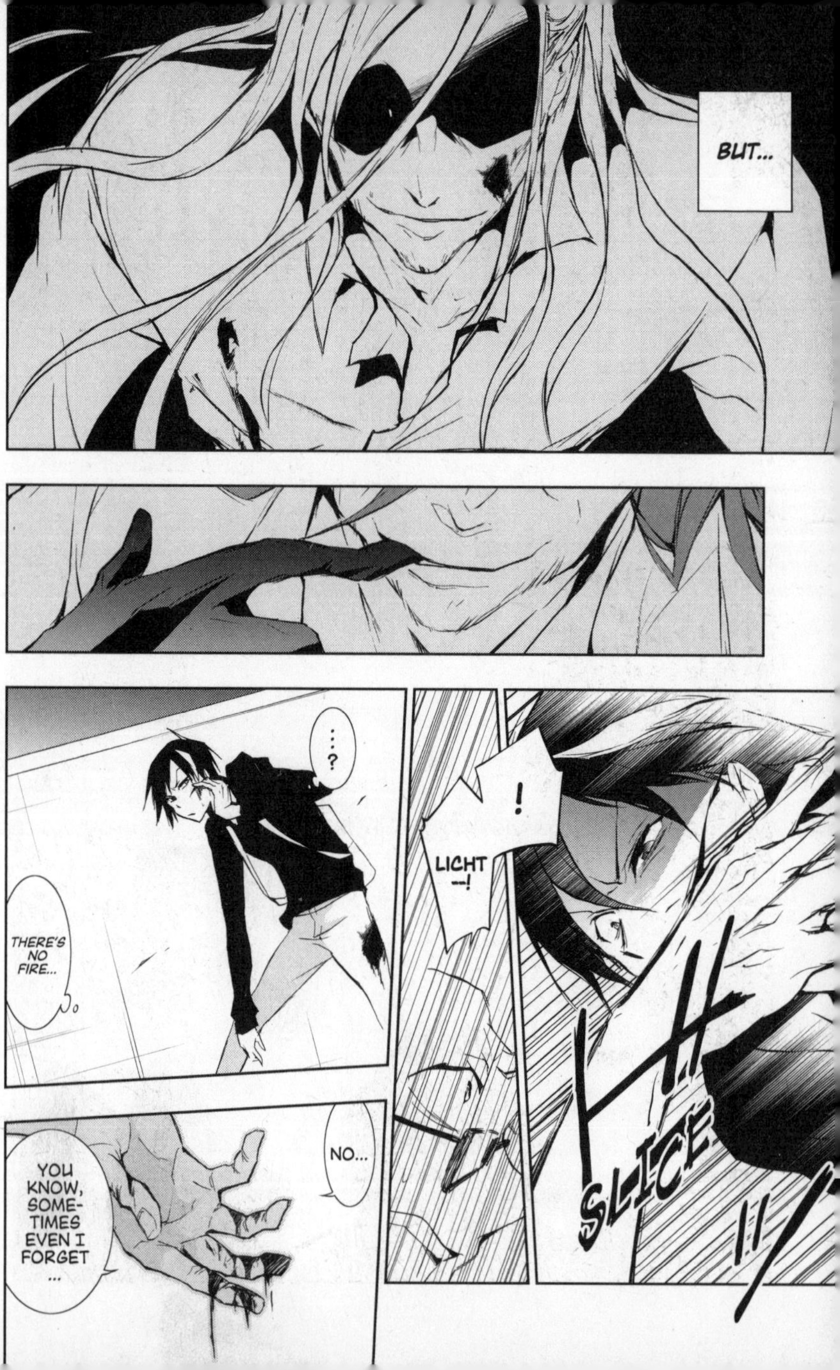
BUT...
!
LICHT --!
SLICE
...?
THERE'S NO FIRE...
NO...
YOU KNOW, SOME-TIMES EVEN I FORGET ...

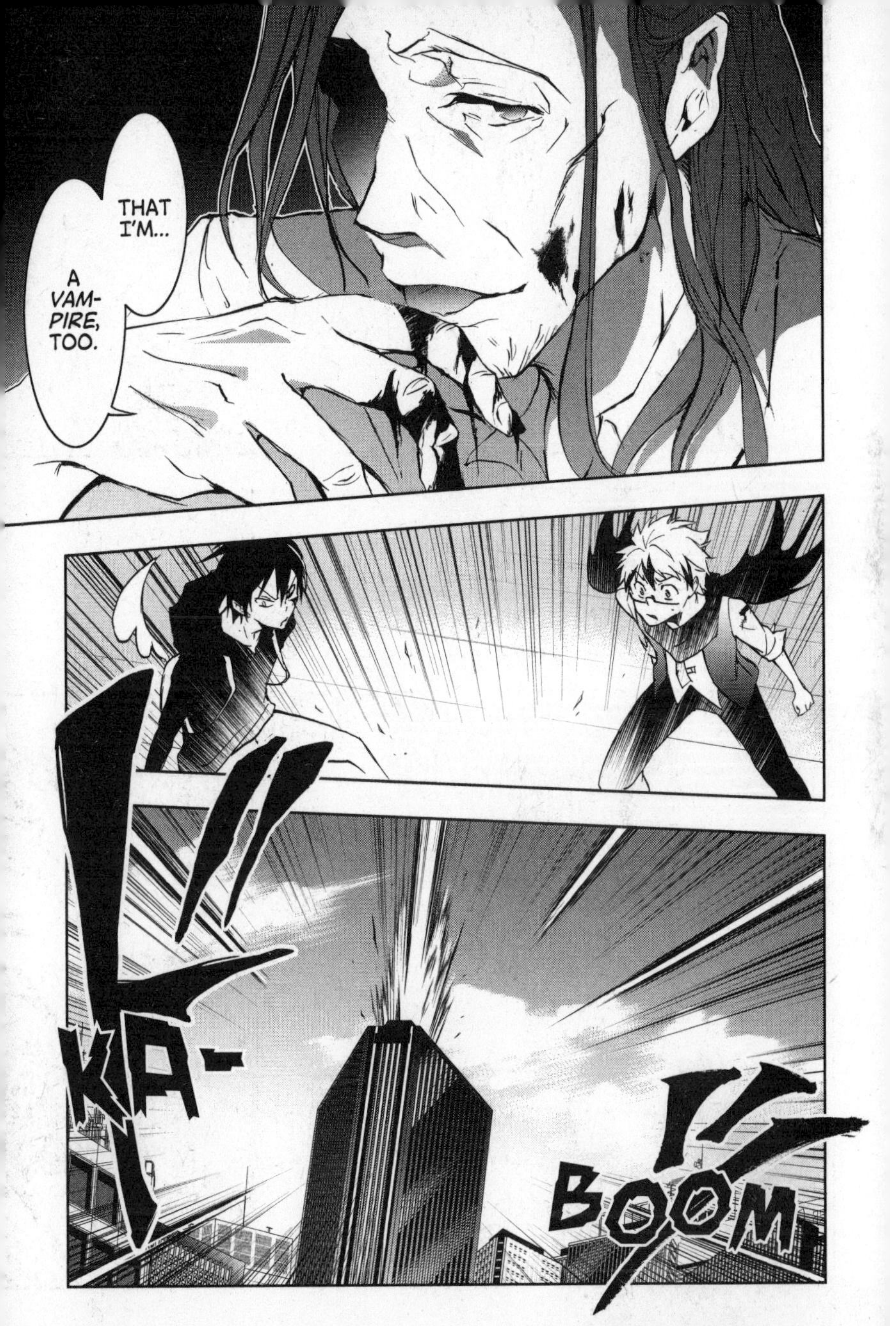
THAT I'M... A VAMPIRE, TOO.
KA-BOOM

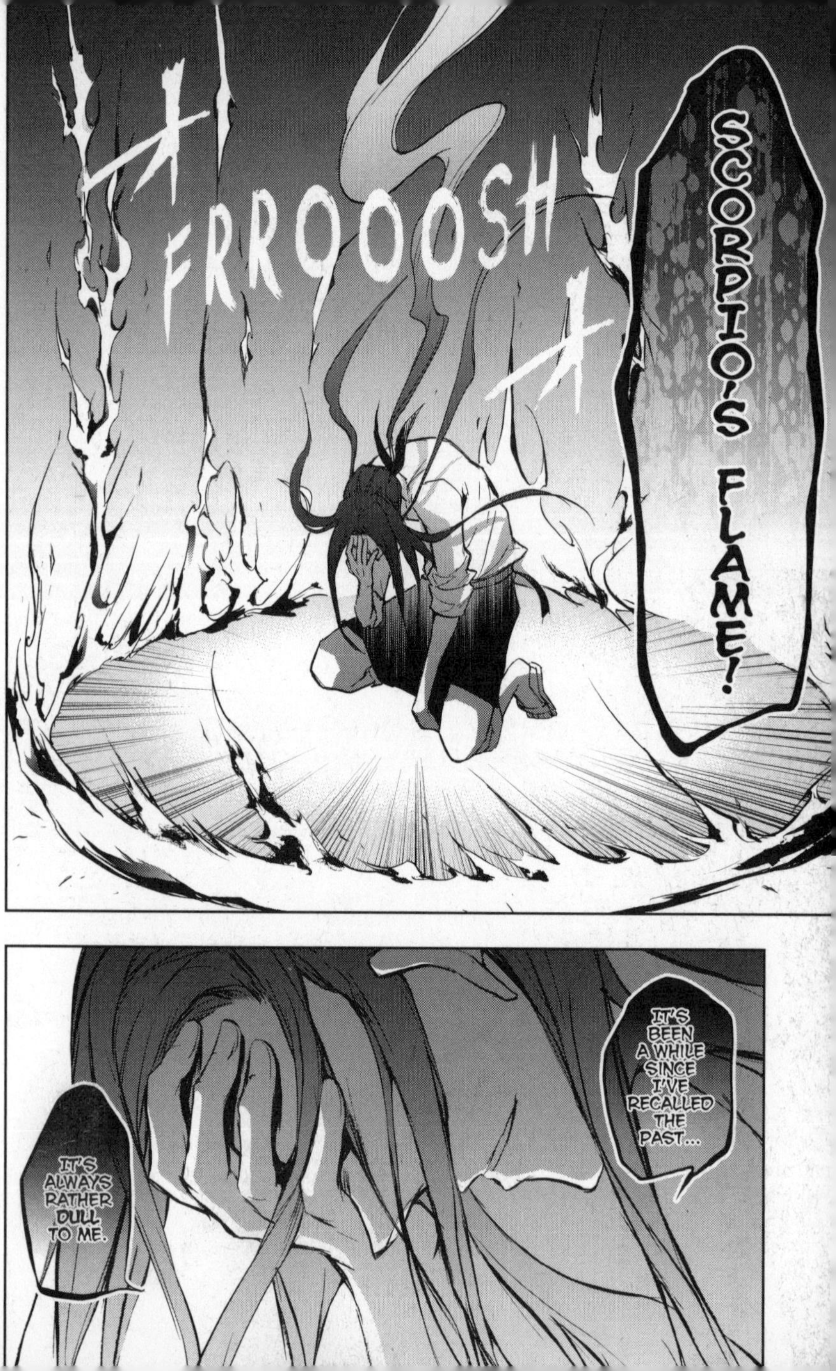
SCORPIO'S FLAME!
FRROOOSH
IT'S BEEN A WHILE SINCE I'VE RECALLED THE PAST...
IT'S ALWAYS RATHER DULL TO ME.

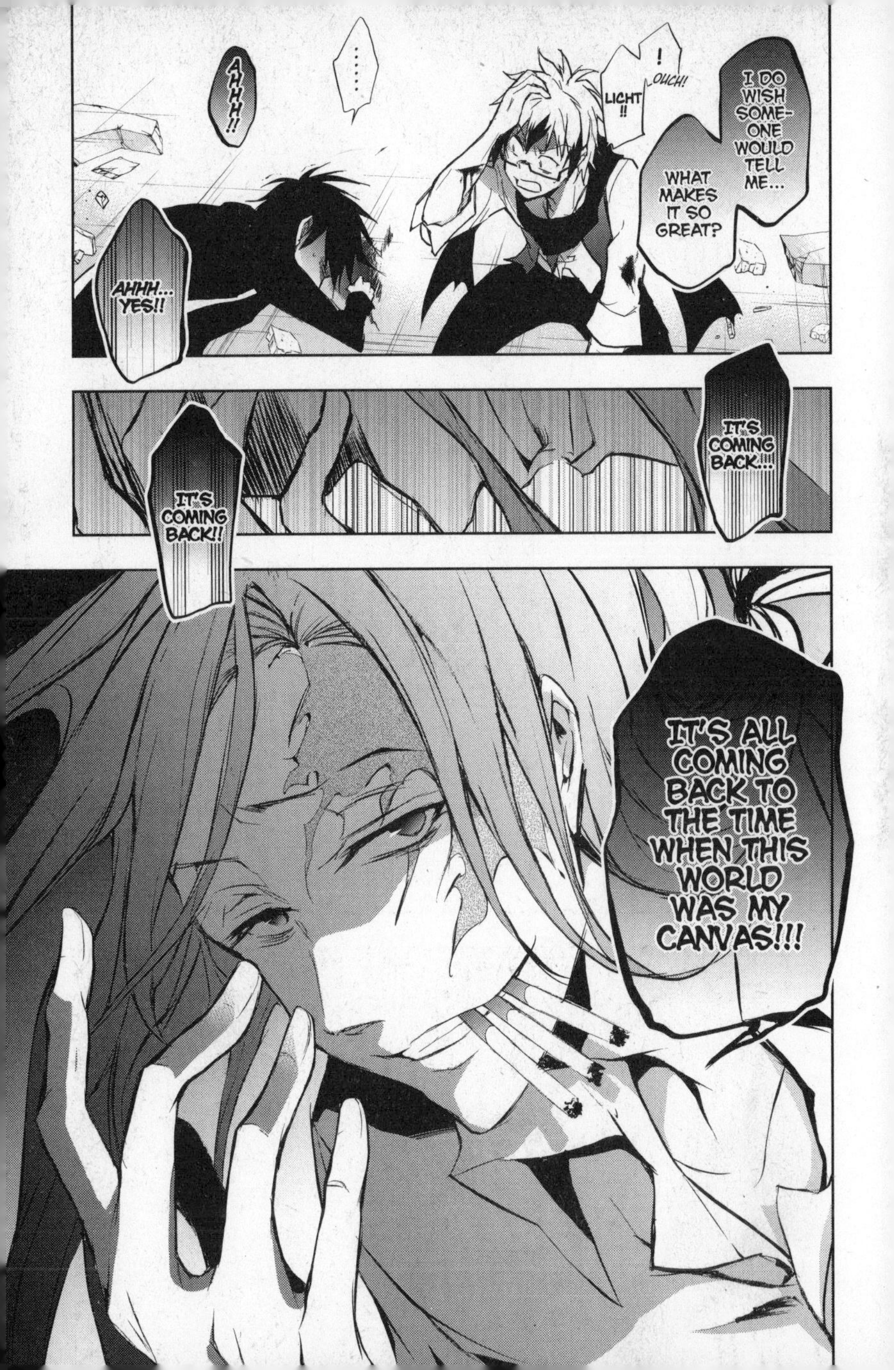
I DO WISH SOMEONE WOULD TELL ME...
WHAT MAKES IT SO GREAT?
!
OUCH!
LICHT!!
......
AHHH!!
AHHH... YES!!
IT'S COMING BACK...
IT'S COMING BACK!!
IT'S ALL COMING BACK TO THE TIME WHEN THIS WORLD WAS MY CANVAS!!!

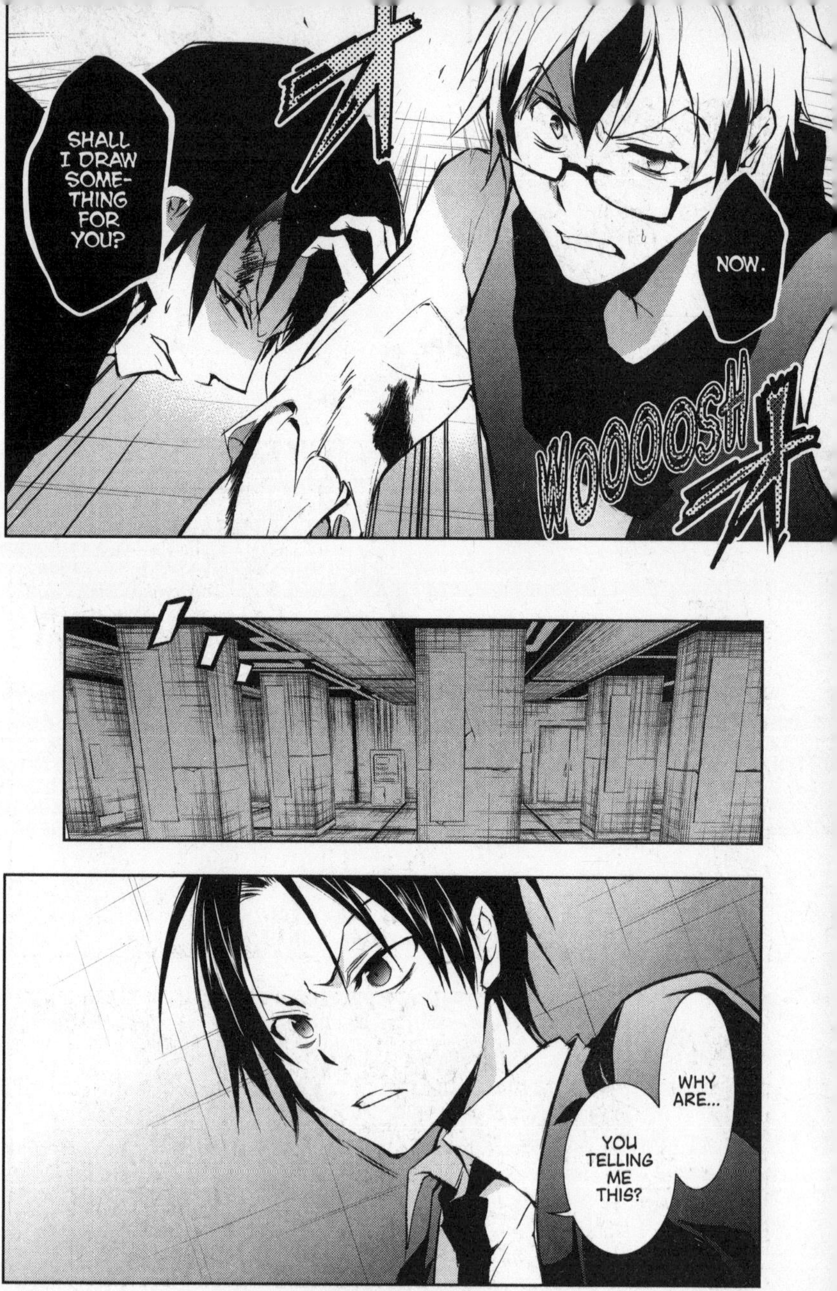
SHALL I DRAW SOME-THING FOR YOU?
NOW.
WOOOOSH
WHY ARE...
YOU TELLING ME THIS?

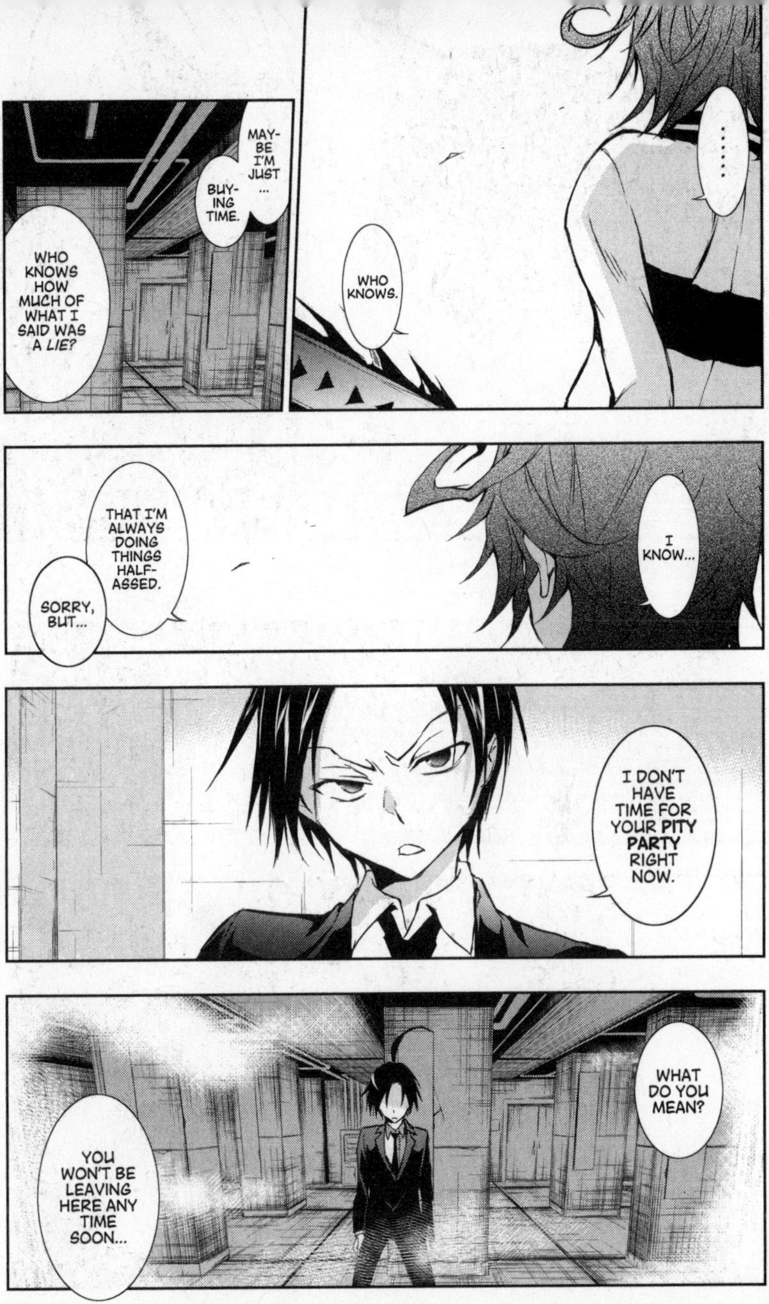
......
WHO KNOWS.
MAYBE I'M JUST ...
BUYING TIME.
WHO KNOWS HOW MUCH OF WHAT I SAID WAS A *LIE*?
I KNOW...
THAT I'M ALWAYS DOING THINGS HALF-ASSED.
SORRY, BUT...
I DON'T HAVE TIME FOR YOUR **PITY PARTY** RIGHT NOW.
WHAT DO YOU MEAN?
YOU WON'T BE LEAVING HERE ANY TIME SOON...

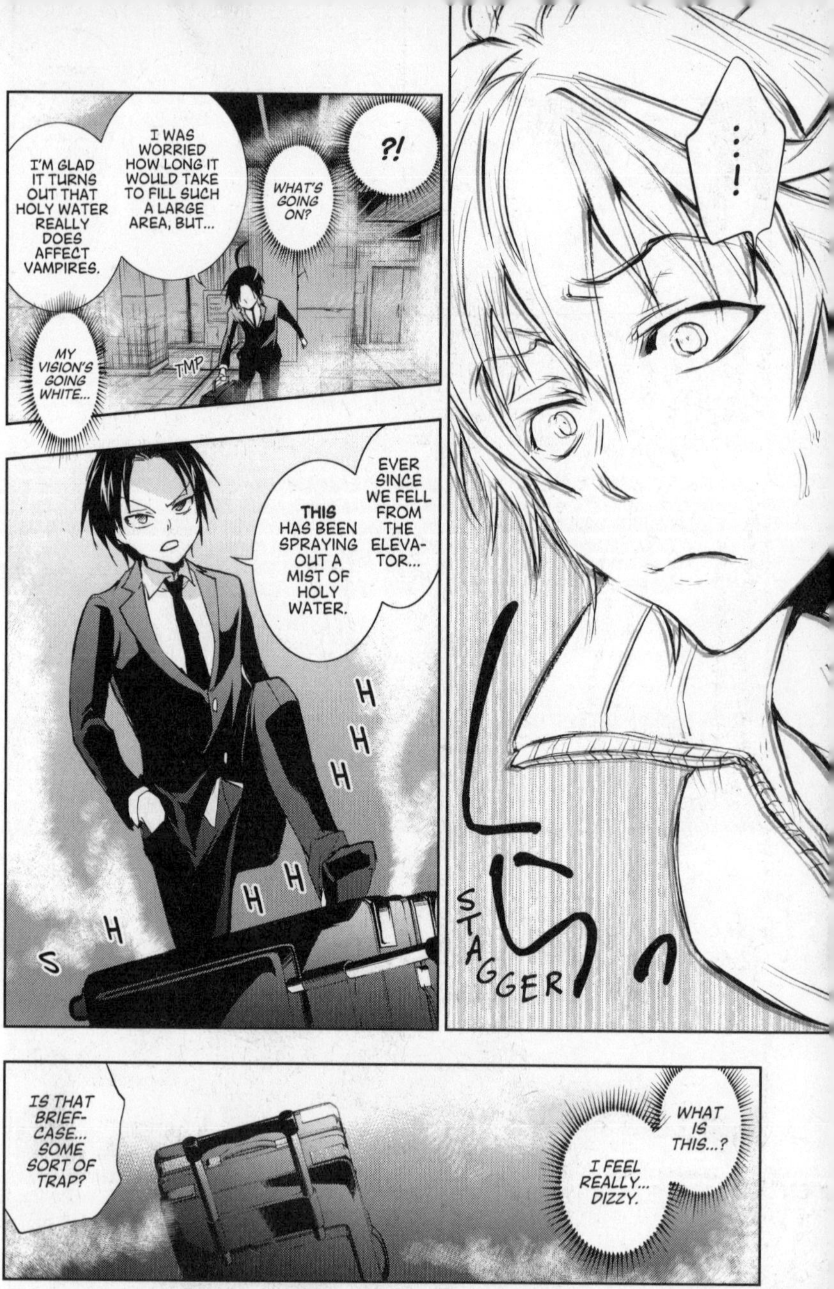
...!
STAGGER
?!
WHAT'S GOING ON?
I WAS WORRIED HOW LONG IT WOULD TAKE TO FILL SUCH A LARGE AREA, BUT...
I'M GLAD IT TURNS OUT THAT HOLY WATER REALLY DOES AFFECT VAMPIRES.
MY VISION'S GOING WHITE...
TMP
EVER SINCE WE FELL FROM THE ELEVATOR...
THIS HAS BEEN SPRAYING OUT A MIST OF HOLY WATER.
SHHHHHHH
WHAT IS THIS...?
I FEEL REALLY... DIZZY.
IS THAT BRIEF-CASE... SOME SORT OF TRAP?

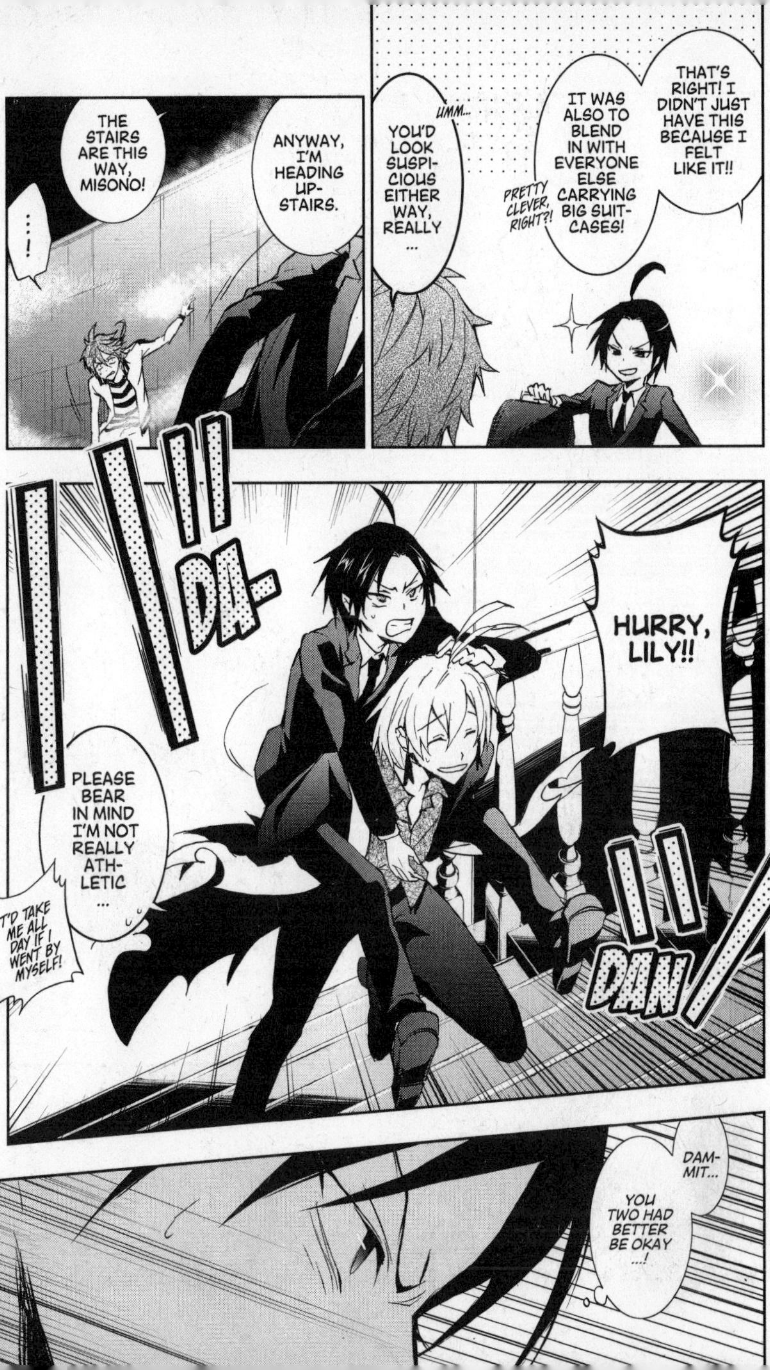
THAT'S RIGHT! I DIDN'T JUST HAVE THIS BECAUSE I FELT LIKE IT!!
IT WAS ALSO TO BLEND IN WITH EVERYONE ELSE CARRYING BIG SUIT-CASES!
PRETTY CLEVER, RIGHT?!
UMM...
YOU'D LOOK SUSPI-CIOUS EITHER WAY, REALLY ...
ANYWAY, I'M HEADING UP-STAIRS.
THE STAIRS ARE THIS WAY, MISONO!
...!
HURRY, LILY!!
DA-
DAN
PLEASE BEAR IN MIND I'M NOT REALLY ATH-LETIC ...
IT'D TAKE ME ALL DAY IF I WENT BY MYSELF!
DAM-MIT...
YOU TWO HAD BETTER BE OKAY ...!

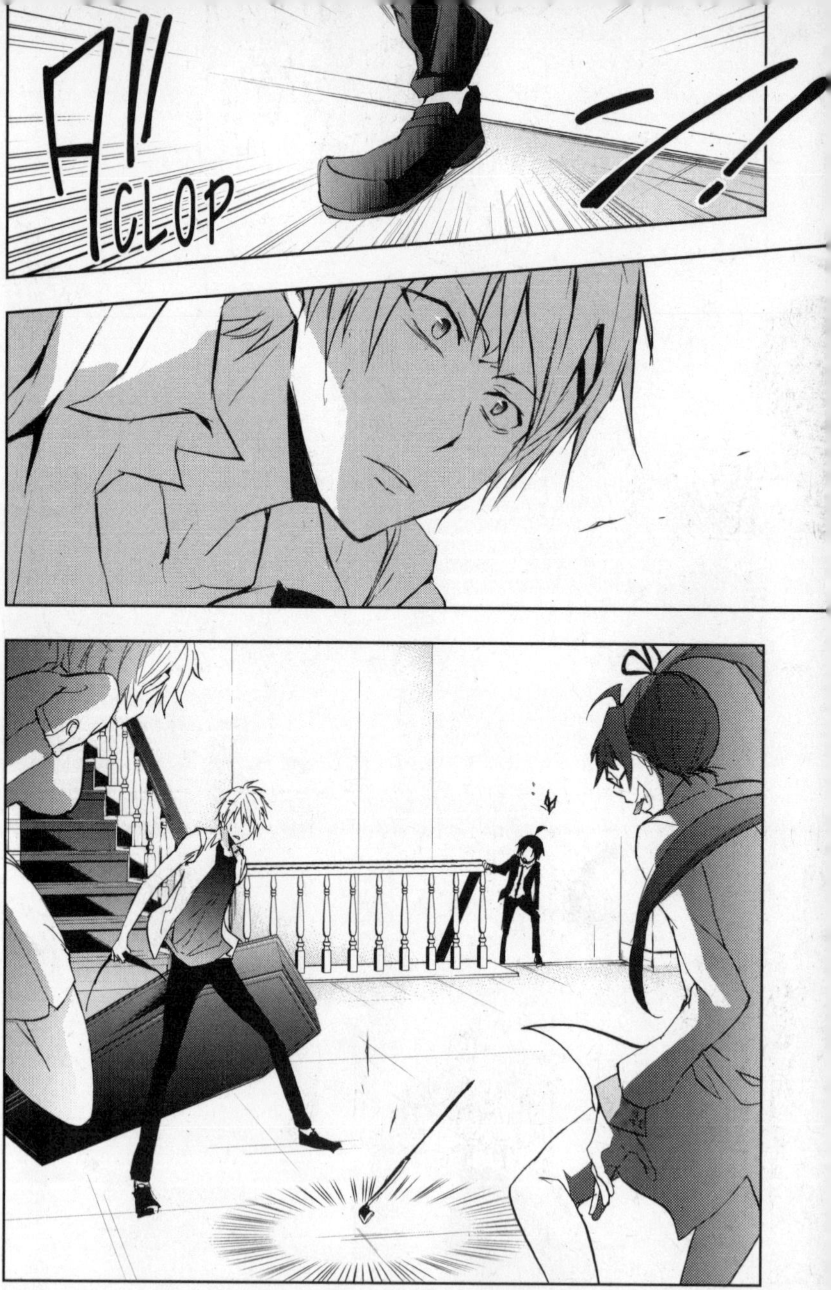
CLOP

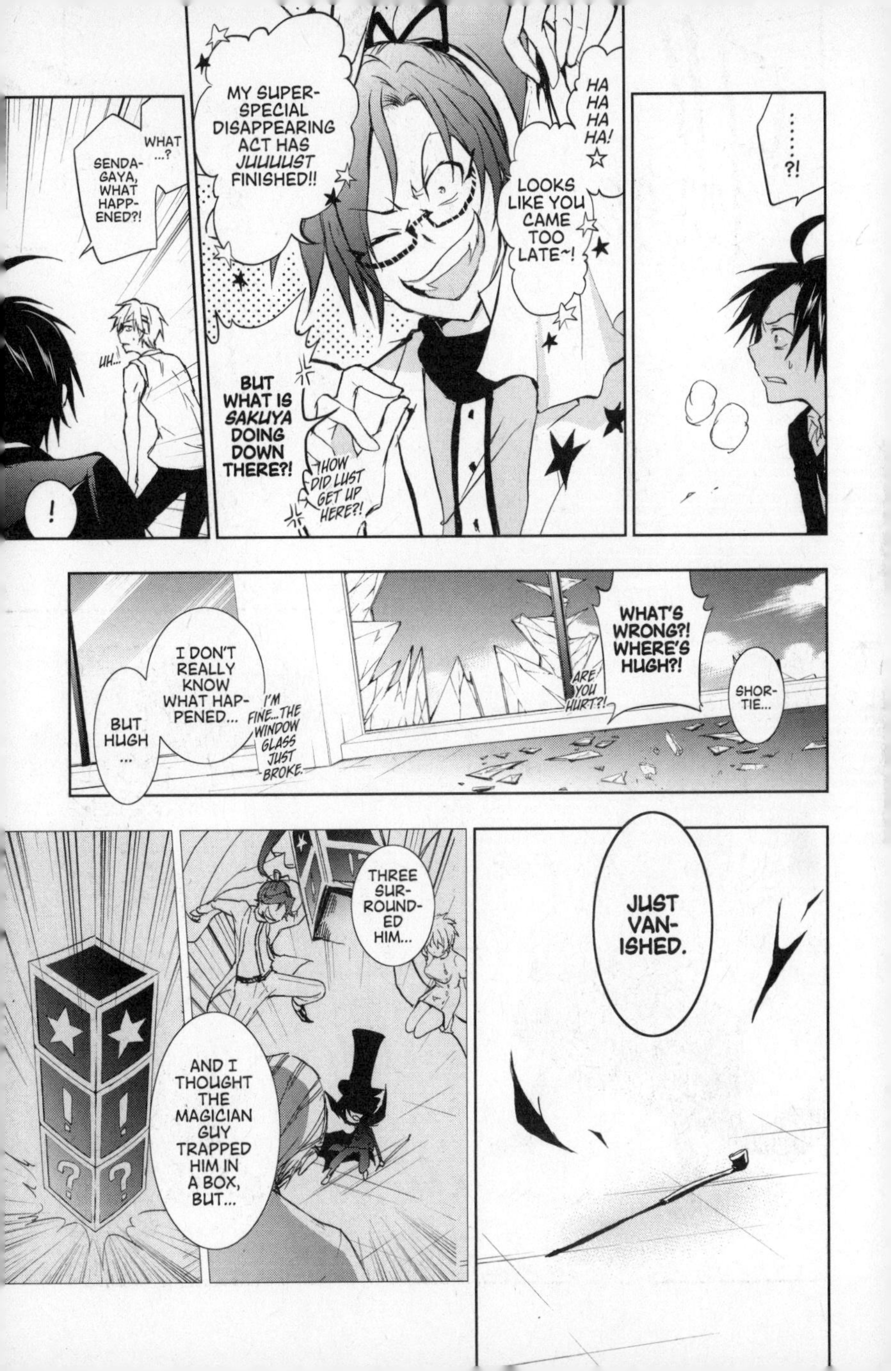
......
?!
HA HA HA HA!
LOOKS LIKE YOU CAME TOO LATE~!
MY SUPER-SPECIAL DISAPPEARING ACT HAS JUUUUST FINISHED!!
BUT WHAT IS SAKUYA DOING DOWN THERE?!
HOW DID LUST GET UP HERE?!
WHAT ...?
SENDA-GAYA, WHAT HAPP-ENED?!
UH...
!
WHAT'S WRONG?! WHERE'S HUGH?!
SHOR-TIE...
ARE YOU HURT?!
I DON'T REALLY KNOW WHAT HAP-PENED...
I'M FINE...THE WINDOW GLASS JUST BROKE.
BUT HUGH ...
JUST VAN-ISHED.
THREE SUR-ROUND-ED HIM...
AND I THOUGHT THE MAGICIAN GUY TRAPPED HIM IN A BOX, BUT...

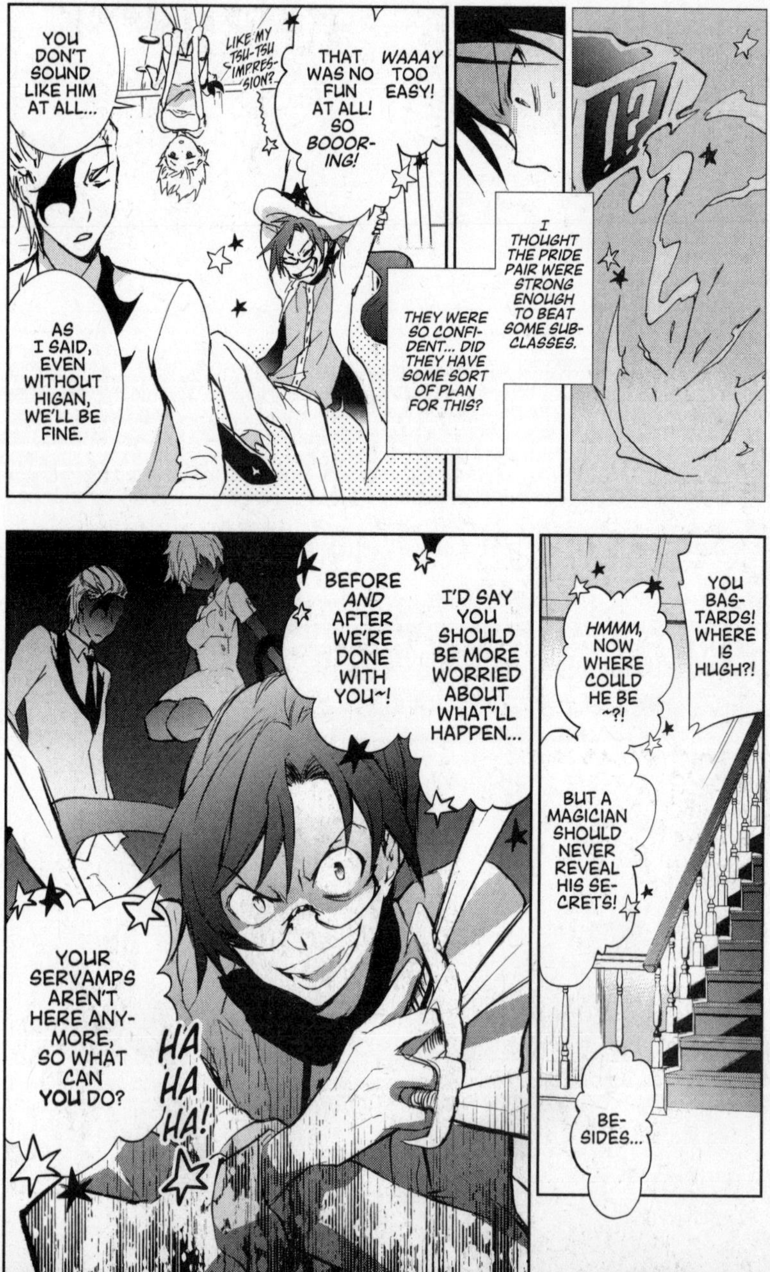
!?
I THOUGHT THE PRIDE PAIR WERE STRONG ENOUGH TO BEAT SOME SUBCLASSES.
THEY WERE SO CONFIDENT... DID THEY HAVE SOME SORT OF PLAN FOR THIS?
WAAAY TOO EASY!
THAT WAS NO FUN AT ALL! SO BOOORING!
LIKE MY TSU-TSU IMPRESSION?
YOU DON'T SOUND LIKE HIM AT ALL...
AS I SAID, EVEN WITHOUT HIGAN, WE'LL BE FINE.
YOU BASTARDS! WHERE IS HUGH?!
HMMM, NOW WHERE COULD HE BE ~?!
BUT A MAGICIAN SHOULD NEVER REVEAL HIS SECRETS!
BESIDES...
I'D SAY YOU SHOULD BE MORE WORRIED ABOUT WHAT'LL HAPPEN...
BEFORE AND AFTER WE'RE DONE WITH YOU~!
YOUR SERVAMPS AREN'T HERE ANYMORE, SO WHAT CAN YOU DO?
HA HA HA!

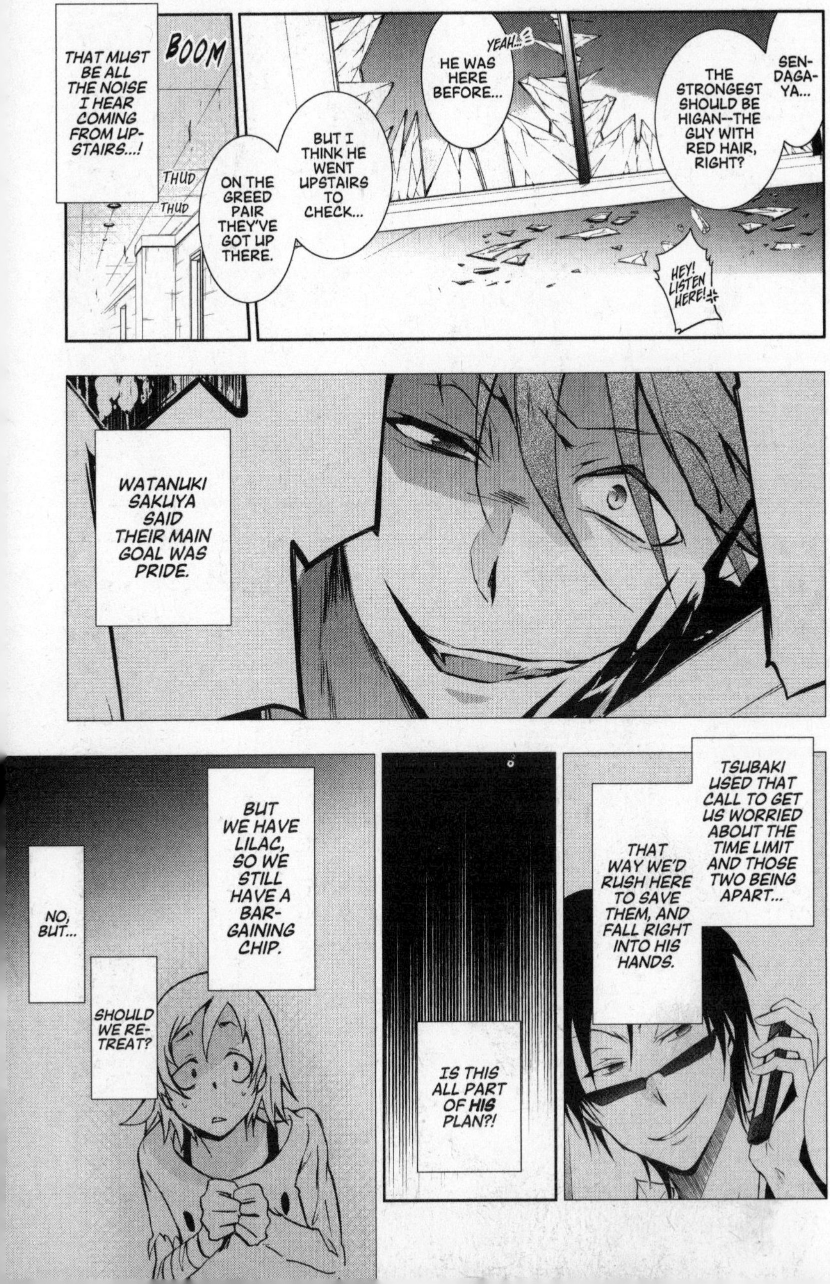
SENDAGAYA...
THE STRONGEST SHOULD BE HIGAN--THE GUY WITH RED HAIR, RIGHT?
YEAH...
HE WAS HERE BEFORE...
BUT I THINK HE WENT UPSTAIRS TO CHECK...
ON THE GREED PAIR THEY'VE GOT UP THERE.
HEY! LISTEN HERE!
BOOM
THAT MUST BE ALL THE NOISE I HEAR COMING FROM UPSTAIRS...!
THUD
THUD
WATANUKI SAKUYA SAID THEIR MAIN GOAL WAS PRIDE.
TSUBAKI USED THAT CALL TO GET US WORRIED ABOUT THE TIME LIMIT AND THOSE TWO BEING APART...
THAT WAY WE'D RUSH HERE TO SAVE THEM, AND FALL RIGHT INTO HIS HANDS.
IS THIS ALL PART OF HIS PLAN?!
BUT WE HAVE LILAC, SO WE STILL HAVE A BARGAINING CHIP.
NO, BUT...
SHOULD WE RETREAT?

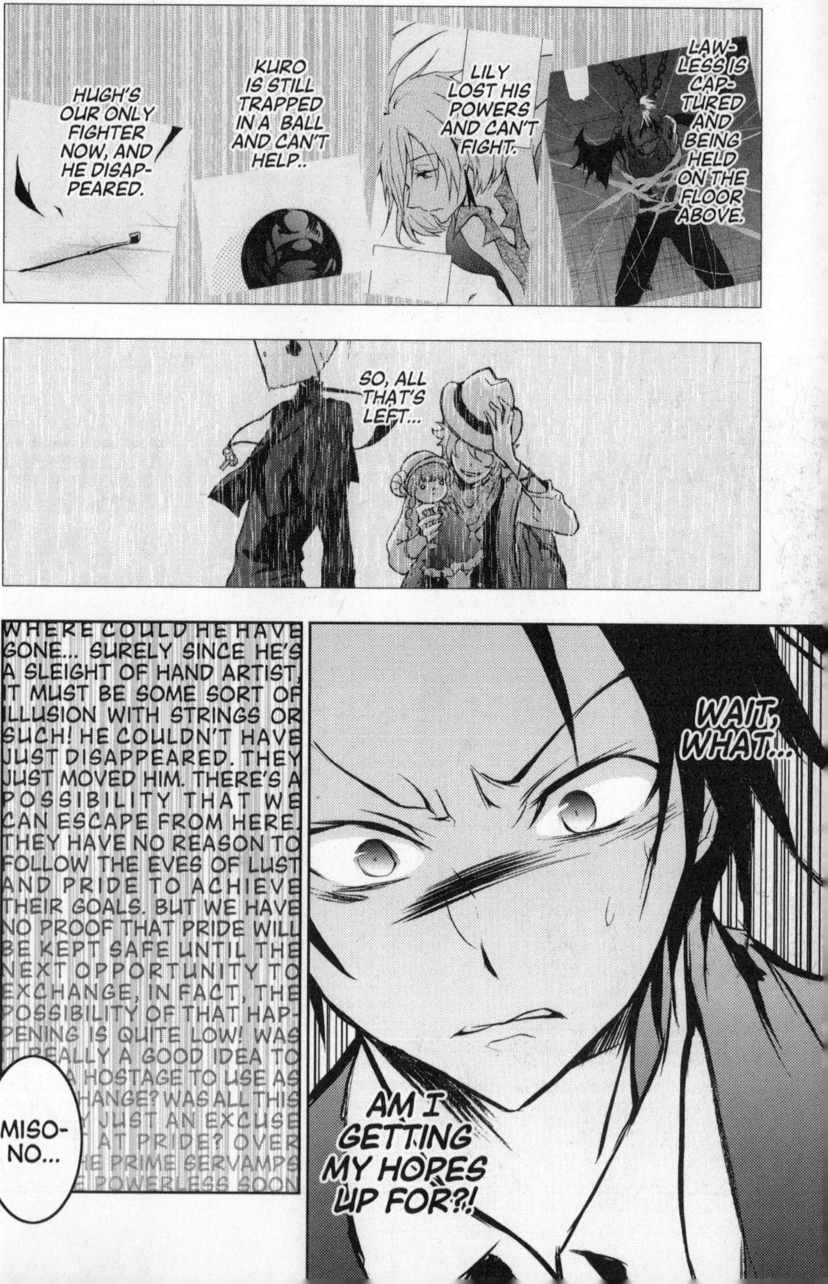
LAW-LESS IS CAP-TURED AND BEING HELD ON THE FLOOR ABOVE.
LILY LOST HIS POWERS AND CAN'T FIGHT.
KURO IS STILL TRAPPED IN A BALL AND CAN'T HELP..
HUGH'S OUR ONLY FIGHTER NOW, AND HE DISAP-PEARED.
SO, ALL THAT'S LEFT...
WAIT, WHAT...
AM I GETTING MY HOPES UP FOR?!
WHERE COULD HE HAVE GONE... SURELY SINCE HE'S A SLEIGHT OF HAND ARTIST, IT MUST BE SOME SORT OF ILLUSION WITH STRINGS OR SUCH! HE COULDN'T HAVE JUST DISAPPEARED. THEY JUST MOVED HIM. THERE'S A POSSIBILITY THAT WE CAN ESCAPE FROM HERE. THEY HAVE NO REASON TO FOLLOW THE EVES OF LUST AND PRIDE TO ACHIEVE THEIR GOALS. BUT WE HAVE NO PROOF THAT PRIDE WILL BE KEPT SAFE UNTIL THE NEXT OPPORTUNITY TO EXCHANGE, IN FACT, THE POSSIBILITY OF THAT HAP-PENING IS QUITE LOW! WAS
REALLY A GOOD IDEA TO
A HOSTAGE TO USE AS
HANGE? WAS ALL THIS
JUST AN EXCUSE
AT PRIDE? OVER
HE PRIME SERVAMPS
POWERLESS SOON
MISO-NO...

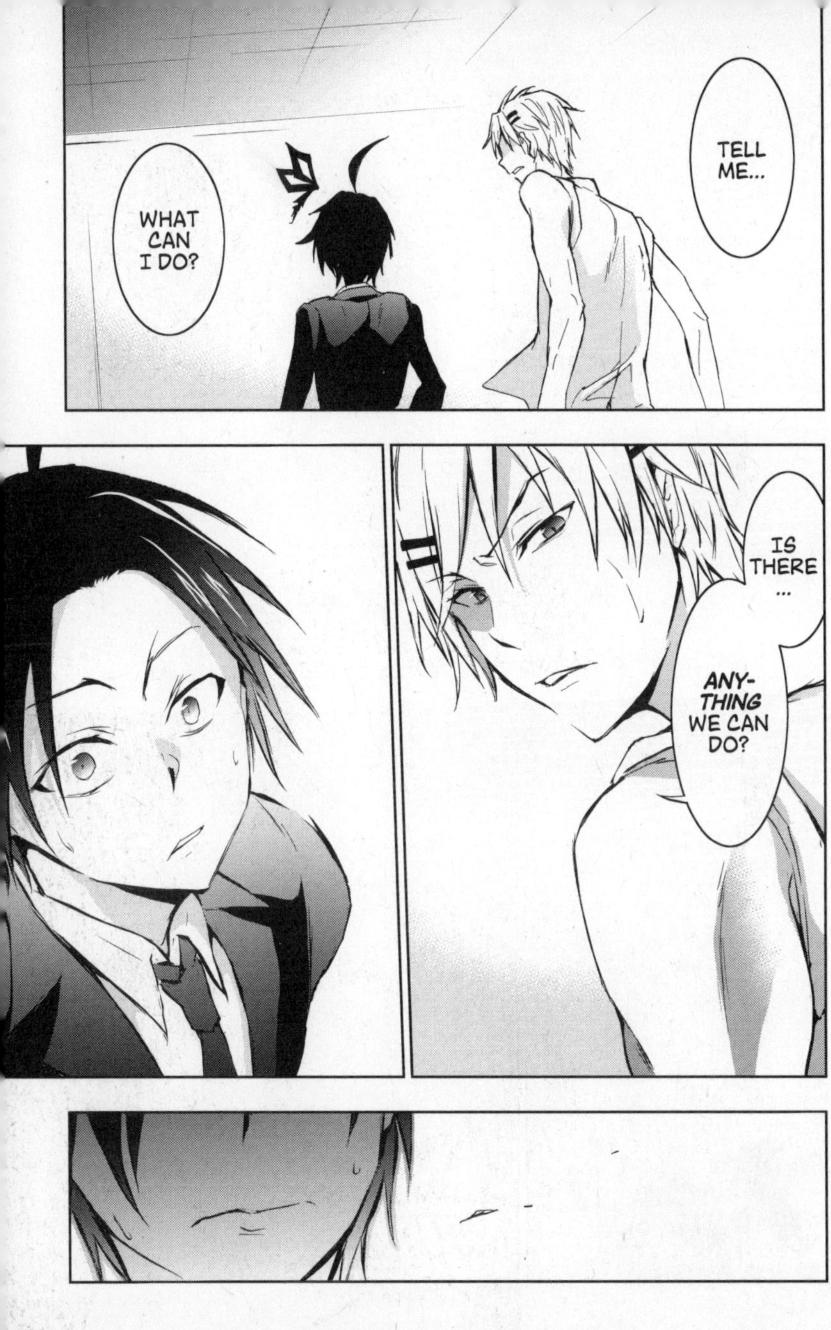
TELL ME...
WHAT CAN I DO?
IS THERE ...
ANYTHING WE CAN DO?

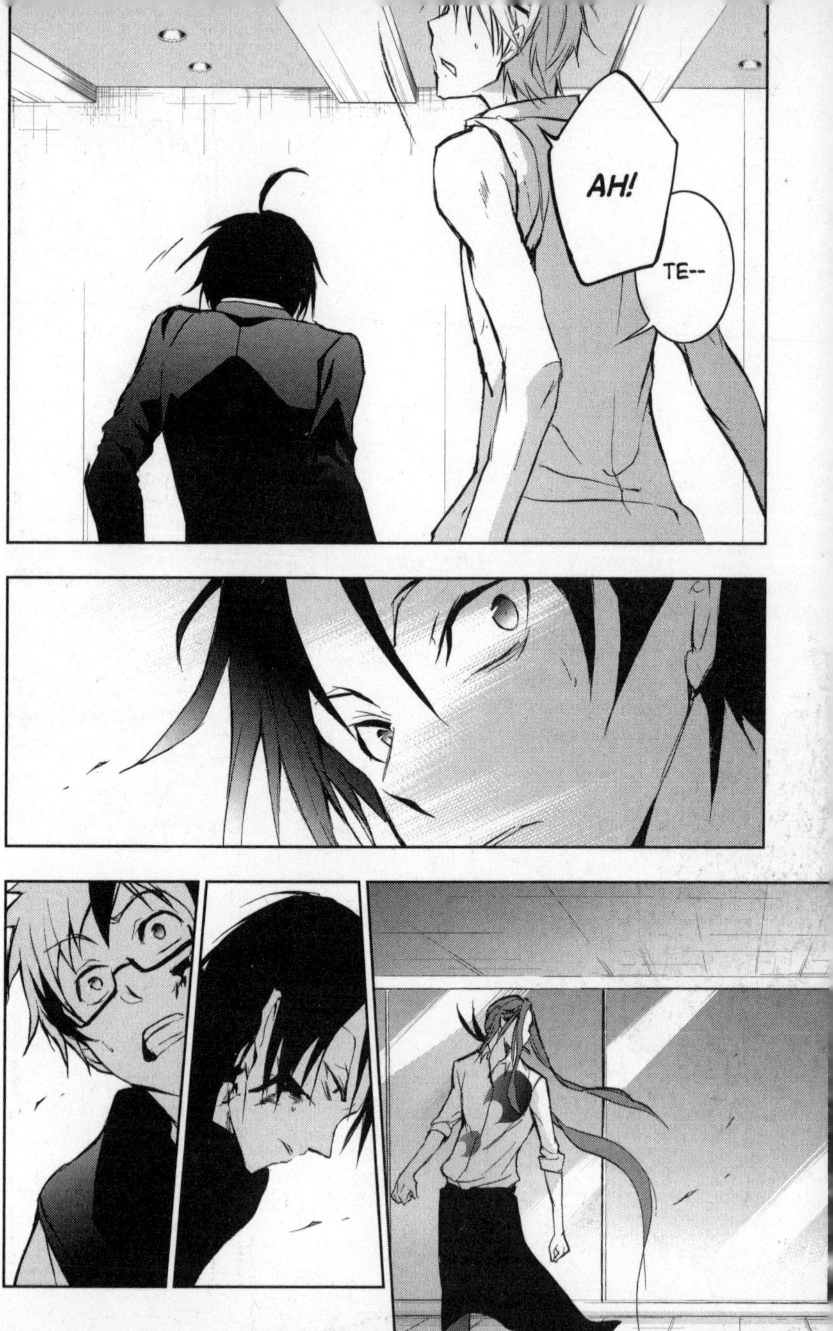
AH!
TE--

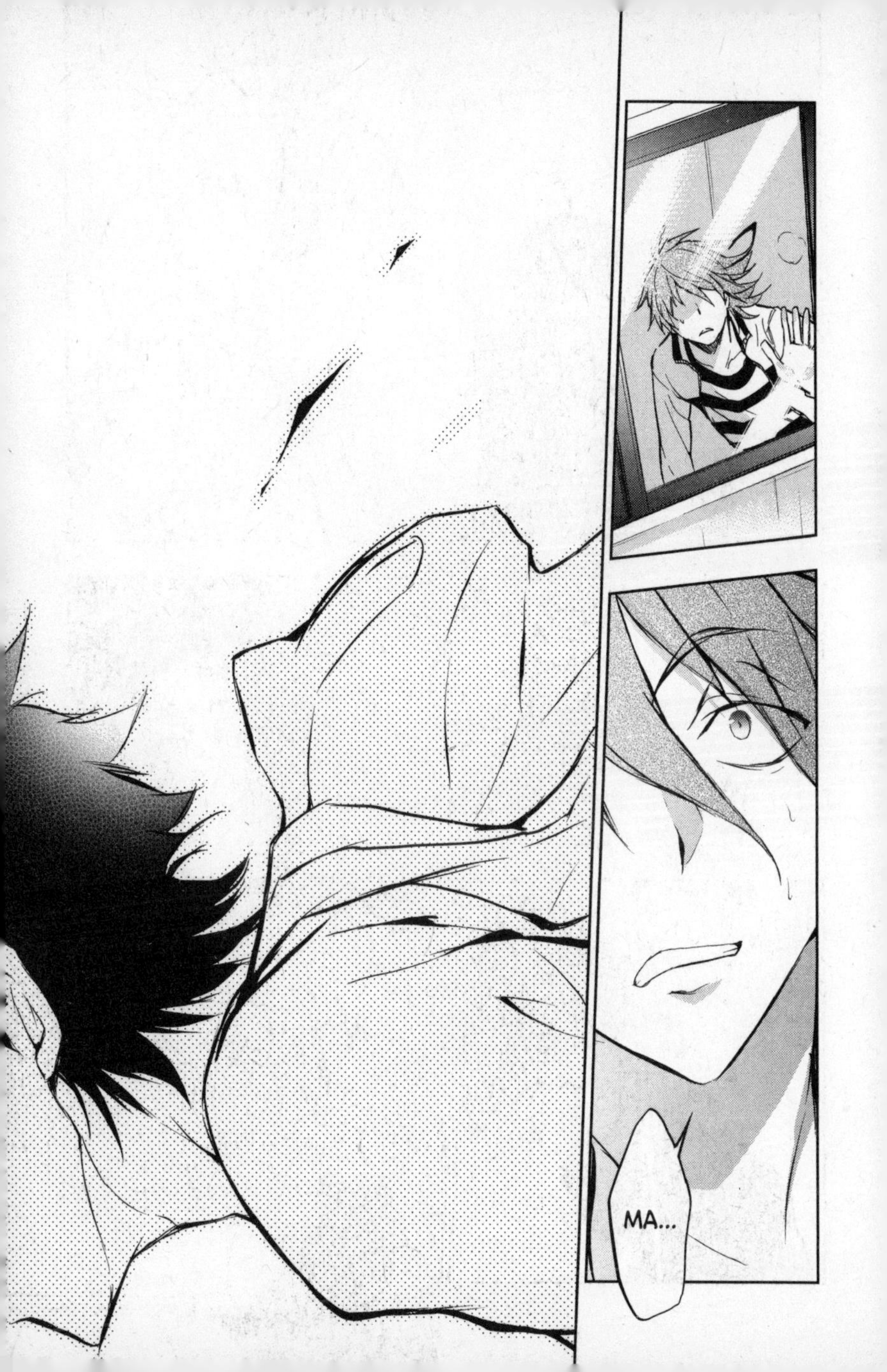
MA...

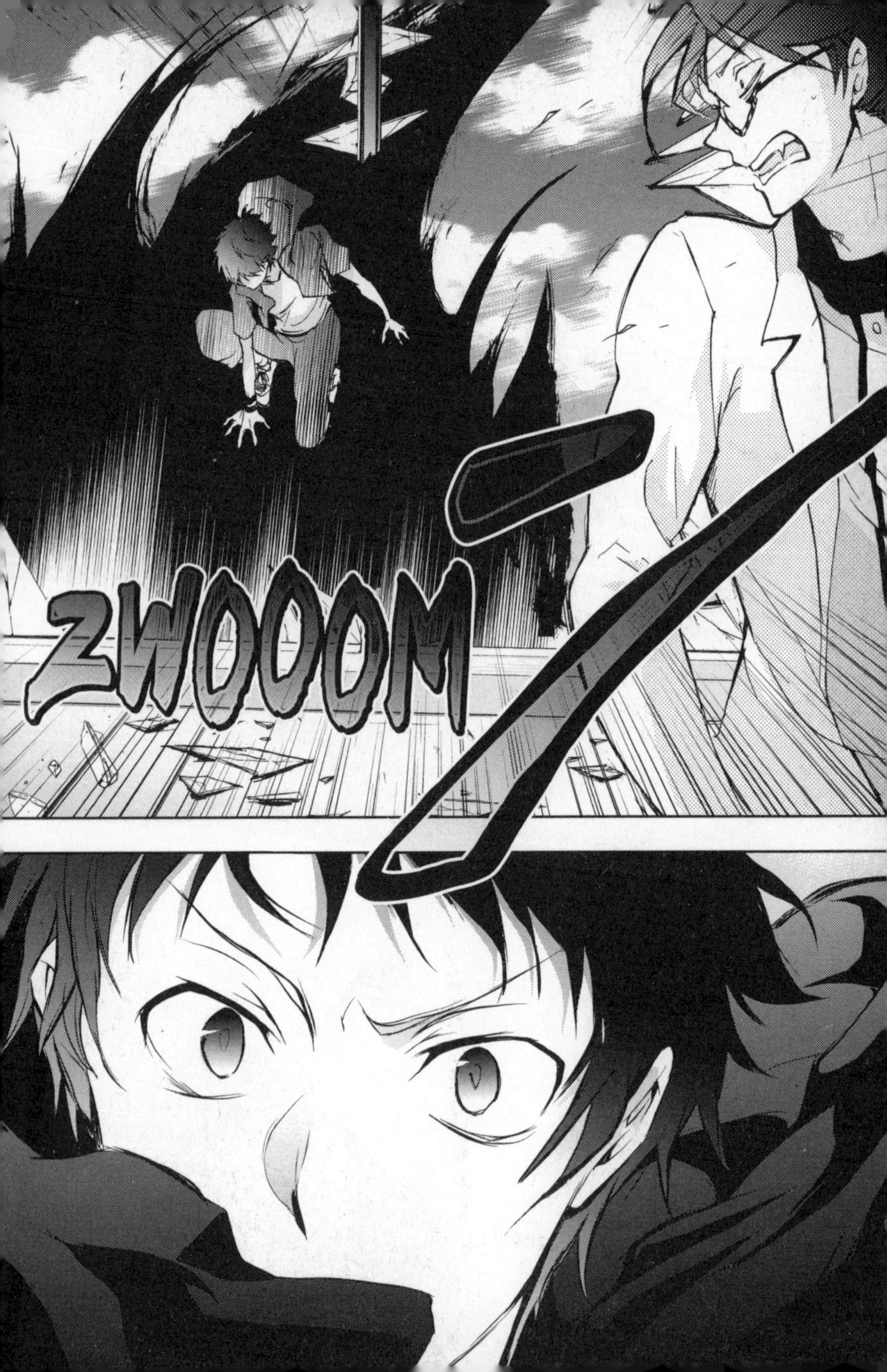
ZWOOOM

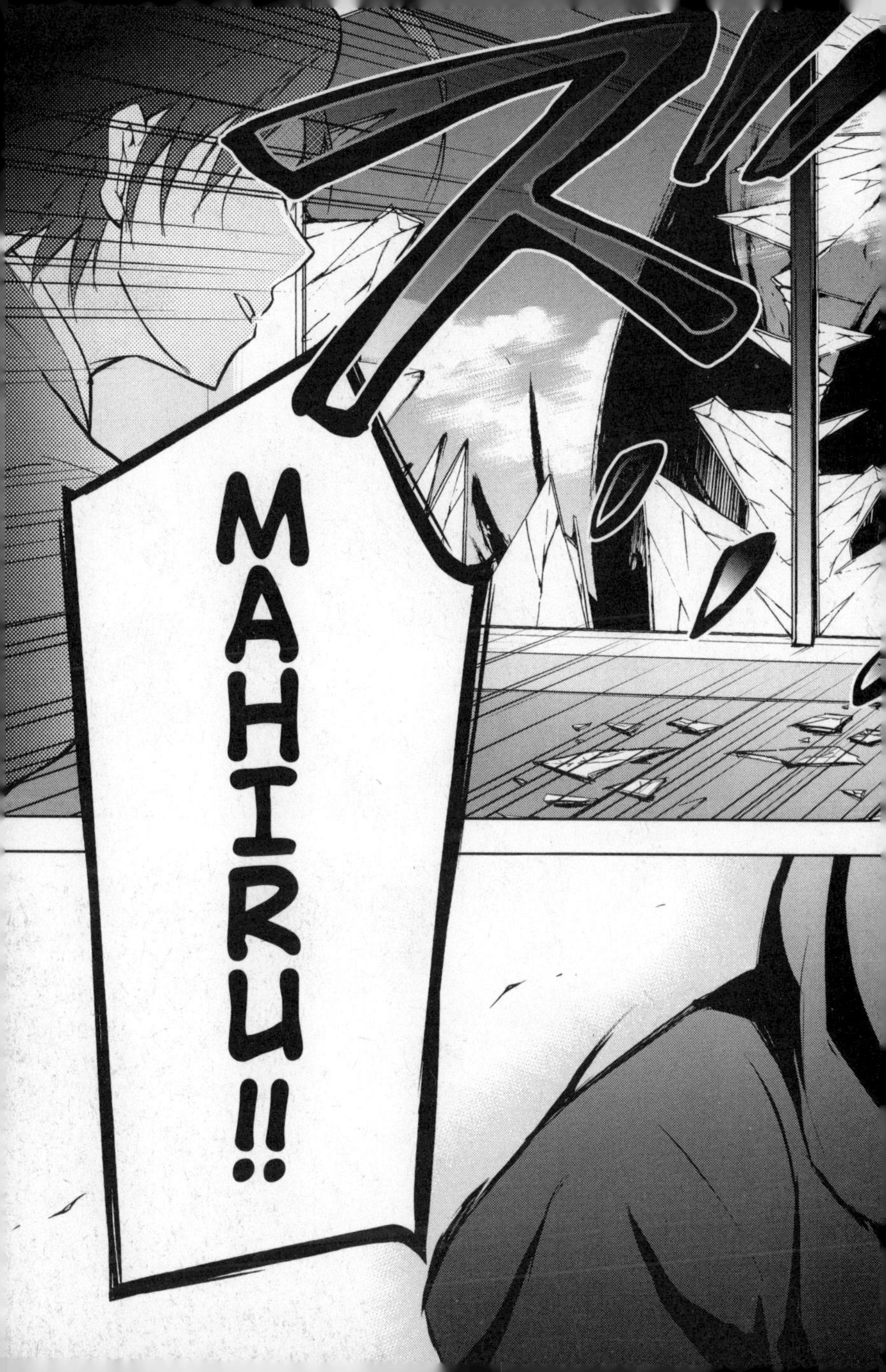
MAHIRU!!

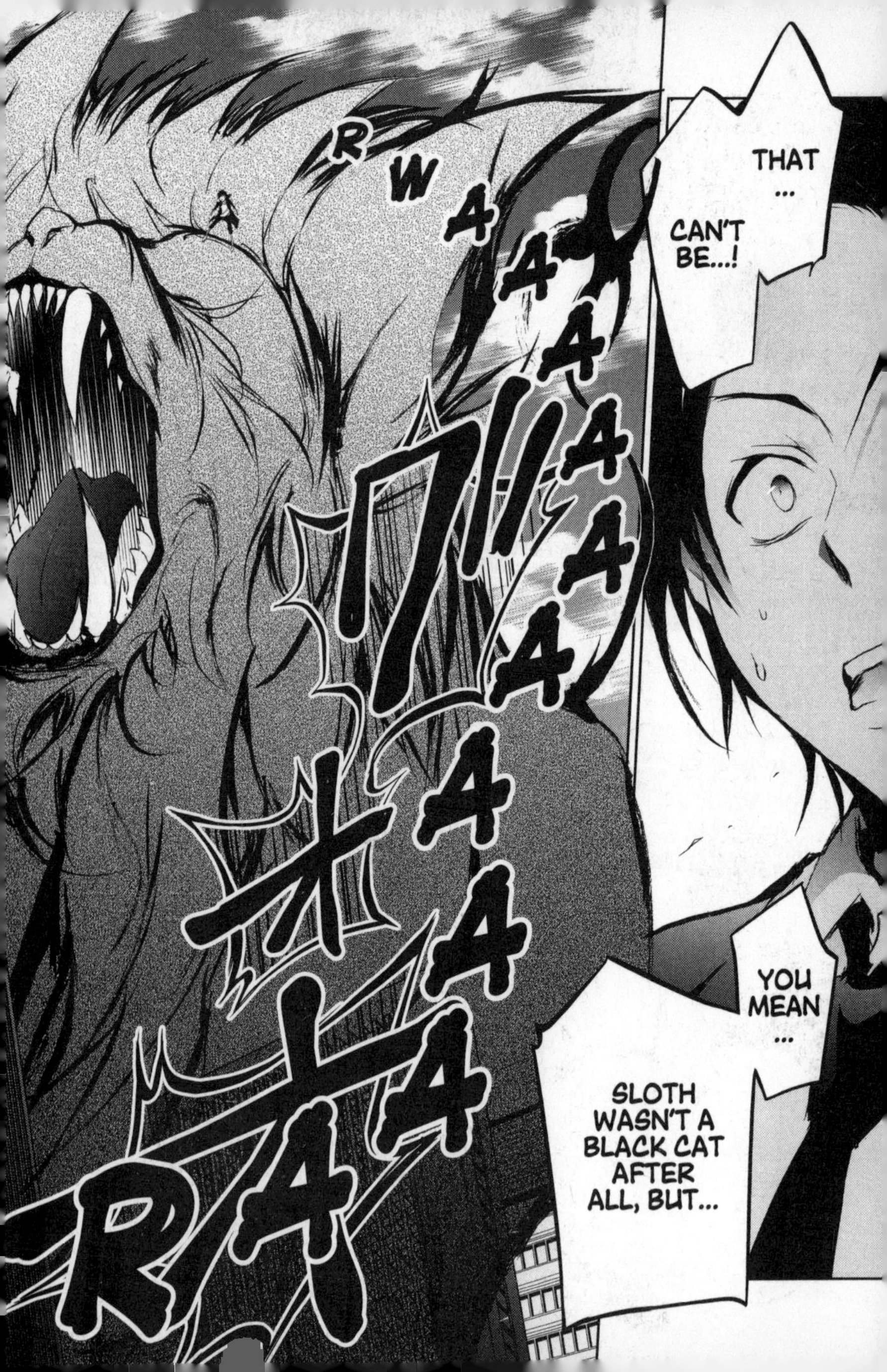
THAT ... CAN'T BE...!
YOU MEAN ...
SLOTH WASN'T A BLACK CAT AFTER ALL, BUT...

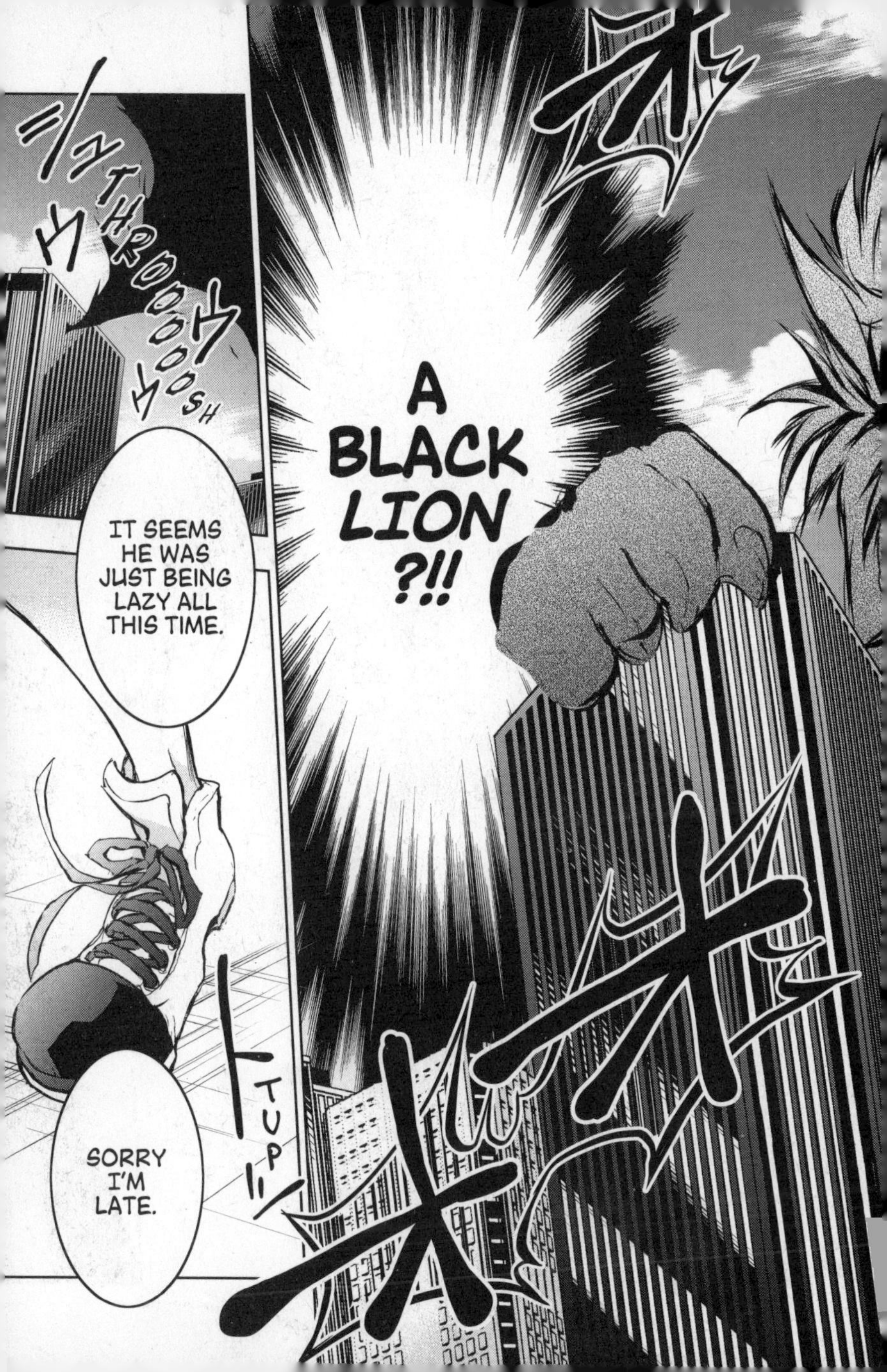
A BLACK LION ?!!
THROOOOOSH
IT SEEMS HE WAS JUST BEING LAZY ALL THIS TIME.
TUP!
SORRY I'M LATE.

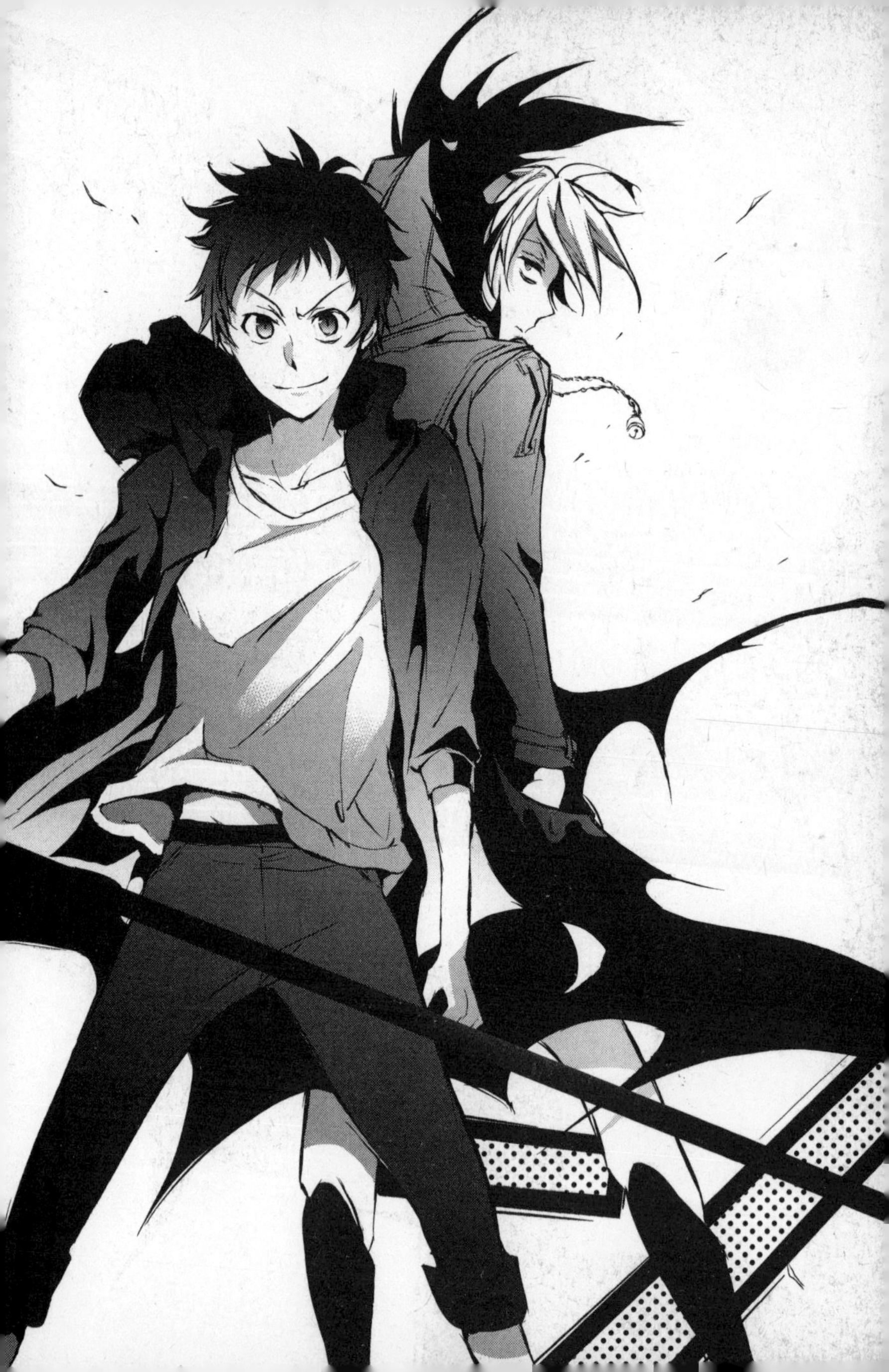

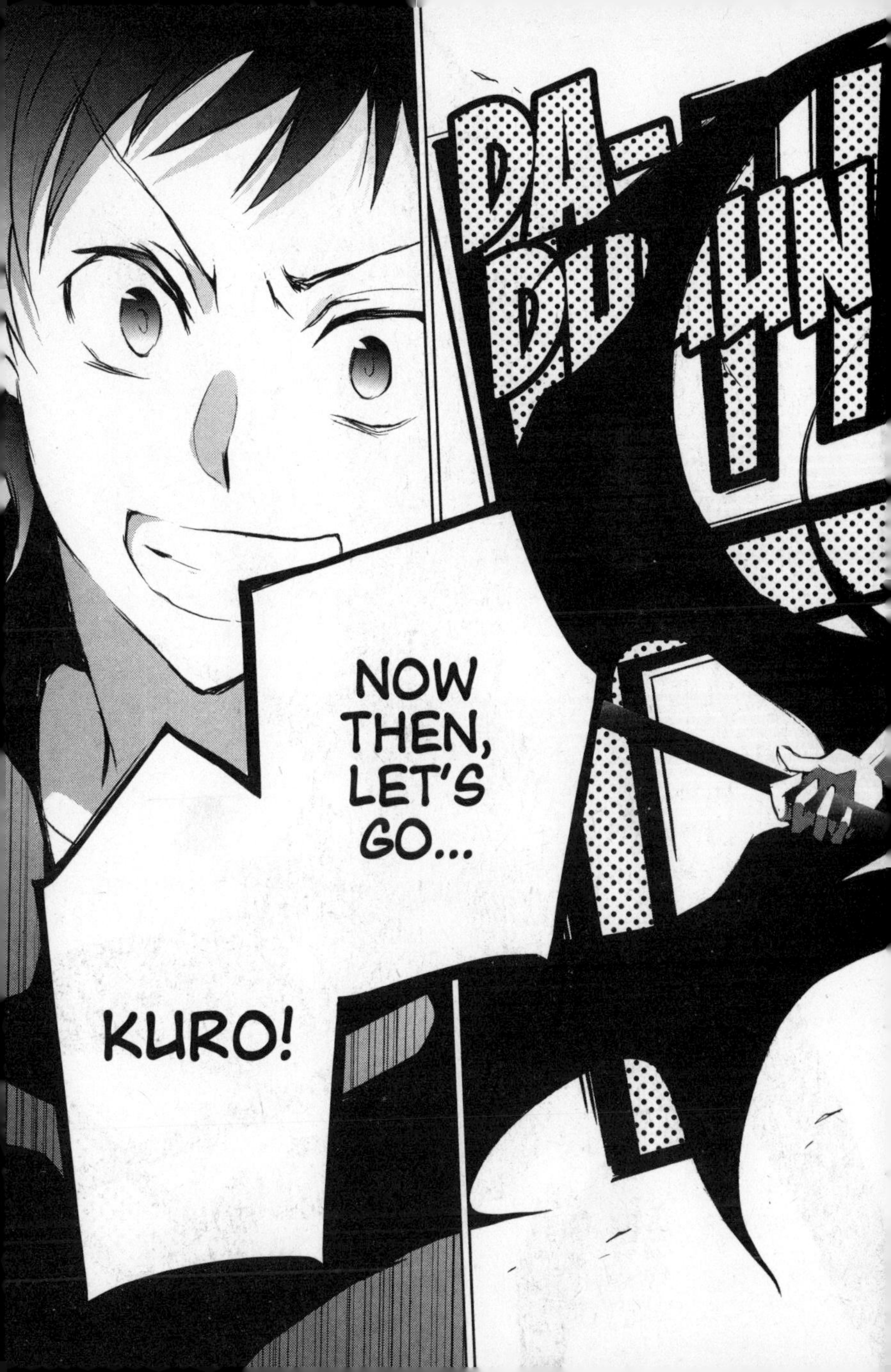
DA-
NOW THEN, LET'S GO...
KURO!

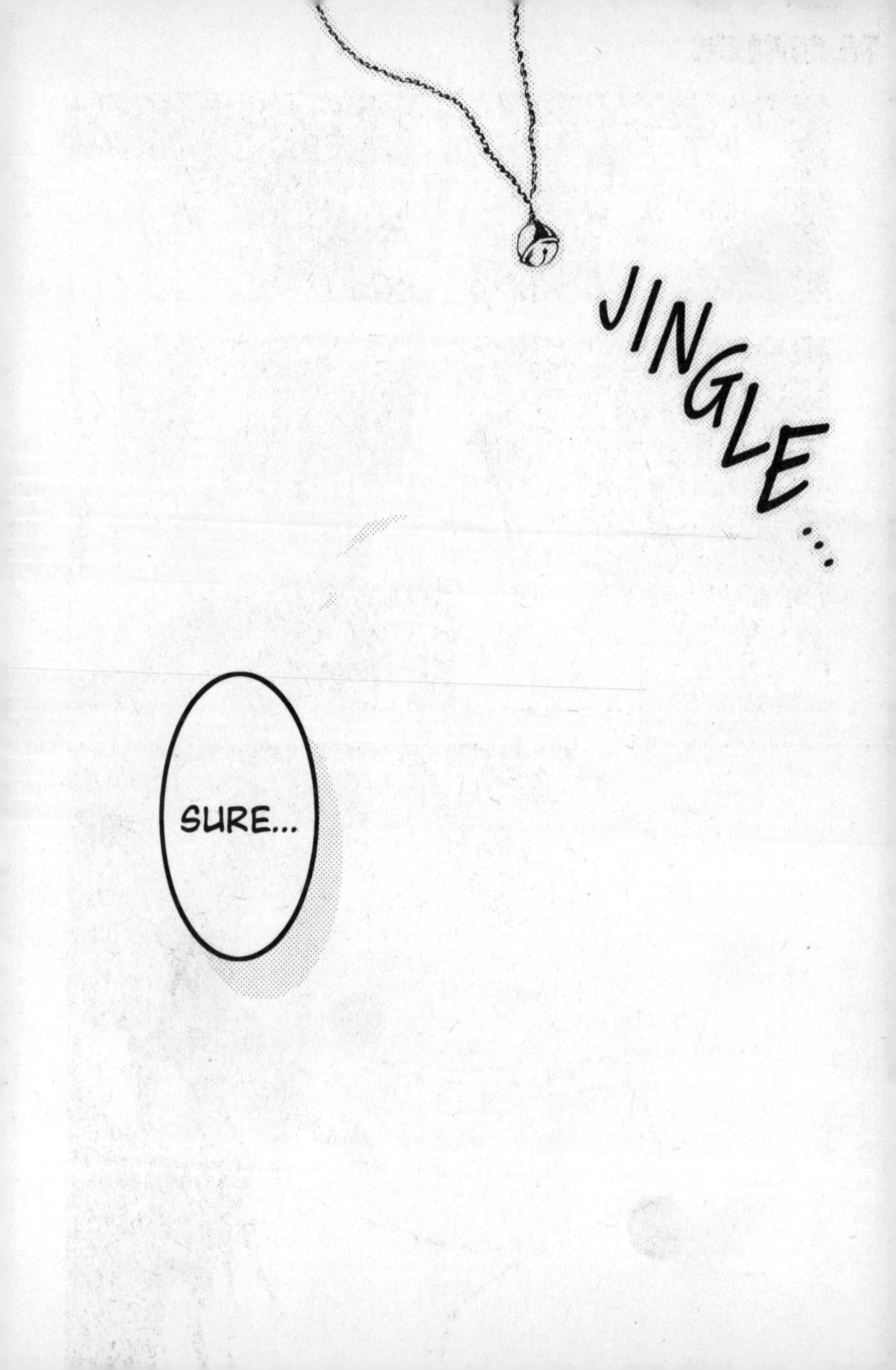
JINGLE...
SURE...

# 36. COWARDS

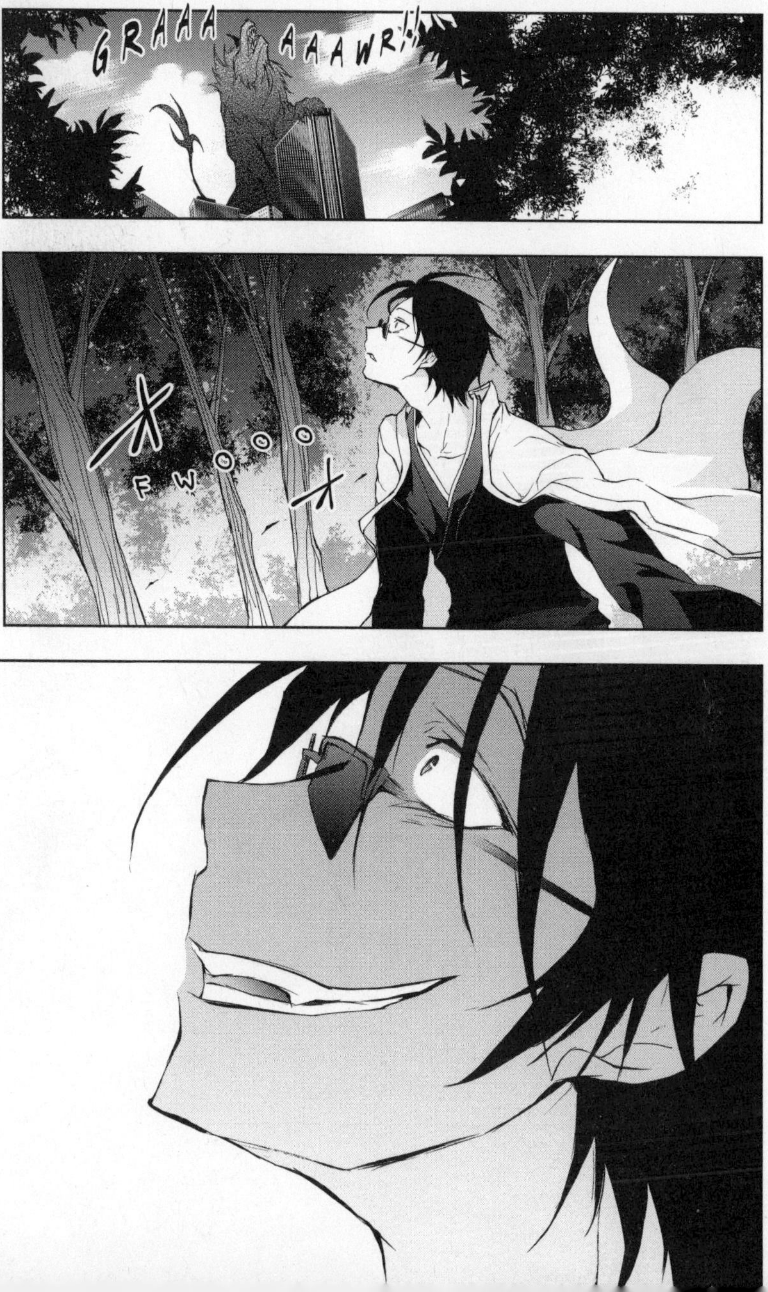
GRAAAAAAWR!!
FWOOOO

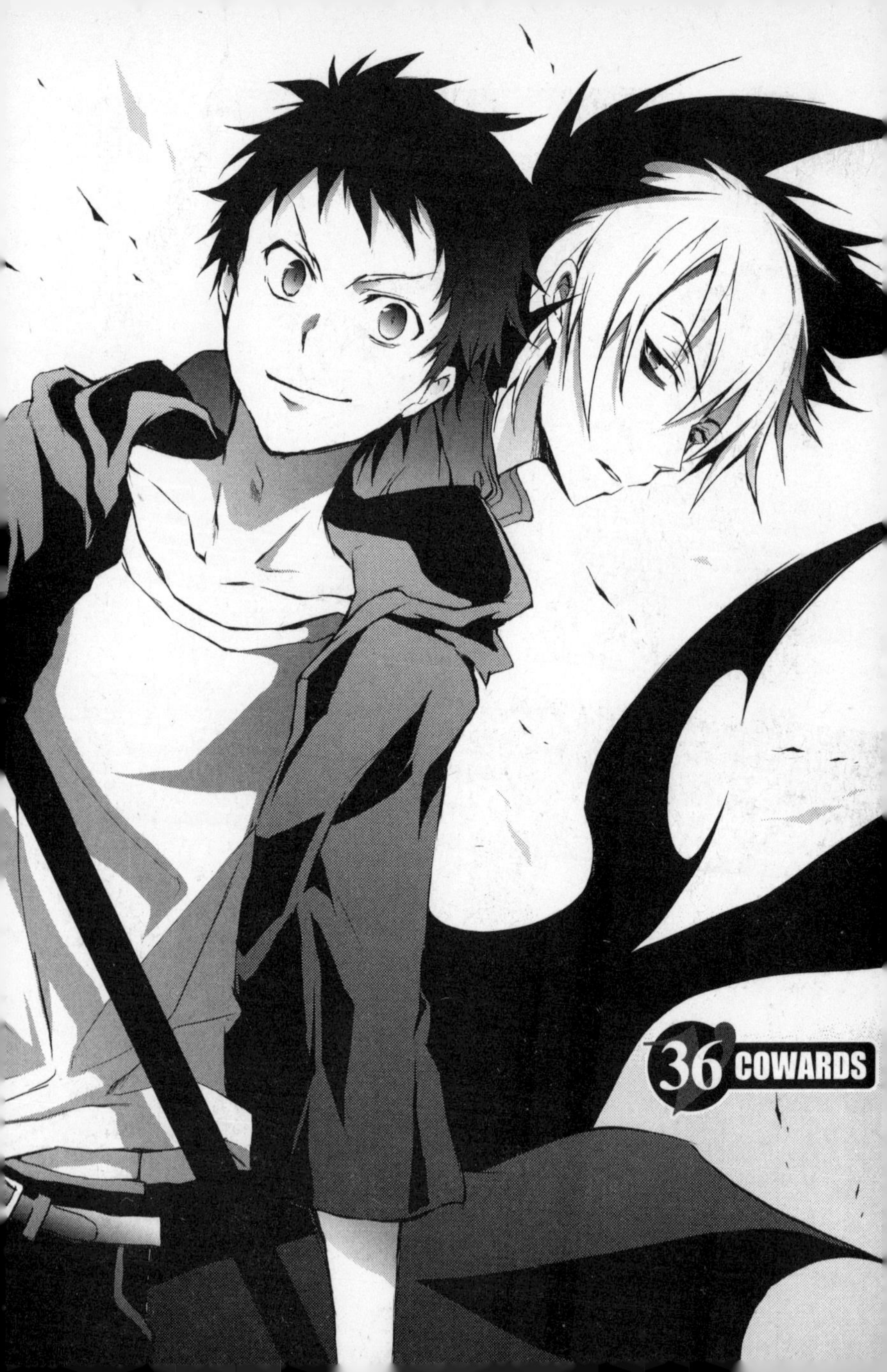
36 COWARDS

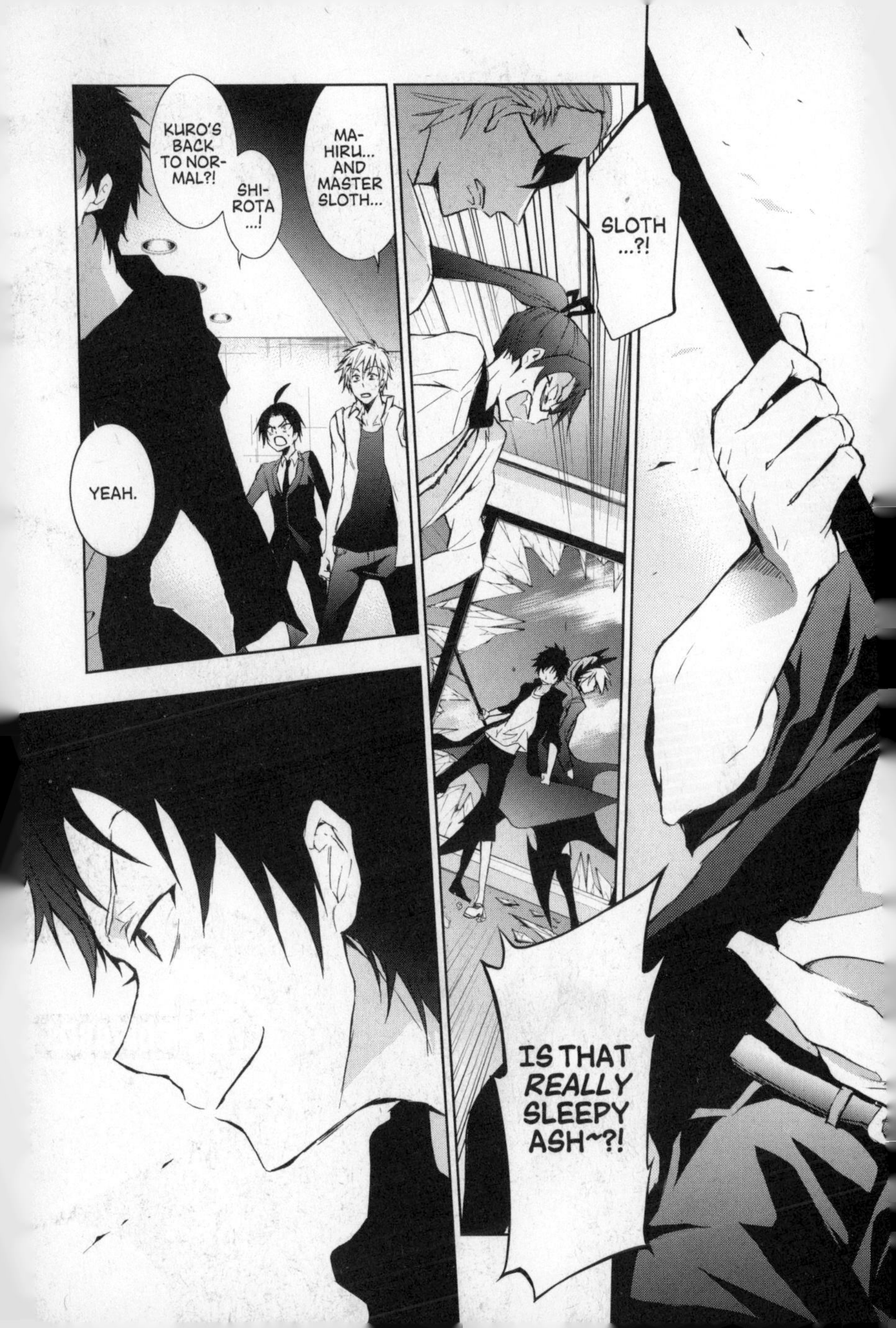
SLOTH ...?!
IS THAT REALLY SLEEPY ASH~?!
MA-HIRU... AND MASTER SLOTH...
KURO'S BACK TO NOR-MAL?!
SHI-ROTA ...!
YEAH.

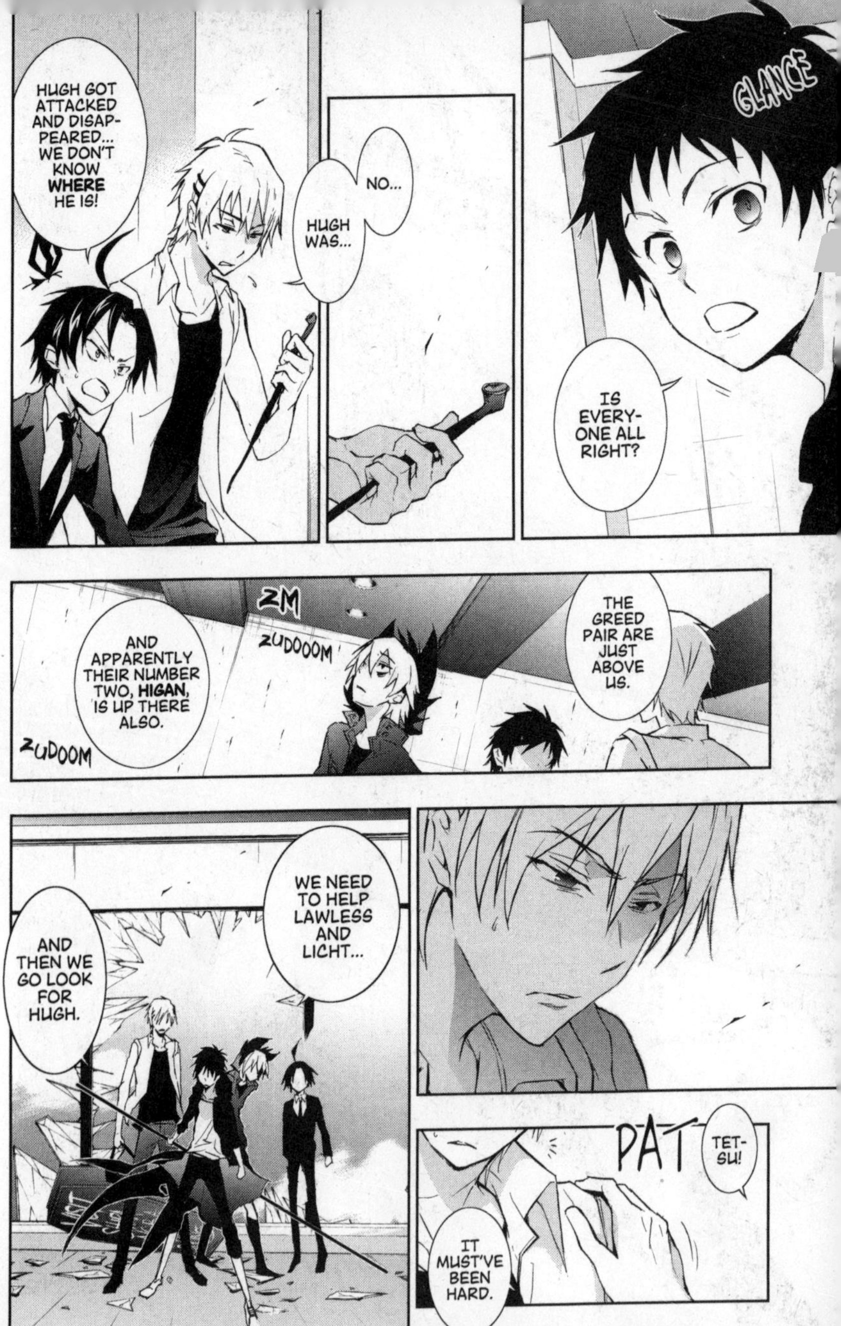
GLANCE
IS EVERY-ONE ALL RIGHT?
NO...
HUGH WAS...
HUGH GOT ATTACKED AND DISAP-PEARED... WE DON'T KNOW **WHERE** HE IS!
THE GREED PAIR ARE JUST ABOVE US.
ZM
ZUDOOOM
AND APPARENTLY THEIR NUMBER TWO, **HIGAN**, IS UP THERE ALSO.
ZUDOOM
PAT
TET-SU!
IT MUST'VE BEEN HARD.
WE NEED TO HELP LAWLESS AND LICHT...
AND THEN WE GO LOOK FOR HUGH.

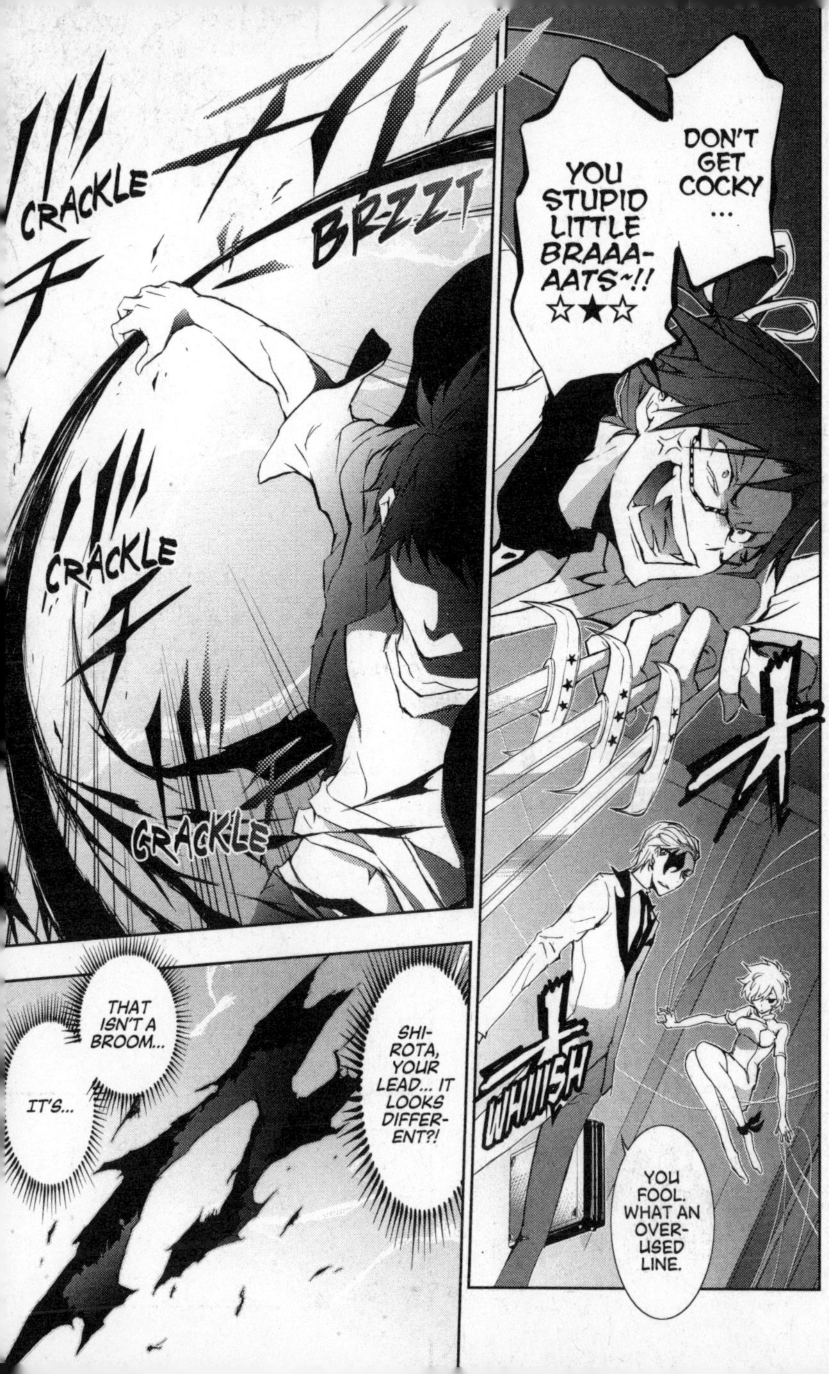
DON'T GET COCKY ...
YOU STUPID LITTLE BRAAAA-AATS~!! ☆★☆
WHIIISH
YOU FOOL. WHAT AN OVER-USED LINE.
BRZZT
CRACKLE
CRACKLE
CRACKLE
SHI-ROTA, YOUR LEAD... IT LOOKS DIFFER-ENT?!
THAT ISN'T A BROOM...
IT'S...

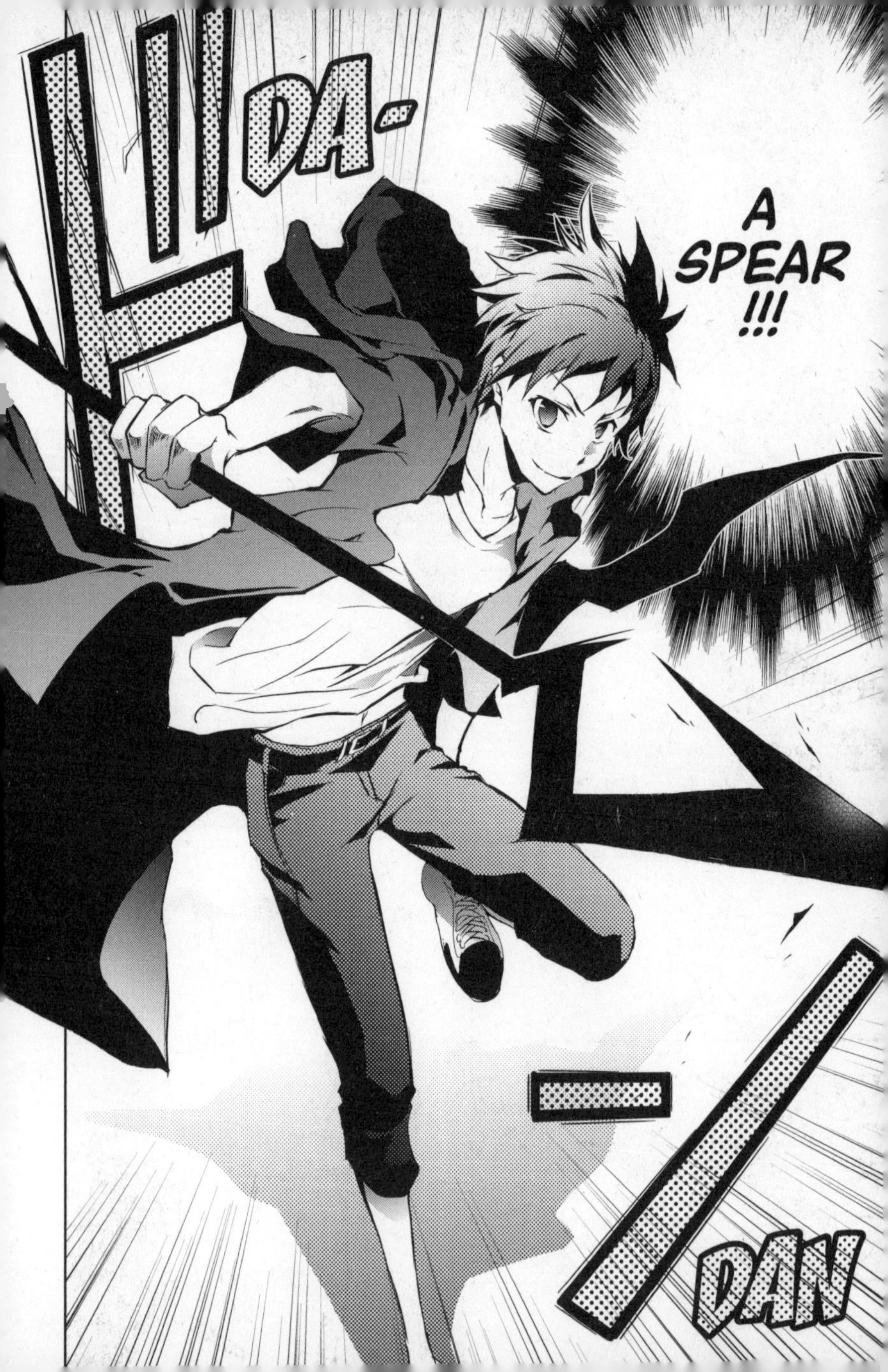
A SPEAR !!!
DA-
DAN

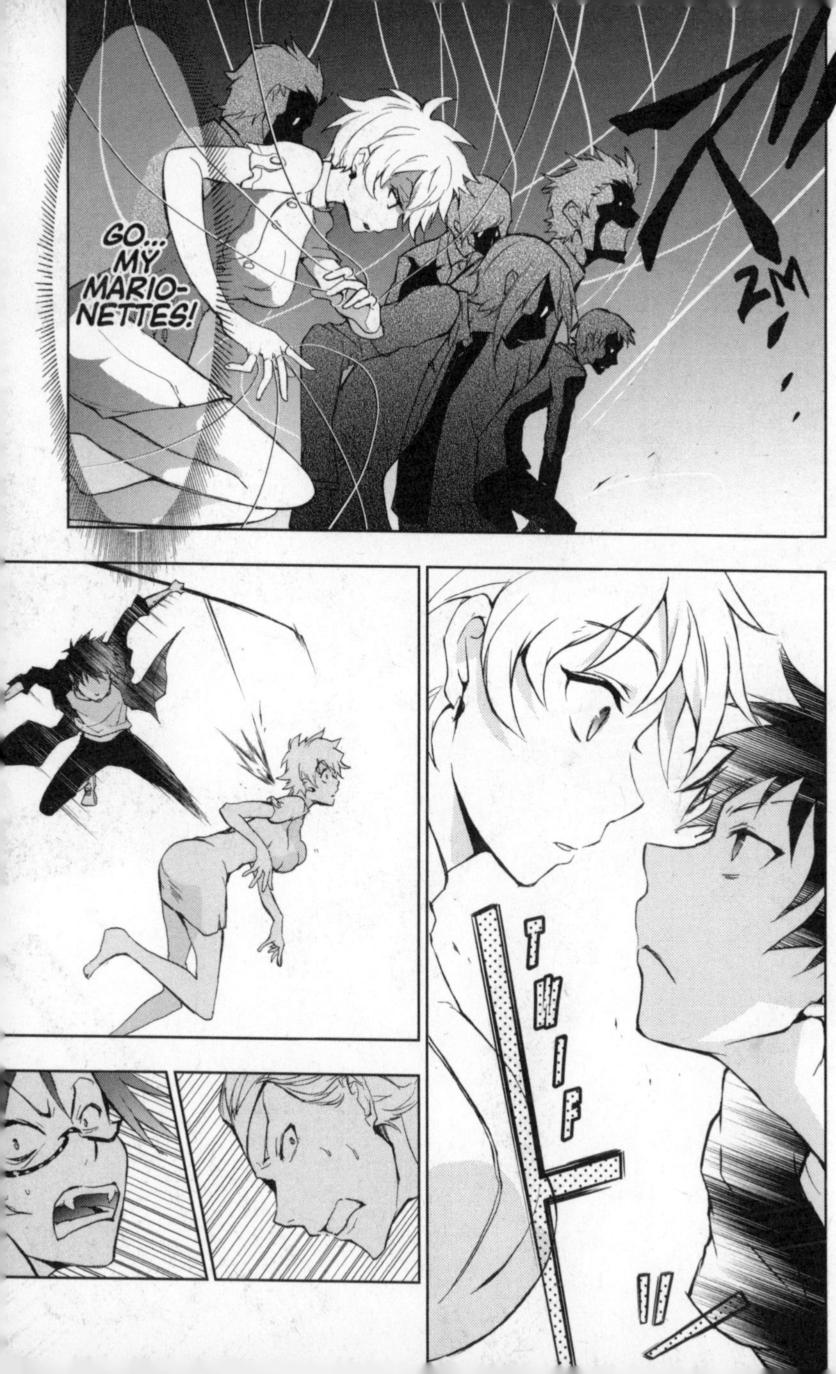
ZM
GO... MY MARIO-NETTES!
THWIF

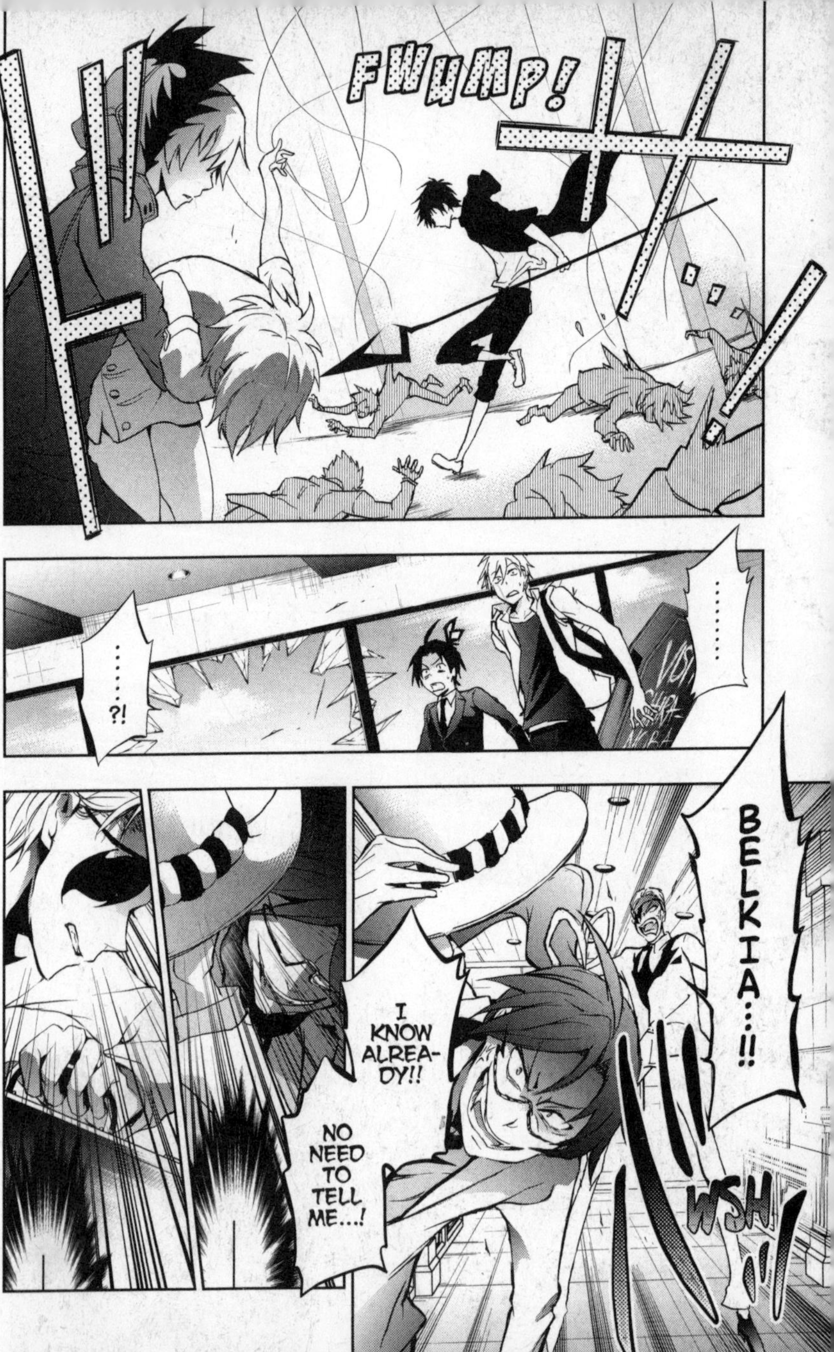
FWUMP!
......
......?!
BELKIA...!!
I KNOW ALREA-DY!!
NO NEED TO TELL ME...!
WSH

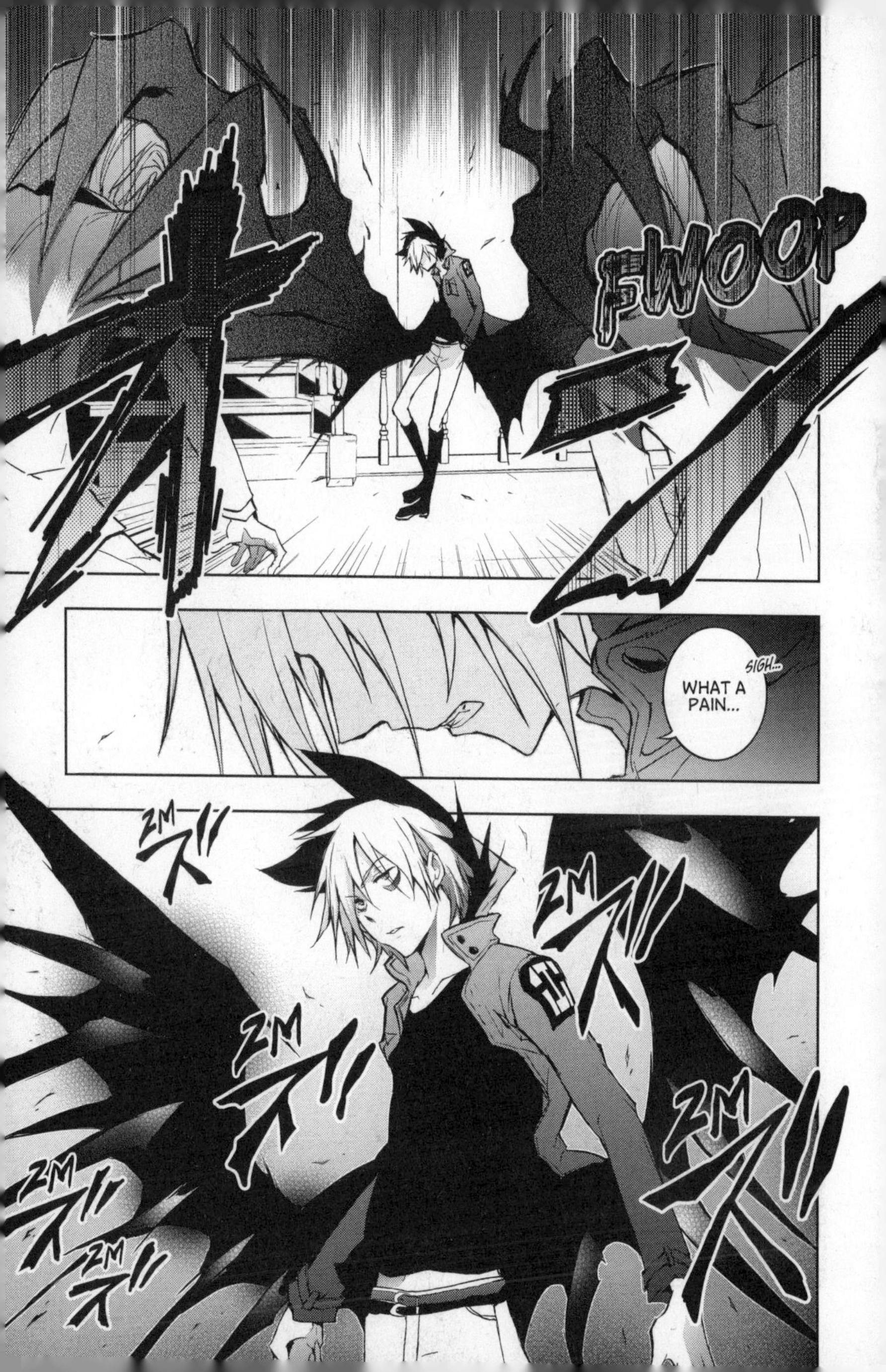
FWOOP
SIGH...
WHAT A PAIN...
ZM
ZM
ZM
ZM
ZM
ZM

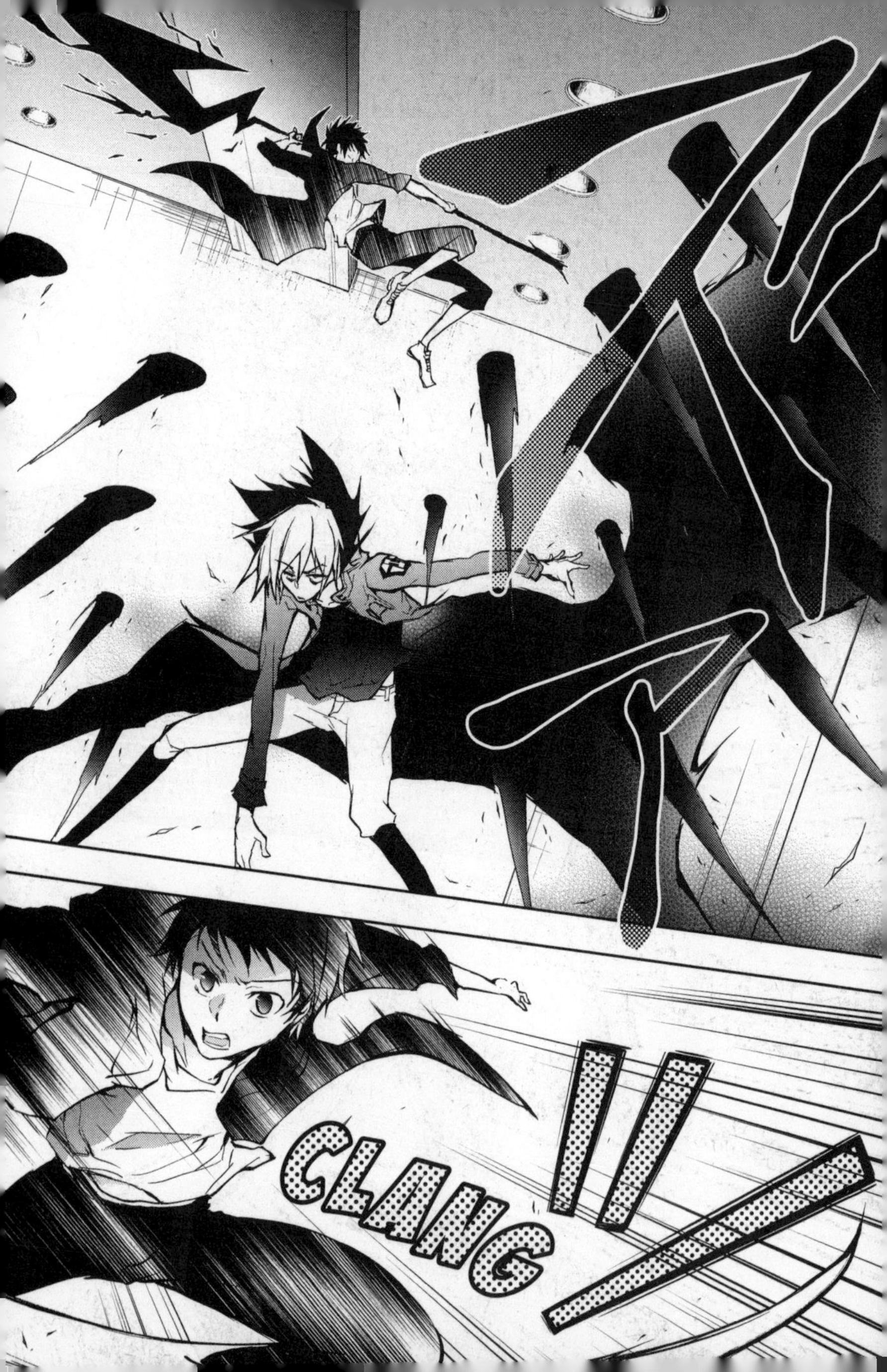
CLANG

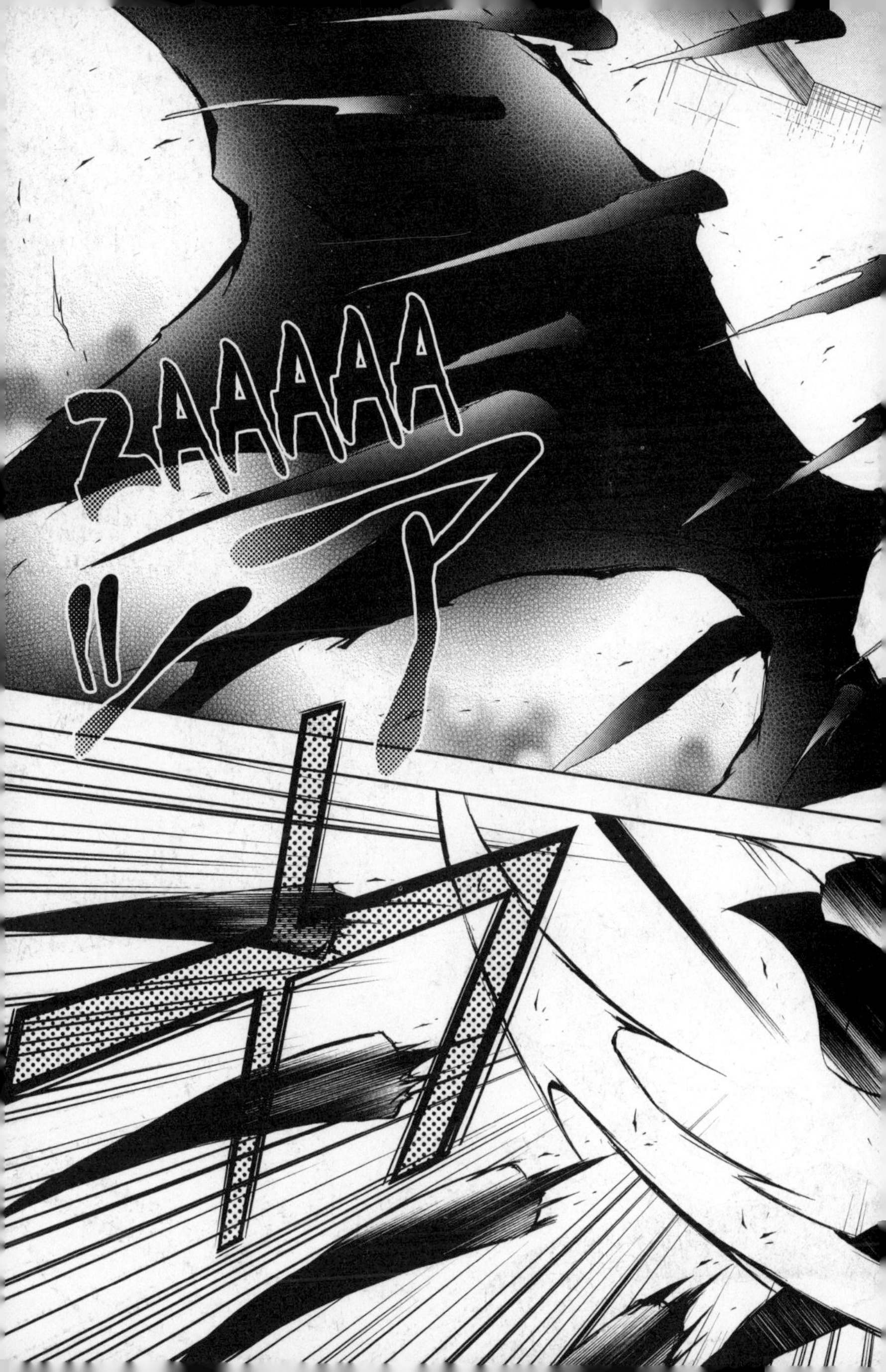
ZAAAAA

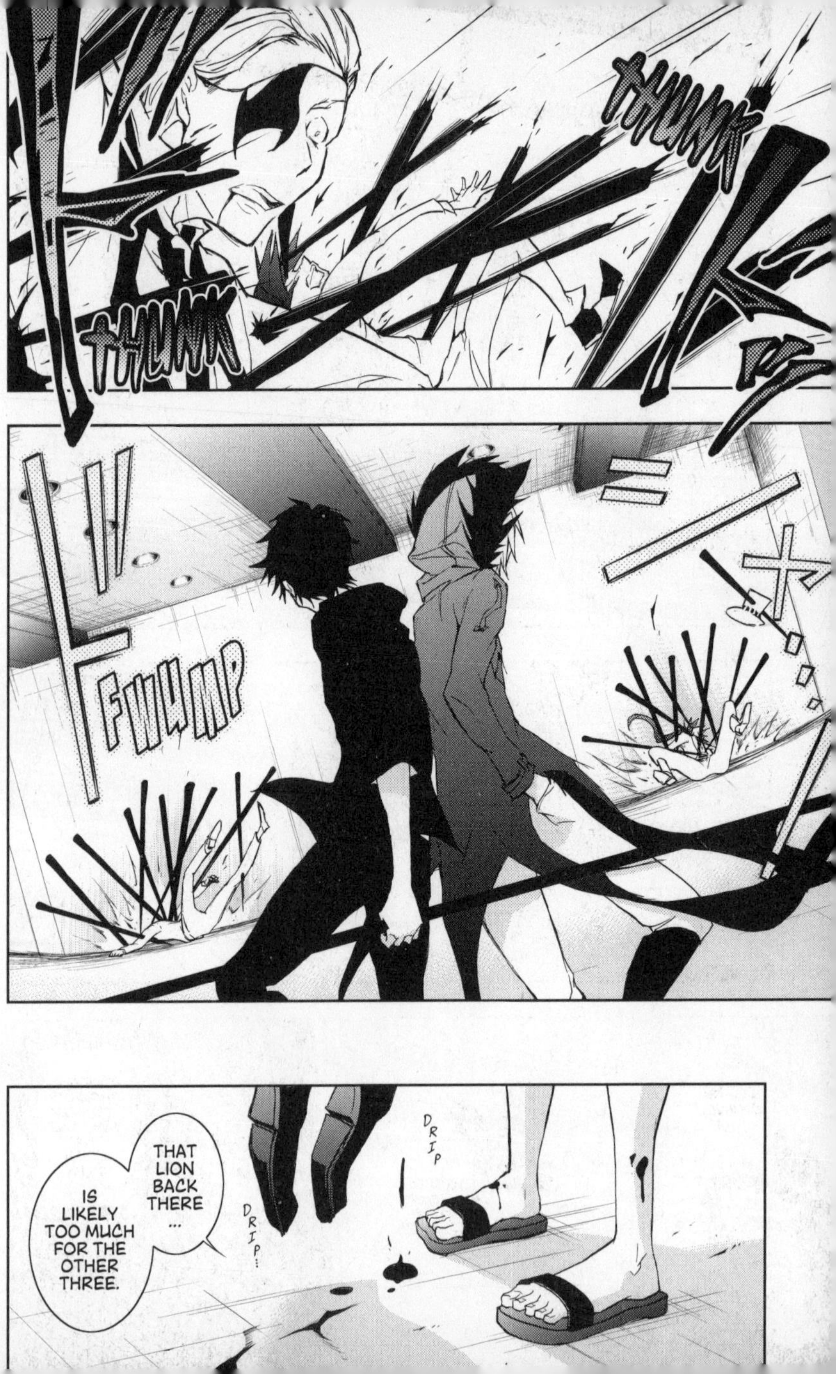
THUNK
THUNK
FWUMP
DRIP
DRIP...
THAT LION BACK THERE ...
IS LIKELY TOO MUCH FOR THE OTHER THREE.

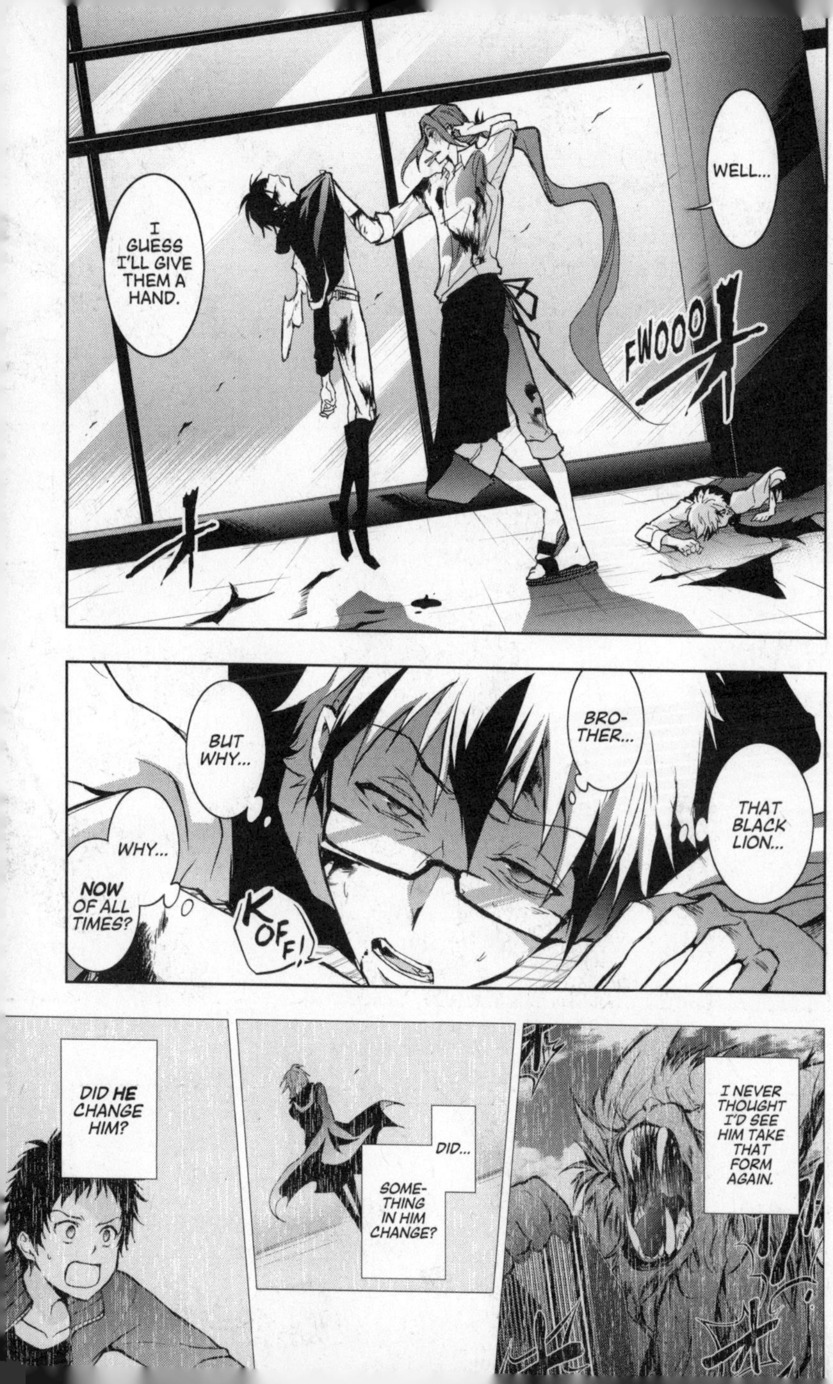
WELL...
I GUESS I'LL GIVE THEM A HAND.
FWOOO
BRO-THER...
THAT BLACK LION...
BUT WHY...
WHY...
KOFF!
NOW OF ALL TIMES?
I NEVER THOUGHT I'D SEE HIM TAKE THAT FORM AGAIN.
DID...
SOME-THING IN HIM CHANGE?
DID HE CHANGE HIM?

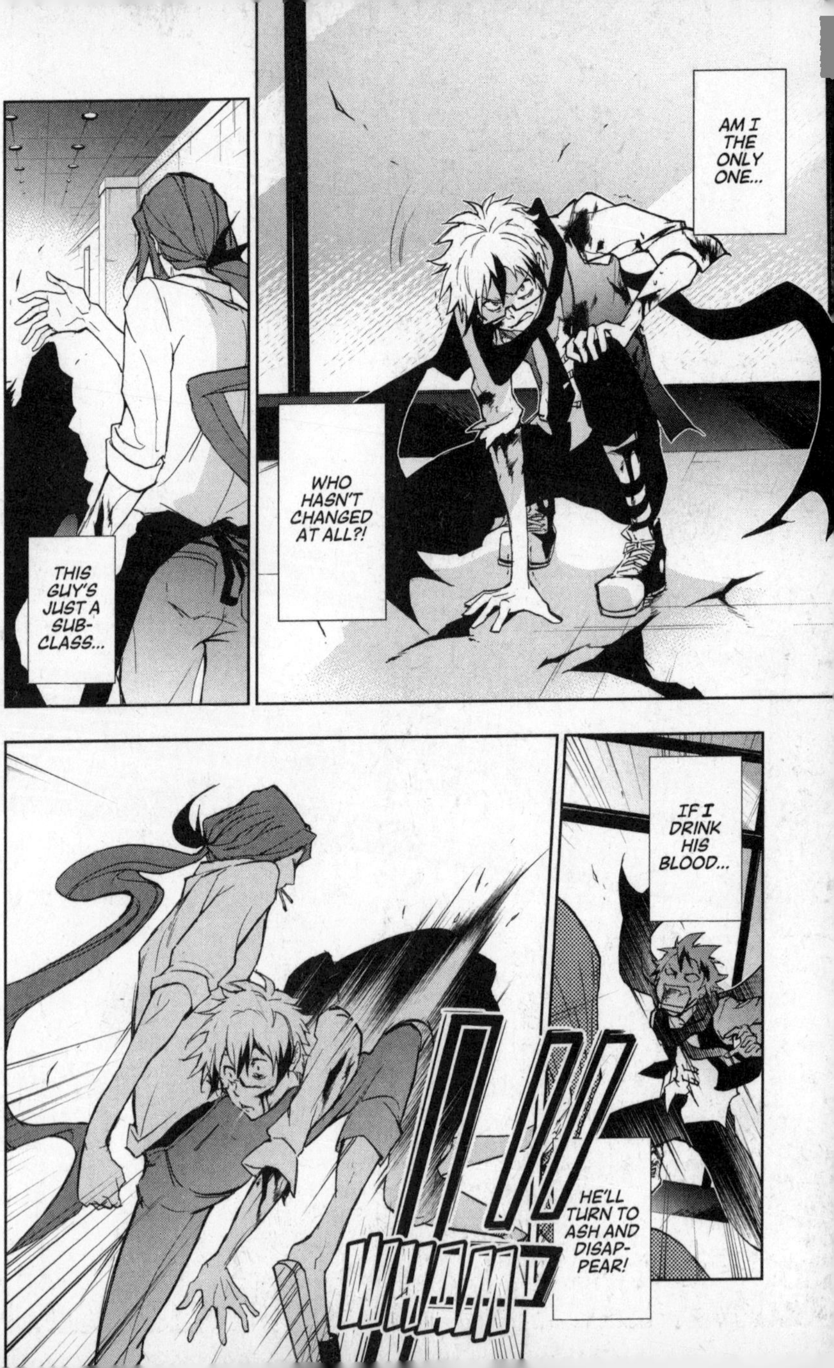
AM I THE ONLY ONE...
WHO HASN'T CHANGED AT ALL?!
THIS GUY'S JUST A SUB-CLASS...
IF I DRINK HIS BLOOD...
HE'LL TURN TO ASH AND DISAP-PEAR!
WHAM

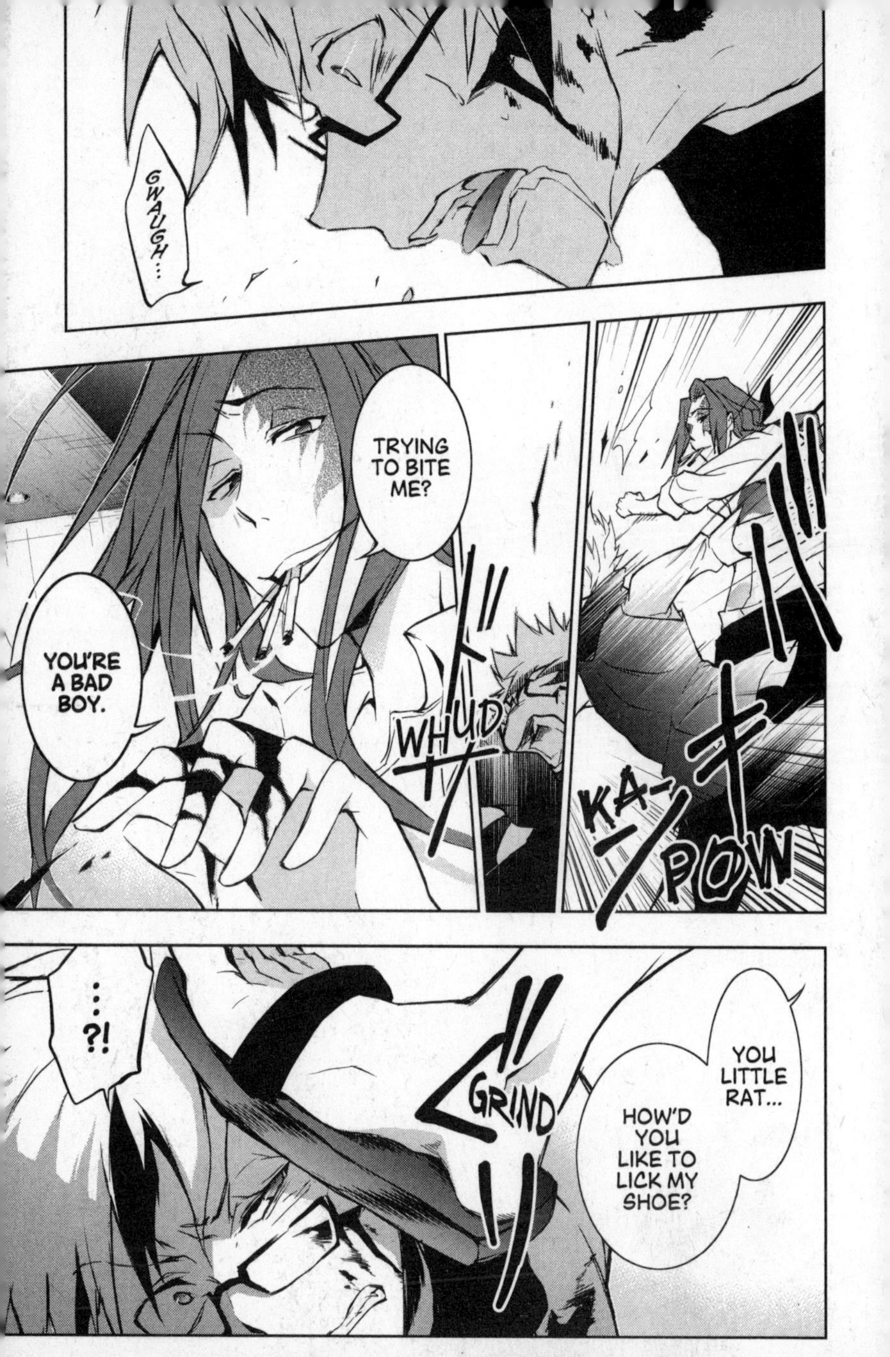
GWAUGH...
KA-
POW
WHUD
TRYING TO BITE ME?
YOU'RE A BAD BOY.
YOU LITTLE RAT...
HOW'D YOU LIKE TO LICK MY SHOE?
GRIND
...?!

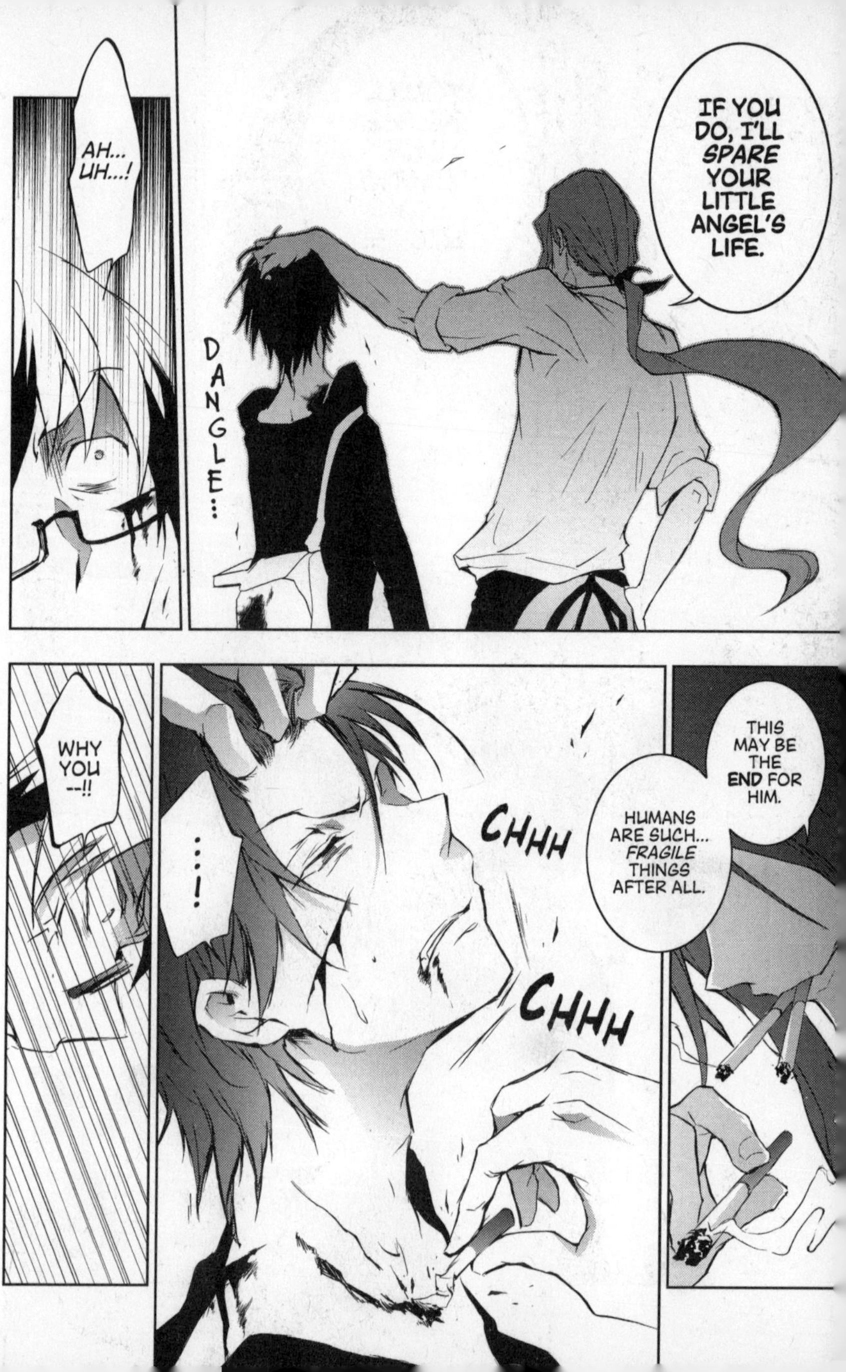
IF YOU DO, I'LL SPARE YOUR LITTLE ANGEL'S LIFE.
DANGLE...
AH... UH...!
THIS MAY BE THE END FOR HIM.
HUMANS ARE SUCH... FRAGILE THINGS AFTER ALL.
CHHH
CHHH
...!
WHY YOU --!!

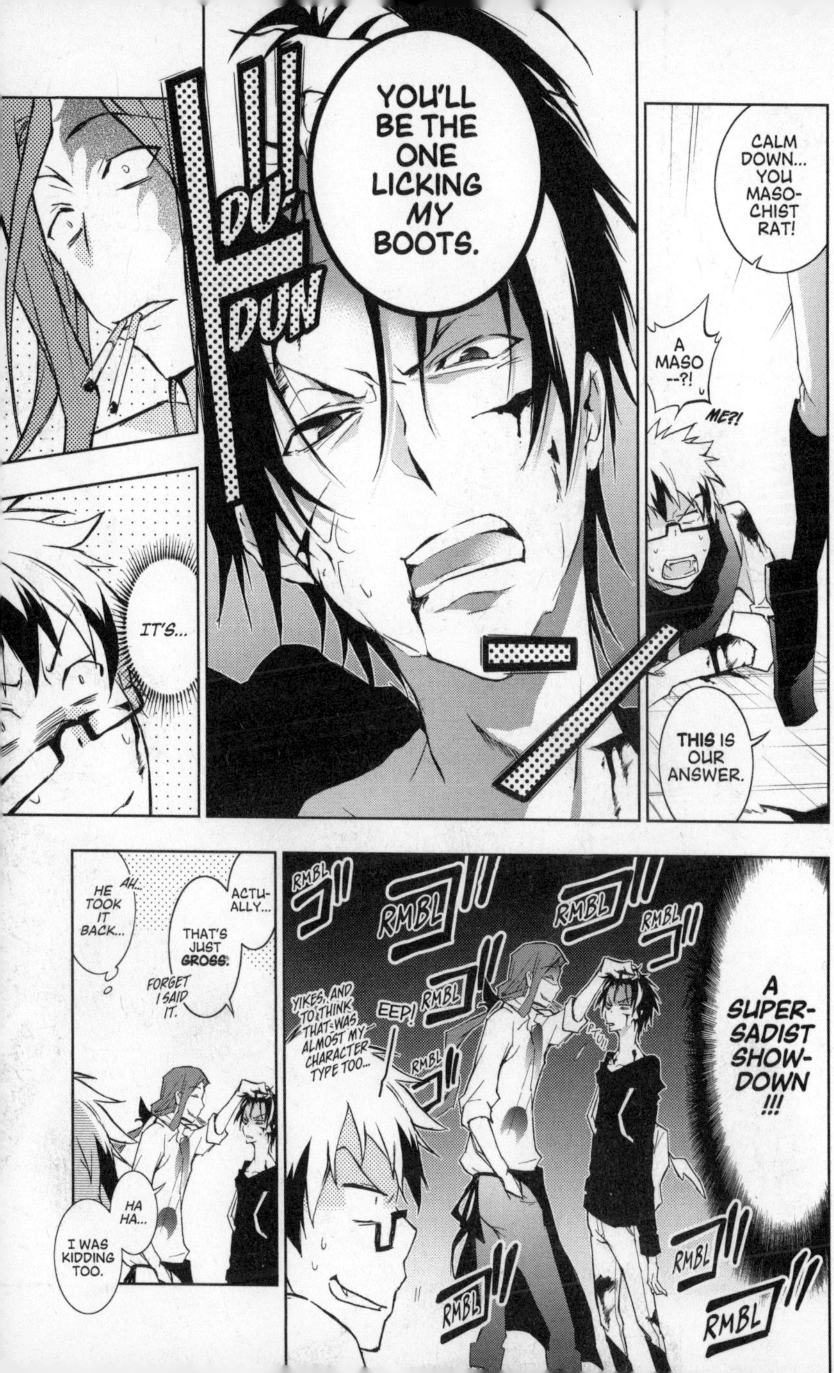
CALM DOWN... YOU MASO-CHIST RAT!
A MASO --?!
ME?!
THIS IS OUR ANSWER.
YOU'LL BE THE ONE LICKING MY BOOTS.
DUN DUN
IT'S...
RMBL
A SUPER-SADIST SHOW-DOWN!!!
YIKES, AND TO THINK THAT WAS ALMOST MY CHARACTER TYPE TOO...
EEP!
RMBL
ACTU-ALLY... THAT'S JUST GROSS.
FORGET I SAID IT.
AH... HE TOOK IT BACK...
HA HA...
I WAS KIDDING TOO.

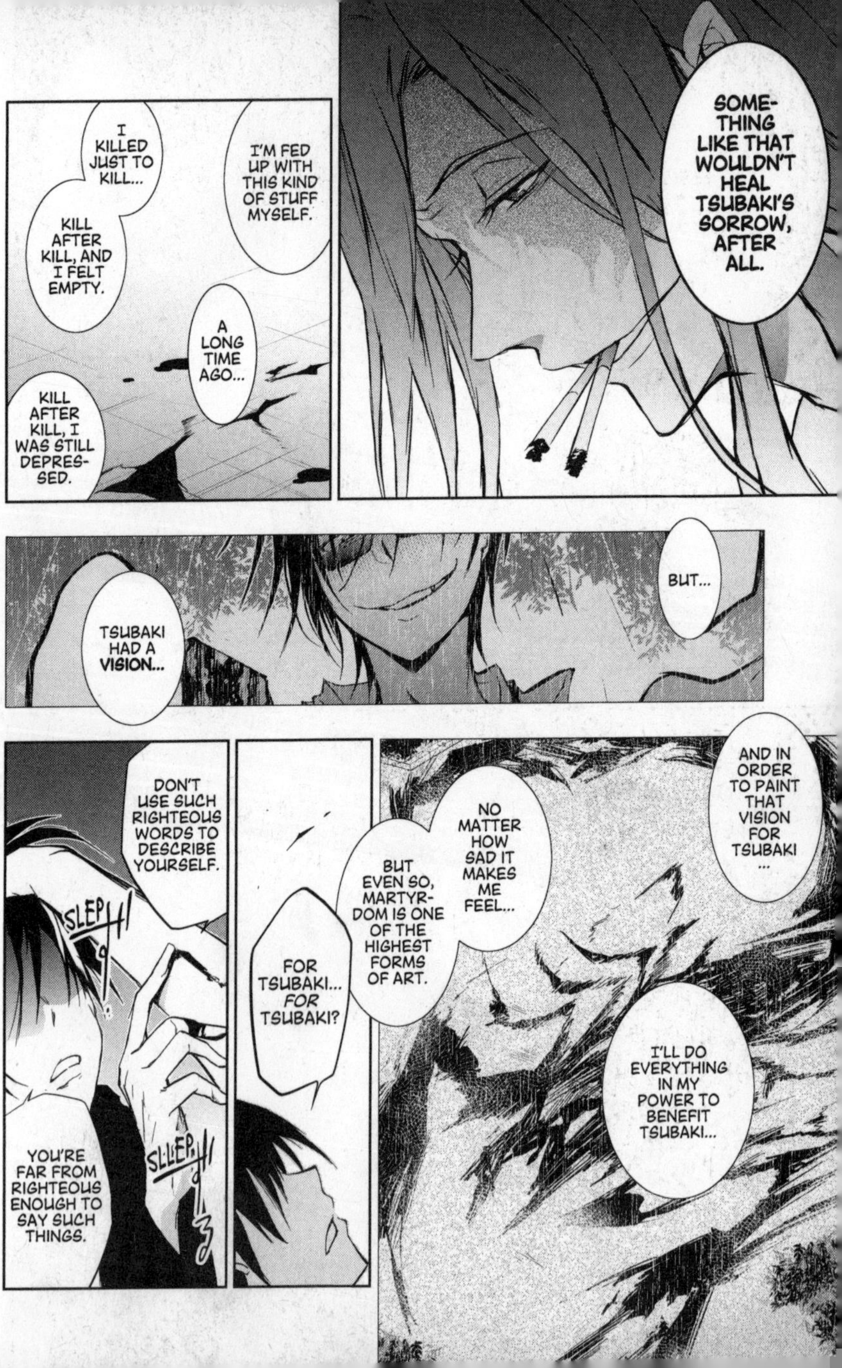
SOMETHING LIKE THAT WOULDN'T HEAL TSUBAKI'S SORROW, AFTER ALL.
I'M FED UP WITH THIS KIND OF STUFF MYSELF.
I KILLED JUST TO KILL...
KILL AFTER KILL, AND I FELT EMPTY.
A LONG TIME AGO...
KILL AFTER KILL, I WAS STILL DEPRESSED.
BUT...
TSUBAKI HAD A **VISION**...
AND IN ORDER TO PAINT THAT VISION FOR TSUBAKI...
I'LL DO EVERYTHING IN MY POWER TO BENEFIT TSUBAKI...
NO MATTER HOW SAD IT MAKES ME FEEL...
BUT EVEN SO, MARTYRDOM IS ONE OF THE HIGHEST FORMS OF ART.
FOR TSUBAKI... *FOR* TSUBAKI?
DON'T USE SUCH RIGHTEOUS WORDS TO DESCRIBE YOURSELF.
SLEP
SLLEP
YOU'RE FAR FROM RIGHTEOUS ENOUGH TO SAY SUCH THINGS.

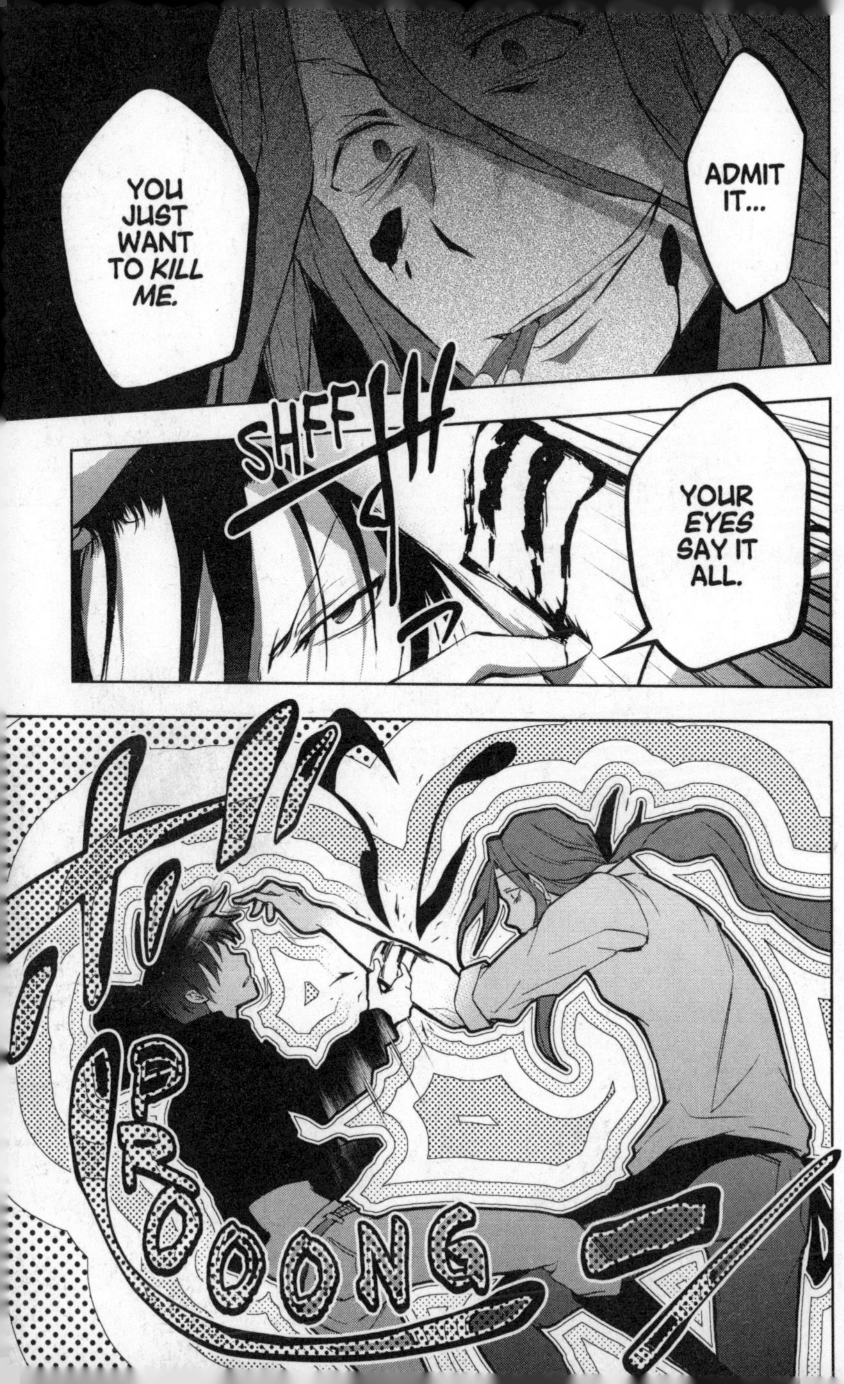
ADMIT IT...
YOU JUST WANT TO KILL ME.
YOUR EYES SAY IT ALL.
SHFF
PROOONG

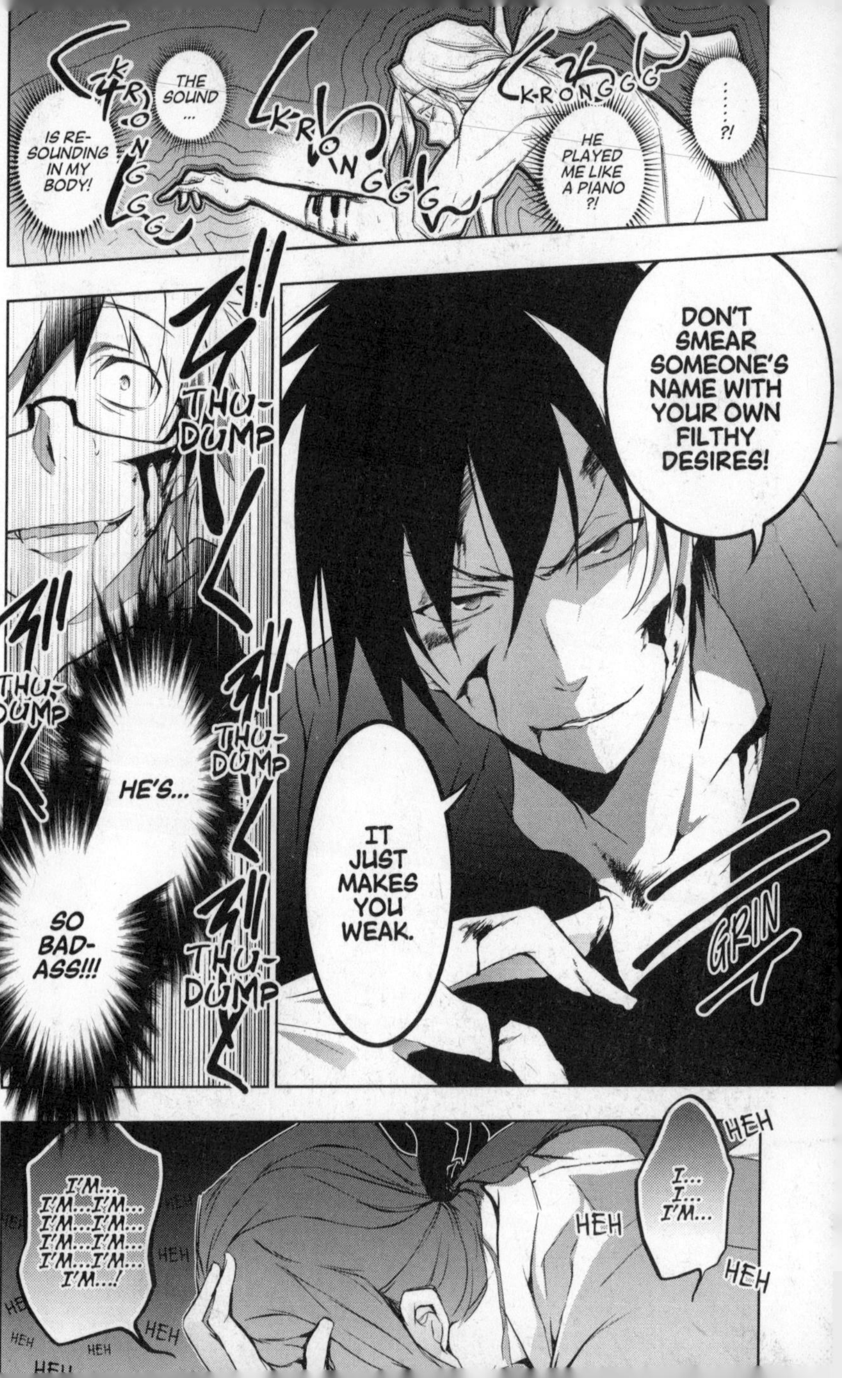
K-R-O-N-G-G-G
......?!
HE PLAYED ME LIKE A PIANO ?!
K-R-O-N-G-G-G
THE SOUND ...
IS RE-SOUNDING IN MY BODY!
K-R-O-N-G-G-G
DON'T SMEAR SOMEONE'S NAME WITH YOUR OWN FILTHY DESIRES!
IT JUST MAKES YOU WEAK.
GRIN
THU-DUMP
THU-DUMP
THU-DUMP
THU-DUMP
HE'S...
SO BAD-ASS!!!
HEH
I... I... I'M...
HEH
HEH
I'M... I'M...I'M... I'M...I'M... I'M...I'M... I'M...I'M... I'M...!
HEH
HEH
HEH
HEH
HEH

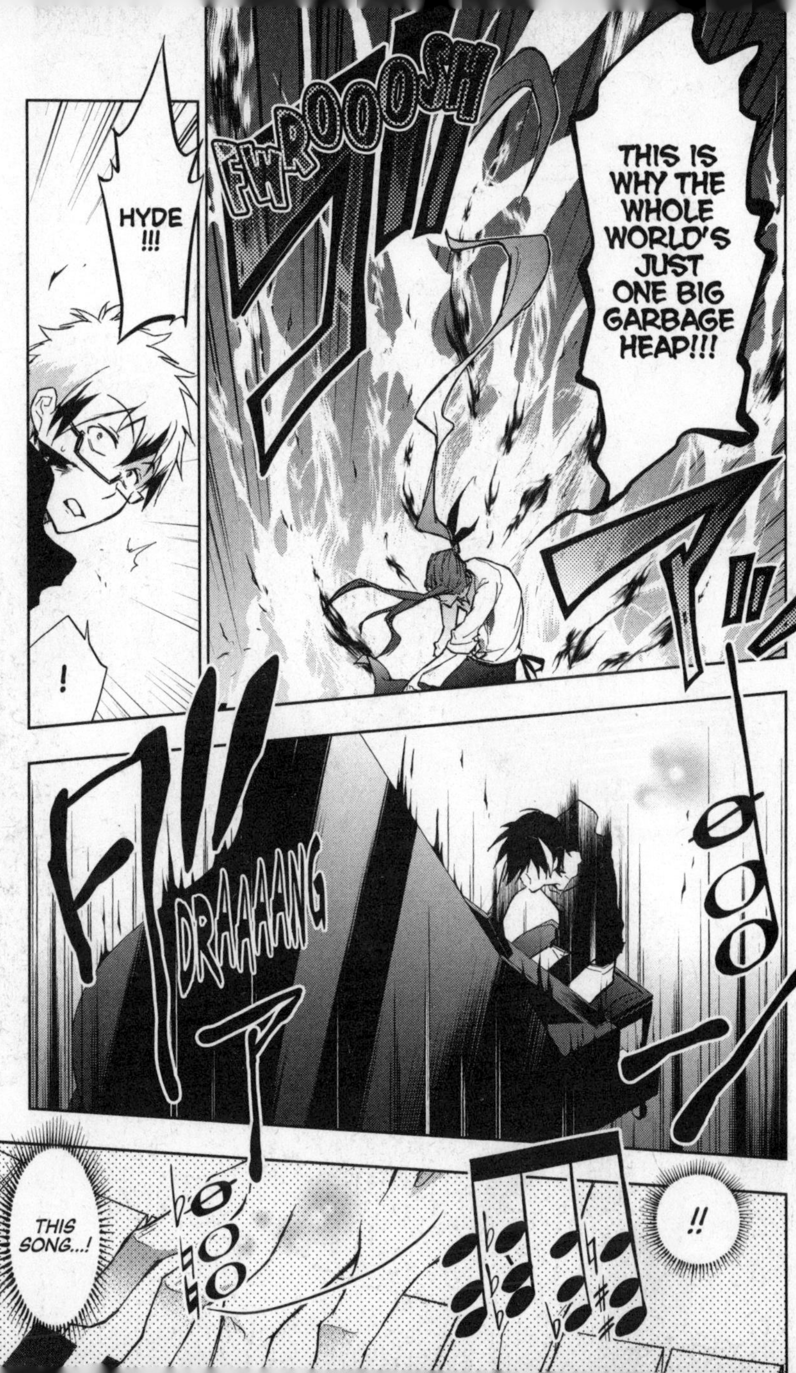
FWROOOSH
THIS IS WHY THE WHOLE WORLD'S JUST ONE BIG GARBAGE HEAP!!!
HYDE !!!
!
DRAAAANG
!!
THIS SONG...!

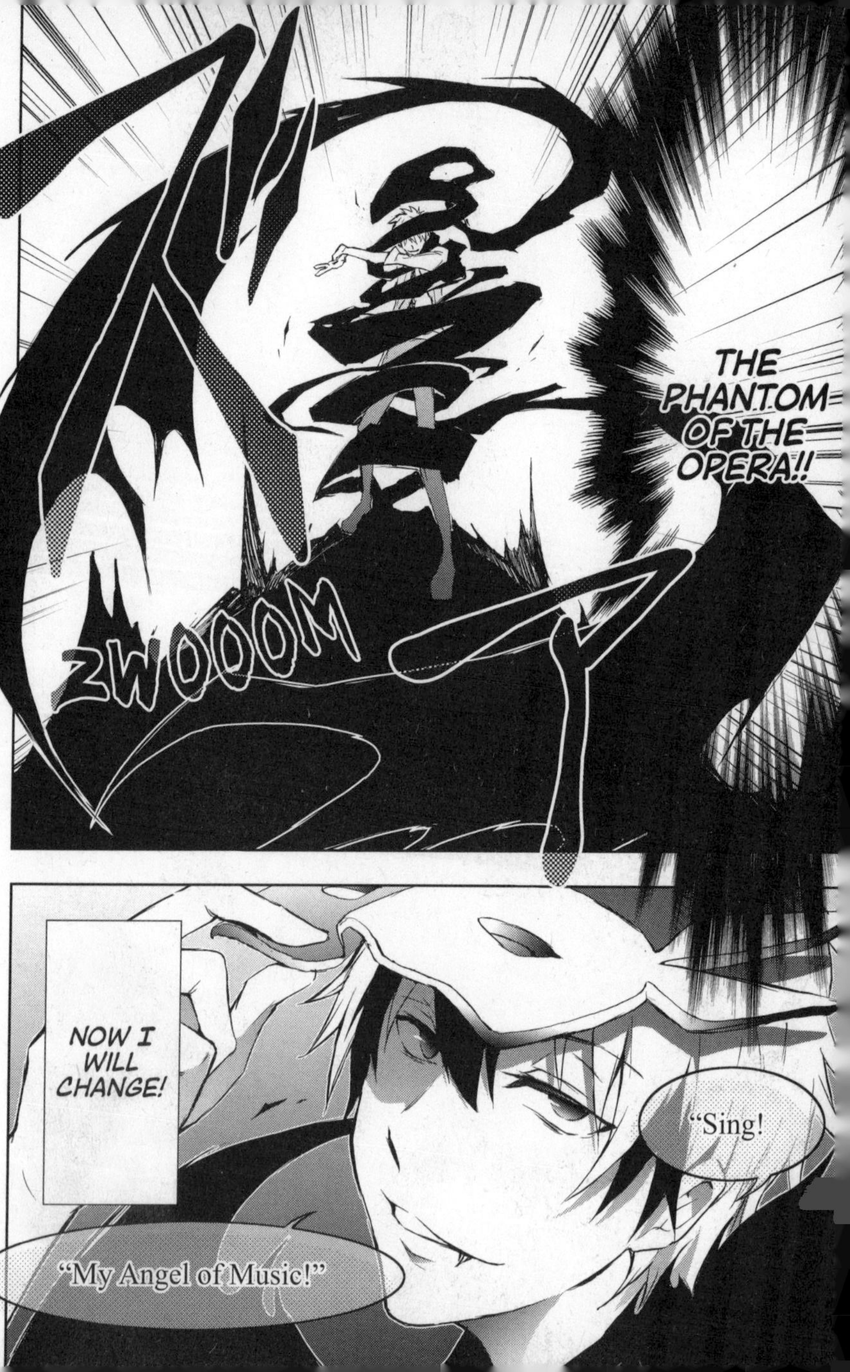
THE PHANTOM OF THE OPERA!!
ZWOOOM
"Sing!
NOW I WILL CHANGE!
"My Angel of Music!"

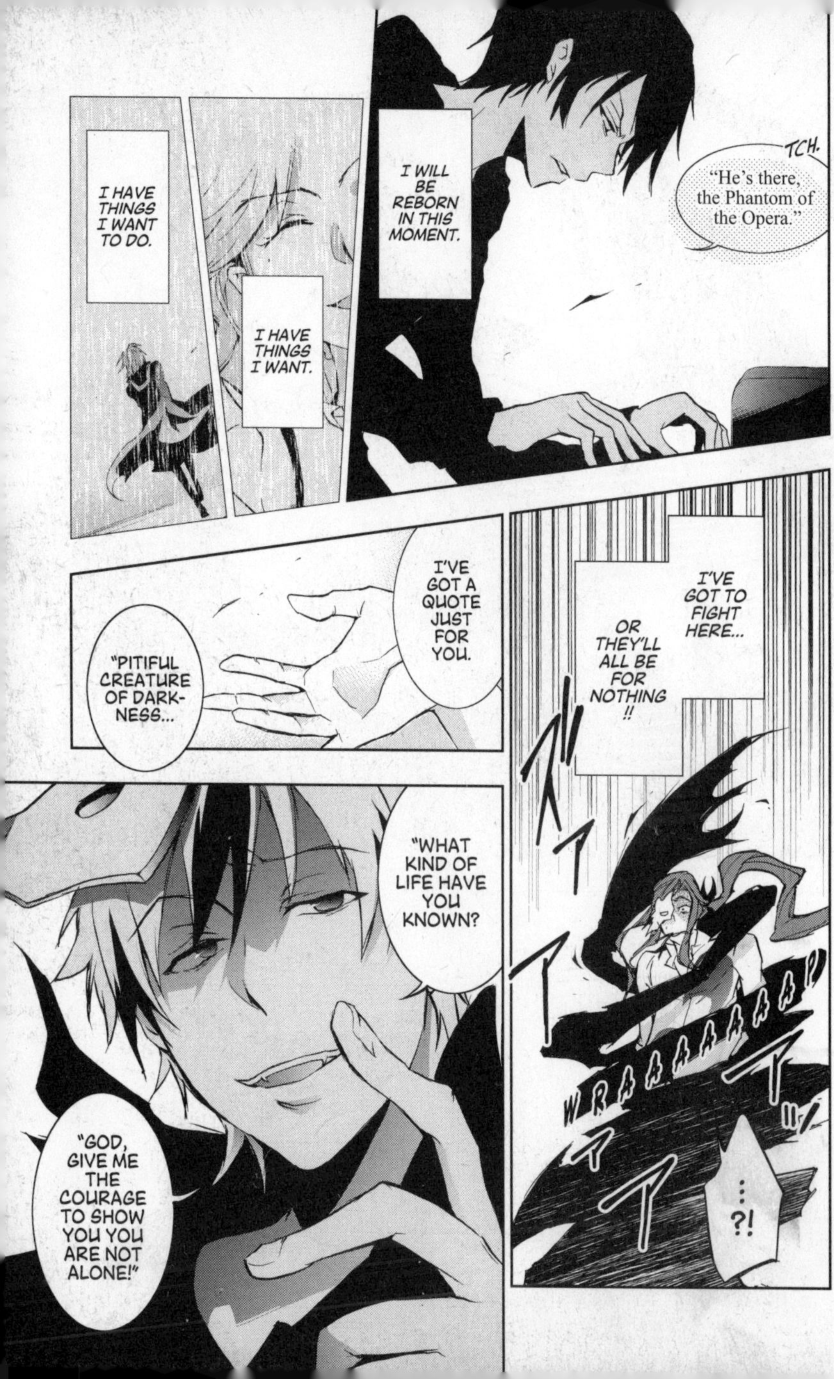
TCH.
"He's there, the Phantom of the Opera."
I WILL BE REBORN IN THIS MOMENT.
I HAVE THINGS I WANT.
I HAVE THINGS I WANT TO DO.
I'VE GOT TO FIGHT HERE...
OR THEY'LL ALL BE FOR NOTHING!!
WRAAAAAAAP!!
...?!
I'VE GOT A QUOTE JUST FOR YOU.
"PITIFUL CREATURE OF DARKNESS...
"WHAT KIND OF LIFE HAVE YOU KNOWN?
"GOD, GIVE ME THE COURAGE TO SHOW YOU YOU ARE NOT ALONE!"

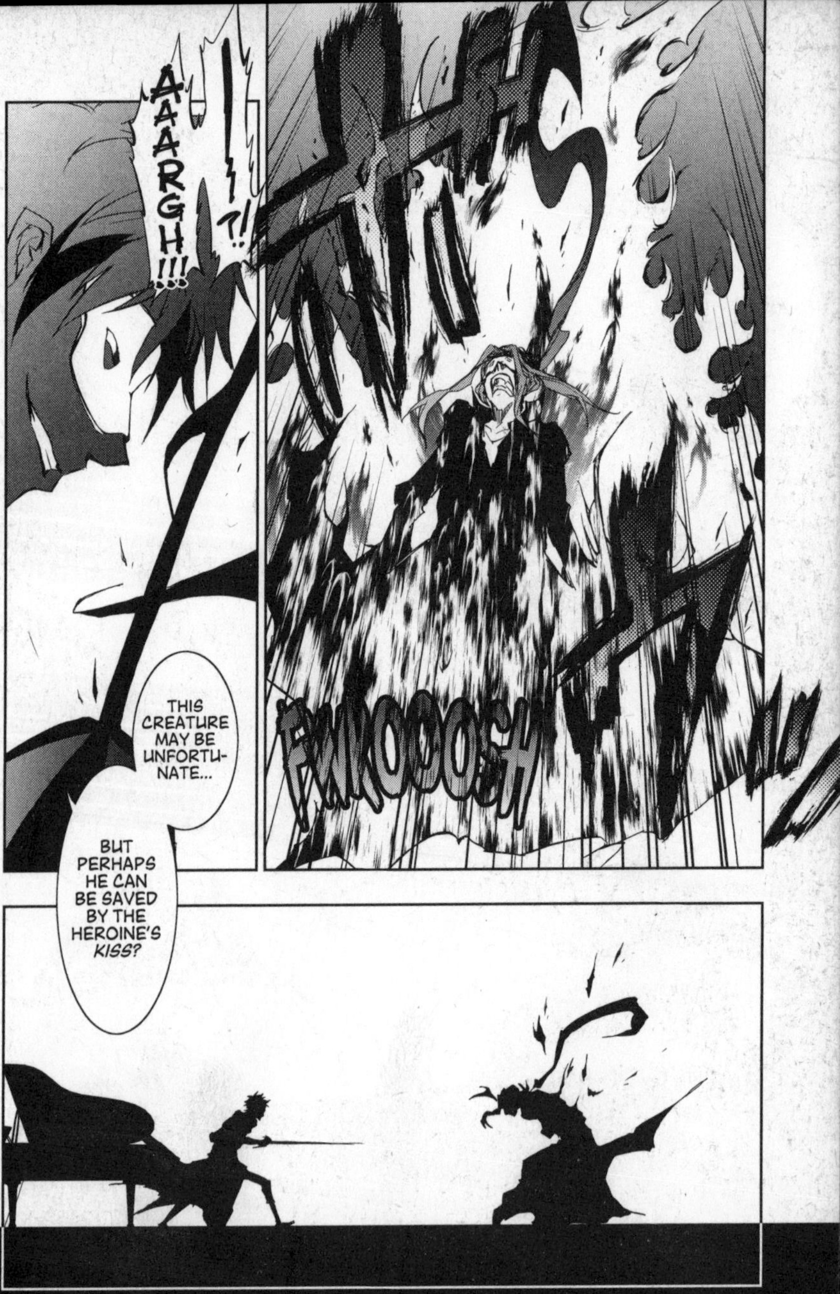
FWOOOSH
!!?
AAARGH!!!
THIS CREATURE MAY BE UNFORTU-NATE...
BUT PERHAPS HE CAN BE SAVED BY THE HEROINE'S *KISS*?

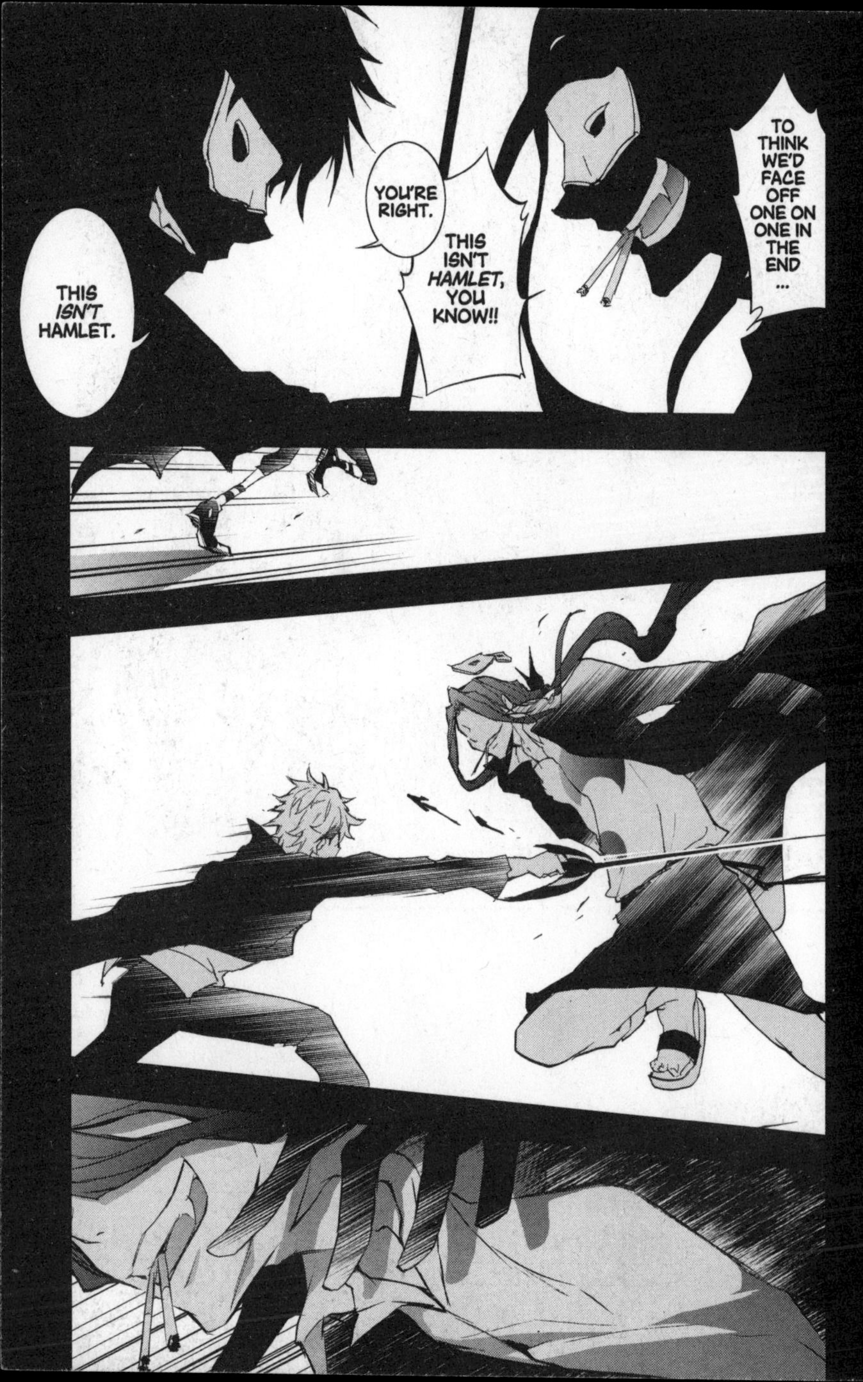

TO THINK WE'D FACE OFF ONE ON ONE IN THE END ...
YOU'RE RIGHT.
THIS ISN'T *HAMLET*, YOU KNOW!!
THIS *ISN'T* HAMLET.

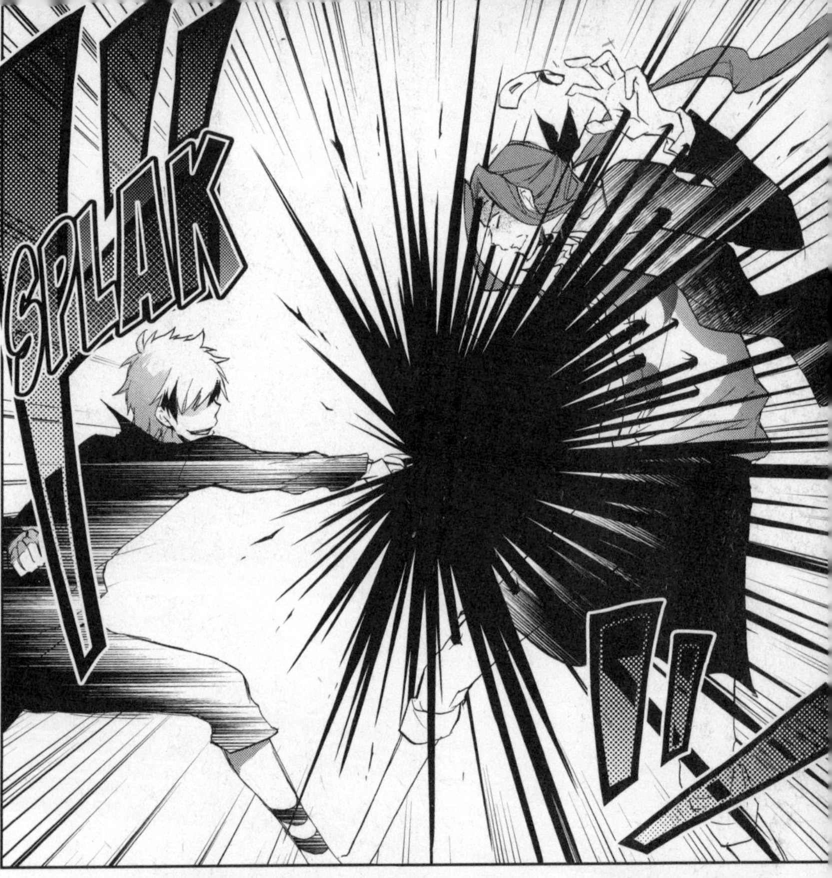
SPLAK

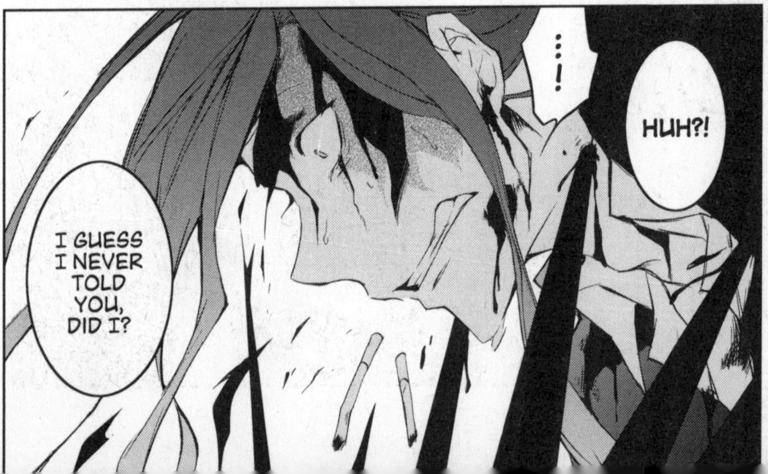
HUH?!
...!
I GUESS I NEVER TOLD YOU, DID I?

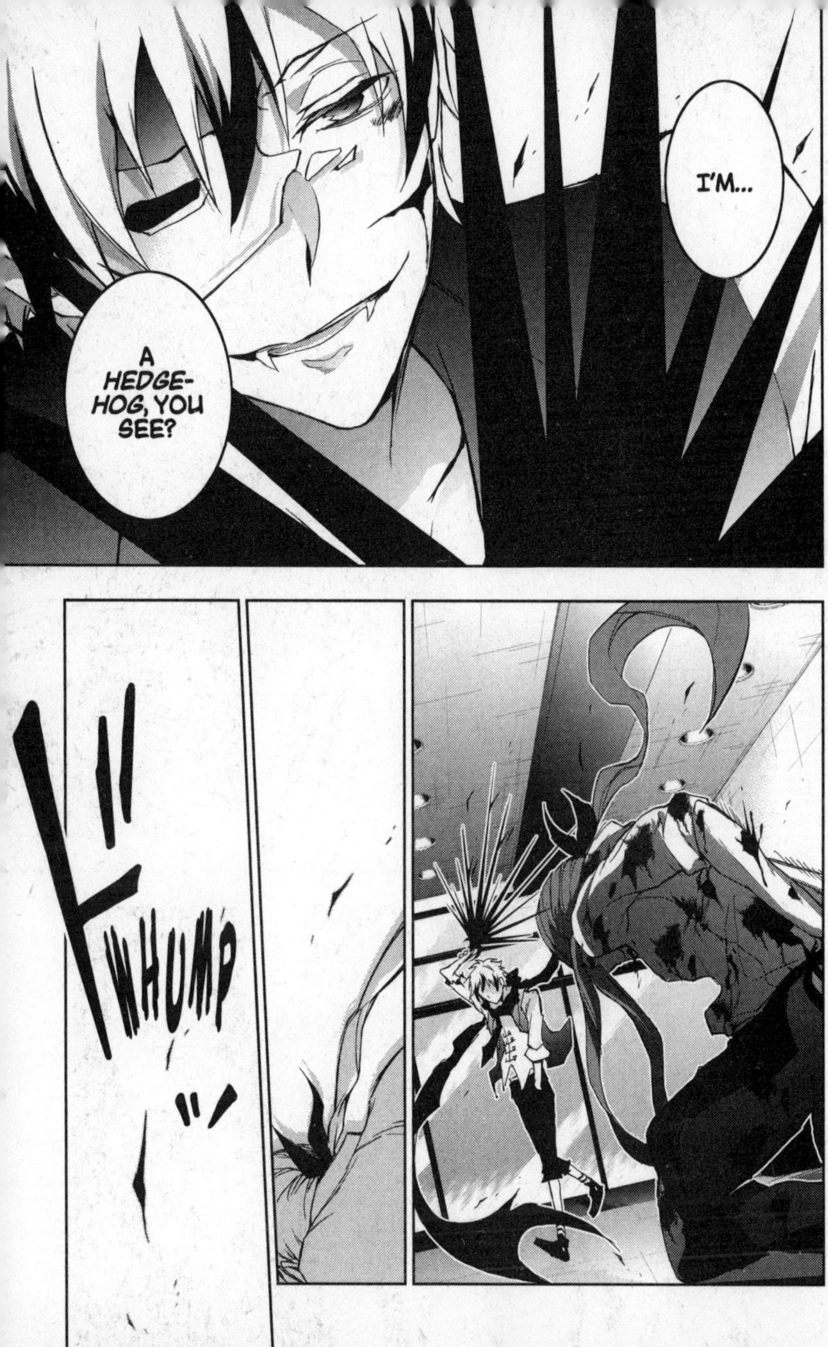
I'M...
A HEDGE-HOG, YOU SEE?
WHUMP

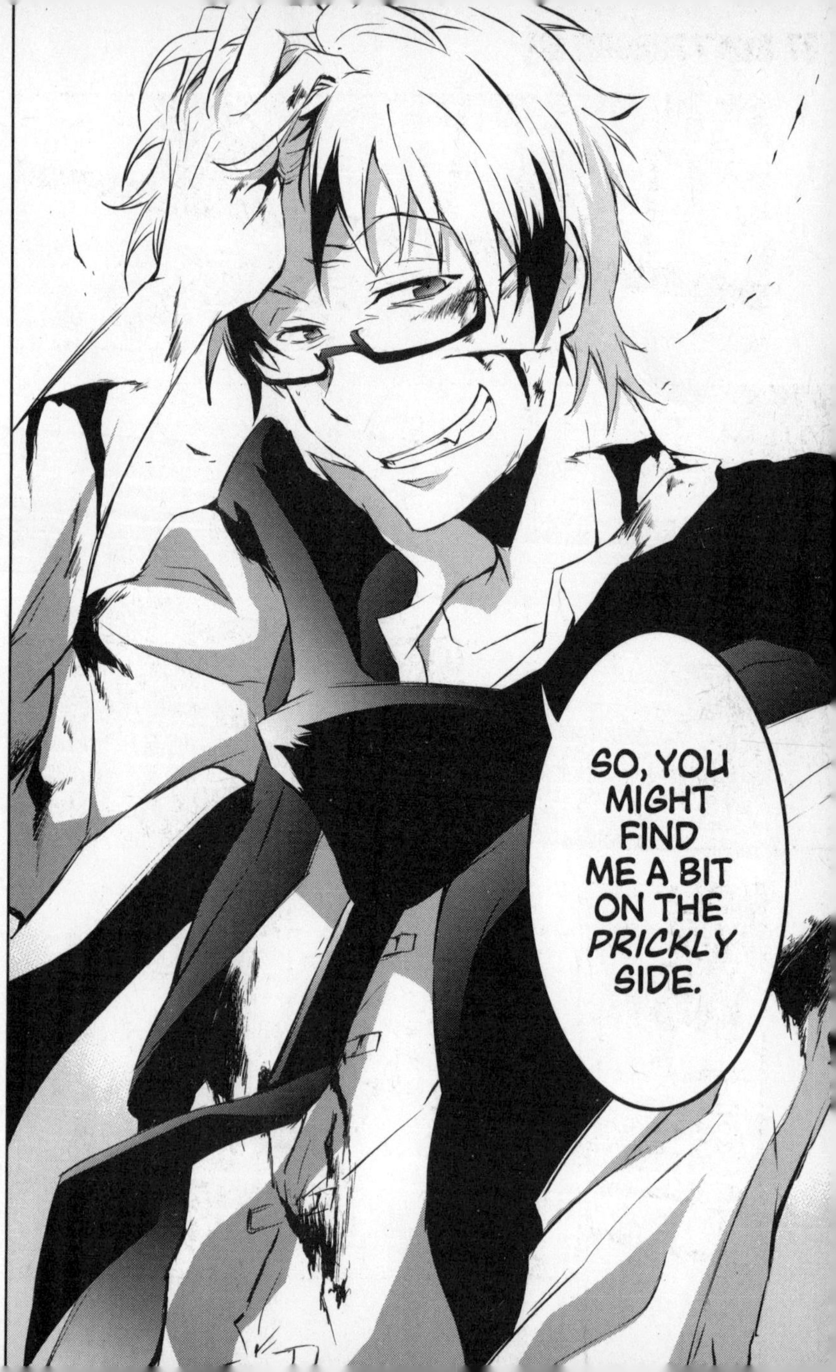
SO, YOU MIGHT FIND ME A BIT ON THE *PRICKLY* SIDE.

# 37. DON'T FORGIVE ME

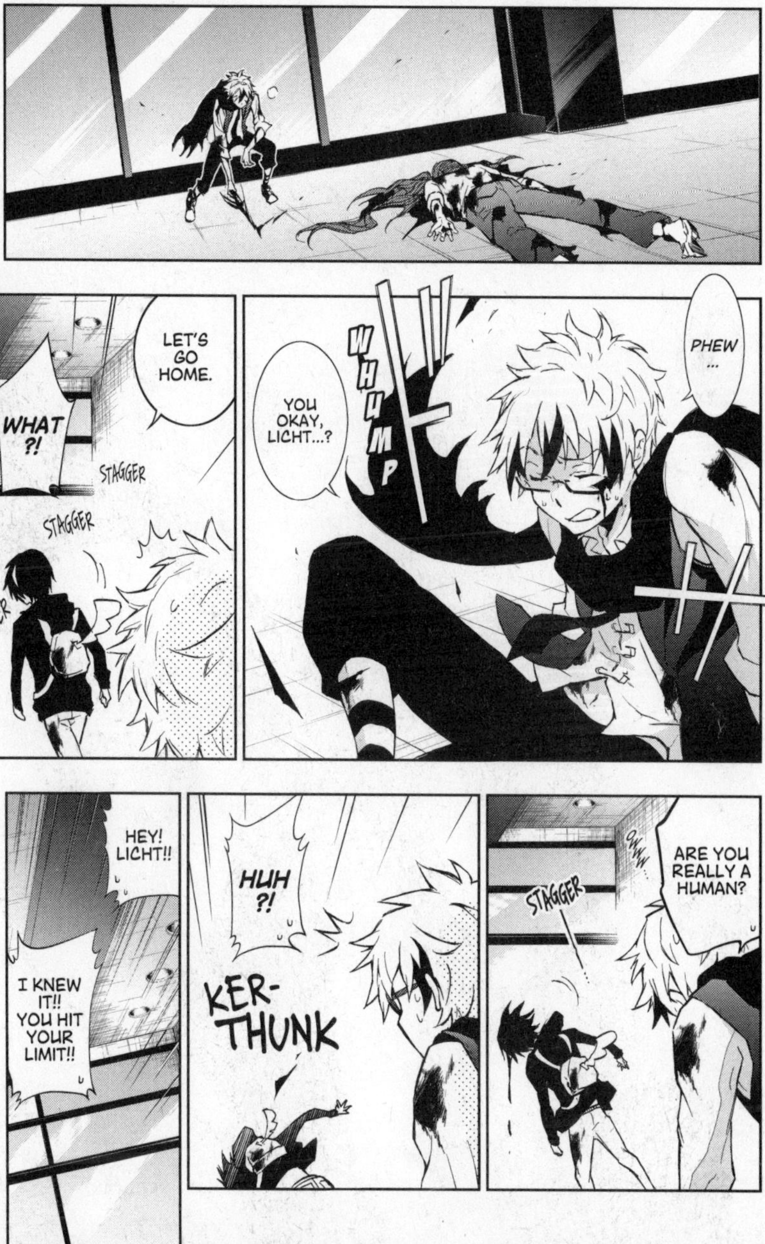
PHEW ...
WHUMP
YOU OKAY, LICHT...?
LET'S GO HOME.
WHAT ?!
STAGGER
STAGGER
STAGGER
ARE YOU REALLY A HUMAN?
OWW...
STAGGER
HUH ?!
KER-THUNK
HEY! LICHT!!
I KNEW IT!! YOU HIT YOUR LIMIT!!

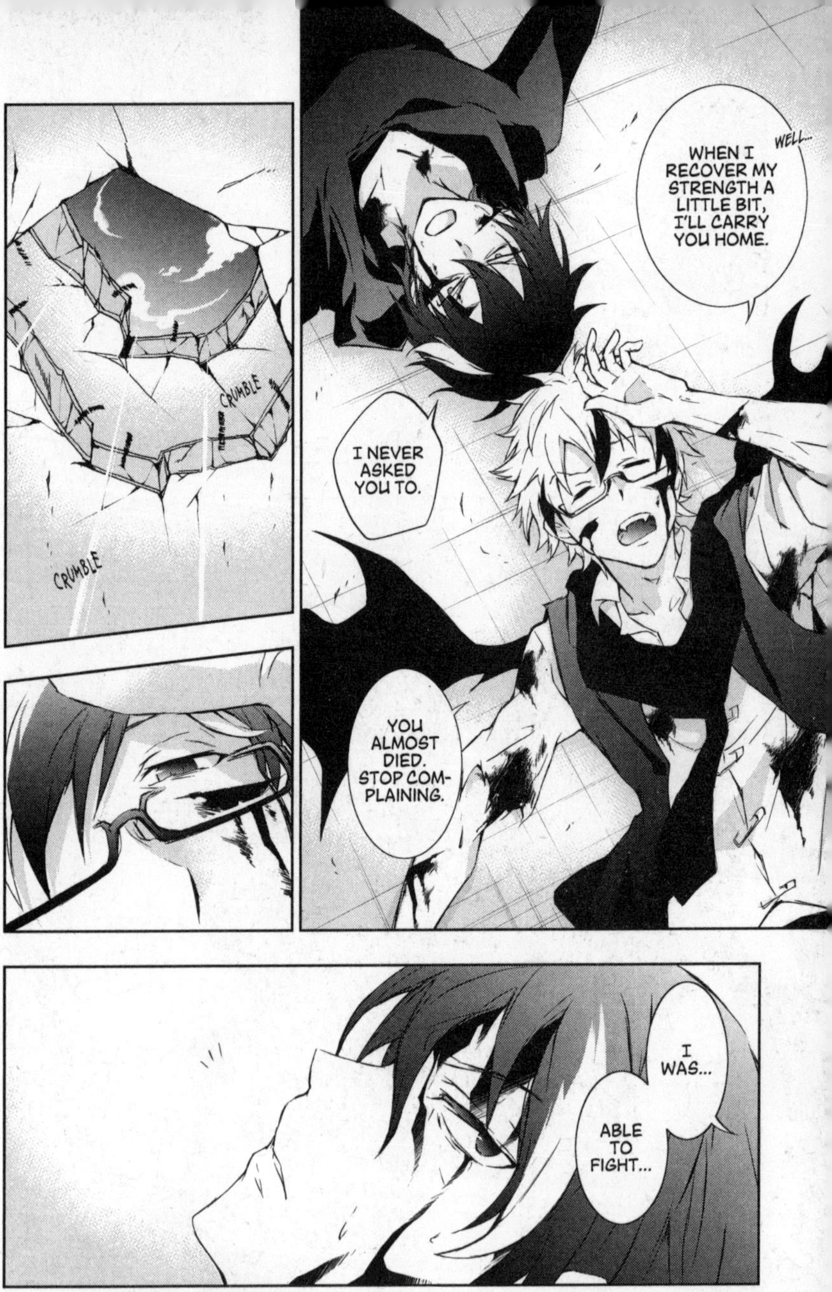
WELL...
WHEN I RECOVER MY STRENGTH A LITTLE BIT, I'LL CARRY YOU HOME.
I NEVER ASKED YOU TO.
YOU ALMOST DIED. STOP COMPLAINING.
CRUMBLE
CRUMBLE
I WAS...
ABLE TO FIGHT...

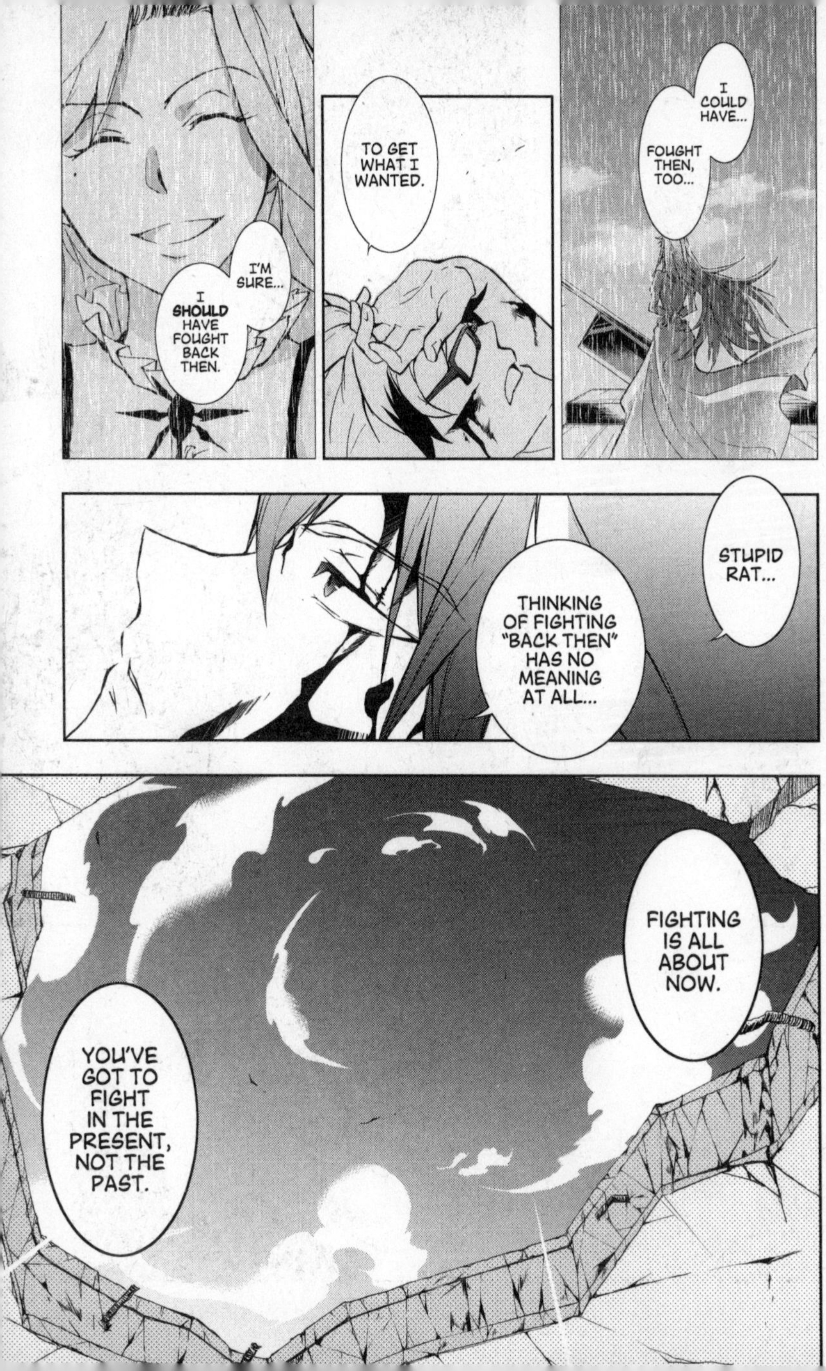
I COULD HAVE...
FOUGHT THEN, TOO...
TO GET WHAT I WANTED.
I'M SURE...
I **SHOULD** HAVE FOUGHT BACK THEN.
STUPID RAT...
THINKING OF FIGHTING "BACK THEN" HAS NO MEANING AT ALL...
FIGHTING IS ALL ABOUT NOW.
YOU'VE GOT TO FIGHT IN THE PRESENT, NOT THE PAST.

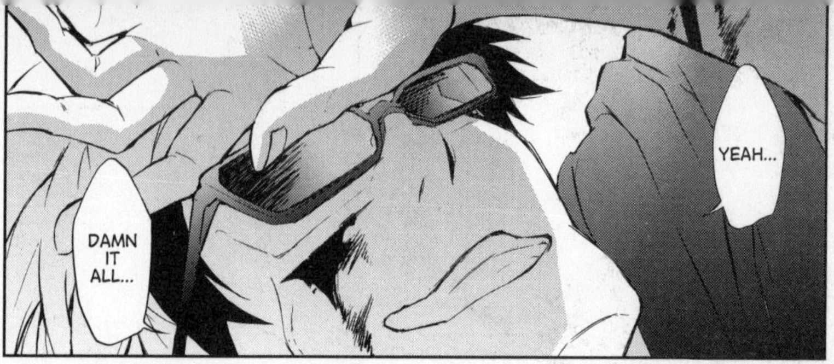
YEAH...
DAMN IT ALL...

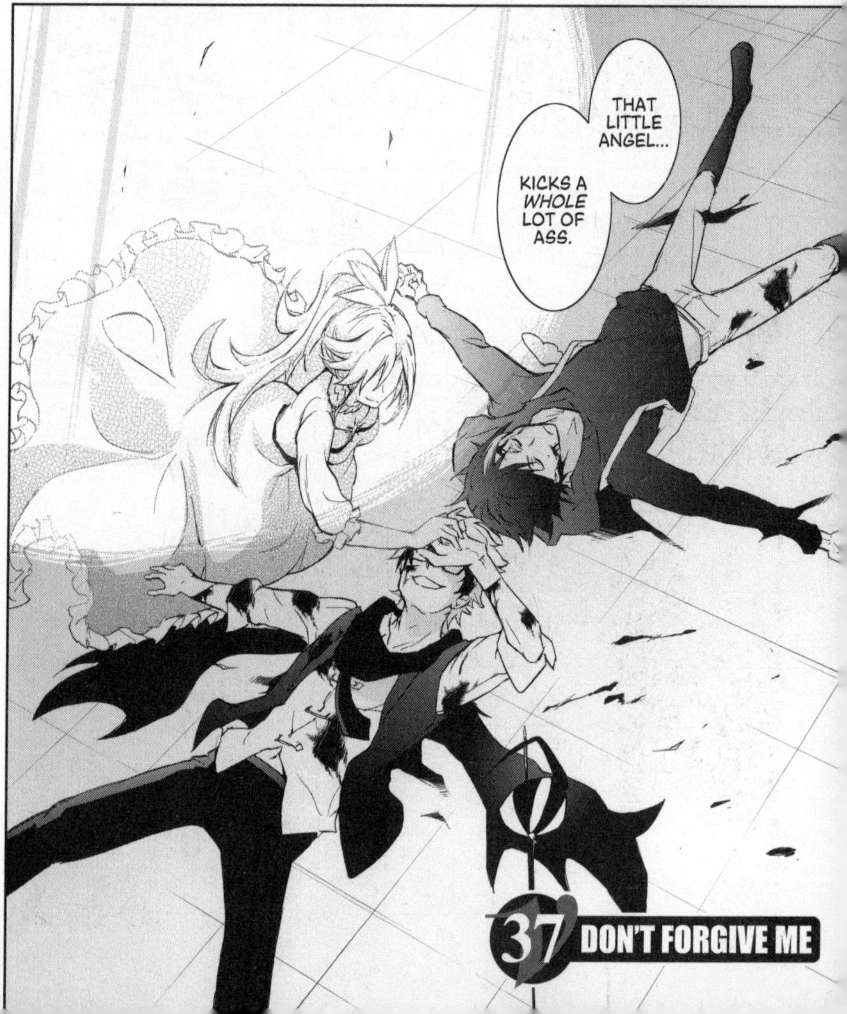
THAT LITTLE ANGEL...
KICKS A *WHOLE* LOT OF ASS.

# 37 DON'T FORGIVE ME

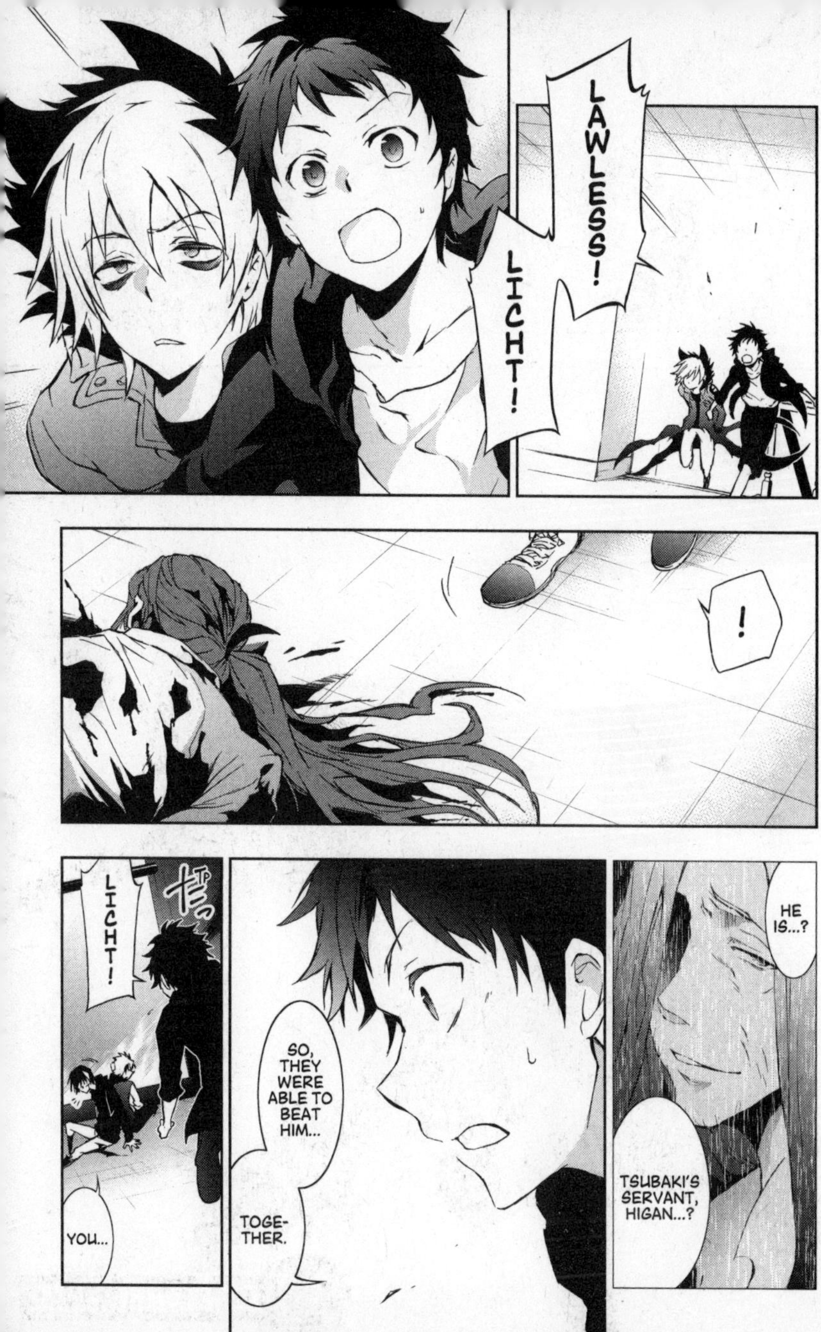
LAWLESS!
LICHT!
!
HE IS...?
TSUBAKI'S SERVANT, HIGAN...?
SO, THEY WERE ABLE TO BEAT HIM...
TOGE-THER.
LICHT!
YOU...

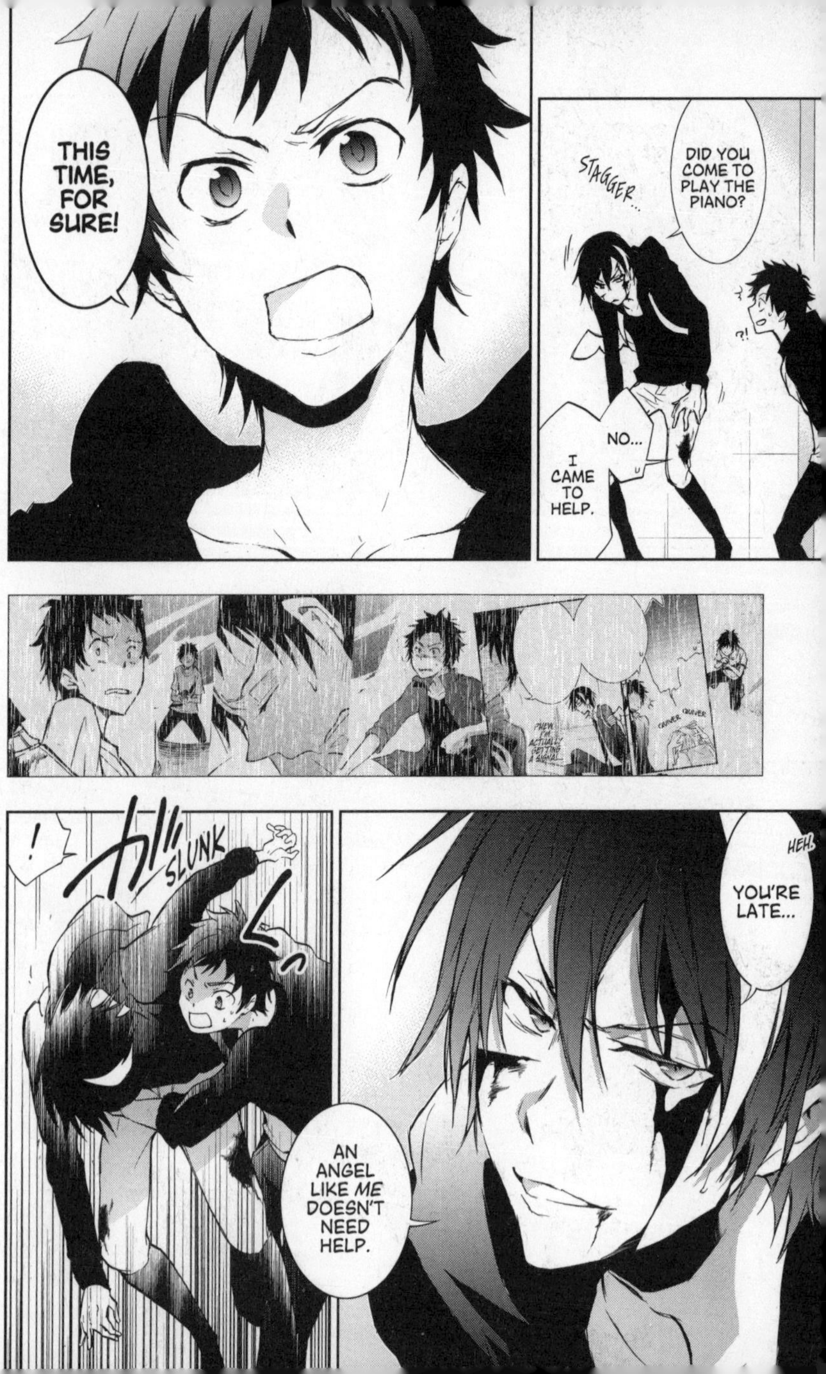
DID YOU COME TO PLAY THE PIANO?
STAGGER...
?!
NO...
I CAME TO HELP.
THIS TIME, FOR SURE!
QUIVER QUIVER
PHEW I'M ACTUALLY GETTING A SIGNAL
HEH.
YOU'RE LATE...
AN ANGEL LIKE *ME* DOESN'T NEED HELP.
!
SLUNK

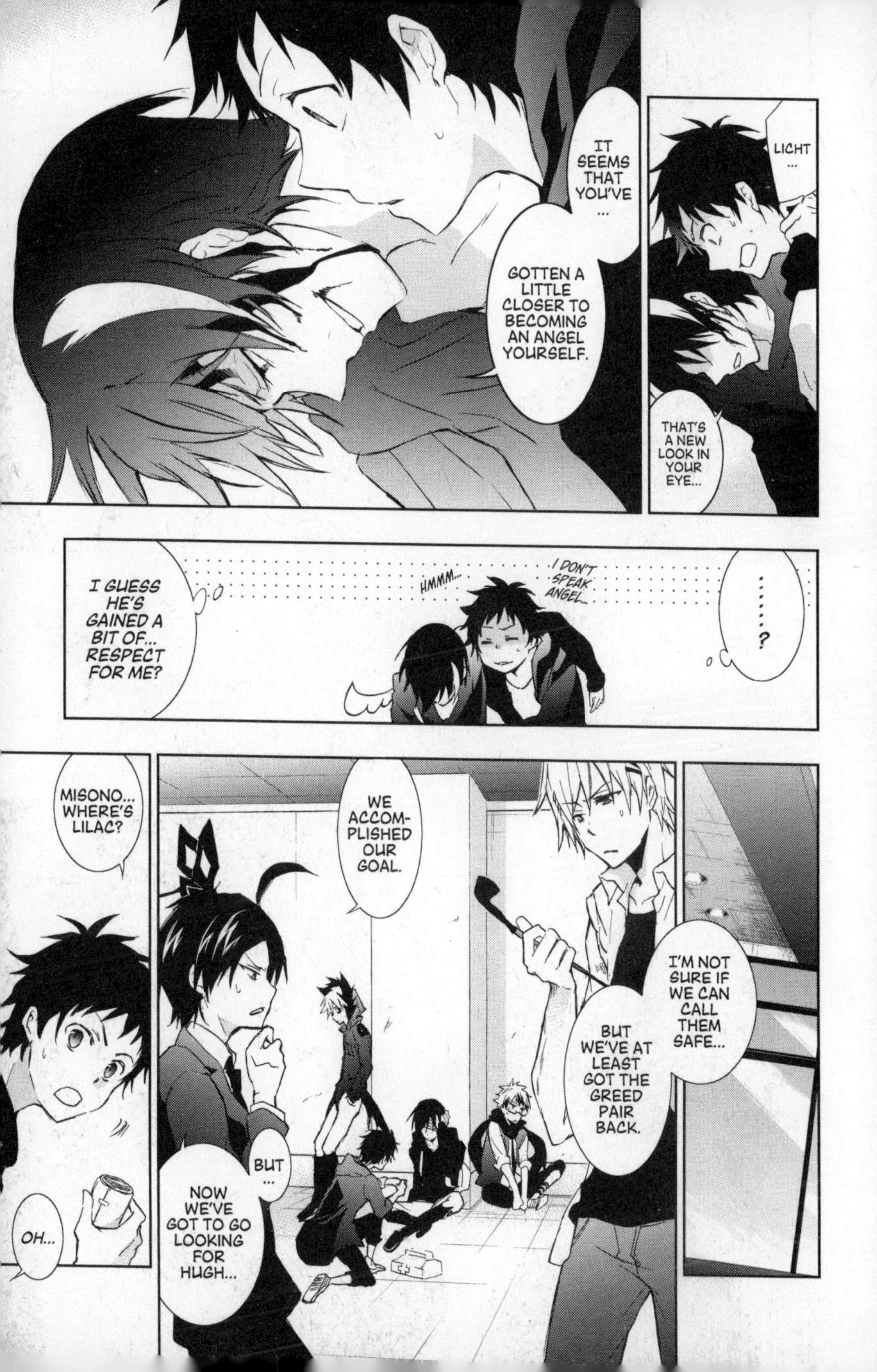
LICHT ...
THAT'S A NEW LOOK IN YOUR EYE...
IT SEEMS THAT YOU'VE ...
GOTTEN A LITTLE CLOSER TO BECOMING AN ANGEL YOURSELF.
......?
I DON'T SPEAK ANGEL...
HMMM...
I GUESS HE'S GAINED A BIT OF... RESPECT FOR ME?
WE ACCOMPLISHED OUR GOAL.
I'M NOT SURE IF WE CAN CALL THEM SAFE...
BUT WE'VE AT LEAST GOT THE GREED PAIR BACK.
BUT ...
NOW WE'VE GOT TO GO LOOKING FOR HUGH...
MISONO... WHERE'S LILAC?
OH...

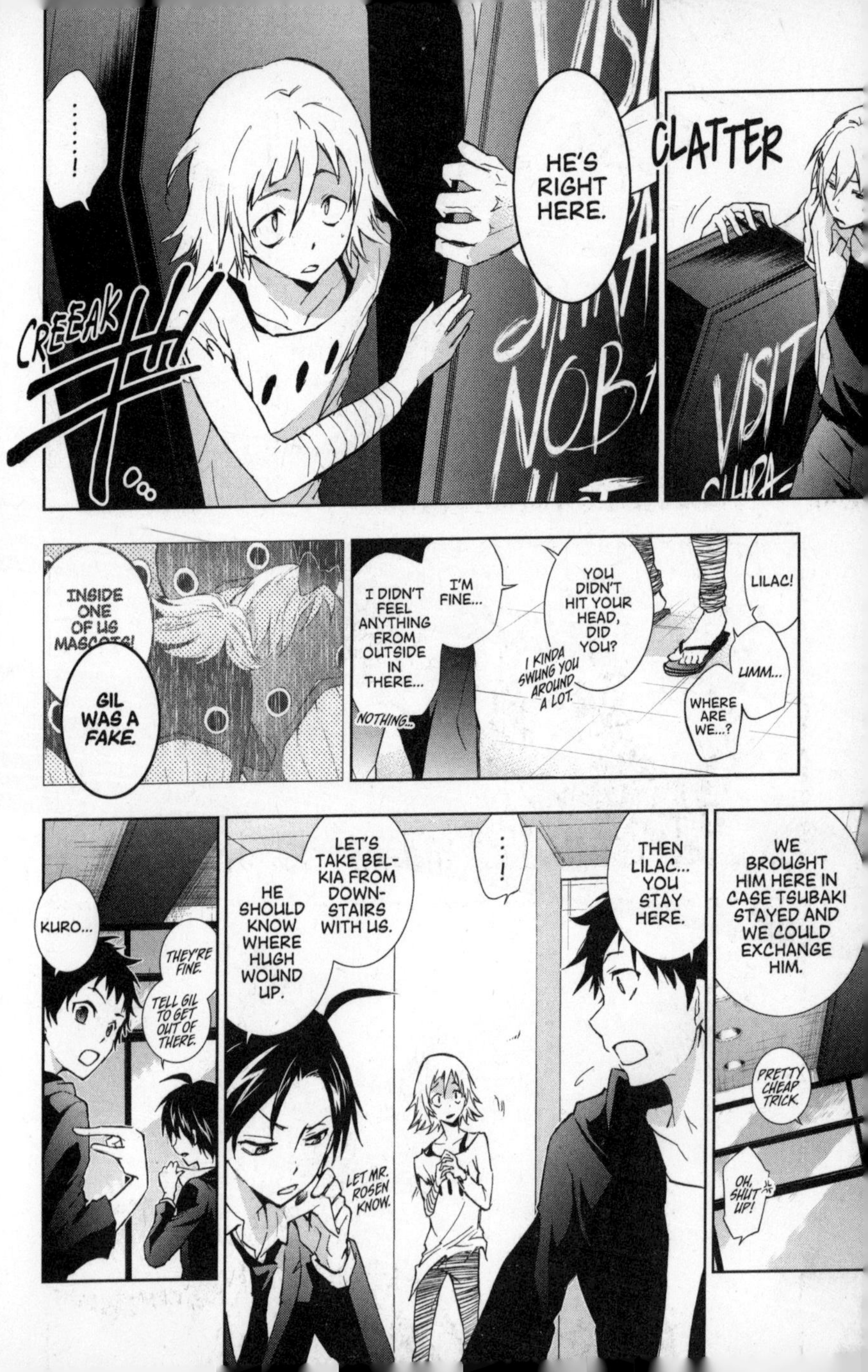
CLATTER
VISIT
HE'S RIGHT HERE.
……!
CREEEAK
LILAC!
UMM...
WHERE ARE WE...?
YOU DIDN'T HIT YOUR HEAD, DID YOU?
I KINDA SWUNG YOU AROUND A LOT.
I'M FINE...
I DIDN'T FEEL ANYTHING FROM OUTSIDE IN THERE...
NOTHING...
INSIDE ONE OF US MASCOTS!
GIL WAS A FAKE.
WE BROUGHT HIM HERE IN CASE TSUBAKI STAYED AND WE COULD EXCHANGE HIM.
PRETTY CHEAP TRICK.
OH, SHUT UP!
THEN LILAC... YOU STAY HERE.
……!
LET'S TAKE BEL-KIA FROM DOWN-STAIRS WITH US.
HE SHOULD KNOW WHERE HUGH WOUND UP.
LET MR. ROSEN KNOW.
KURO...
THEY'RE FINE.
TELL GIL TO GET OUT OF THERE.

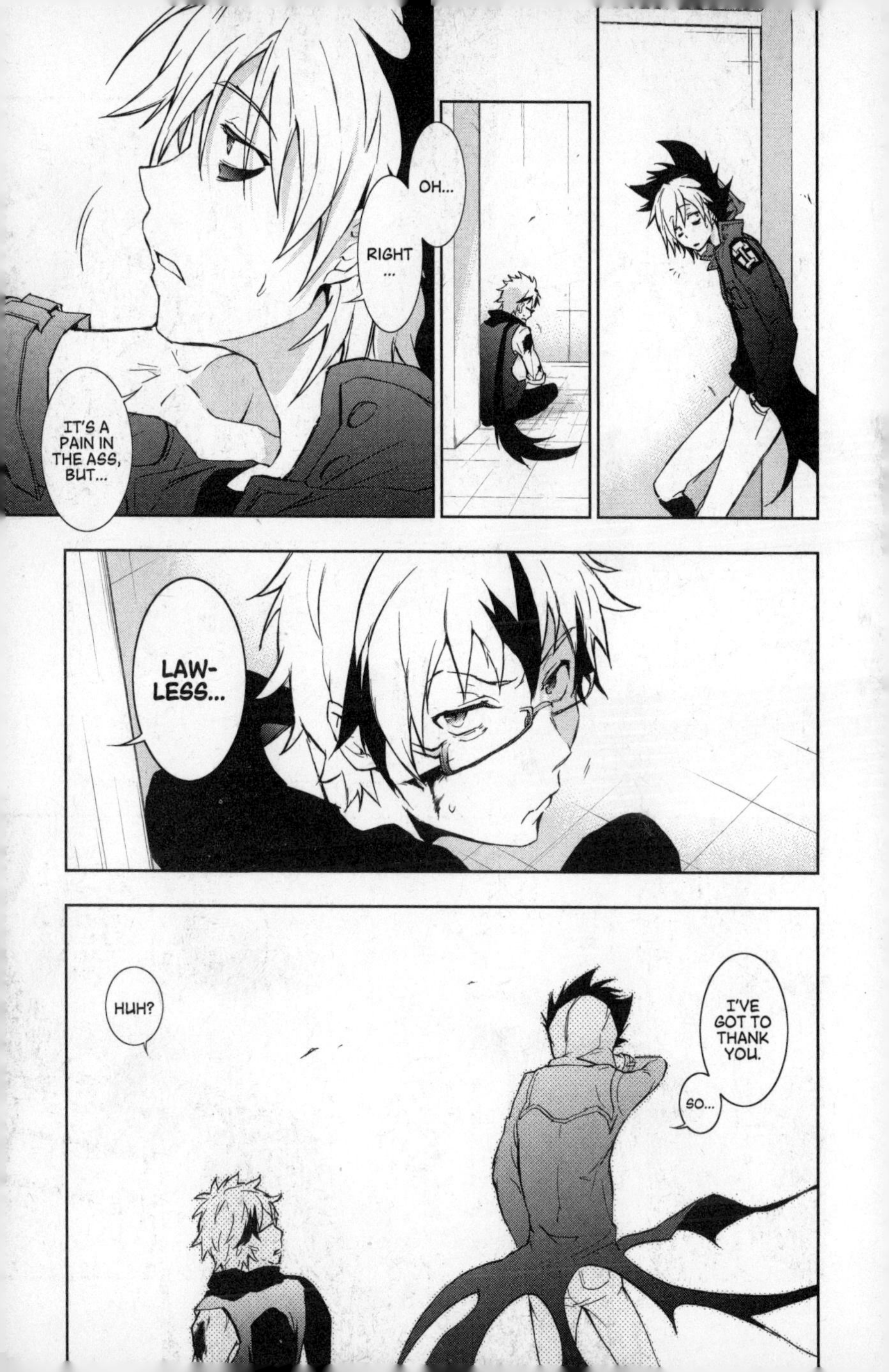
OH...
RIGHT ...
IT'S A PAIN IN THE ASS, BUT...
LAW-LESS...
I'VE GOT TO THANK YOU.
SO...
HUH?

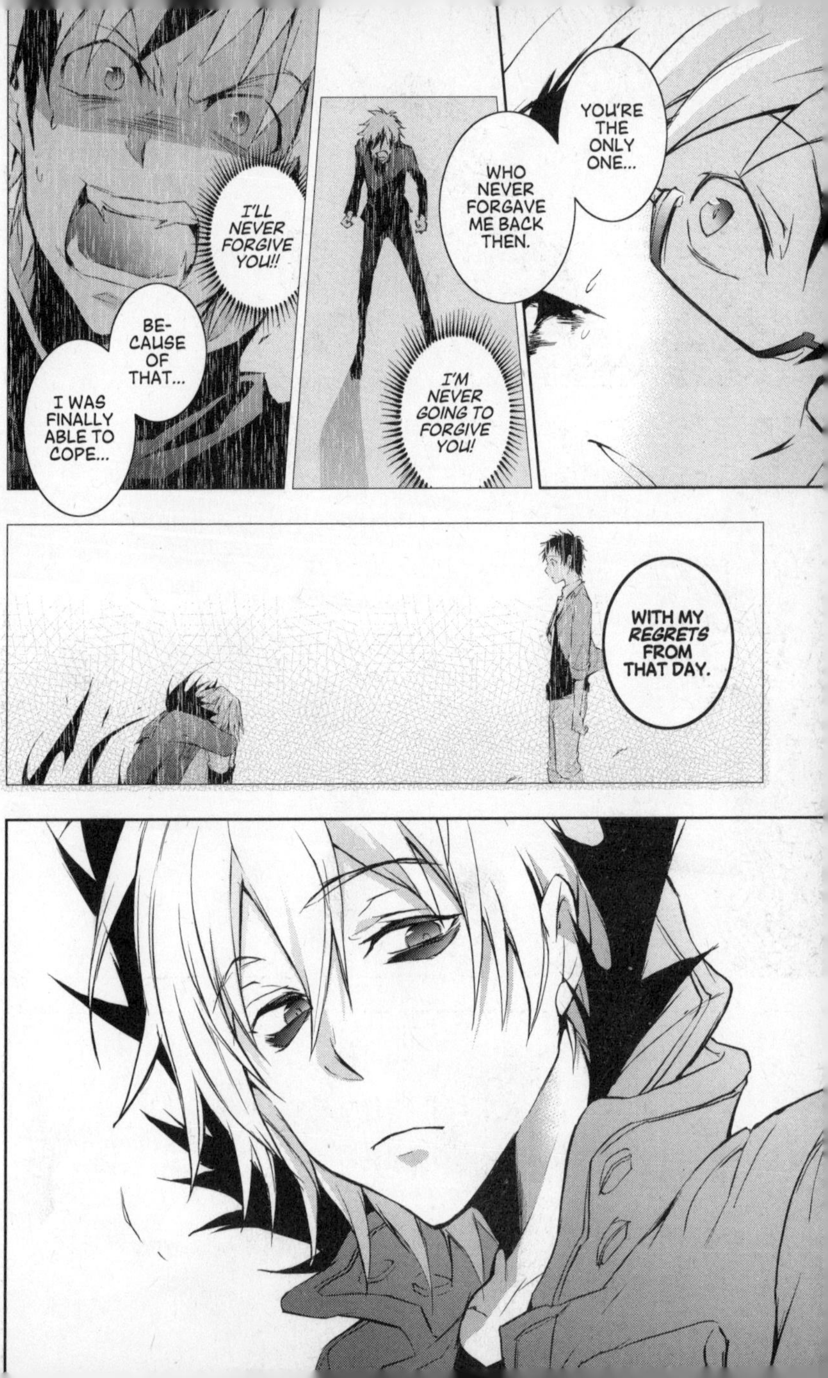
YOU'RE THE ONLY ONE...
WHO NEVER FORGAVE ME BACK THEN.
I'M NEVER GOING TO FORGIVE YOU!
I'LL NEVER FORGIVE YOU!!
BE-CAUSE OF THAT...
I WAS FINALLY ABLE TO COPE...
WITH MY *REGRETS* FROM THAT DAY.

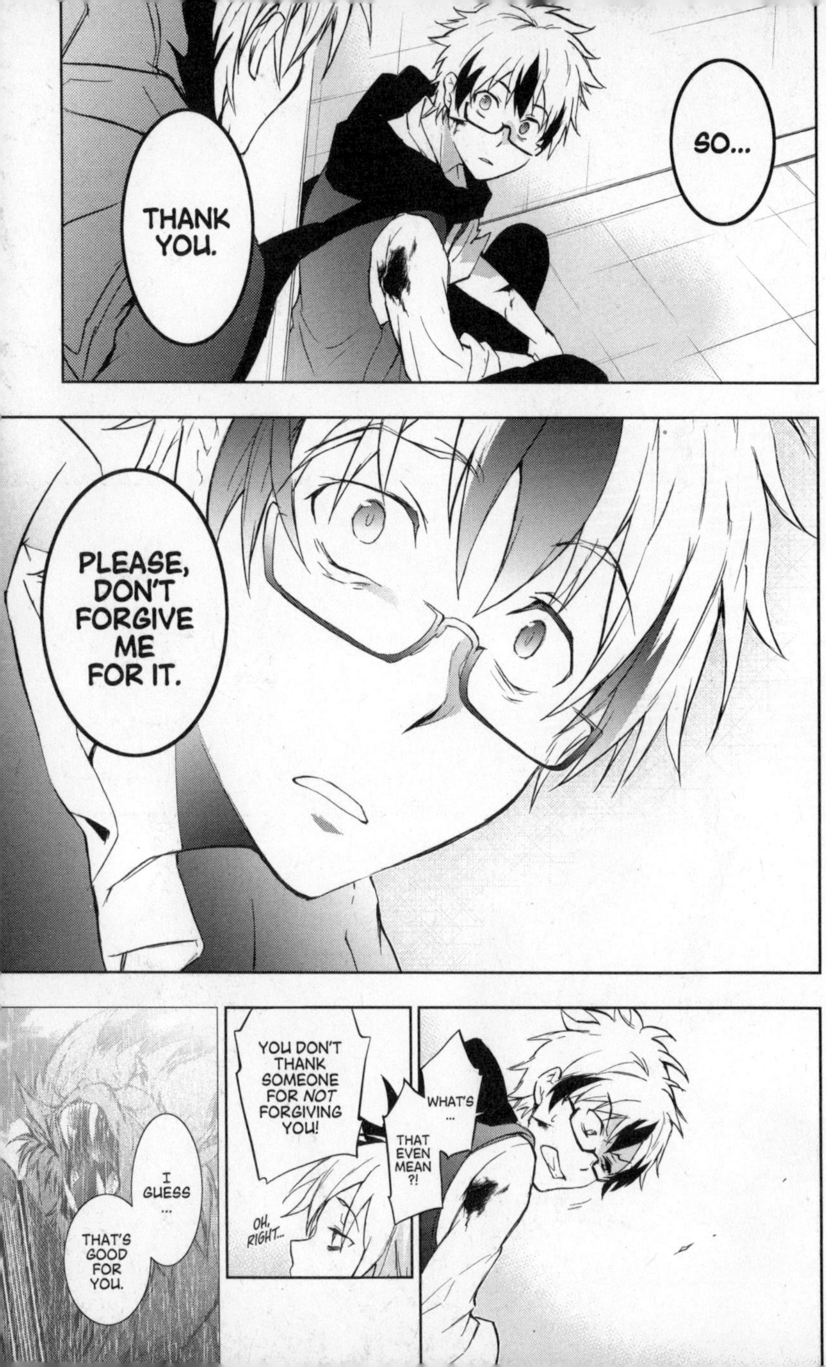
SO...
THANK YOU.
PLEASE, DON'T FORGIVE ME FOR IT.
WHAT'S ... THAT EVEN MEAN?!
YOU DON'T THANK SOMEONE FOR *NOT* FORGIVING YOU!
OH, RIGHT...
I GUESS ... THAT'S GOOD FOR YOU.

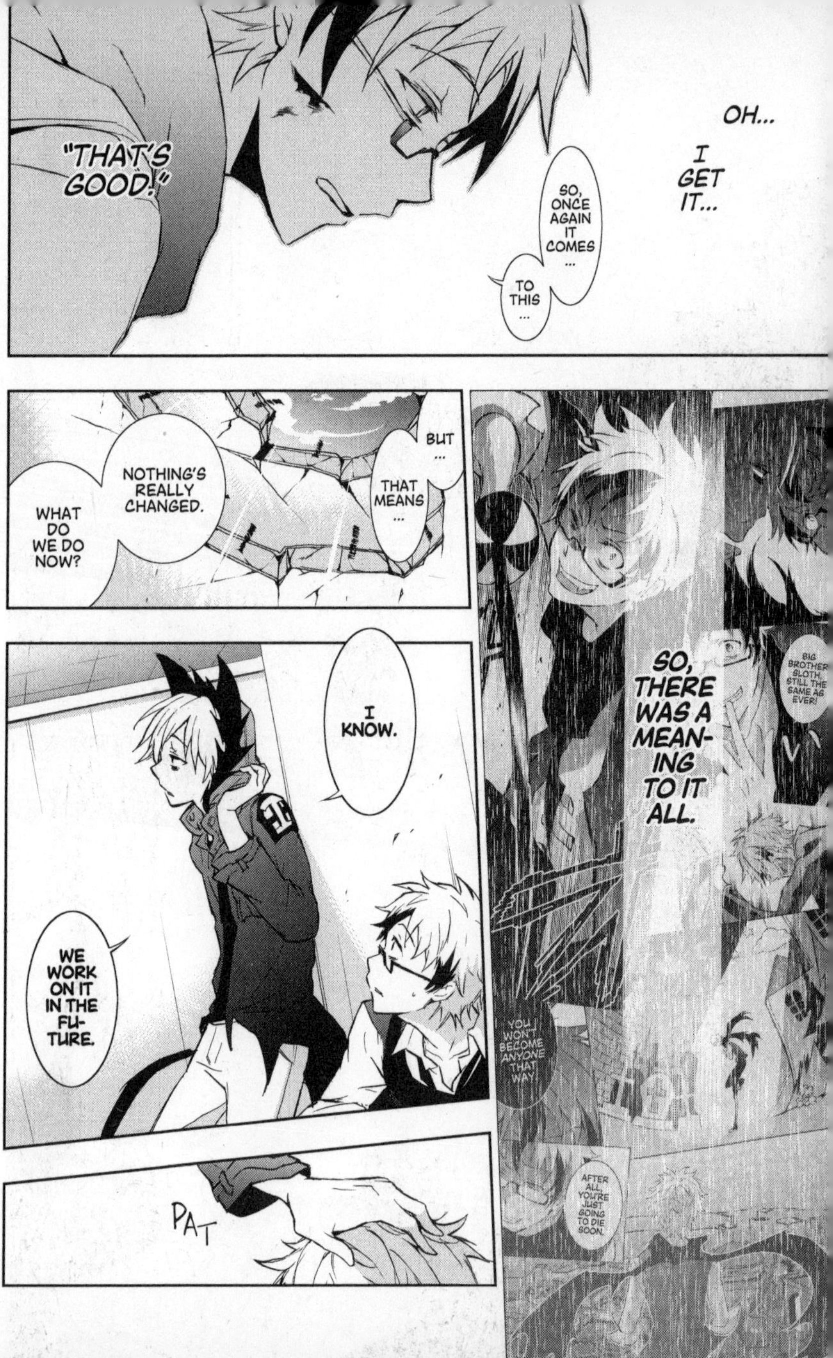
OH...
I GET IT...
SO, ONCE AGAIN IT COMES...
TO THIS...
"THAT'S GOOD!"
BIG BROTHER SLOTH, STILL THE SAME AS EVER!
SO, THERE WAS A MEANING TO IT ALL.
YOU WON'T BECOME ANYONE THAT WAY.
AFTER ALL, YOU'RE JUST GOING TO DIE SOON.
BUT...
THAT MEANS...
NOTHING'S REALLY CHANGED.
WHAT DO WE DO NOW?
I KNOW.
WE WORK ON IT IN THE FUTURE.
PAT

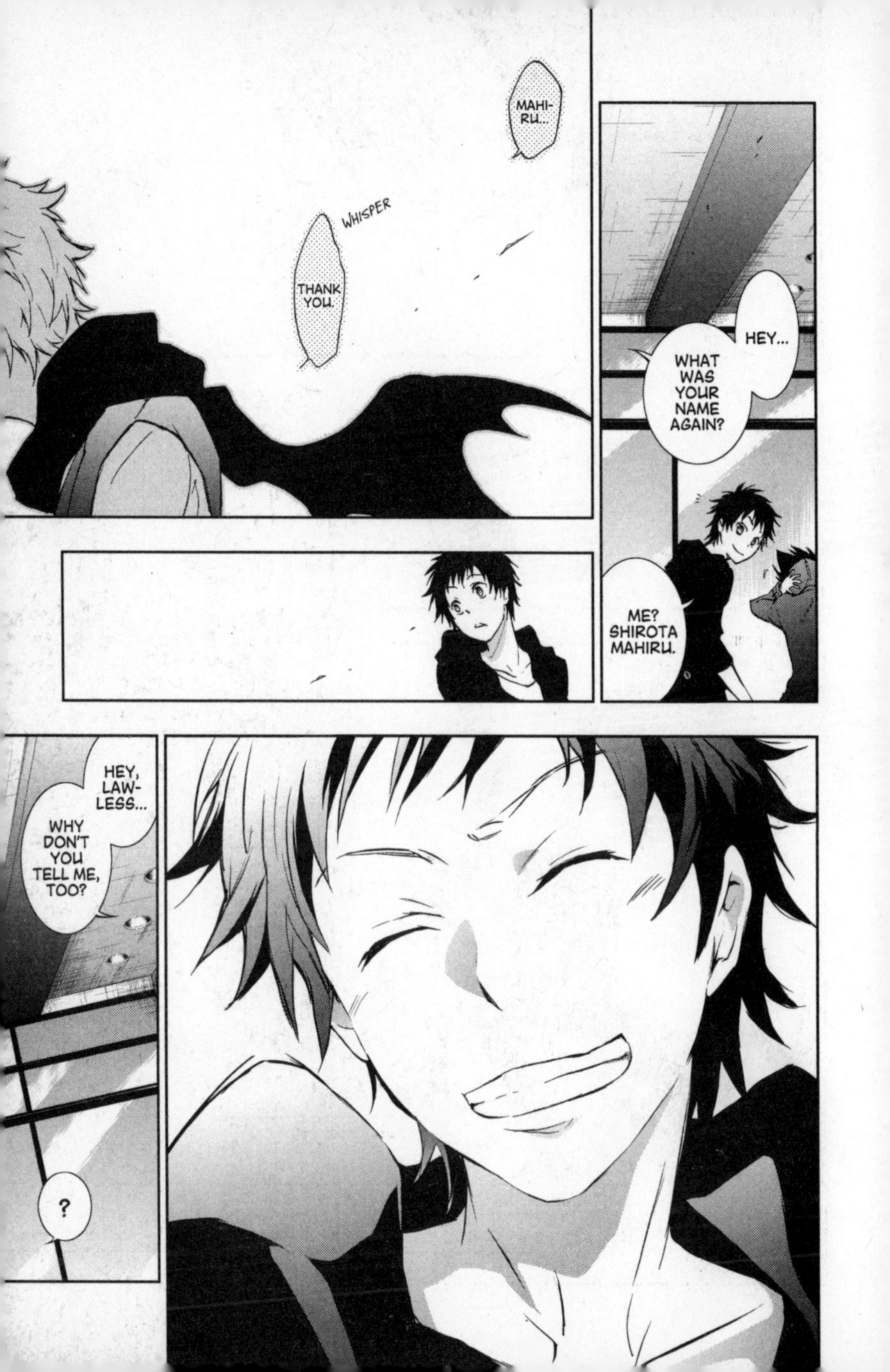
HEY...
WHAT WAS YOUR NAME AGAIN?
ME? SHIROTA MAHIRU.
MAHI-RU...
WHISPER
THANK YOU.
HEY, LAW-LESS...
WHY DON'T YOU TELL ME, TOO?
?

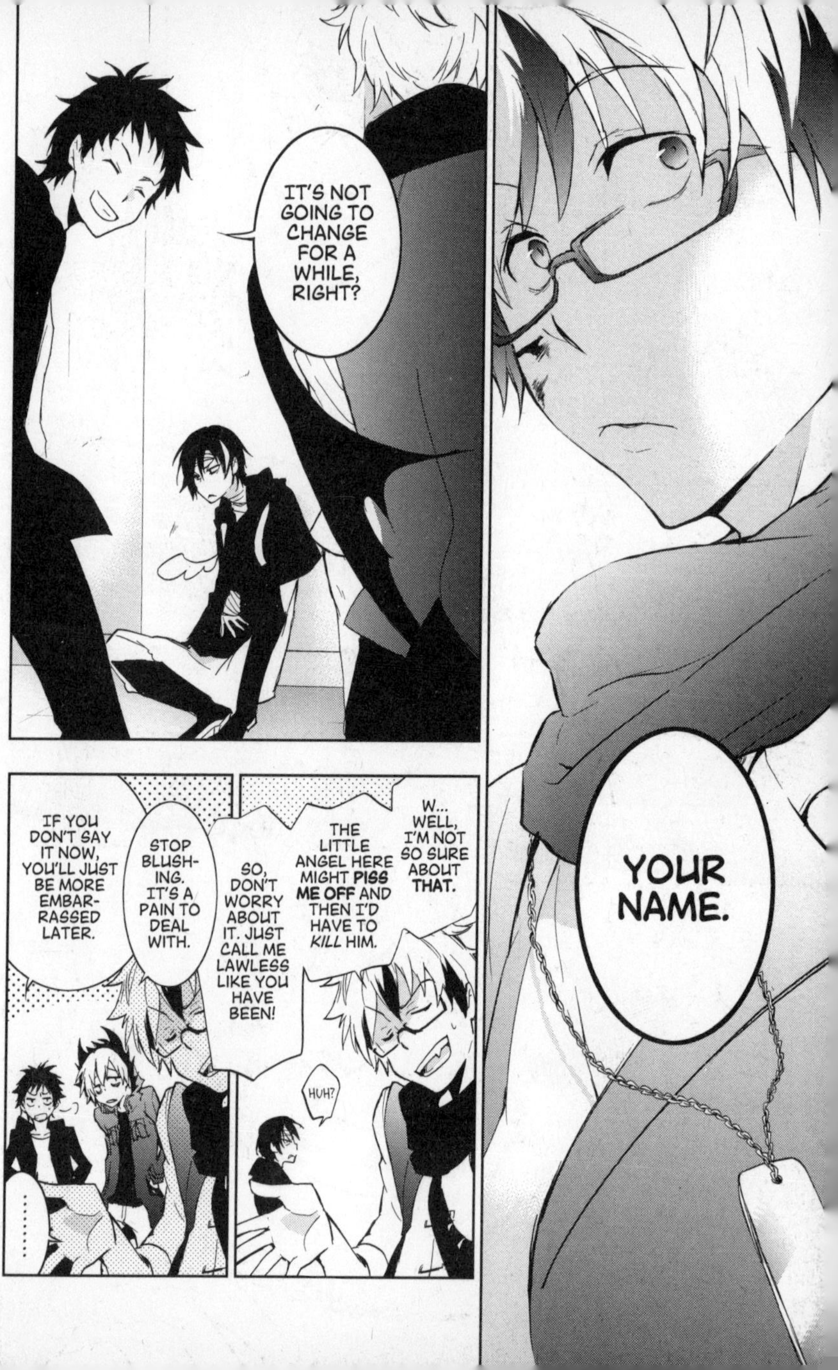
YOUR NAME.
IT'S NOT GOING TO CHANGE FOR A WHILE, RIGHT?
W... WELL, I'M NOT SO SURE ABOUT THAT.
THE LITTLE ANGEL HERE MIGHT PISS ME OFF AND THEN I'D HAVE TO KILL HIM.
SO, DON'T WORRY ABOUT IT. JUST CALL ME LAWLESS LIKE YOU HAVE BEEN!
HUH?
STOP BLUSHING. IT'S A PAIN TO DEAL WITH.
IF YOU DON'T SAY IT NOW, YOU'LL JUST BE MORE EMBARRASSED LATER.
......

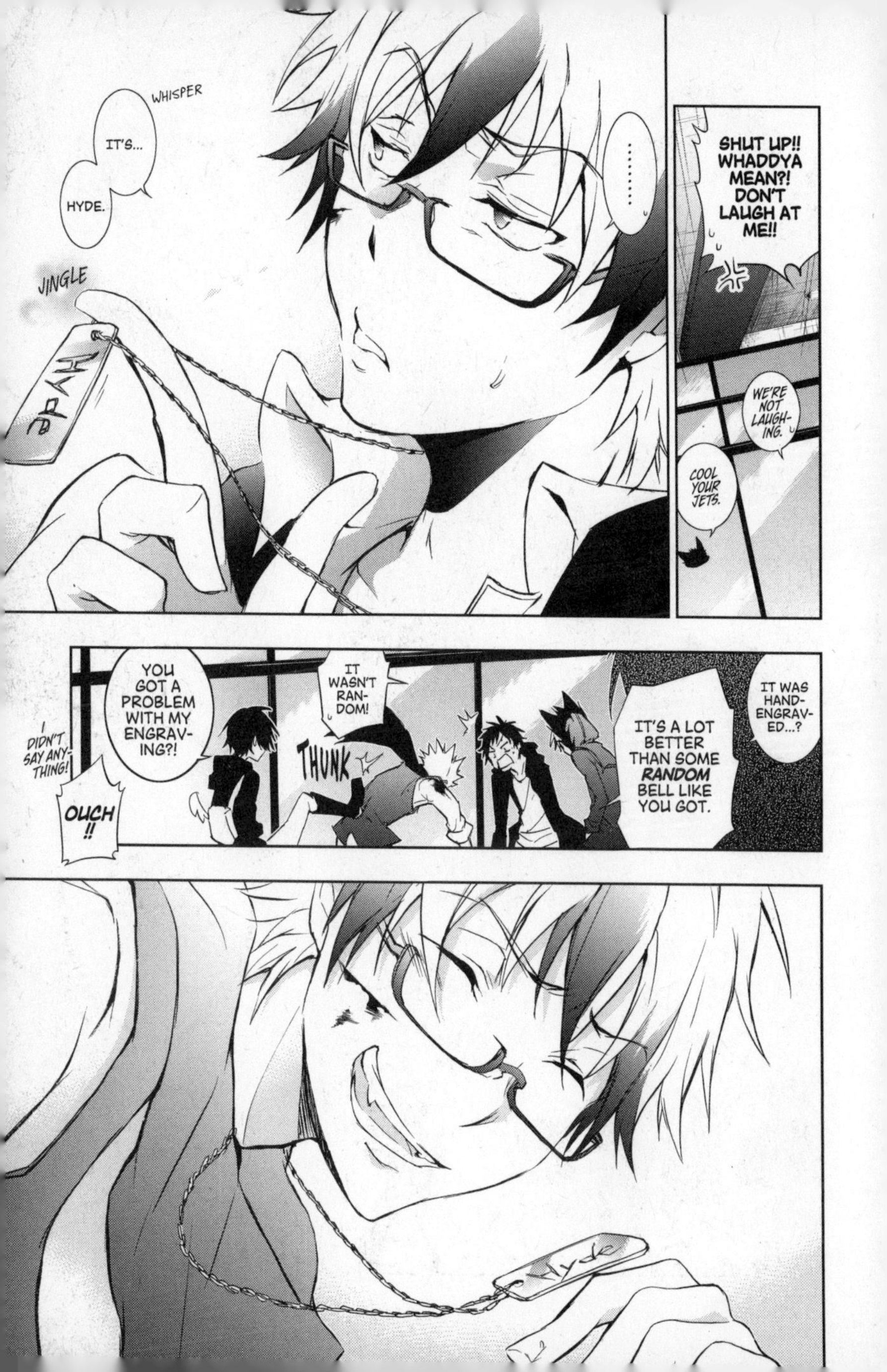
SHUT UP!! WHADDYA MEAN?! DON'T LAUGH AT ME!!
WE'RE NOT LAUGHING.
COOL YOUR JETS.
......
WHISPER
IT'S... HYDE.
JINGLE
Hyde
IT WAS HAND-ENGRAVED...?
IT'S A LOT BETTER THAN SOME RANDOM BELL LIKE YOU GOT.
IT WASN'T RANDOM!
THUNK
YOU GOT A PROBLEM WITH MY ENGRAVING?!
I DIDN'T SAY ANYTHING!
OUCH!!
Hyde

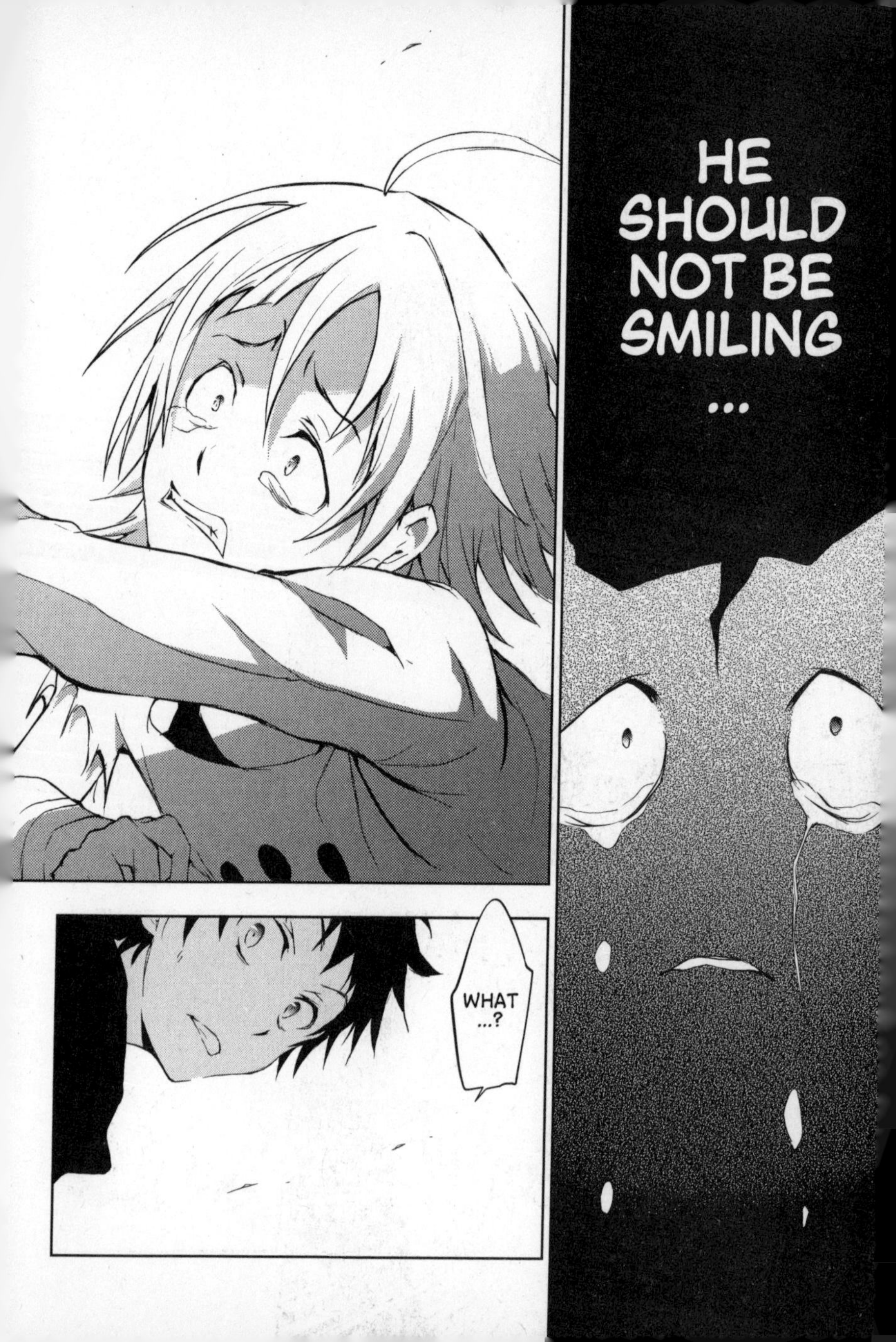
HE SHOULD NOT BE SMILING ...
WHAT ...?

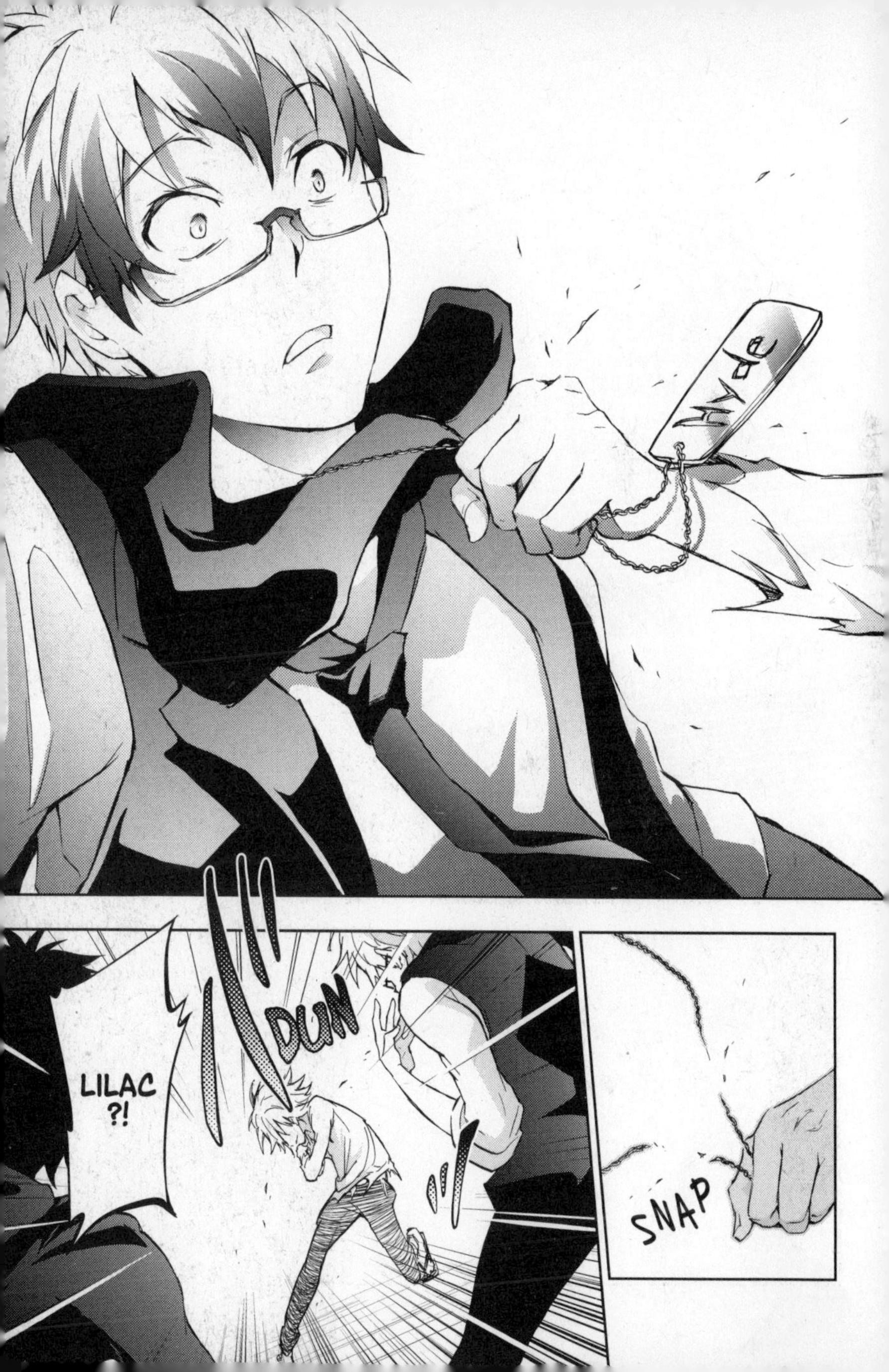
SNAP
DUN
LILAC ?!

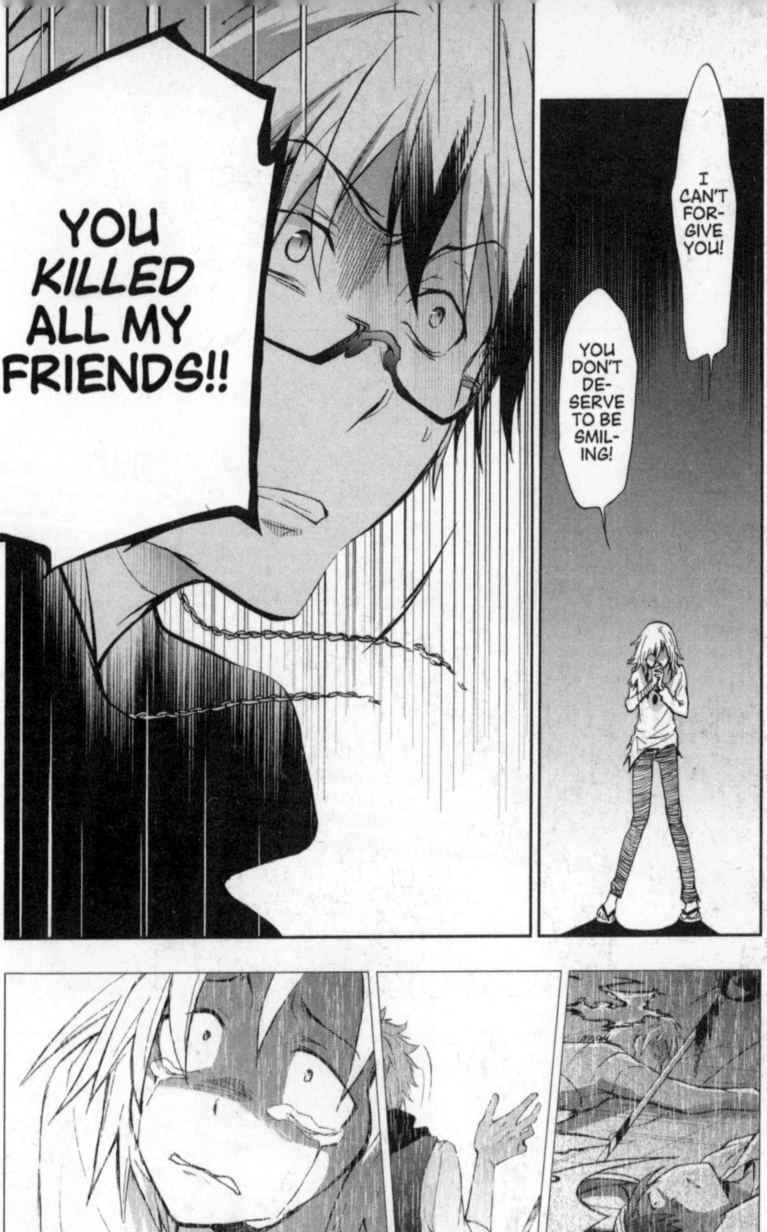
I CAN'T FORGIVE YOU!
YOU DON'T DESERVE TO BE SMILING!
YOU *KILLED* ALL MY FRIENDS!!

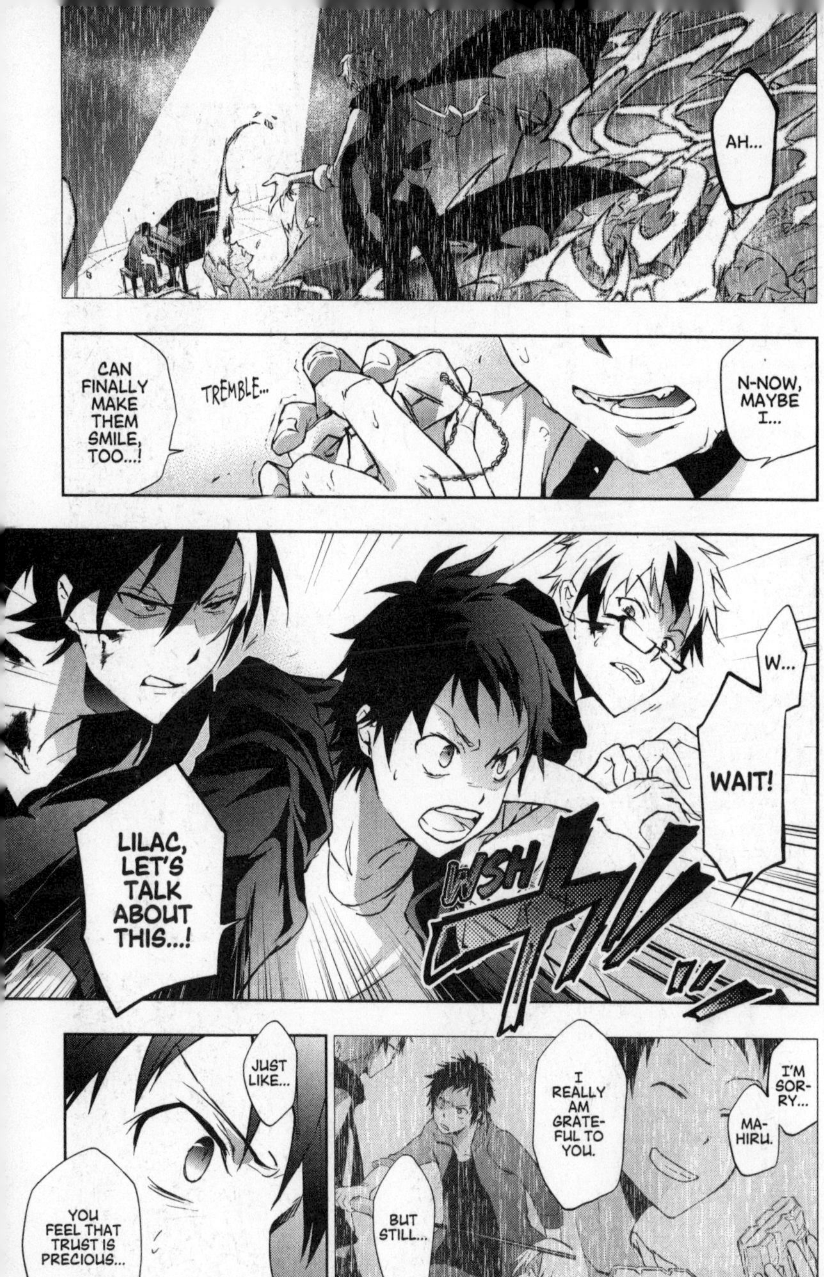
AH...
N-NOW, MAYBE I...
TREMBLE...
CAN FINALLY MAKE THEM SMILE, TOO...!
W...
WAIT!
WSH
LILAC, LET'S TALK ABOUT THIS...!
I'M SORRY...
MAHIRU.
I REALLY AM GRATEFUL TO YOU.
BUT STILL...
JUST LIKE...
YOU FEEL THAT TRUST IS PRECIOUS...

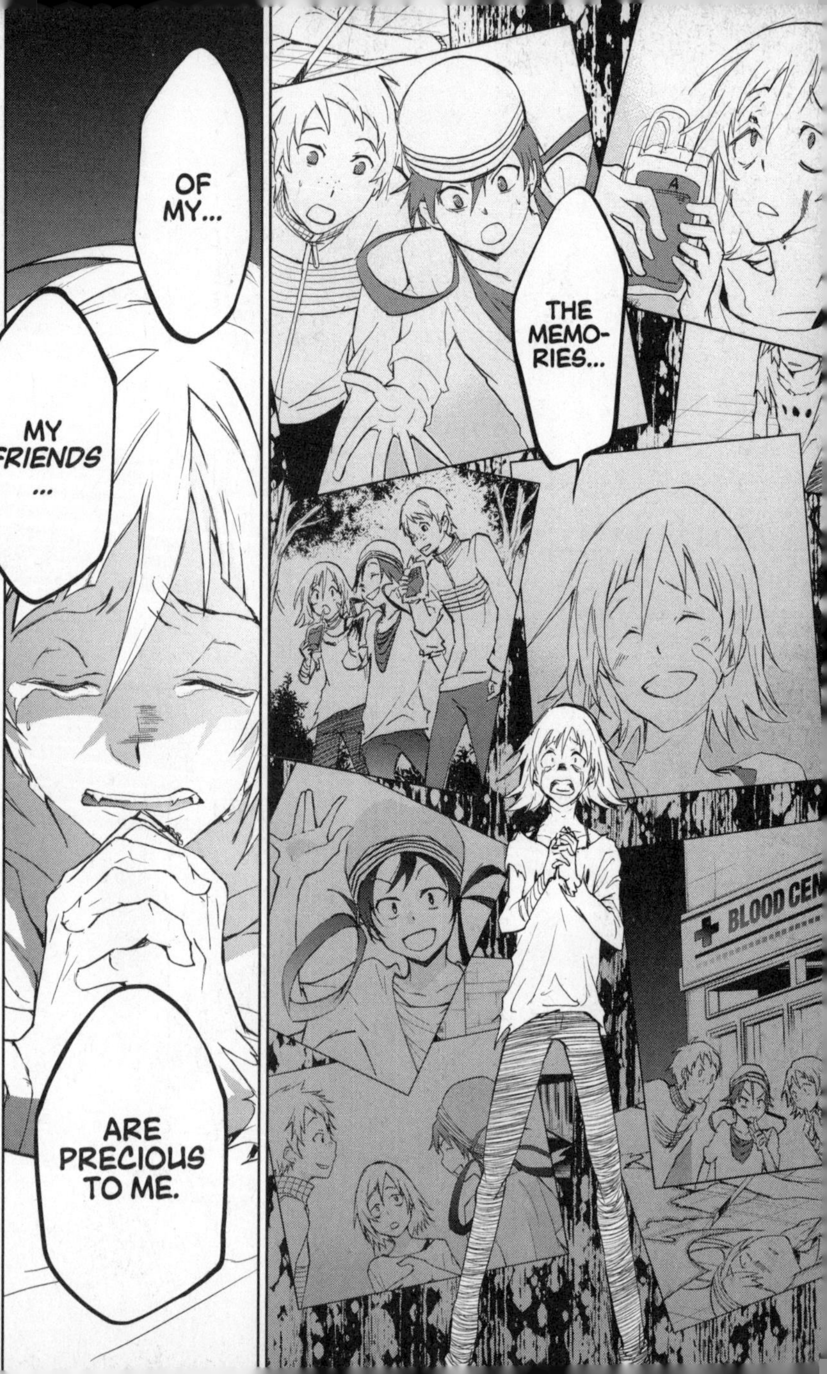
THE MEMORIES...
BLOOD CEN
OF MY...
MY FRIENDS ...
ARE PRECIOUS TO ME.

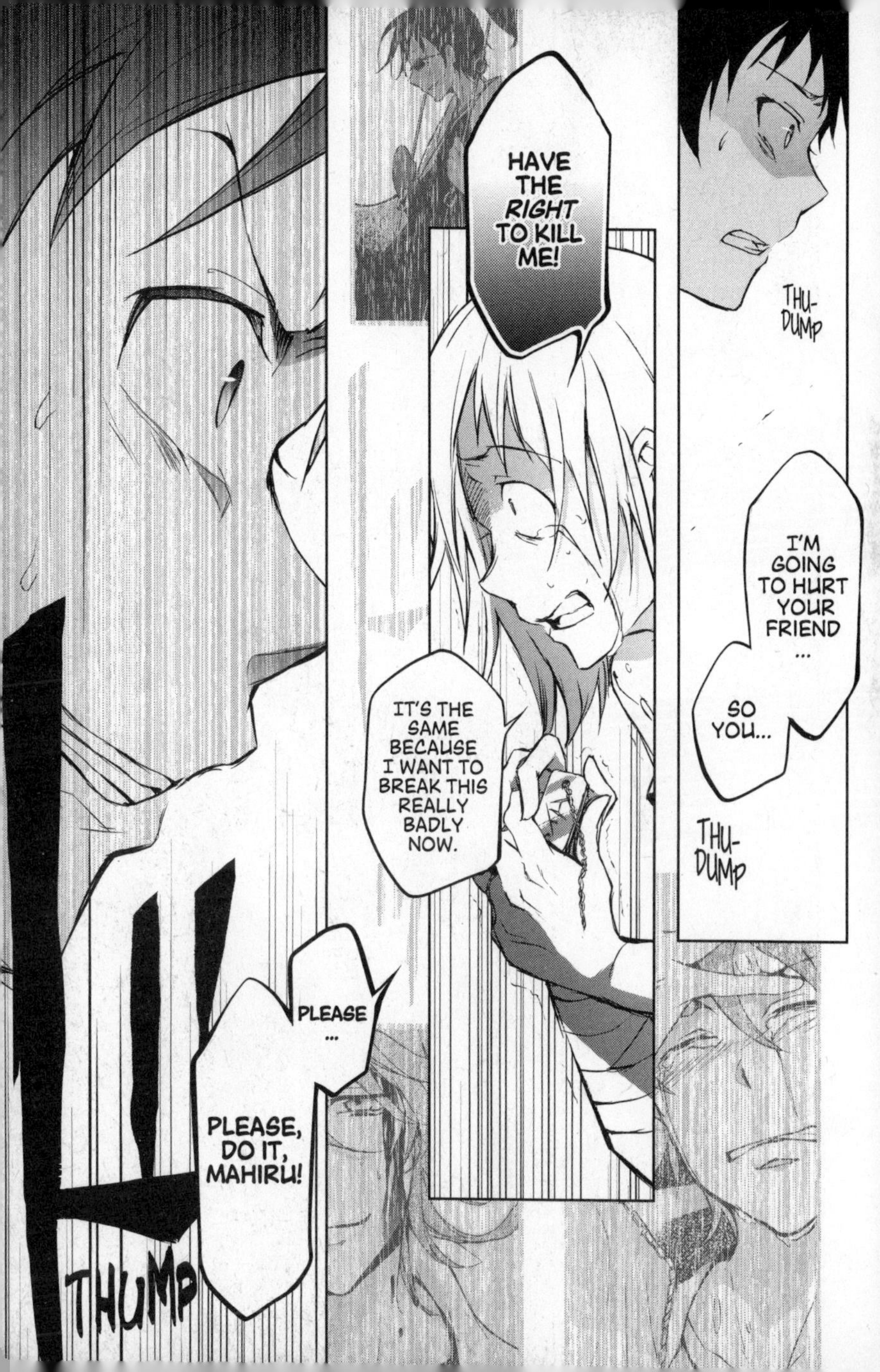
HAVE THE *RIGHT* TO KILL ME!
THU-DUMP
I'M GOING TO HURT YOUR FRIEND ... SO YOU...
THU-DUMP
IT'S THE SAME BECAUSE I WANT TO BREAK THIS REALLY BADLY NOW.
PLEASE ...
PLEASE, DO IT, MAHIRU!
THUMP

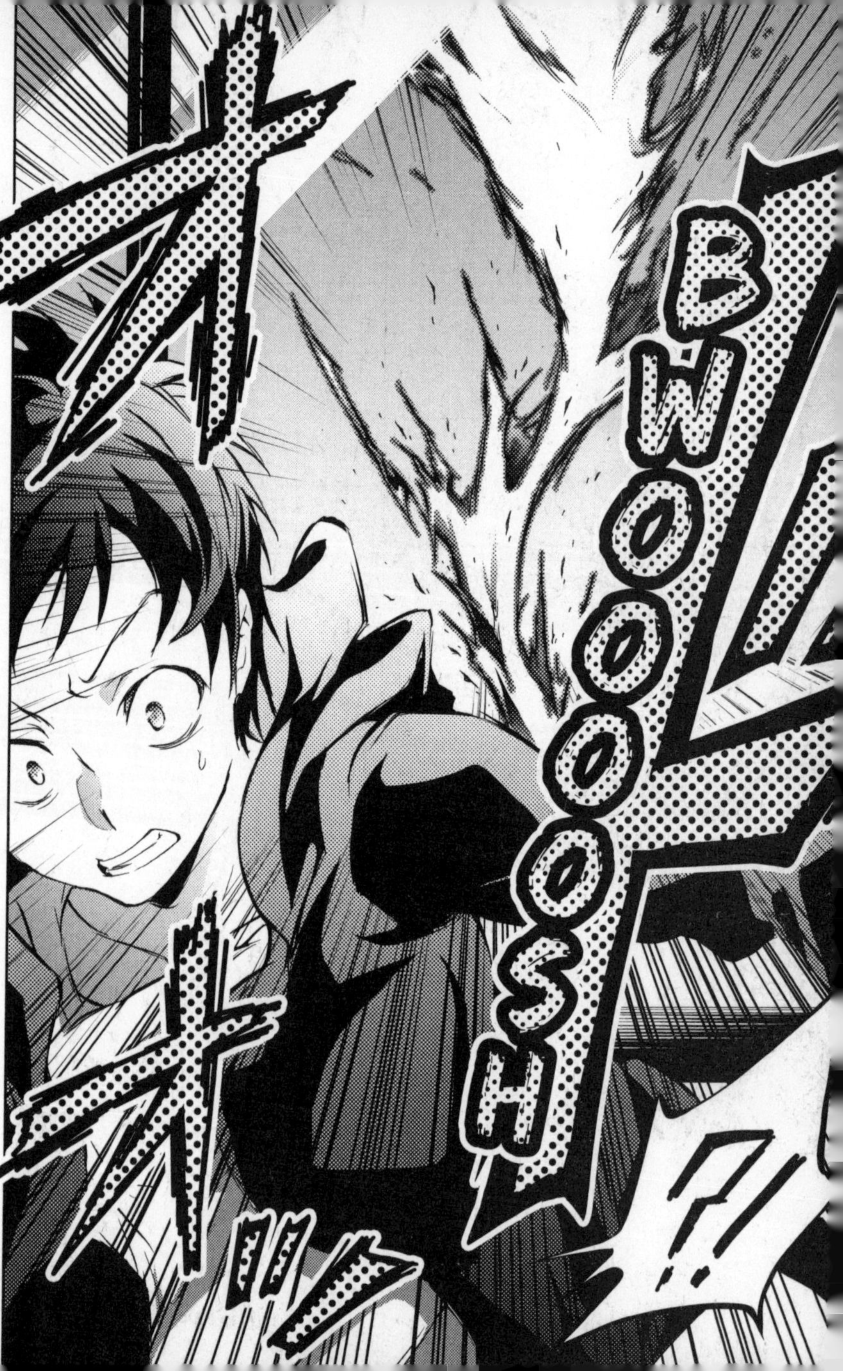
BWOOOOOSH
?!

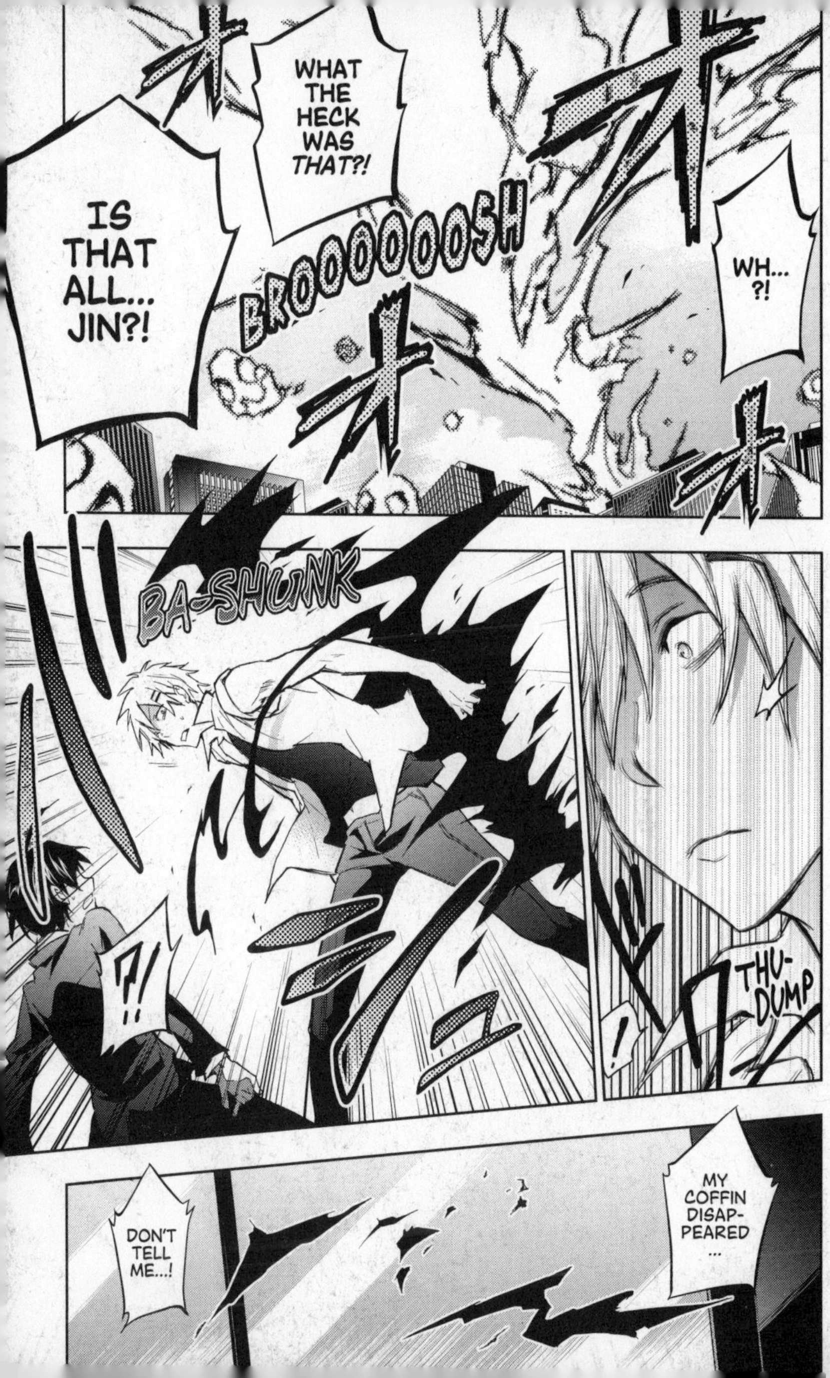
WH...?!
WHAT THE HECK WAS THAT?!
BROOOOOOOSH
IS THAT ALL... JIN?!
THU-DUMP
!
BA-SHUNK
?!
MY COFFIN DISAPPEARED...
DON'T TELL ME...!

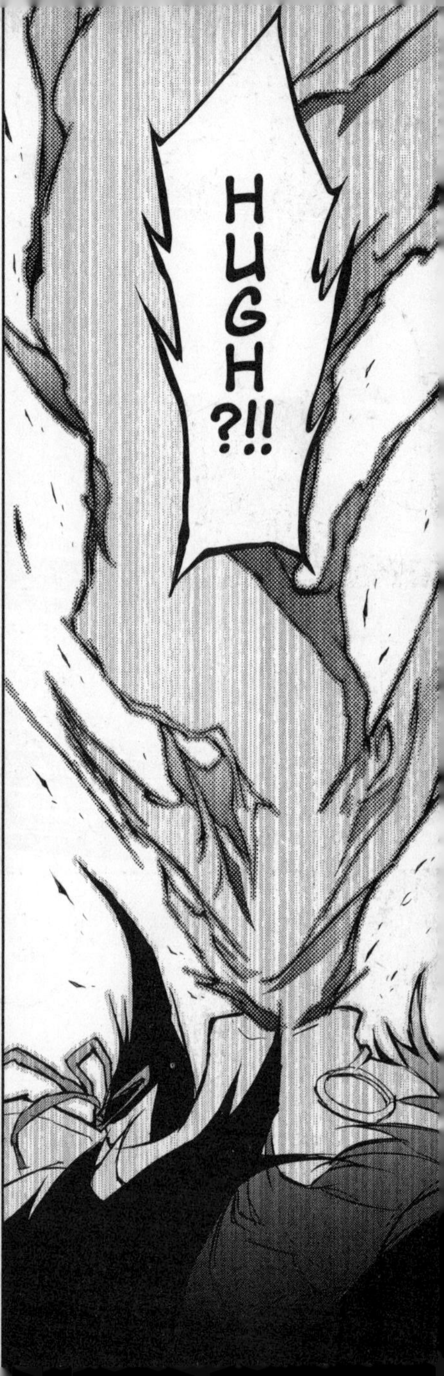
HUGH?!!

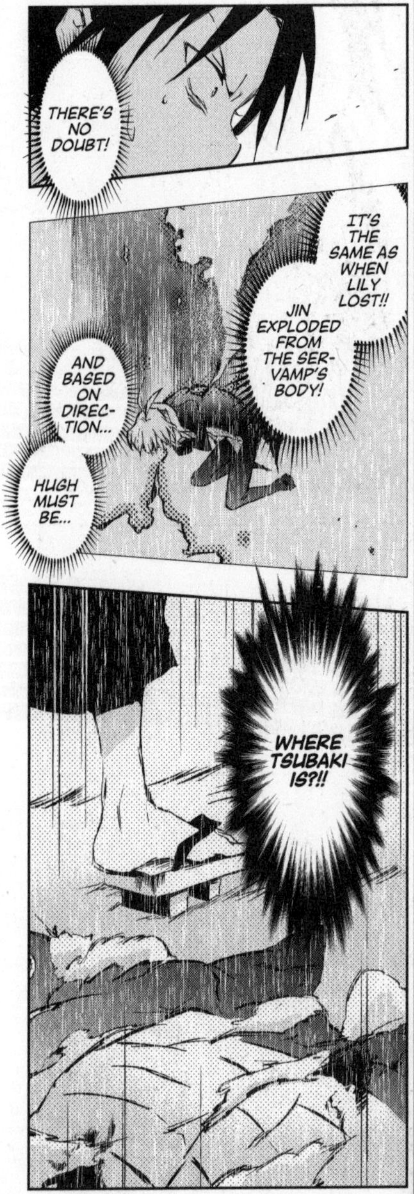
THERE'S NO DOUBT!
IT'S THE SAME AS WHEN LILY LOST!!
JIN EXPLODED FROM THE SER-VAMP'S BODY!
AND BASED ON DIRECTION...
HUGH MUST BE...
WHERE TSUBAKI IS?!!

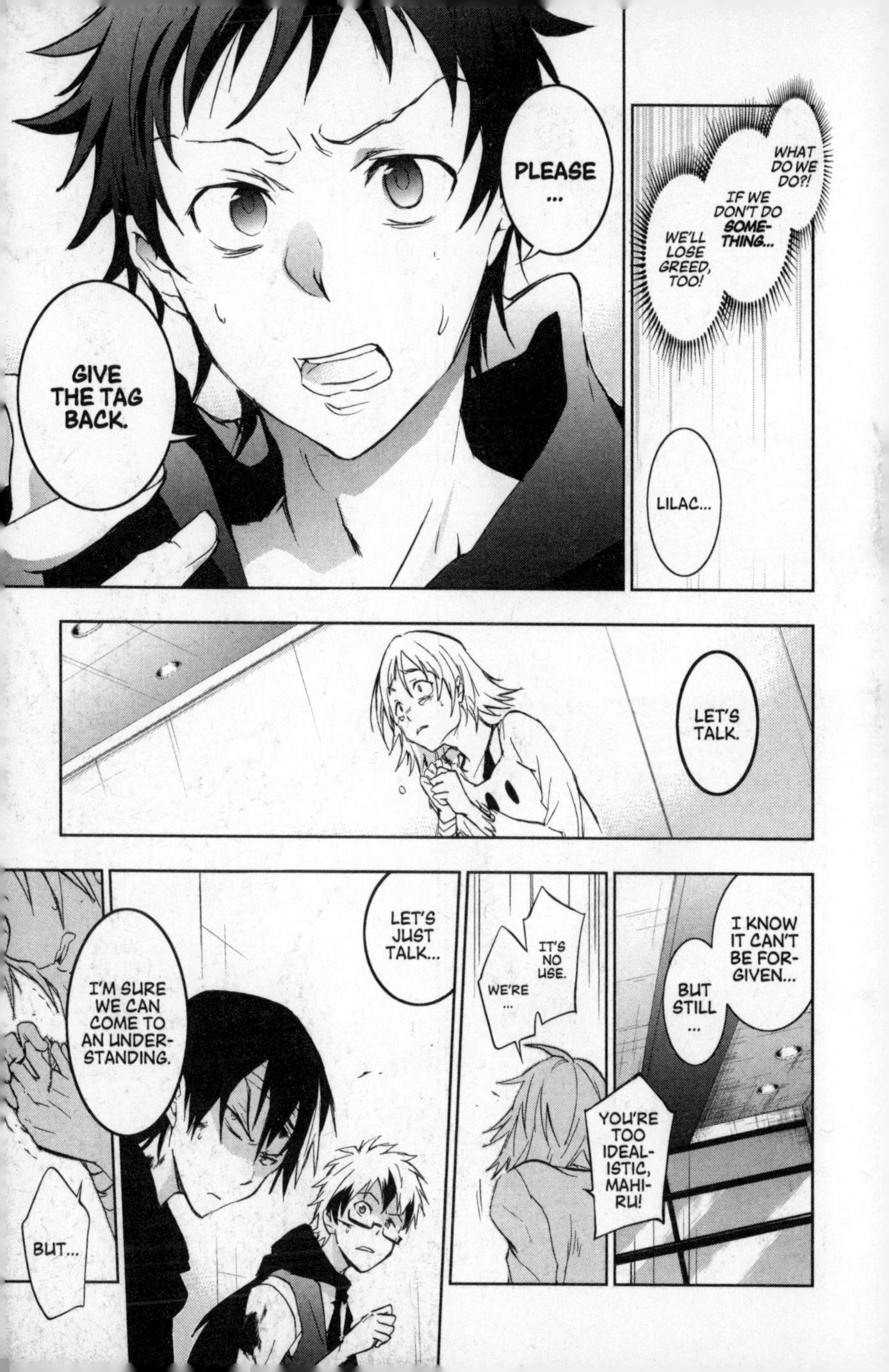
WHAT DO WE DO?!
IF WE DON'T DO SOMETHING...
WE'LL LOSE GREED, TOO!
LILAC...
PLEASE...
GIVE THE TAG BACK.
LET'S TALK.
I KNOW IT CAN'T BE FORGIVEN...
BUT STILL...
YOU'RE TOO IDEALISTIC, MAHIRU!
IT'S NO USE.
WE'RE...
LET'S JUST TALK...
I'M SURE WE CAN COME TO AN UNDERSTANDING.
BUT...

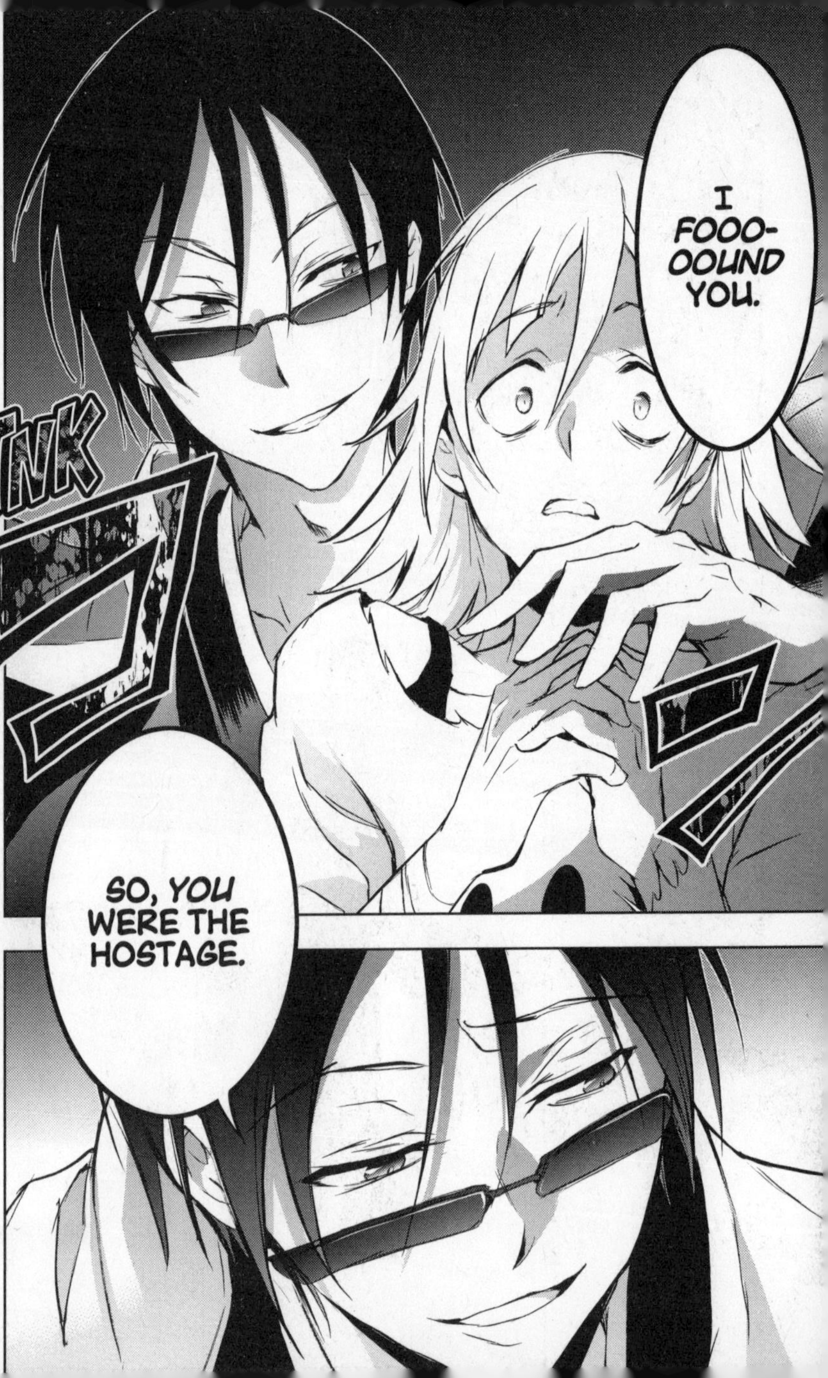
I FOOO-OOUND YOU.
TINK
SO, YOU WERE THE HOSTAGE.

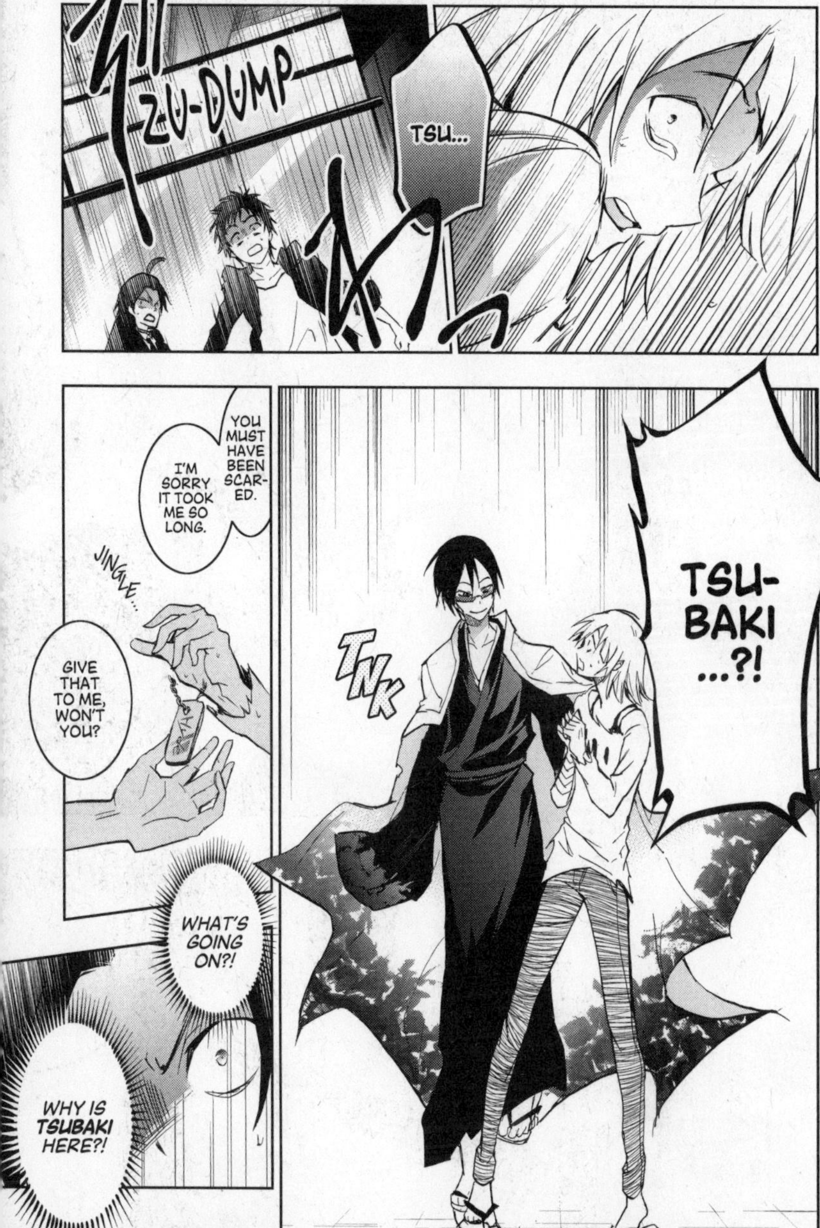
TSU...
ZU-DUMP
TSU-BAKI ...?!
TNK
YOU MUST HAVE BEEN SCAR-ED.
I'M SORRY IT TOOK ME SO LONG.
JINGLE...
GIVE THAT TO ME, WON'T YOU?
WHAT'S GOING ON?!
WHY IS TSUBAKI HERE?!

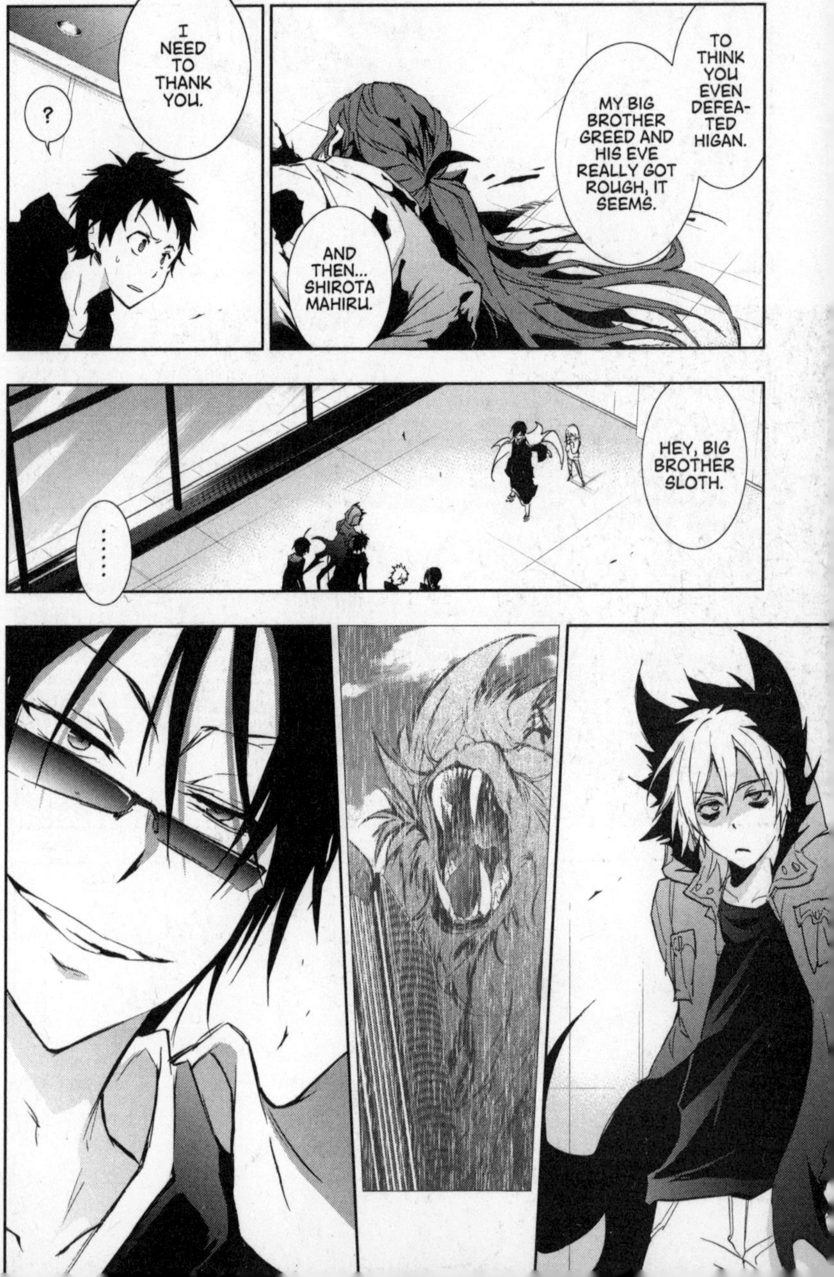
TO THINK YOU EVEN DEFEATED HIGAN.
MY BIG BROTHER GREED AND HIS EVE REALLY GOT ROUGH, IT SEEMS.
AND THEN... SHIROTA MAHIRU.
I NEED TO THANK YOU.
?
HEY, BIG BROTHER SLOTH.
......

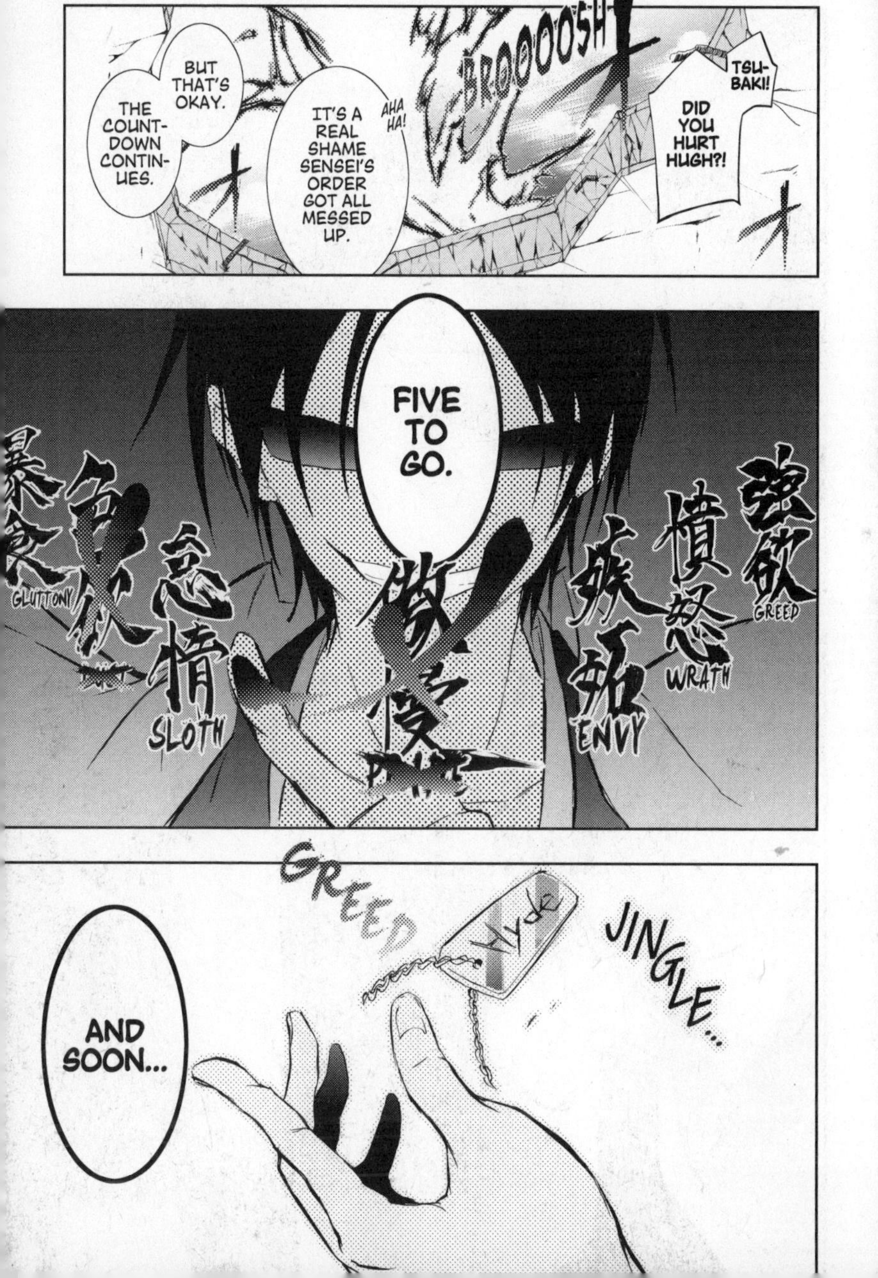
TSU-BAKI!
DID YOU HURT HUGH?!
BROOOOSH
AHA HA!
IT'S A REAL SHAME SENSEI'S ORDER GOT ALL MESSED UP.
BUT THAT'S OKAY.
THE COUNT-DOWN CONTIN-UES.
強欲
GREED
憤怒
WRATH
嫉妬
ENVY
FIVE TO GO.
怠惰
SLOTH
GLUTTONY
GREED
Hyde
JINGLE...
AND SOON...

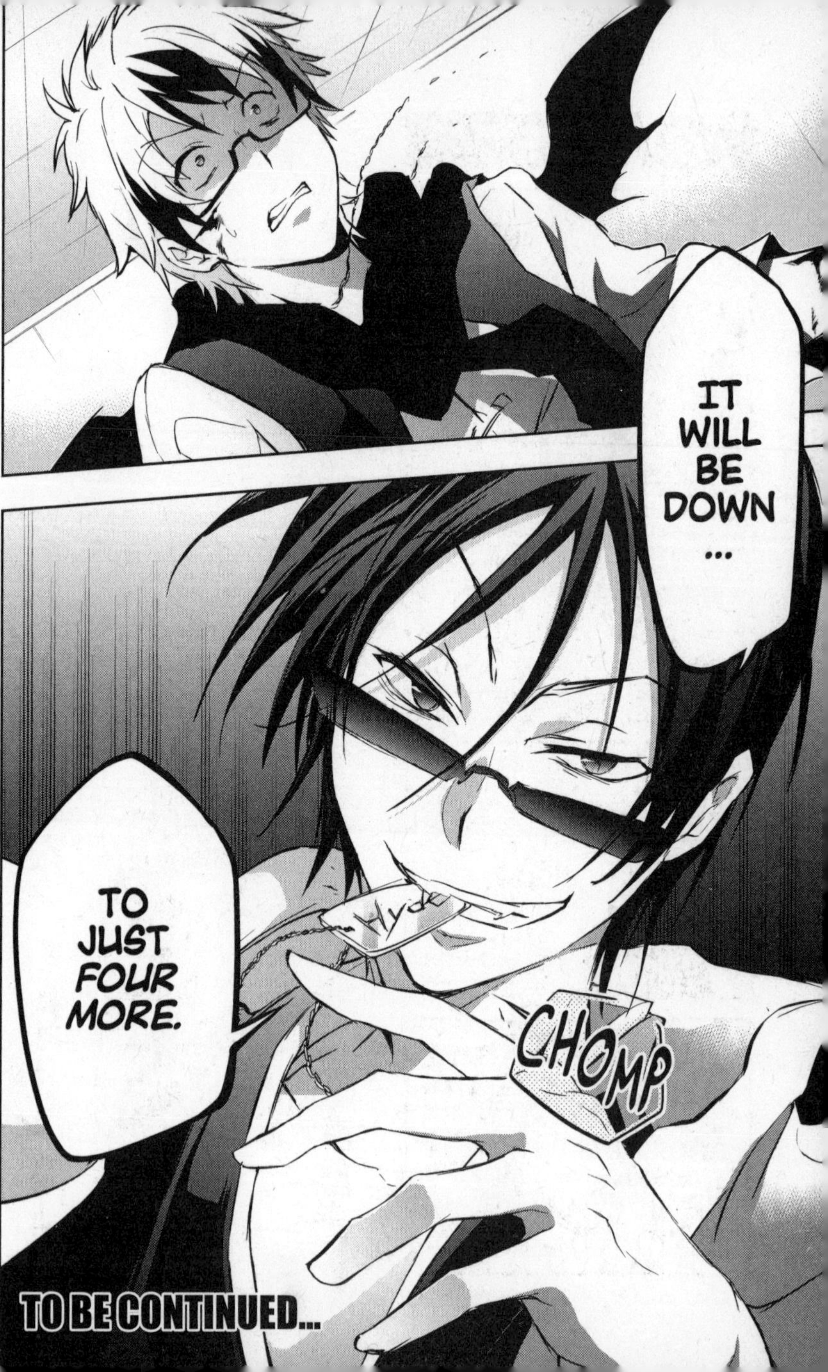
IT WILL BE DOWN ...
TO JUST FOUR MORE.
CHOMP
TO BE CONTINUED...

OMAKE 4-KOMA

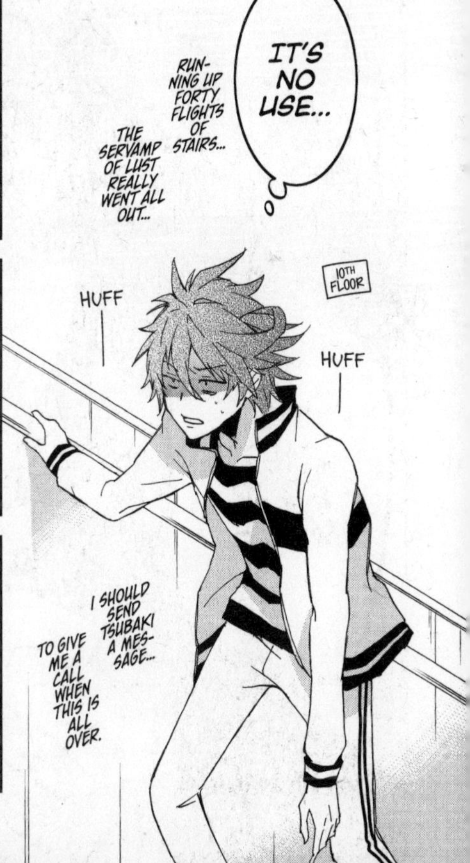
IT'S NO USE...
RUNNING UP FORTY FLIGHTS OF STAIRS...
THE SERVAMP OF LUST REALLY WENT ALL OUT...
10TH FLOOR
HUFF
HUFF
I SHOULD SEND TSUBAKI A MESSAGE...
TO GIVE ME A CALL WHEN THIS IS ALL OVER.

## VILLAIN

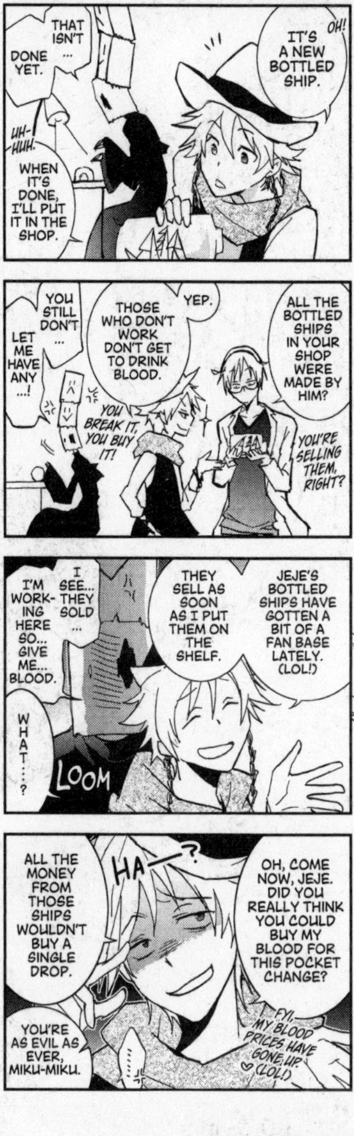
OH! IT'S A NEW BOTTLED SHIP.
THAT ISN'T ... DONE YET.
UH-HUH. WHEN IT'S DONE, I'LL PUT IT IN THE SHOP.
ALL THE BOTTLED SHIPS IN YOUR SHOP WERE MADE BY HIM?
YOU'RE SELLING THEM, RIGHT?
YEP.
THOSE WHO DON'T WORK DON'T GET TO DRINK BLOOD.
YOU STILL DON'T ... LET ME HAVE ANY ...!
YOU BREAK IT, YOU BUY IT!
JEJE'S BOTTLED SHIPS HAVE GOTTEN A BIT OF A FAN BASE LATELY. (LOL!)
THEY SELL AS SOON AS I PUT THEM ON THE SHELF.
I SEE... THEY SOLD ...
I'M WORKING HERE SO... GIVE ME... BLOOD.
WHAT....?
LOOM
OH, COME NOW, JEJE. DID YOU REALLY THINK YOU COULD BUY MY BLOOD FOR THIS POCKET CHANGE?
HA—?
ALL THE MONEY FROM THOSE SHIPS WOULDN'T BUY A SINGLE DROP.
FYI, MY BLOOD PRICES HAVE GONE UP. ♥ (LOL!)
YOU'RE AS EVIL AS EVER, MIKU-MIKU.
......

## HOW TO RAISE AN ANGEL

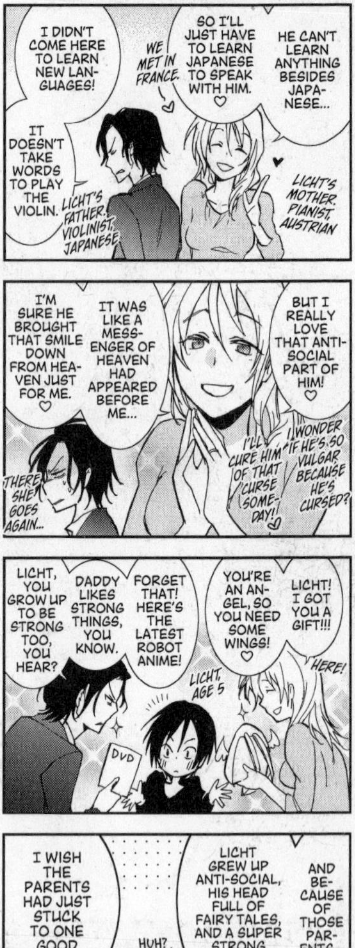
HE CAN'T LEARN ANYTHING BESIDES JAPANESE...
SO I'LL JUST HAVE TO LEARN JAPANESE TO SPEAK WITH HIM.
WE MET IN FRANCE.
I DIDN'T COME HERE TO LEARN NEW LANGUAGES!
LICHT'S MOTHER. PIANIST. AUSTRIAN
IT DOESN'T TAKE WORDS TO PLAY THE VIOLIN.
LICHT'S FATHER. VIOLINIST. JAPANESE
BUT I REALLY LOVE THAT ANTI-SOCIAL PART OF HIM!
IT WAS LIKE A MESSENGER OF HEAVEN HAD APPEARED BEFORE ME...
I'M SURE HE BROUGHT THAT SMILE DOWN FROM HEAVEN JUST FOR ME.
I WONDER IF HE'S SO VULGAR BECAUSE HE'S CURSED?
I'LL CURE HIM OF THAT CURSE SOMEDAY!
THERE SHE GOES AGAIN...
LICHT! I GOT YOU A GIFT!!!
YOU'RE AN ANGEL, SO YOU NEED SOME WINGS!
FORGET THAT! HERE'S THE LATEST ROBOT ANIME!
DADDY LIKES STRONG THINGS, YOU KNOW.
LICHT, YOU GROW UP TO BE STRONG TOO, YOU HEAR?
HERE!
LICHT, AGE 5
DVD
AND BECAUSE OF THOSE PARENTS...
LICHT GREW UP ANTI-SOCIAL, HIS HEAD FULL OF FAIRY TALES, AND A SUPER STRONG LITTLE ANGEL.
I WISH THE PARENTS HAD JUST STUCK TO ONE GOOD SIDE...
HUH?
RATHER THAN BIRTHING THIS VIOLENT ANGEL.
AGE 18

## TSUBAKI AND SAKUYA 3

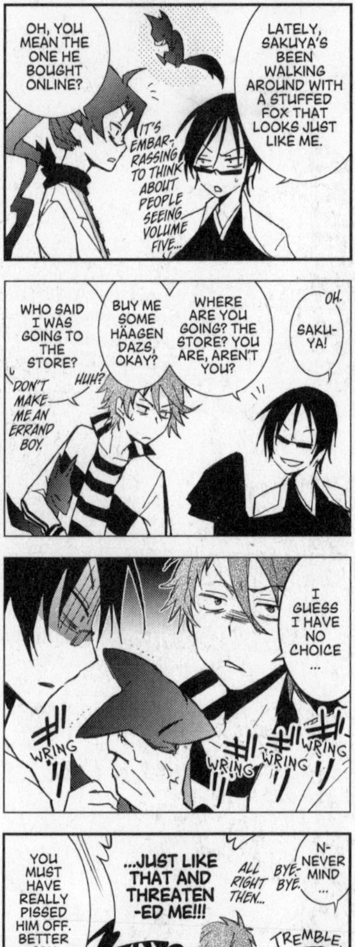
LATELY, SAKUYA'S BEEN WALKING AROUND WITH A STUFFED FOX THAT LOOKS JUST LIKE ME.
OH, YOU MEAN THE ONE HE BOUGHT ONLINE?
IT'S EMBARRASSING TO THINK ABOUT PEOPLE SEEING VOLUME FIVE...
OH. SAKUYA!
WHERE ARE YOU GOING? THE STORE? YOU ARE, AREN'T YOU?
BUY ME SOME HÄAGEN DAZS, OKAY?
WHO SAID I WAS GOING TO THE STORE?
HUH?
DON'T MAKE ME AN ERRAND BOY.
I GUESS I HAVE NO CHOICE ...
WRING
WRING
WRING
WRING
N-NEVER MIND ...
BYE-BYE.
ALL RIGHT THEN...
...JUST LIKE THAT AND THREATEN-ED ME!!!
YOU MUST HAVE REALLY PISSED HIM OFF. BETTER SAY SORRY.
TREMBLE...